MOVING SUBJECTS, MOVING OBJECTS

Material Mediations: People and Things in a World of Movement

Edited by **Birgit Meyer** (Department of Religious Studies and Theology, Utrecht University) and **Maruška Svašek** (School of History and Anthropology, Queens University, Belfast)

During the last few years, a lively, interdisciplinary debate has taken place between anthropologists, art historians and scholars of material culture, religion, visual culture and media studies about the dynamics of material production and cultural mediation in an era of intensifying globalization and transnational connectivity. Understanding 'mediation' as a fundamentally material process, this series provides a stimulating platform for ethnographically grounded theoretical debates about the many aspects that constitute relationships between people and things, including political, economic, technological, aesthetic, sensorial and emotional processes.

Volume 1
Moving Subjects, Moving Objects: Transnationalism, Cultural Production and Emotions
Edited by Maruška Svašek

Volume 2
Growing Artefacts, Displaying Relationships: Yams, Art and Technology amongst the Nyamikum Abelam of Papua New Guinea
Ludovic Coupaye

In Preparation
Objects and Imagination: Perspectives on Materialization and Meaning
Edited by Øivind Fuglerud and Leon Wainwright

MOVING SUBJECTS, MOVING OBJECTS

Transnationalism, Cultural Production and Emotions

Edited by

Maruška Svašek

berghahn
NEW YORK · OXFORD
www.berghahnbooks.com

Published in 2012 by
Berghahn Books
www.berghahnbooks.com

Library of Congress Cataloging-in-Publication Data
Moving subjects, moving objects : transnationalism, cultural production
and emotions / edited by Maruška Svašek.
    p. cm.
Includes bibliographical references and index.
 ISBN 978-0-85745-323-5 (hardback) -- ISBN 978-1-78238-512-7
(paperback) – ISBN 978-0-85745-324-2 (ebook)
 1. Ethnopsychology. 2. Emotions. 3. Transnationalism. 4. Material
culture. I. Svašek, Maruška.
 GN502.M69 2012
 306--dc23

                                                          2011046315

British Library Cataloguing in Publication Data
A catalogue record for this book is available from the British Library

Printed on acid-free paper

ISBN: 978-1-78238-512-7 paperback
ISBN: 978-0-85745-324-2 ebook

CONTENTS

LIST OF FIGURES AND TABLES

Figures

Tables

ACKNOWLEDGEMENTS

The initial idea for this book came out of the conference 'Migrant Art, Artefacts and Emotional Agency' that took place at Queens University, Belfast, in 2007. The conference was one in a series of three, funded by the AHRC in the 'Diasporas, Migration and Identities' programme. Early versions of four chapters in this book were presented at that conference, namely chapters by Sameera Maiti, Deborah Schultz, Leon Wainwright and Maruška Svašek.

INTRODUCTION

AFFECTIVE MOVES:
TRANSIT, TRANSITION AND TRANSFORMATION

Maruška Svašek

> We find it familiar to consider objects as useful or aesthetic, as necessities or vain indulgences. We are on less familiar ground when we consider objects as companions to our emotional lives or as provocations to thought.
>
> —Sherry Turkle

The principal aim of this volume is to explore the emotional dimensions of subject and object mobility. Mobility or 'transit' (see below) are terms used to describe the different processes at play when people and things cross geographical, social and cultural boundaries as they move through time and space. Emotional dynamics are part and parcel of these processes. By exploring the different ways in which mobile individuals relate emotionally to changing material environments, and by investigating how transportable objects evoke feelings in distinct socio-geographical milieux, the book aims to contribute to recent debates about globalization, cultural production and emotions.

The contributors comprise seven anthropologists, two art historians, one historian and one sociologist, who draw on discussions that cut across the fields of anthropology, sociology, cultural studies and art history, and build on recent debates in emotions research. The chapters engage with theoretical perspectives that focus on the social and emotional agency of images and artefacts – for example, those introduced by Freedberg (1989) and Gell (1998). The authors explore transnational experiences through the perspective of material culture, by analysing cases from sometimes diverse and sometimes strongly interconnected regions in Europe, Africa, the United States, Asia and the Caribbean.

The book addresses the theme by focusing on examples of object and subject mobility and emotional interaction. The first four chapters concentrate on the different ways in which distinct individuals and groups of migrants produce and interact emotionally with specific artefacts. The subsequent four chapters explore the capacity of material things to increase feelings of well-being and belonging. The three remaining chapters focus on artistic fields of production, and the ways in which mobile artists deal with and instrumentalize emotions in their work. This introduction will also outline numerous other themes connecting individual chapters and perspectives that are woven into the structure of the book.

Transit, Transition and Transformation

This introductory chapter presents the emotional dimensions of subject and object mobility within an overall conceptual framework that, as in previous works (Svašek 2007b, 2009), employs the terms transit, transition and transformation to investigate these processes.[1] These terms help to shed light on the emotional significance of cultural and material production in an interconnected world.

Transit and Transition

To illustrate the use of the first two concepts, 'transit' and 'transition', consider a necklace with a crucifix for sale at a Christian pilgrimage site. Buying the commodity, a passing pilgrim might identify the object as desirable, possibly aesthetically pleasing, and also as a religious artefact that symbolizes both his faith and the suffering of Christ. Perceived as a meaningful and sacred artefact it has the ability to evoke spiritual engagement. Although related to a wider religious doctrine, the object's meaning will become more personalized as it becomes part of the buyer's life. At the same time, its fluctuating emotional efficacy will be shaped by the changing predicament and mood of its owner. In moments of crisis it may become a focus of intense prayer that stimulates feelings of hope and confidence, while at other moments it may be consciously hidden under clothing, or touched out of nervous habit, or simply forgotten about.

In the example above, 'transit', which describes the movements of people, objects and images through time and space, would refer to both the pilgrim and the crucifix. Transit describes the changing social, cultural and spatial environments constituted by objects and individuals before and after coming into contact with each other, as well as the process and occasion by which contact is made. In this instance the object (the crucifix) and subject (the pilgrim) come into contact at a pilgrimage souvenir shop. This results in an exchange of ownership whereby pilgrims themselves provide part of the crucifix's new context, while the crucifix adds to the visual, social and religious profile of the pilgrim.

By contrast, changes that occur in the perceived value or meaning of the object, namely the crucifix, and the process by which this happens, are referred to as its 'transition'. Transition identifies transit-related changes in the meaning, value and emotional efficacy of objects and images as opposed simply to changes in their location or ownership. Hence in this case the perceived value of the souvenir, mass-produced to generate profit for a vendor, becomes a personal memento of religious significance when purchased by the pilgrim. The concepts of transit and transition are interdependent, and hence a future change in one is likely to affect a change in the other. If, in an extension to the example of transit, the pilgrim were to take a flight to a non-Christian country, or a country where all religions were officially banned, the significance of the crucifix both for the pilgrim and others around him would change in a further act of transition.

As concrete examples of how the significance of an object, such as a crucifix, can be radically altered by this process of transition, consider the following cases. In 2006 a media storm was triggered in Britain when an airport check-in worker, Nadia Eweida, was suspended after refusing to remove a crucifix from around her neck, which it was claimed breached the British Airways dress code. Eweida claimed she was a victim of an unfair attack on her Christian identity:

> I will not hide my belief in the Lord Jesus. British Airways permits Muslims to wear a headscarf, Sikhs to wear a turban and other faiths religious apparel. Only Christians are forbidden to express their faith. I am a loyal and conscientious employee of British Airways, but I stand up for the rights of all citizens ... I am not ashamed of my faith.[2]

A fierce public debate ensued, with supporters of Eweida claiming that the British Airways dress code harmed her personal well-being and undermined her personal integrity, which was inextricably bound up with her Christian beliefs. They similarly claimed Christians were being treated unfairly when compared with other religious groups. Other 'crucifix' cases quickly came to light, such as that of a nurse similarly suspended for refusing to remove a necklace, and the whole debate came to a head when it was revealed that the country's most prominent news presenter, Fiona Bruce, had also been issued with instructions to hide her crucifix from view by the BBC.

The ensuing, often emotional debates about identity, personal freedom, legal rights, employment regulations, moral duty and the government's intent to remove religion from certain public places, all focused on the processes of transit and transition. Wearing the crucifix in private, it was claimed, had a different significance to when it was worn in more public spaces, such as while working as a representative of a company or reading the news to the nation. Jon Snow, another of the country's prominent news readers, criticized Bruce for wearing the crucifix in front of the camera, claiming that: 'I am allowed to wear unspeakably bright ties. But there is a world of difference there [to wearing a crucifix] that we should be assertive about. My ties are abstract – I do not believe in wearing anything that represents any kind of statement' (Pook 2006). The BBC ultimately resolved the issue by providing guidelines that were intended to allow a crucifix to be worn if it was done in such a way as to underpin the idea among viewers that it was of private importance to the wearer and connected with their personal beliefs, rather than having a wider political or religious meaning. To that end, newsreaders were informed that a crucifix should be neither 'large' nor 'shiny' (Sherwin 2006).

The artist Andres Serrano arguably provoked even more fierce debate over his use of the crucifix in 1997 when he appropriated the religious iconography of the cross for an art installation entitled *Piss Christ*. The work, a photograph of a crucifix submerged in the artist's urine, shocked many viewers. Some visitors who saw the work at an exhibition at the National Gallery of Victoria in Australia expressed their outrage by pulling the picture off the wall and vandalizing it with a hammer. They clearly did not accept the artist's aesthetic approach, regarding it as a malign misappropriation of a symbol of religious importance. As a result, the exhibition was closed. In 2011 the art work was destroyed when a thousand French Catholics marched through the city of Avingnon to the gallery that exhibited the work and attacked it with hammers (Chrisafis 2011).

After the attack in 1997, Serrano criticized the viewers' emotional reaction, denying their claim that his work ridiculed a sacred Christian symbol. In an interview with the art critic, Coco Fusco, he noted: 'One of the things that always bothered me was the fundamentalist labelling of my work as "anti-Christian bigotry". As a former Catholic, and as someone who even today is not opposed to being called a Christian, I felt I had every right to use the symbols of the Church and resented being told not to' (Fusco 2002).

The above examples show that object transition can lead to passionate debates about people's intentionality, and that emotions often function as mediators of social norms, an important point of departure in this book. It also demonstrates that object/image perception implies 'a particular sensorial or somatic experience' that can be deeply rooted in viewers' sense of moral judgement (Verrips 2008: 215; Joy and Sherry 2003; Yi-Fu Tuan 2005; Walker 1999). In addition, it illustrates how controversies arising from a perceived change in the significance of an object in a particular context can reveal power struggles within and between specific social fields or particular groups (Zolberg and Cherbo 1997). When British Airways and the BBC banned the wearing of crucifixes by their employees, the debate that erupted centred not only on the struggle between state control and personal freedom, but also on the struggle between religious groups where there was a perceived inequality in how their religious identities were respected and tolerated. In the case of the backlash generated by the artist Serrano, the field of 'postmodern contemporary art', supported by critics and other artists, found itself pitted against religious groups bent on protecting Christianity and its sacred symbols.

Transit and Transformation

The perspective proposed in this introduction not only uses the concepts of 'transit' and 'transition', but also introduces the notion of 'transformation'. Transformation refers to transit-related changes in human subjects, specifically in terms of their status, identity formation and emotional subjectivity. In our initial example of the pilgrimage, a process of change takes place when individuals, who might range in social status from bank executives to lollipop men, assume the identity of pilgrims during their spiritual journey. In their enactment and experience of 'pilgrim-ness', individuals tend to de-emphasize social differences of age, nationality, ethnicity, gender, class and profession in order to feel connected through similar emotional engagement. In other words, in transformation, their situated identities and emotional subjectivities change, either temporarily or leading to a more permanent personal change (Conradson and McKay 2007).

In Chapter 3, Eddy Plasquy presents a striking example of this process in his analysis of the engagement by Spanish Catholic migrants with a statue of the Virgin Mary of El Rocío at a religious event in Belgium. Creating and participating in the festival, the migrants appropriate elements of Spanish culture in the diasporic environment, and feel momentarily united as a group of people with a shared geographical and cultural background, an experience that increases their sense of 'home away from home'.

Connecting Transition and Transformation

But how can we explore the experiences of specific individuals, such as Plasquy's Spanish migrants, as they engage with material things that exist in, are taken to or disappear from concrete socio-historical and spatial settings? The framework proposed in this introductory chapter seeks to address this issue by linking the perspectives of 'object transition' and 'subject transformation.' The central assumption is that human beings are beings in the world, perceiving themselves in relation to their human and non-human environments (Merleau-Ponty 1996; Ingold 2000). To stay with the example of the pilgrimage, this implies that the transformation of individuals into Christian devotees can only be understood if examined in tandem with the transition of artefacts into devotional objects. The two processes, in other words, are dialectically related.

It is important to note that in the case of a pilgrimage to a specific church, for example, these processes are often highly staged. Two- and three-dimensional religious depictions at these sites have normally been commissioned and spatially contextualized by religious authorities, so as to stimulate feelings of religious piety. Visiting pilgrims to the sites are part of this performative process. By lighting candles and praying before religious icons they perform the ritualistic behaviour expected of them and serve to complete the scene. Their knowledge of Christian doctrine and familiarity with ritualistic gestures shape their emotional habitus. Their almost identical sensorial involvement with the sacred objects informs their emotional experience of how it feels to belong to a congregation of worshippers.

Dialogic relationships between transition and transformation in religious fields of mobility are explored in three chapters of this book. In Chapter 3, Plasquy is interested in the emotional efficacy of the statue of Virgin Mary of El Rocío within a Spanish community in Belgium, and analyses the ways in which diasporic identities are enacted through rituals focused on religious artefacts. In Chapter 2, Burrell focuses on the importance of particular artefacts and foods to Polish migrant workers in the UK during the Christmas period. Forced to improvise in their new country of residence, they experiment with familiar and unfamiliar traditions, thereby shaping their transnational sense of selfhood. In Chapter 5, Grønseth explores how religious artefacts increase feelings of well-being amongst Buddhist Tamil refugees working in the fishing industry in Norway. In all three cases, the sentiments evoked by the artefacts not only mediate attachments to the homeland but also mark their users' identities as members of minorities that connect through religion.

Mobility and Emotions

The framework of transit, transition and transformation makes connections between two types of 'movement': firstly, mobility through time and space; and secondly, emotional dynamics. The first type of movement has spatial dimensions that are intrinsic to 'being-in-and-thus-moving-through-the-world'. All humans pass through various stages of life and are necessarily in motion – whether walking, driving, sailing, flying, or being pushed in a pram or a wheelchair. As Tim Ingold (2000) has pointed out, motion is central to perceptual experience, not only because people build perceptual knowledge as they move through time and space, but also because they make scanning movements from fixed locations as they perceive the space around them. Objects and images are also at least potentially geographically mobile; things move (drift, float, roll) or are moved (pushed, carried, thrown, transmitted) from one location to the next, and some have prominent 'social lives' (Appadurai 1986), 'careers' (Zolberg 1990) or 'cultural biographies' (Kopytoff 1986).

The latter terms point to connections between geographical and social mobility. Consider, for example, a painting that increases in value, meaning and impact when appearing in increasingly prestigious venues at increasingly important periods in the exhibition calendar. The artwork not only increases in monetary value but is also attributed a position in art history as an important work of superior aesthetic quality, thereby increasing its ability to impress particular audiences. Art-related transitions are also often influenced by political dynamics, as pointed out in Chapter 10 by the art historian Leon Wainwright. The analysis shows how in Trinidad the 'careers' of artworks by Indo-Trinidadian artists have developed against the background of colonialism and nationalism. While these ideologies have inspired some artists, others have experienced them as a stifling burden on their creativity.

Learning about the changing human and non-human environment is central to people's perceptual experience of the world. Building on Ingold's approach to perception, Kay Milton has suggested that this cognitive process can be understood as an inherently emotional phenomenon. Emotions, in her approach, are defined as 'ecological phenomena that link us to our environment and enable us to learn from them' (Milton 2002: 37). Also focusing on the role played by emotions, Svašek connects these insights in Chapter 11 to Gell's theory of object agency (Gell 1998) in an analysis of audience perception of an art performance by a Ghanaian migrant artist.

Milton's perspective is useful when analysing subjects and objects in transit, as learning about, remembering and anticipating the impact of changing material environments (an art gallery, a church, somebody's home, a new country) generate transformations in mobile selves. Consider, for example, a Northern Irish elderly lady with little travel experience on a visit to London. Turning a corner, she suddenly spots the Swaminarayan temple in Neasden (see Figure 0.1). No doubt she will be taken by surprise, as the building, a good example of what Durant and Lord have called

Figure 0.1: Swaminarayan Temple in London, 2010. Photograph by Maruška Svašek.

'migratory aesthetics' (Durant and Lord 2007: 12), stands out from the surrounding architecture through its contrasting features. The experience might generate an array of emotional judgements, partly depending on her political views on immigration issues.

In the case of *Piss Christ*, embodied memories of devotion triggered outrage in some Christians when they saw the symbol submerged in urine. The shock of the unexpected and the sense of moral righteousness generated a physical reaction to, and negative evaluation of, the material environment. A focus on these emotional dynamics can produce insights into the ways in which bodies in time and space change as people are affected by the objects they perceive, as well as their own acts of perception.

Examining 'Emotions'

It is important to note that theoretical definitions of emotions differ from everyday uses of the term. Ideas of emotivity also differ widely from one society to the next, and in some societies a concept of emotions, as would most commonly be understood by the term 'emotions' in English, is entirely absent (Lutz 1988; Wierzbicka 2004). In other words, emotional processes are at least partially culturally constituted, informed by situated social practices (Myers 1986; Lynch 1990). Even when emotional dynamics are explored in English-speaking settings, local understandings and usage of the term might differ, and should not be confused with conceptual approaches. The authors of this volume avoid naively using emic notions of emotions in their research, clearly outlining their theoretical approaches in their analyses. They also seek to escape the limitations of approaches that have regarded emotions as either physical processes (passions) or cultural constructions (knowledge), an ongoing interdisciplinary debate beyond the scope of this introduction.[3] As Leavitt (1996) has argued, people in all societies create associations between cultural meanings and physical feelings, and it is precisely in these connections where something recognizable as 'emotions' happens.[4]

While emotions are intrinsic to human life (Lutz and White 1986; Parkinson 1995; Nussbaum 2001; Milton 2005; Wulff 2007), emotional processes can strongly differ in intensity and outcome. Using the metaphor of movement and impact, they might, for example, be perceived as sudden, sharp scratches, as overwhelming forces, or as slow processes of entanglement within or between individuals. In Chapter 11, Svašek describes how a small Irish girl in the audience of an art performance bursts into tears when the performer unexpectedly screams. The instant physical reaction is radically different from the growing feelings of irritation felt by Tibetan traders when confronted with haggling Indian customers, described by Timm Lau in Chapter 4.

Named emotions, for example 'fear', can also have different embodied meanings in different contexts. Fear of being mugged while walking in a dark street, for example, is markedly different from fear of teenage pregnancy. In Chapter 6, Sameera Maiti examines elderly Karen migrants in the Andaman Islands and their anxiety about the loss of skills amongst the younger generation. While the physiological symptoms of fright (increased heartbeat, higher blood pressure) might have similarities in each of the three cases, the discourses and practices associated with them are quite different (see also Svašek 2005a: 12).

The examples of fear allude to the complex relationship between emotional dynamics and subjectivity. A large body of literature has been written about this topic in the often overlapping fields of psychology, sociology, anthropology, cultural studies and human geography. In the following section, I shall introduce a selection of relevant perspectives that tie in with the analytical framework of transit, transition and transformation.

Emotions as Discourses

Lutz and Abu-Lughod (1990) introduced a culturalist approach to emotions, arguing that discourses of emotions and emotivity produce knowledge about self and society that may create, maintain or challenge power relations and thus influence subjectivity. To express fear, for example, can be prescriptive and evaluative of the roles of specific individuals or social groups, and punishment for the transgression of social norms can turn fear into an instrument of control, influencing the behaviour and self-perception of mobile individuals. Wikan (1990: 32) noted that in Bali, fear is regarded as a dangerous state in which people are more likely to be victim to sorcery, a notion that constructs individuals as vulnerable beings who need to balance precautions and risks.

On the Andaman Islands, discourses of anxiety over the lack of interest of younger Karen in traditional weaving, pottery and other crafts produce an image of the youngsters as victims of modernity. The older generation argues that craft production helps maintain psychological balance and harmony within the family, increasing experiences of well-being. In Chapter 6, Sameera Maiti shares the concerns of the older Karen, appropriating a discourse of 'threat' in a plea for the protection of a culturally diverse heritage.

Anxiety over cultural extinction is also apparent amongst Tibetan knitwear traders living in India, as Timm Lau points out in Chapter 4. While the discourse feeds into Tibetan perceptions of Indian merchants and customers as 'bad people', competing narratives construct the merchants as people who can also be trustworthy. Judgemental constructions of others not only shape direct interaction, but are also distributed through newspapers and other media. Emotions, in this case, circulate within affective economies, 'align[ing] subjects with some others and against other others' (Ahmed 2004a: 117). Discourses of fear can also produce knowledge in relation to immigration – for example, when immigrants are described as a risk to the well-being of local populations, or as polluting and destabilizing elements that should be avoided (Ahmed 2004b: 124; Hall 2010: 889; Radford 2010: 900).

In Chapter 7, Enrico Milič exemplifies this process in an analysis of discourses of rootedness that circulate in a diasporic Italian community through a globally distributed journal. The community consists of Italian families who were expelled from the island now known as Lošinj (currently part of Croatia) after the Second World War, and who use photographs, framed by texts, to share feelings of love for the island and strengthen and evoke resentment about their predicament. His study confirms the view of numerous scholars that affective dimensions should be included in analytic approaches to photography (Barthes 2000; Miller 2003; Edwards 2010). As Edwards (2010) has argued, such an analysis should go beyond textual analysis and accept that photographs have meanings that are multi-sensory and emotionally negotiated.

Emotions as Practices

Discourses of emotions are often played out through emotional practices that can have a strong performative dimension (Parkinson 1995). Imagine a mother who feigns a show of fright at the image of a snake in a book she is reading with her child. Managing her feelings, she employs emotional expression to pass judgement on a situation she regards as dangerous, teaching her child how to evaluate her environment. Numerous authors have emphasized this normative dimension of emotional dynamics, arguing that emotional acts can function as 'appraisals' or 'judgements' (Solomon 1983; Nussbaum 2001) or as 'concern-based construals' (Roberts 2003). Josephides has argued that people's feelings can be understood as 'mood-inducing action-motivators' that function as 'evaluators, diagnosticians and interpreters of social standing' (Josephides 2005: 81).

In Chapter 1, Fiona Parrott gives a telling example of emotional practice. A London-based Spanish father performs parental love for his two daughters, carefully instructing them how to cook paella. His action is double-edged: on the one hand, it positively evaluates their interest in their 'Spanish side'; on the other, his effort is an attempt to counterbalance what he sees at their 'cold, English mentality'.

Arlie Hochschild introduced the term 'emotion work' to explore people's efforts to manage feelings when conforming to (or resisting) dominant cultural expectations within particular social settings (Hochschild 1983). Various scholars have taken this perspective to analyse the emotional dimensions of migration – international transit and transformation. Exploring the emotion work of Irish nurses in the UK, for example, Louise Ryan demonstrated how 'the culture of migration created a pragmatism and stoicism in Irish society that under-estimated the emotional cost associated with migration' (Ryan 2008: 311). The Irish nurses, changed by the experience of migration, downplayed feelings of homesickness when talking to their kin in Ireland, and tried to hide feelings of distress related to failing marriages. The conscious non-display of particular feelings also resulted from expectations around transnational care giving (see also Baldock 2000; Baldassar, Baldock and Wilding 2006; Wilding 2006).[5]

Emotions as Embodied Experiences

The perspective of 'embodied experience' explores physical aspects of emotional experience and subjectivity, analysing the perceptual process of sensation and interpretation, and exploring the multi-sensorial interaction of bodies in space (Csordas 1990, 1994; Lock 1993; Lyon 1995). As people appear in and co-create different social environments, their embodied dispositions are partly shaped by their discursive constructions of each other (Hall 2010: 890). Deleuze (1998) has focused on the potential intensity of human experience, defining 'affect' as an interactional embodied process that appears as a result of relational encounters between people in changing life worlds.

People apprehend human and non-human environments through multi-sensorial engagement. As Amanda Wise noted, spending longer periods of time in specific environments, people's senses can become 'habituated, linking ... bodies to experiences, sensations and emotions' (Wise 2010: 933), and in this way places may come to evoke what Raymond Williams termed 'structures of feeling' (ibid.: 933). Familiar sensorial experiences, in other words, can trigger a strong sense of home, and these experiences may be reproduced in new places (Cierraad 1999). In 2009 and 2010, numerous first-generation Indian migrants who had settled in Northern Ireland told me about their increased sense of belonging whenever they entered the Indian Community Centre in Belfast. From the outside the building appears to be just one of the many churches in the city (see Figure 0.2); inside, however, visitors find a consecrated temple space on the ground floor that houses Hindu deities (see Figure 0.3). These objects are not only seen, but also experienced multi-sensorially. As Mitchell (2005a, 2005b) has argued, situational perceptions of images and artefacts do not only involve the sense of vision. In the case of the Belfast temple, during ritual occasions the space is also filled with the smell of incense, the sight of small burning flames and the sound of chanting.

The perspective of bodily perception and interaction in space is central to Chapter 8 by Maggie O'Neill. She analyses a community project in which refugees based in Britain walked around their present places of residence, using the environment as a multi-sensorial trigger of reminiscence. In cooperation with other migrants, they translated their sometimes painful experiences of pre-migration life in their homelands and relocation to Britain into collaborative art works. In many cases, their engagement had a positive transformative impact, increasing their

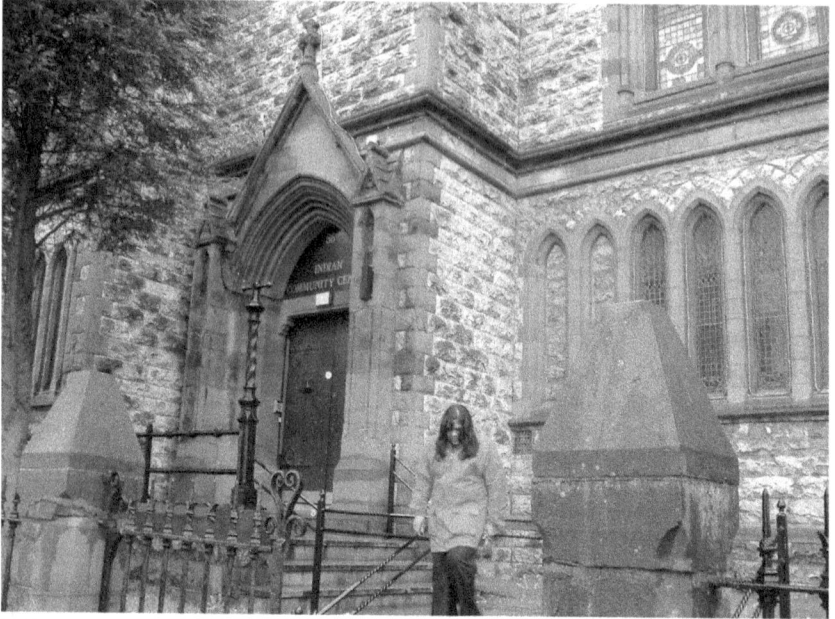

Figure 0.2: Indian Community Centre, Belfast, 2007. Photograph by Maruška Svašek.

Figure 0.3: Hindu deity in the temple of the Indian Community Centre, Belfast, 2007. Photograph by Maruška Svašek.

sense of belonging in Britain. The potential 'healing' power of creative engagement has also been central to art therapeutic practices (Matravers 1998; Hogan 2010).

Subjectivity and Multiple Attachments

Emotional processes do not solely occur when individuals share space and time with each other or with objects, but also occur when they are engaged in inner dialogues, recalling or imagining other people, past selves, places and other phenomena. Exploring the connection between emotional dynamics, memory and imagination is crucial when analysing people in transit and transformation (Casey 1987; Bhatia and Ram 2004; Svašek 2005b, 2008, 2010). Mobile people, perceived as relational multiple selves, are often attached to people in distant homes or to objects and places they might never see again. They 'carry along' memories and feelings from earlier times and places, and are to some extent conditioned by emotional discourses and practices already learned (Svašek and Skrbiš 2007: 373). They might also find new 'affective possibilities' in current places of residence that also influence the ideas they hold about their own identity and the way they experience the world (Conradson and Latham 2007; see also Davidson et al. 2005). In Chapter 1, Fiona Parrott illustrates the latter process when she describes how a London-based gay man from New Zealand pointed out to her that his transformation into a 'freer' person was directly enabled by his years spent in the city. Preparing to return to his home country, he planned to take most of the possessions that he had acquired in the UK with him as a reminder of his new-found identity, hoping that they would strengthen him to maintain his new sense of self.

All the chapters in this volume show that the unavoidable dynamics of multiple attachments and detachments, part and parcel of 'de/territorialisation' (Inda and Rosaldo 2002: 14), can make human mobility a particularly intense emotional and transformative experience.[6] Focusing on material culture, the contributors demonstrate that these attachments can be strengthened, hampered or undermined through engagement with objects and images that have the potential to actively trigger a myriad of feelings.

Objects and Emotions: Impact and Agency

The above demonstrates that a theoretical focus on emotional processes can provide insights into the experiences, motivations and values of human beings. But what about objects? How useful is it to extend the perspective of emotions to artefacts and images? Is this anything more than a sort of quasi poetic personification? And how should we conceptualize emotions when exploring subject–object relationships?

In the examples provided earlier about crucifixes, it has already been highlighted how objects in transit from one place and context to another can evoke strong emotional reactions in different social, artistic and political spheres. There are countless examples of how artefacts can directly affect people's embodied feelings, often in a uniform manner. In the political economy of the Trobriand Islands for instance, painted canoes have a specific strategic function, evoking awe, admiration and a willingness to trade (Malinowski 1922; Campbell 2001, 2002). Ghanaian Christians argue that visual depictions of evil, such as the devil, wield their own evil powers of influence, and consequently trigger feelings of fear (Meyer 2008: 85). The potential power of objects and images is also apparent in political fields. In pre-invasion Iraq, for example, statues of Saddam Hussein elicited strong feelings of pride in political supporters, and anger and contempt in their opponents (al-Khalil 1991).

The art historian David Freedberg (1989) has argued that some images are so powerful that they produce an almost instant emotional reaction. *Massacre of the Innocents*, a group of sculpted figures in the Chapel of the Innocents (one of forty-five chapels built between the late fifteenth and early seventeenth centuries in the Italian town of Varallo), depicts the scene of mothers grieving beside the corpses of their children. Commenting on its powerful impact on viewers, Freedberg argued that 'we spontaneously draw back from the bloodied bodies of the infants, and ... the pain that registers on the faces of the distraught mothers becomes, perhaps only momentarily, the pain we feel ourselves' (ibid.: 200).

Drawing on Freedberg's insights, Alfred Gell (1992, 1998) outlined a theoretical perspective that is extremely useful when exploring such reactions, as it conceptualizes people's interaction with objects as relational processes of causality and intentionality. Undermining the idea that humans fully control their man-made environments, Gell argued that, '[t]he immediate "other" in a social relationship does not have to be another "human being" ... Social agency can be exercised relative to "things" and social agency can be exercised by "things"' (Gell 1998: 17). Things, in other words, have similar potentials as human beings, operating as 'agents' or 'patients' in causal networks. As Gell explained:

> if my car breaks down in the middle of the night, I am in the 'patient' position and the car is the 'agent'. If I should respond to this emergency position by shouting at, or maybe even punching or kicking my unfortunate vehicle, then I am the agent and the car is the patient, and so on. (ibid.: 22)

The description of the driver's reaction highlights emotional causality in object–subject interaction. The effect of the breakdown does not evoke a directionless state of rage in the driver but rather directs his anger at the car. In the process, the vehicle is physically experienced and imagined as an intentional player in a field of emotional interaction.

Focusing on the impact of objects through an '"action"-centred approach', Gell's theory rejects a linguistically inspired analysis of objects 'as if' they were texts (ibid.: 6), an approach that some authors have rejected as too radical (Campbell 2001; Weiner 2001; Layton 2003; Leach 2007). Shirley Campbell (2001: 120), for example, has pointed out that this unconditional dismissal of symbolic and semiotic approaches to material culture risks ignoring findings provided by earlier research. In the past, she argued, aesthetic and semiotic investigations have been utilized to create insights into the impact of object production on social interaction and consequential activity, so a complete rejection of these methods would be missing an opportunity. Weiner similarly stated that,

> We can easily jettison a consideration of autonomous or discrete artistic meaning ... without throwing out the bath water of aesthetics or language or signs. Aesthetics is not restricted to a consideration of how a notion of beauty or sensory fitness is achieved in any given tradition. The notion of such sensory appropriateness is just one part of a more general process by which a community gives cognizance to its conventional forms. (Weiner 2001: 16)

It could be argued, however, that Gell's approach does not stimulate a disinterest in iconography per se, but rather urges researchers to examine the interrelated dynamics of cognition and reactive perception (d'Alleva 2001; Thomas 2001; Svašek 2007b).[7] People are partially responsive to the power of objects because they have learnt to perceive the world in a particular way. Meaning and impact, in other words, are embedded in, and produced by, perceptual and sensorial interaction with the material environment. The concept of transition, central to the approach in this chapter, seeks to provide a perspective that links these dimensions. In addition, it draws attention to processes of commoditization, as objects' meanings and effects are also influenced by changing market values.

Extending Primary Agency across Time and Space

From Gell's perspective, material objects have secondary agency as human beings are able to extend their primary agency through them (Gell 1998: 21). This idea stipulates that primary agency is mediated by 'indexes', defined as 'material entities which motivate inferences, responses or interpretations' (Thomas 2001: 4). An Indian mother may, for example, send a poster depicting the Hindu deity Ganesh to her UK-based son to be displayed in his home. The image not only brings the perceived power of Ganesh (who is invested with the power to remove unwanted obstacles) to the house, but also makes the mother's well-wishing presence felt through the index. By displaying the deity in his lounge, the son responds to his mother's intentions, but also enacts his own will as a primary agent. He might wish, for example, that the display emphasizes his Indian origins, both to himself and visitors.

Gifts brought along from the homeland to new places may also 'stand for' distant loved ones, and multi-sensorial engagement with 'objects from home' may be an important way for migrants to evoke positive memories of far-away places and people (Attan 2006; Fortier 2000; Burrell 2008; Svašek 2008: 221), and inform a sense of transnational 'extended self' (Belk 1988). The emotional impact of gifts from home is addressed in Chapter 2 by Kathy Burrell, who convincingly argues that gift giving is an embodiment of social relationships, and that the practice of finding and sending Christmas presents implies emotion work.

In transition, gifts have the potential to trigger evocative stories, as demonstrated by the following example. In 2007, a Chinese woman from Singapore, who had settled in a Northern Irish town with her Chinese husband, showed me a clock her mother had given her as a present when she was younger (see Figure 0.4).

Figure 0.4: Helen's clock in her Northern Irish home, 2007. Photograph by Maruška Svašek.

She sent me the following explanatory text a few days later:

> The teddy bears below the clock are having a picnic. My family used to go on lots of picnics when my brother and I were little. Sometimes my cousins would come along. I have lots of cousins. The car would be full of squealing children but it didn't matter because I was one of them. The clock is really from Mum. In our culture, people don't usually give clocks and watches because it means to send somebody off (to death). We're not superstitious though. Mummy loves it when we put to use the gifts she's given us. Very suitably, the clock is encased in a large suitcase. I missed my family a lot when I first arrived in Northern Ireland. I would call Mum a couple of times a week. I've travelled a lot and lived away from home quite a bit but it always feels raw when you leave your loved ones again.

The account demonstrates how memory and imagination surrounding material culture can help to sustain an emotional relationship with distant kin, triggering nostalgic stories as well as evoking feelings of homesickness.

Csikszentmihalyi and Rochberg-Halton have argued that the physicality or the 'unique concreteness and permanence' of artefacts explains why, in some cases, tangible things may help people to experience existential continuity (Csikszentmihalyi and Rochberg-Halton 1981: 14 ; Drazin 2001; Pennartz 1999). This offers a perspective on consumption that is more optimistic than the one offered by Baudrillard (1996[1968]) and Colin Campbell (1987), who have argued that, driven by a desire for self-realization and domination through possessions, consumers in capitalist societies are caught in endless cycles of longing and desire that cannot but lead to frustration and disappointment (Woodward 2007: 142).

A wide variety of consumption goods, including furniture, decorations, and works of art, can indeed be used to create more permanent material and social environments (Steedman 1982; Bourdieu 1984; Halle 1993). In the case of migrants, decorating one's home with objects brought from the homeland can increase a sense of a continuous transnational self, as also apparent in the example of Helen's clock (Parkin 1999; Attan 2006; Walsh 2006; Miller 2008). Some of the chapters that follow demonstrate the importance of active engagement with objects, such as amulets, foodstuffs and hand-made household items, to allow momentary experiences of non-fractured identity.

While moving concrete possessions from one location to another (or relocating them within the same home space) can contribute to a sense of continuity, it can also disrupt a sense of existential permanence as 'things out of place' might come to stand for 'people out of place'. The rupture of relocation may, however, also be experienced as a welcome change, allowing 'momentary disarray' and opening up space for a new sense of self (Garvey 2001: 66; Miller 2008). It should of course not be forgotten that contradictory demands with regard to the various uses of domestic space may also create tensions between family members (Munro and Madigan 1999).

Offering a visual depiction of distant people and places, photographs are specifically powerful emotional and mnemonic devices, as shown in Chapter 7 by Enrico Milič in his analysis of an Italian diasporic journal. Taken away from the homeland, personal photographs are transformational as they are given new meanings and gain new effects, as also apparent in the discussion by Deborah Schultz in Chapter 9 of photographic appropriations by the artist Arnold Daghani.

Figure 0.5: Lion dance performance in Belfast, 2007. Photograph by Maruška Svašek.

Diasporic Transformations and Transitions

Diasporic groups often use material culture to create sites of affective engagement that create and emphasize shared identities and highlight ongoing connections with the homeland. Work by Fortier (2000) and Baldassar (2001), for example, analyses processes of inter-generational transmission of attachment to Italy among Italian migrant families, and highlights the role of material culture. Diasporic Poles in the UK consume 'traditional Polish' foodstuffs with their children to strengthen their feelings for Poland, as shown in Chapter 2 by Kathy Burrell. In Chapter 10, Leon Wainwright critically analyses expectations of diasporic cultural transmission through artistic practices in Trinidad.

Migrant groups frequently use material culture 'from home' to draw the attention of local residents, aiming to influence their emotional perceptions. In 2007, for example, a Chinese lion dance was performed in Belfast on a busy spot in front of the City Hall to mark and celebrate Chinese New Year (see Figure 0.5). The performance also aimed to provoke positive feelings from the local Irish audience towards the Chinese minority. At a time when racist attacks were on the rise, political representatives of the Chinese community supported such public activities, hoping that they would help to tackle racism. Interestingly, while the very visible musicians were of Chinese origin, some of the dancers inside the Lion costume were actually local Irish boys, who were trained in Chinese dance traditions. The outfit transformed them into mediators of Chinese diasporic agency.

Diasporic transitions and transformations can have strong political connotations as pointed out by Clare Harris (2001) in a study of Tibetan Buddhist icons. She argued that:

> Due to the dispersal of Tibetan bodies in various locations around the globe, an artefactual diaspora has also been generated. Since the first decade of exile (1960+) photographic reproductions of the Dalai Lama have been deployed to consecrate domestic shrines in which he may stand alone or among a selection of photographed 'root gurus' and other reincarnated Tibetan Buddhist teachers. (ibid.: 185–86)

The images, she noted, do not only evoke religious feelings, but mediate anger about the Dalai Lama's imposed exile, and bolster a communal sense of resilience and protest against Chinese politics. As secondary agents, the photographs extend the agency of both the Dalai Lama and his political supporters.

Subject–Object Ambiguity

As numerous authors have noted (Latour 1994; Pinney and Thomas 2001; Henare, Holbraad and Wastell 2007; Svašek 2007a), a strict analytic distinction between subjects and objects is problematic as people in specific times and places experience different levels of permeability between themselves and the material world around them. The model of transition and transformation provides a similar perspective, as it regards relationships between people and things as a mutually constitutive process. In the words of Daniel Miller, artefacts are 'active [participants] in a process of social self-creation in which they are directly constitutive of our understanding of ourselves and others' (Miller 1987: 215; Miller 1998).

It must, however, be acknowledged that the range of possible ways in which people understand their interaction with material realities is vast. At one end of the spectrum, a car mechanic changing a tire, or a scientist doing an experiment with a particular substance, might consider the objects in question as empirical realities separate from their own being. Contrast these examples with a Hindu priest who maintains a personal and spiritual relationship with three-dimensional depictions of Hindu deities (*murtis*) through intense ritual, bodily and multi-sensorial engagement. In numerous temple traditions, the *murtis* have quite realistic features (see Figure 0.3), and the priests wake, wash, feed and dress them on a daily basis. Devotees interact with the *murtis* through *darshan*, a ritual practice of gazing in the eyes of religious idols (Eck 1998). The practice is grounded in the perception of direct communication between the worshipping devotee and the blessing god. Gell noted that this process assumes both object agency and a willingness to be affected: '*Darshan* is ... very much a two-way affair. The gaze directed by the god towards the worshipper confers his blessing; conversely, the worshipper reaches out and touches the god. The result is union with the god, a merging of consciousness according to the devotionalist interpretation' (Gell 1998: 117).

Christopher Pinney introduced the term 'corpothetics' to describe the sensory and bodily engagement Hindus have with religious images, contrasting this mode of perception with the 'disembodied absorption' of appreciation through explanation, typical of modernist rationalism (Pinney 2001: 158–61; see also Latour 1994). Hindu children are introduced to corpothetic perception at a young age, accompanying their parents as they perform *darshan* in front of home shrines and in temples around the world (see Figure 0.6).

It must be stressed that people who experience the merging of inner and outer realities are normally aware that people and things also exist as separate phenomena with different material characteristics. Hindu worshippers know that a stone deity might break if it falls over. Human beings are also commonly aware that durable material possessions can 'outlive' people, a realization that highlights their mortality. This dynamism alludes to an added complexity of transition and transformation that is worth exploring but not further discussed in this volume.

Transition and Transformation in Fields of Art

Gell's anthropological theory is not only relevant to anthropologists studying material culture (Pinney and Thomas 2001; Pederson 2007) but is also

Figure 0.6: A family in London in 2010 in a Hindu temple devoted to Lord Murugan. Photograph by Maruška Svašek.

of immediate interest to art historians (Osborne and Tanner 2007: 1). To explore the agency of works of art in a world of object and subject mobility, it is vital to take a process-based, relativist approach which acknowledges that art is itself a 'set of historically specific ideas and practices that have shifted meanings across the course of the centuries' (Errington 1998: 103; see also Anheier and Isar 2010). The concept of 'art worlds' is useful here, as it examines forms of co-operation between artists and others involved in the art trade in connection with the fluctuating popularity of artistic genres. Becker loosely defined the term as 'a way of talking about people who routinely participate in the making of art works' (Becker 1982: 161–62). His approach emphasized that artistic prestige and aesthetic values are, at least in part, actively produced in art markets. He also stressed the importance of examining the interaction between key players operating in these markets. From the perspective of Pierre Bourdieu (1984), the process of art production and consumption is informed by aesthetic preferences that reproduce culturally and politically embedded social distinctions. Cultural producers operating in specific professional fields learn to acquire and use field-specific types of cultural capital (knowledge), social capital (contacts) and symbolic capital (valued possessions, reputations and experience) (see also Wolff 1981; Lang and Lang 1988). What can be added is the necessity to require 'emotional capital', embodied knowledge of emotional discourses and practices that dominate in specific art worlds.

Errington (1998) coined the terms 'art by intention' and 'art by appropriation' to draw an analytic distinction between artefacts created with the specific purpose of being displayed as contemporary art, and objects and images created for a different purpose but given the status of art by art dealers and museum curators.[8] Her aim was to emphasize their active and sometimes aggressive involvement in the selective nature of object transition (ibid.: 78, 277). Knowledge production through object and image transition has been an important part of political processes, such as nation building, the creation of colonial empires and the project of multiculturalism (Clifford 1988; MacClancy 1997; Gosden and Knowles 2001).

Numerous authors (e.g., Binkley and Darish 1998; Davis 1997; Stocking 1985; Price 1989; Clifford 1991; Karp and Levine 1991; Karp, Mullen Kraemer and Levine 1992) have explored how artefacts, collected from all over the world, have been classified as 'art' or 'culture' in art museums or museums of ethnography, or have moved from one category to another – for example, from 'craft' into 'art' (Attfield 2000; Auther 2010). Important questions need to be asked that deal with hierarchies and inequalities in fields of cultural production and consumption, and explore related processes of transit and transition. Why, for example, would a Peruvian pot be classified as an ethnographic artefact while a painting by Picasso is exhibited as a work of art? Why would a mounted giraffe appear in the taxidermy section of a natural history museum, while a dissected cow by Damien Hirst be put up for sale in an art gallery? Why are specific artefacts commoditized in specific markets?[9]

The recontextualization of objects and images in spatial and discursive contexts creates conditions for particular types of emotional engagement without fully determining the outcome. In the colonial period, exhibitions in Europe of 'primitive' cultural products made in Asia, Africa and Australia often reinforced feelings of superiority or triggered misplaced, patronizing empathy in European viewers (Barringer and Flynn 1998; Binkley and Darish 1998). When some of these works were later re-evaluated and appropriated as works of art, their makers were often not consulted or even informed about the transitional process. As Sally Price pointed out: 'Although scholars occasionally put native aesthetic criteria under a microscope for social scientific study, African villagers are rarely asked to advise exhibit organisers about which masks merit the epithet of "masterpiece", and South American Indians do not generally serve as consultants about which feather headdresses deserve centre stage in museums' (Price 1989: 87).

Towards the end of the twentieth century, museums that were keen to transform museum spaces into sites of contact and dialogue started taking an approach that was more collaborative (Kuo Wei Tchen 1992; Peers and Brown 2003). The project 'Talking in Colour', for example, curated and organized in 2003 by the art historian Shan McAnena at the Naughton Art Gallery in Belfast, consulted Fante flag makers about the inclusion of specially commissioned copies of existing sacred flags in the exhibition. Two flag makers were also invited over to Belfast and employed to work with local Northern Irish community groups. In this dialogical process, all participants needed to interpret each other's intentions, adjusting work methods as they co-produced new forms and meanings (Svašek 2007: 210–16).

Appropriation is a common strategy in artistic production, with artists borrowing ideas from various sources. As Arnd Schneider (2003, 2004) has argued, this process can be hegemonic, reinforcing existing inequalities, or by contrast can create a more balanced dialogue. A good example of mutual appropriation is the cooperation between the Indian Kathakali actor Kalamandalam Vijayakumar and his English wife, the artist Kalamandalam Barbara Vijayakumar, a textiles and fashion graduate from the Winchester School of Art. The couple first met when Barbara travelled to India in the 1970s to study the make-up technique of Kathakali, a 500-year-old theatre genre performing Hindu epic stories that first developed in the temples of Kerala. Graduating from the prestigious Kerala Kalamandalam, she became the first female Kathakali make-up artist, skilled in applying make-up for all the different Kathakali characters. The thick and colourful make up includes the application of *chutti*, paper shapes that are attached to the face with thick rice paste (see Figure 0.7).

Returning to Britain in 1979, Barbara experimented with her newly learned skills, creating colourful sculptural costumes and Kathakali-inspired facial make-up that included *chutti*-like features (see Figure 0.8). She established Centre Ocean Stream, a group of four contemporary dancers who, wearing the costumes and the make-up, performed slowly moving visual compositions. The end result was quite different to the often fierce physical body language of the Kathakali actors.

Appropriation took place in what can be regarded as the opposite direction when Kalamandalam Vijayakumar came over to Britain in 1987. Having gained a postgraduate diploma in 1986 as a Kathakali actor at Kerala Kalamandalam, and having toured throughout Kerala and India as member of the Kerala Kalamandalam Troupe, he had enough experience to start performing in the UK, with Barbara as main organizer and *chutti* artist. Together, they founded the Kala Chethena Company, which brings over actors and musicians from Kerala for two-month tours on an annual

Figure 0.7: Padmasree Kalamandalam Gopi, preparing for a Kathakali performance in Liverpool in 2010, with *chutti* make-up created by Kalamandalam Barbara Vijayakumar. Photograph by Maruška Svašek.

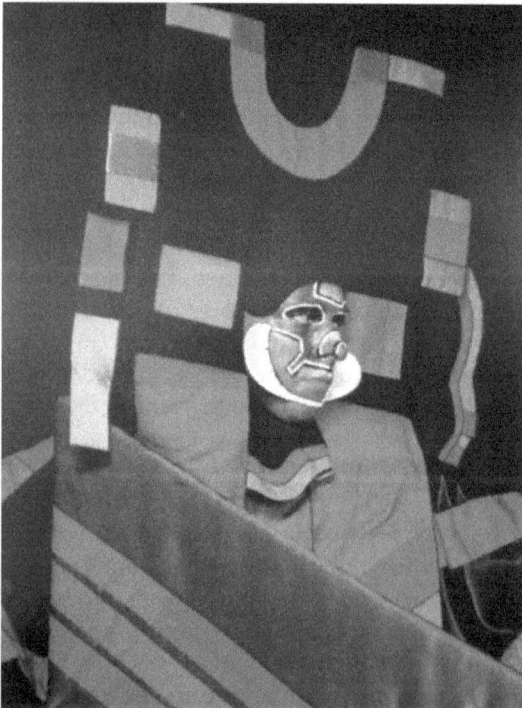

Figure 0.8: Detail from a 1988 poster advertising a Centre Ocean Stream performance, showing the performer Julian Harrow. Photograph courtesy of Centre Ocean Stream.

basis. Initially, Vijayakumar presented only traditional stories, though adapted for Western audiences who expected shows to last no longer than an hour and a half. Responding to possibilities and limitations in the British context, he introduced more radical changes when, together with Barbara, he developed Kathakali workshops for schools and community groups, created a show based on the story of Snow White, and developed a sign-language for deaf people inspired by the hand gestures of the Indian *mudras*. In the process, his role as a Kathakali performer clearly changed.

As the examples of the Fante flag makers and Kathakali artists demonstrate, the issue of transit and transition raises questions about the changing identities of object producers as they operate in different fields. Chapter 8 focuses on what could be called 'artists by appropriation'. Maggie O'Neill examines a project in which migrants and refugees, most of them non-artists, are temporarily transformed into art producers during a community project. This group of people can be contrasted with artists by intention, who are central in the final three chapters. In these later contributions, Deborah Schultz, Leon Wainwright and Maruška Svašek follow Hungarian, Trinidadian and Ghanaian artists on their career paths. Their analyses show how the shifting and at times contradictory meanings and impact of artworks inform processes of identity construction and transformation in ways that are comparable to the transition and transformation dynamics discussed in earlier chapters.

Outline of the Book

The contributors to this book analyse a number of processes, which offer prime material for analysing transit, transition and transformation. Migration is the main focus of Chapters 1 to 8, while Chapters 9 to 11 concentrate on transit and transition in artistic fields. Chapter 8 connects the two major themes as it deals with an art project organized for refugees.

Migration

When exploring the theme of migration, material culture and emotions, it must be highlighted that the socio-economic background of transnational migrants varies greatly, ranging from members of the affluent propertied class who seek to further their careers abroad to poor migrants and political refugees who are forced to leave their homelands for economic or political reasons. Their migratory situation also influences the ways in which they engage with particular objects and images. To give an example, refugees who flee war-torn countries or hunger-stricken zones often have little time and opportunity to take anything with them. This stands in sharp contrast with expat diplomats who are in a position to relocate many of their possessions, while also being able to frequently travel back and forth to their home countries.[10]

The authors in this book focus on various types of mobile people who, because of their different predicaments and life trajectories, have different and changing material and emotional links to their homelands. The groups include migrant workers in the UK (Chapters 1 and 2) and Belgium (Chapter 3), refugees in India (Chapter 4), Norway (Chapter 5) and Britain (Chapter 8), diasporic communities in India (Chapter 6), Italy (Chapter 7) and Trinidad (Chapter 10), and mobile artists who have moved from Romania to France (Chapter 9) and from Ghana to the US (Chapter 11).

The contributions demonstrate that individual migrants use and are affected by objects in many different ways. Chapter 1 by Fiona Parrott focuses on artefacts in the homes of migrants who live in a cosmopolitan street in South London. The choice of street is interesting as it groups together people from different parts of the world, turning it into a complex setting of transnational movement and emotional engagement. A dynamic assembly of artefacts is intertwined with the personal trajectories of their owners. Parrott also shows that while interaction with artefacts brought from the homeland can bring comfort, it might also generate unintentional, emotional effects that increase feelings of non-belonging. In addition, the chapter demonstrates that objects and images may reinforce contradictory attachments, helping people to manage and negotiate connections in their homeland and new place of residence.

Material culture's ability to evoke feelings of connectivity and well-being is central to Kathy Burrell's analyses in Chapter 2. Burrell analyses Polish migrants' experiences of Christmas in the UK, and focuses on the material embodiment of migrant identity, specifically through foodstuffs and ritual artefacts. She stresses the emotional intensity of the Christmas experience, with its strong associations of home, family life and friendship. The chapter highlights that ritual interaction with Christmas decorations and special food is a multi-sensorial experience that creates links between past and present. In this process, the connection between memories and emotions are as vital as the multi-sensorial dimensions of subject–object interaction. Seeing, holding, smelling and tasting wafers, for example, not only triggers nostalgic feelings, but can also create a sense of shared Polishness and increase experiences of positive transnational belonging while abroad from the nation state.

Ritual events like Christmas clearly offer migrants the opportunity to create a sense of 'home away from home'. As Eddy Plasquy points out in Chapter 3, object-focused religious rituals may also help migrants to appropriate traditions specific to localities in the homeland, intensifying diasporic identity formation and forging new bonds between diasporas and communities in their countries of origin. Plasquy's contribution focuses on efforts by Spanish migrants in the Belgium town of Vilvoorde to organize events based on the Catholic celebration of the Virgin Mary of El Rocío. The analysis traces the historical roots of the tradition and explores its reinvention and transformation in the context of Vilvoorde. Plasquy demonstrates how, in transit and transition, the image of the Virgin, embodied by several versions of the statue, has diverse and changing emotional impact on the organizers of and participants in the procession. As the celebrations have grown each year, attracting an increasing number of non-Spanish visitors, the object has become a mediator of positive emotional interaction between the Spanish migrants of Vilvoorde and other Spanish and non-Spanish communities.

As Plasquy points out, when exploring the lives of migrants we should not limit ourselves to studying migrant groups in isolation but also investigate relations between migrants and other individuals. This is also the opening argument of Timm Lau's analysis of interactions between India-based Tibetan refugees, who are active in the sweater trade, and their Indian suppliers and customers in Chapter 4. Lau points out that the sweaters function as active mediators of emotional dynamics. In transit and transition between the Indian manufacturers and the Tibetan market stalls, the commodities (sweaters) are important agents, shaping relations of trust between individual traders. This is essential in a business riddled with risk. Concrete examples show that the sweaters can also become mediators of distrust and anger. Lau explains how Tibetan traders comment on the exploitative relationship between themselves and the Indian merchants, and describes how irritated and frustrated Tibetan salesmen can become when faced with hard-nosed Indian customers. Tibetan traders' risk management also has a religious component. Before trade expeditions, many traders perform Buddhist divinatory rituals and place blessed grains in bundles of sweaters that are being prepared for sale. Relying on the protective capacity of ritual implements, traders also wear protective amulets.

Amulets are also worn by Hindu Tamil refugees in Anne Sigfrid Grønseth's contribution (Chapter 5). As do the following two chapters, this chapter explores the capacity of objects to increase personal feelings of well-being and positive belonging. Grønseth's analysis describes how Tamils in exile have resettled in Norwegian fishing villages along the Arctic coast. Despite being economically integrated into the Norwegian community, they feel isolated and lost in their new surroundings. They suffer both physically and mentally from their separation from their homeland, and long for the physical company of their relatives and their former local gods. Grønseth's informants invoke their presence through objects such as amulets, strings, pictures of the gods and kitchen utensils used specially for ritual practices. Embodied engagement with these artefacts increases the refugees' sense of well-being. Interaction between subjects and objects, Grønseth argues, generates positive emotions and sensations as the multi-sensorial experience connects the refugees to their kin, deities and places of origin. Embodied ritual practices, in other words, evoke potentially healing memories of home, and strengthen the inner presence of a familiar, 'understanding' world. In addition, manipulating 'things', with the intention of protecting distant family members, gives the Tamils an increased sense of agency that counters their feelings of disempowerment.

The potential power of objects to increase people's well-being is also discussed by Sameera Maiti in Chapter 6 in an analysis of artefact production by Karen migrants who live on the Andaman Islands. Supporting her older informants, Maiti laments what she sees as the 'sad state' of traditional Karen arts and crafts. When the Christian Karen migrated from Burma in the 1920s in an attempt to escape poverty, the similar environmental and climatic conditions on the islands enabled them to continue producing their traditional dwellings, household items and tools. As in the case of the Tamil refugees, the resulting artefacts had an added emotional impact, triggering feelings of positive re-embeddedness and transnational connectivity. Development policy and ideologies of modernization in independent India, however, began to hamper the production of the traditional arts and crafts. The most senior Karen, who still produce traditional artefacts, stressed that their embodied engagement with raw materials (through carving, weaving and plaiting) enhanced their personal well-being and stimulated a harmonious social sphere. Younger generations of Karen, however, have been reluctant to learn the skills, regarding them as 'outdated'. Their desire for 'modern' mass-produced goods has also been triggered by the arrival of new Indian settlers. Interestingly, some youngsters have recently shown an interest in the 'old-fashioned' skills as part of their strategy to gain the status as a 'scheduled tribe'. Traditional production processes, in other words, have been objectified as active agents in an emotionally charged struggle for political and economic gain.

In Chapter 7 by Enrico Milič, identity politics are also played out through material culture. In this case, Italians who left the island of Lussìn (now Lošinj) after the end of the Second World War produce a diasporic journal in which they reminisce about their lost island. In an intricate process of object transit and transition, old photographs of 'Italian life' on the island are collected by the editors, reproduced and recontextualized in the journal, then distributed to Lussignani exiles and their descendants who have settled in different corners of the world. As visual catalysts, the photographs are meant to have a powerful emotional impact, evoking nostalgic memories of specific people and places, as well as engendering feelings of anger about what is regarded by many as an unjust historical fate. Milič argues that the editors of the journal are only partially successful. While the leaders of the diasporic island community use the journal to multiply and justify their call for economic and political rights on the island, most readers and contributors are not interested in these claims, but use the publication as a network through which they can share visual and textual stories about a common past. In both cases, the journal empowers the diasporic Italians, increasing their sense of well-being through material 'evidence' of rootedness and an increased notion of transnational connectivity.

Art Production

Mobilizing people to tell a story about their past is also an important aim of the art project analysed by Maggie O'Neill in Chapter 8. The people participating in the project were refugees and migrants who settled in Britain. They were asked to tell stories about locations 'back home' while walking around in their present place of residence. The resulting stories were often moving, bringing up evocative topics such as love for particular landscapes, homesickness and fear of persecution. After the walks, guided by professional artists, the narrators created visual objects around the themes of 'home' and 'belonging'. Often in combination with fragments of their stories, the resulting artefacts were displayed as 'installations' in a gallery space. The case study is fascinating in terms of its complexity regarding transit, transition and transformation. It involved the relocation of individuals to Britain, turning them into 'refugees', 'migrants' and 'minorities'. In the context of the walk and the exhibition they took on the role of 'artists'. Members of the public interacted with their productions in different ways, being touched for different reasons. One of the aims of the project was to increase the personal well-being of participants. As O'Neill argues, their largely positive feedback showed that many rated their involvement positively as it allowed them to share and visualize feelings about past and present experiences of belonging and non-belonging.

The three remaining chapters discuss the life and work of professional artists who moved abroad, or are descendents of migrants, and explore the emotional meaning and impact of their paintings, sculptures and other artistic productions. The artist Arnold Daghani (1909–1985) left communist Romania in 1958 in an attempt to develop his career outside the limitations of a politically controlled art world. In Chapter 9, Deborah Schultz describes how Daghani's displacement led him to reflect on his past experiences as a prisoner in a slave-labour camp in Ukraine in 1942/43. Survivor guilt came to haunt his drawings and writings. Texts and visual imagery, combined in some of his productions, collapsed time and spatial distance, expressing and evoking remembered and re-experienced emotions. Daghani's art 'books', or folios, crossed both artistic and physical boundaries, having travelled with him on his journeys and 'outliving' the artist. Schultz points out that, as powerful affective agents and objects in transit through time and space, they have moved viewers whose experience differs radically from that of the creator of the work.

In Chapter 10, Leon Wainwright follows the stylistic and iconographic subject matter of the Trinidadian artist Shastri Maharaj (b.1953), exploring how changing demands for ethnic difference are constructed and challenged by the artist in his artworks. The perspective of transit, transition and transformation is useful, he argues, as it pushes the analysis beyond the textual metaphor of translation, and puts the spotlight on the contradictions and tensions of lived experience. In the context of Trinidad, individual

'Indo-Trinidadian' artists like Maharaj have developed their careers against the backdrop of this complexity, responding to various cultural forces stemming from nationalist ideology, their own diasporic embeddedness in East-Indian transnationalism, and the globally spread myth of artistic freedom. Wainwright is interested in the emotional pressures this has put on the artist, and compares the 'everydayness' of the artist's career with the lived Indianness of Indo-Trinidadian popular culture. Ethnicity and creole nationalism turn out to be problematic and politicized categories of analysis, providing a grid that is too static to capture the reality and emotional complexity of cultural production and reception. The chapter shows how artists like Maharaj are immersed in an emotional nexus where they cater for, play with and defy demands for an easily readable 'ethnic' and 'national creole' visual language.

In Chapter 11, the final contribution to this volume, Maruška Svašek discusses the US-based Ghanaian artist and performer George Hughes, who also challenges existing discourses of ethnic and artistic identity in his performance piece 'What You Perceive Is What You Conceive'. She describes how Hughes plays with the notion of 'the primitive African', confronting his audience in Belfast with his half-naked, painted and masked body, interspersing the show with loud screams. Transforming himself into a stereotype, he does, however, also challenge and escape the image, appropriating other objects such as robotic dogs, and dancing to a combination of different musical styles. Focusing on audience perception, the analysis demonstrates that previous knowledge and emotional memories and expectations influence the ways in which individual audience members experience and interpret cultural productions.

Throughout the book, we see that subject–object dialectics and the emotional interaction of mobile primary and secondary agents shape human experience. The detailed case studies aim to stimulate further interdisciplinary research in this field of study.

Notes

1. This Introduction was developed as part of the project 'Creativity and Innovation in a World of Movement', financially supported by the HERA Joint Research Programme. The programme is co-funded by AHRC, AKA, DASTI, ETF, FNR, FWF, HAZU, IRCHSS, MHEST, NWO, RANNIS, RCN, VR and The European Community FP7 2007-2013, under the Socio-economic Sciences and Humanities programme. I am grateful for the financial and intellectual support of both AHRC and HERA. I would also like to thank Birgit Meyer, Justin I'Anson-Sparks and two anonymous reviewers for their insightful comments on an earlier version of this chapter.
2. *London Evening Standard*, 2006, Retrieved 29 September 2010 from: http://www. thisislondon.co.uk/news/article-23370734-christian-ba-employee-to-take-legal-action-over-suspension-for-wearing-cross.do.
3. For a more in-depth discussion of this debate, see Lutz and White (1986), Lynch (1990), Leavitt (1996), Milton (2005) and Svašek (2005a).
4. See also Fiona Parrott's discussion of Leavitt's approach in Chapter 1 of this volume.

5. In a book edited by Ehrenreich and Hochschild (2003), the authors focus on the emotional labour performed by migrant women in the context of global economic and gender inequalities. These migrants, mostly women who leave their children behind, travel abroad to work as nannies, domestic workers, care workers and sex workers in more affluent countries. Parreñas (2001, 2005), Constable (2003) and Lindio-McGovern (2003) and have explored how female Filipino workers negotiate long-distance intimate relationships with their children, and Zarembka (2003) has analysed this process amongst female Bolivian migrants. Although not at the centre of these studies, the cases demonstrate that material objects, in the form of letters, presents and money sent home to buy food, clothes and household items, are important agents of transnational care.

6. Inda and Rosaldo (2002: 14) pointed out that globalizing processes of deterritorialization ('the general weakening of the ties between culture and place') and reterritorialization ('reinscribing culture in new time–space contexts') happen simultaneously. The term de/territorialization captures this double movement, emphasizing that '[t]here is no dislodging of everyday meanings from their moorings in particular localities without their simultaneous reinsertion in fresh environments' (ibid.: 15). See also Gilroy (1991), Wolf (2002), Ahmed et al. (2003) and Wise and Chapman (2005).

7. Building on Gell's approach and discussing the significance of metaphor and metonym in Tahitian visual representations, d'Alleva (2001) has argued that these symbolic forms are cognized through a broad range of perceptual and conceptual processes. This makes them powerful presences that 'stimulate the mind, provoking the imagination and creating understanding in sometimes new and unexpected ways' (ibid.: 82).

8. The terms were based on the concepts of art by destination and art by metamorphosis used by André Malraux (1965). Jacques Maquet applied these terms in his theory of aesthetic consciousness (Maquet 1971; see also Maquet 1986: 18), and a few years later Nelson Graburn (1976) used the terminology in his classification of ethnic and tourist art. Arjun Appadurai (1986) also used the terms as building blocks in his theory of commoditization. Shelley Errington subsequently renamed them by replacing the words 'destination' and 'metamorphosis' with 'intention' and 'appropriation' respectively.

9. Commoditization in existing and newly developed (partially overlapping) global markets of 'contemporary art', 'souvenirs', 'ethnic art', and so on, has shaped the transition of many local products (Maquet 1971; Coote and Shelton 1992; Hart 1995; Marcus and Myers 1995; Mullin 1995; Steiner 1995). Mobile object and image producers, in other words, have to deal with local, regional or national markets that might or might not be connected through global networks, and might have different systems of value (Steiner 1994; Hart 1995).

10. Since the 1990s, a growing number of scholars have used the concept 'transnationalism' to analyse the predicaments of migrants, defined as 'the processes by which immigrants forge and sustain multi-stranded social relations that link together their societies of origin and settlement' (Basch, Glick Schiller and Blanc Szanton 1994: 7; see also Appadurai 1990; Glick Schiller, Basch and Blanc Szanton 1995; Lie 1995; Hannerz 1996; Inda and Rosaldo 2002; Vertovec 2004; Lechner 2009: 210–13). Numerous scholars have explored the emotional dimensions of transnational relatedness and belonging, acknowledging the centrality of emotional dynamics to diasporic identity formation, social life and political struggle (Ahmed et al. 2003; Svašek and Skrbiš 2007). For research on the emotional dimensions of the experiences of refugees, see, e.g., Marx (1990), Davis (1992), Sommers (2001), Cernea and McDowell (2002) and Marfleet (2005). Some of the refugees who participated in the art project analysed in Chapter 8 by Maggie O'Neill refer to feelings of fear and uncertainty that urged them to leave their homelands, and feelings of grief relating to the people and things they had to leave behind.

References

Ahmed, S. 2004a. *The Cultural Politics of Emotion*. Edinburgh: Edinburgh University Press.

———— 2004b. 'Affective Economies', *Social Text* 22(2): 117–39.

Ahmed, S., C. Castañeda, A. Fortier and M. Sheller (eds). 2003. *Uprootings/ Regroundings: Questions of Home and Migration*. Oxford: Berg.

Al-Khalil, S. 1991. *The Monument: Art, Vulgarity and Responsibility in Iraq*. Berkeley: University of California Press.

Anheier, H., and Y.R. Isar (eds). 2010. *Cultural Expression, Creativity and Innovation*. London: Sage.

Appadurai, A. 1990. 'Global Ethnoscapes: Notes and Queries for a Transnational Anthropology', in R. Fox (ed.), *Recapturing Anthropology*. Santa Fe, NM: School of American Research Press, pp. 191–210.

———— (ed.) 1986. *The Social Life of Things: Commodities in Cultural Perspective*. Cambridge: Cambridge University Press.

Attan, C. 2006. 'Hidden Objects in the World of Cultural Migrants: Significant Objects Used by European Migrants to Layer Thoughts and Memories', in K. Burrell and P. Panayi (eds), *Histories and Memories: Migrants and their History in Britain*. London: I.B. Tauris, pp. 171–90.

Attfield, J. 2000. *Wild Things: The Material Cultures of Everyday Life*. Oxford: Berg.

Auther, E. 2010. *String Felt Thread: The Hierarchy of Art and Craft in American Art*. Minneapolis: University of Minnesota Press.

Baldassar, L. 2001. *Visits Home: Migration Experiences between Italy and Australia*. Melbourne: Melbourne University Press.

Baldassar, L., C. Baldock and R. Wilding. 2006. *Families Caring Across Borders: Migration, Ageing and Transnational Caregiving*. London: Palgrave Macmillan.

Baldock, C. 2000. 'Migrants and their Parents: Caregiving from a Distance', *Journal of Family Issues* 21(2): 205–24.

Barringer, T., and T. Flynn (eds). 1998. *Colonialism and the Object: Empire, Material Culture and the Museum*. London: Routledge.

Barthes, R. 2000. *Camera Lucida*, trans. R. Howards. London: Vintage.

Basch, L., N. Glick Schiller and C. Blanc-Szanton. 1994. *Nations Unbound: Transnational Projects, Postcolonial Predicaments, and Deterritorialised Nation-States*. Amsterdam: Gordon and Breach.

Baudrillard (1996[1968]) *The System of Objects*, trans. J. Benedict. London: Verso

Becker, H.S. 1982. *Art Worlds*. Berkeley: University of California Press.

Belk, Russell W. 1988. 'Possessions and the Extended Self', *The Journal of Consumer Research* 15: 139–65.

Bhatia. S., and A. Ram. 2004. 'Culture, Hybridity and the Dialogical Self: Cases from the South Asian Diaspora', *Mind, Culture and Activity* 11(3): 224–40.

Binkley, D.A., and P.J. Darish. 1998. '"Enlightened but in Darkness": Interpretations of Kuba Art and Culture at the Turn of the Twentieth Century', in E. Schildkrout and C.A. Keim (eds.), *The Scramble for Art in Central Africa*. Cambridge: Cambridge University Press, pp. 37–62.

Bourdieu, P. 1984. *Distinction: A Social Critique of the Judgement of Taste*, trans. R. Nice. London: Routledge and Kegan Paul.

Burrell, K. 2008. 'Managing, Learning and Sending: The Material Lives and Journeys of Polish Women in Britain', *Journal of Material Culture* 13: 63–83.

Campbell, C. 1987. *The Romantic Ethic and the Spirit of Modern Consumerism*. Oxford: Basil Blackwell.

Campbell, S.F. 2001. 'The Captivating Agency of Art: Many Ways of Seeing', in C. Pinney and N. Thomas (eds), *Beyond Aesthetics: Art and the Technologies of Enchantment*. Oxford: Berg, pp. 117–36.

———— 2002. *The Art of Kula*. Oxford: Berg.

Casey, E.S. 1987. *Remembering: A Phenomenological Study*. Bloomington: Indiana University Press.

Cernea, M., and C. McDowell. 2002. *Risks and Reconstruction: Experiences of Resettlers and Refugees*. Oxford: Berghahn.

Chrisafis, A. 2011. 'Attack on "Blasphemous" Art Work Fires Debate on Role of Religion in France', *Guardian*, 18 April. Retrieved 2 June 2011 from: http://www.guardian.co.uk/world/2011/apr/18/andres-serrano-piss-christ-destroyed-christian-protesters.

Cierraad, I. 1999. *At Home: An Anthropology of Domestic Space*. New York: Syracuse University Press.

Clifford, J. 1988. *The Predicament of Culture: Twentieth-century Ethnography, Literature, and Art*. Cambridge, MA: Harvard University Press.

———— 1991. 'Four Northwest Coast Museums: Travel Reflections', in I. Karp and S.D. Levine (eds), *Exhibiting Cultures: The Poetics and Politics of Museum Display*. Washington: Smithsonian Institution, pp. 212–54.

Conradson, D., and A. Latham. 2007. 'The Affective Possibilities of London: Antipodean Transnationals and the Overseas Experience', *Mobilities* 2(2): 167–74.

Conradson, D., and D. McKay. 2007. 'Translocal Subjectivities: Mobility, Connection, Emotion', *Mobilities* 2(2): 231–54.

Constable, N. 2003. 'Filipina Workers in Hong Kong Homes: Household Rules and Relations', in B. Ehrenreich and A.R. Hochschild (eds), *Global Women: Nannies, Maids, and Sex Workers in the New Economy*. New York: Metropolitan and Own, pp. 115–41.

Coote, J., and A. Shelton (eds). 1992. *Anthropology, Art and Aesthetics*. Oxford: Oxford University Press.

Csikszentmihalyi, M., and E. Rochberg-Halton. 1981. *The Meaning of Things: Domestic Symbols and the Self*. Cambridge: Cambridge University Press.

Csordas, T.J. 1990. 'Embodiment as a Paradigm for Anthropology', *Ethos* 18(1): 5–47.

_____ (ed.) 1994. *Embodiment and Experience: The Existential Ground of Culture and Self*. Cambridge: Cambridge University Press.

D'Alleva, A. 2001. 'Captivation, Representation, and the Limits of Cognition: Interpreting Methaphor and Metonymy in Tahitian Tamau', in C. Pinney and N. Thomas (eds), *Beyond Aesthetics: Art and the Technologies of Enchantment*. Oxford: Berg, pp. 79–96.

Davis, J. 1992. 'The Anthropology of Suffering', *Journal of Refugee Studies* 5(2): 149–61.

Davidson, J., L. Bondi and M. Smith (eds). 2005. *Emotional Geographies*. Aldershot: Ashgate.

Deleuze, G. 1998. *Essays Critical and Clinical*, trans. D.W. Smith and M.A. Greco. London: Verso.

Drazin, A. 2001. 'A Man Will Get Furnished: Wood and Domesticity in Urban Romania', in D. Miller (ed.), *Home Possessions*. Oxford: Berg, pp. 173–200.

Durant, S., and C.M. Lord. 2007. 'Essays in Migratory Aesthetics: Cultural Practices Between Migration and Art-making', in S. Durrant and C.M. Lord (eds), *Essays in Migratory Aesthetics: Cultural Practices Between Migration and Art-making*. Amsterdam: Rodopi, pp. 11–20.

Eck, D.L. 1998. *Darshan*. New York: Columbia University Press.

Edwards, E. 2010. 'Photographs and History: Emotions and Materiality', in S. Dudley (ed.), *Museum Materialities: Objects, Engagements, Interpretations*. London: Routledge, pp. 21–38.

Ehrenreich, B., and A.R. Hochschild (eds). 2003. *Global Woman: Nannies, Maids, and Sex Workers in the New Economy*. New York: Metropolitan and Own.

Errington, S. 1998. *The Death of Authentic Art and Other Tales of Progress*. Berkeley: University of California Press.

Fortier, A. 2000. *Migrant Belongings: Memory, Space, Identity*. Oxford: Berg.

Freedberg, D. 1989. *The Power of Images*. Chicago: University of Chicago Press.

Fusco, C. 2002. 'Shooting the Klan: An Interview with Andres Serrano'. Retrieved 16 November 2004 from: http://www.community arts.net/readingroom/archive/ca/fusco-serrano.php.

Garvey, P. 2001. 'Organized Disorder: Moving Furniture in Norwegian Homes', in D. Miller (ed.), *Home Possessions: Material Culture behind Closed Doors*. Oxford: Berg.

Gell, A. 1998. *Art and Agency: An Anthropological Theory*. Oxford: Clarendon Press.

_____ 1992. 'The Enchantment of Technology and the Technology of Enchantment', in J. Coote and A. Shelton (eds), *Anthropology, Art and Aesthetics*. Oxford: Oxford University Press.

Gilroy, P. 1991. 'It Ain't Where You're From, It's Where You're At: The Dialectics of Diasporic Identification', *Third Text* 13: 3–16.

Gosden, C., and C. Knowles. 2001. *Collecting Colonialism: Material Culture and Colonial Change*. Oxford: Berg.

Graburn, N. (ed.) 1976. *Ethnic and Tourist Arts: Cultural Expressions from the Fourth World*. Los Angeles: University of California Press.

Hall, A. 2010. '"These People Could Be Anyone": Fear, Contempt (and Empathy) in a British Immigration Removal Centre', *Journal of Ethnic and Migration Studies* 36(6): 881–98.

Halle, D. 1993. *Inside Culture: Art and Class in the American Home*. Chicago: University of Chicago Press.

Hannerz, U. 1996. *Transnational Connections: Culture, People, Places*. London: Routledge.

Harris, C. 2001. 'The Politics and Personhood of Tibetan Buddhist Icons', in C. Pinney and N. Thomas (eds.), *Beyond Aesthetics: Art and the Technologies of Enchantment*. Oxford: Berg, pp. 180–200.

Hart, L.M. 1995. 'Three Walls: Regional Aesthetics and the International Art World', in G.E. Marcus and F.R. Myers (eds), *The Traffic in Culture: Refiguring Art and Anthropology*. Berkeley: University of California Press.

Henare, A., M. Holbraad and S. Wastel (eds). 2007. *Thinking through Things: Theorising Artefacts Ethnographically*. New York: Routledge.

Hochschild, A.R. 1983. *The Managed Heart: Commercialization of Human Feeling*. Berkeley: University of California Press.

Hogan, S. 2010. 'Routes to Interiorities: Art Therapy and Knowing Anthropology', *Visual Anthropology* 23(2): 158–74.

Inda, J., and R. Rosaldo (eds). 2002. *The Anthropology of Globalisation: A Reader*. Oxford: Blackwell.

Ingold, T. 2000. *The Perception of the Environment*. London: Routledge.

Josephides, L. 2005. 'Resentment as a Sense of Self', in K. Milton and M. Svašek (eds), *Mixed Emotions: Anthropological Studies of Feeling*. Oxford: Berg, pp. 71–90.

Joy, A., and J.F. Sherry. 2003. 'Speaking of Art as Embodied Imagination: A Multisensory Approach to Understanding Aesthetic Experience', *Journal of Consumer Research* 30: 259–83.

Karp, I., and S.D. Levine (eds). 1991. *Exhibiting Cultures: The Poetics and Politics of Museum Display*. Washington: Smithsonian Institution.

Karp, I., C. Mullen Kraemer and S.D. Levine. 1992. *Museums and Communities: The Politics of Public Culture*. Washington: Smithsonian Institution Press.

Kopytoff, I. 1986. 'The Cultural Biography of Things: Commoditization as Process', in A. Appadurai (ed.), *The Social Life of Things: Commodities in Cultural Perspective*. Cambridge: Cambridge University Press, pp. 64–91.

Kuo Wei Tchen, J. 1992. 'Creating a Dialogic Museum: The Chinatown History Museum Experiment', in I. Karp, C. Mullen Kraemer and S.D. Levine (eds), *Museums and Communities: The Politics of Public Culture.* Washington: Smithsonian Institution Press, pp. 285–326.

Lang, G., and K. Lang. 1988. 'Recognition and Reknown: The Survival of Artistic Reputations', *American Journal of Sociology* 94: 79–109.

Latour, B. 1994. *We Have Never Been Modern.* New York: Prentice Hall.

Layton, R. 2003. 'Art and Agency: A Reassessment', *Journal of the Royal Anthropological Institute* 9: 447–64.

Leach, J. 2007. 'Differentiation and Encompassment: A Critique of Alfred Gell's Theory of the Abduction of Creativity', in A. Henare, M. Holbraad and S. Wastel (eds), *Thinking through Things: Theorising Artefacts Ethnographically.* New York: Routledge, pp. 167–88.

Leavitt, J. 1996. 'Meaning and Feeling in the Anthropology of Emotions', *American Ethnologist* 23(3): 514–39.

Lechner, F.J. 2009. *Globalization: The Making of World Society.* Malden, MA: Wiley-Blackwell.

Lie, J. 1995. 'From International Migration to Transnational Diaspora', *Contemporary Sociology* 24(4): 303–6.

Lindio-McGovern, L. 2003. 'Labour Export in the Context of Globalization', *International Sociology* 18(3): 513–34.

Lock, M. 1993. 'Cultivating the Body: Anthropology and Epistemologies of Bodily Practice and Knowledge', *Annual Review of Anthropology* 22: 133–55.

Lutz, C.A. 1988. *Unnatural Emotions: Everyday Sentiments on a Micronesian Atoll and Their Challenge to Western Theory.* Chicago and London: University of Chicago Press.

Lutz, C.A., and L. Abu-Lughod (eds). 1990. *Language and the Politics of Emotion.* Cambridge: Cambridge University Press.

Lutz, C.A., and G.M. White. 1986. 'The Anthropology of Emotions', *Annual Review of Anthropology* 15: 405–36.

Lynch, O.M. 1990. *Divine Passion: The Social Construction of Emotion in India.* Berkeley: University of California Press.

Lyon, M.L. 1995. 'Missing Emotion: The Limitations of Cultural Constructionism in the Study of Emotion', *Cultural Anthropology* 10(2): 244–63.

MacClancy, J. 1997. *Contesting Art: Art, Politics and Identity in the Modern World.* Oxford: Berg.

Malinowski, B. 1922. *Argonauts of the Western Pacific.* London: Routledge and Kegan Paul.

Malraux, A. 1967[1965] *Museum without Walls: The Voices of Silence*, trans. Stuart Gilbert and Francis Price. London: Secker and Warburg.

Maquet, J. 1979[1971] *Introduction to Aesthetic Anthropology.* Malibu, CA: Undena Publications.

_____ 1986. *The Aesthetic Experience: An Anthropologist Looks at the Visual Arts*. New Haven, CT and London: Yale University Press.

Marcus, G.E., and F.R. Myers. 1995. 'The Traffic in Art and Culture: An Introduction', in G.E. Marcus and F.R. Myers (eds), *The Traffic in Culture: Refiguring Art and Anthropology*. Berkeley: University of California Press, pp. 1–54.

Marfleet, P. 2005. *Refugees in a Global Era*. London: Palgrave Macmillan

Marx, E. 1990. 'The Social World of the Refugee: A Conceptual Framework.' *Journal of Refugee Studies* 3: 189–203.

Matravers, D. 1998. *Art and Emotion*. Oxford: Clarendon Press.

Merleau-Ponty, M. 1996[1945]. *La Phenomenologie de la perception*. Paris: Gallimard.

Meyer, B. 2008. 'Powerful Pictures: Popular Christian Aesthetics in Southern Ghana', *Journal of the American Academy of Religion* 76(1): 82–110.

Miller, D. 1987. *Material Culture and Mass Consumption*. Oxford: Blackwell.

_____ (ed.) 1998. *Material Cultures: Why Some Things Matter*. Chicago: University of Chicago Press.

_____ (ed.) 2001. *Home Possessions: Material Culture behind Closed Doors*. Oxford: Berg.

_____ 2008. *The Comfort of Things*. Cambridge: Polity.

Miller, N.K. 2003. '"Portraits of Grief". Telling Details and the Testimony of Trauma', *Differences* 18: 112–35.

Milton, K. 2005. 'Meanings, Feelings and Human Ecology', in K. Milton and M. Svašek (eds), *Mixed Emotions: Anthropological Studies of Feeling*. Oxford: Berg, pp. 25–42.

_____ 2002. *Loving Nature. Towards an Ecology of Emotion*. London and New York: Routledge.

Mitchell, W.J.T. 2005a. 'There Are No Visual Media', *Journal of Visual Culture* 4(2): 257–66.

_____ 2005b. *What Do Pictures Want? The Lives and Loves of Images*. Chicago: University of Chicago Press.

Mullin, M.H. 1995. 'The Patronage of Difference: Making Indian Art "Art, Not Ethnology"', in G.E. Marcus and F.R. Myers (eds), *The Traffic in Culture: Refiguring Art and Anthropology*. Berkeley: University of California Press, pp. 166–200.

Munro, M., and R. Madigan. 1999. 'Negotiating Space in the Family Home', in I. Cierraad (ed.), *At Home: An Anthropology of Domestic Space*. New York: Syracuse University Press, pp. 107–17.

Myers, F. 1986. *Pintupi County, Pintupi Self: Sentiment, Place, and Politics among Western Desert Aborigines*. Washington, DC: Smithsonian Institution Press.

Nussbaum, M.C. 2001. *Upheavals of Thought: The Intelligence of Emotions*. Cambridge: Cambridge University Press.

Osborne, R., and J. Tanner (eds). 2007. *Art's Agency and Art History*. Oxford: Blackwell.

Parkin, D. 1999. 'Mementoes as Transitional Objects in Human Displacement', *Journal of Material Culture* 4(3): 303–20.

Parkinson, B. 1995. *Ideas and Realities of Emotion*. London: Routledge.

Parreñas, R.S. 2001. 'Mothering from a Distance: Emotions, Gender, and Inter-generational Relationships in Filipino Transnational Families', *Feminist Studies* 27(2): 361–90.

_____ 2005. 'Long-distance Intimacy: Class, Gender and Intergenerational Relations Between Mothers and Children in Filipino Transnational Families', *Global Networks* 5(4): 317–36.

Pedersen, M.A. 2007. 'Talismans of Thought: Shamanist Ontologies and Extended Cognition in Northern Mongolia', in A. Henare, M. Holbraad and S. Wastel (eds), *Thinking through Things: Theorising Artefacts Ethnographically*. New York: Routledge, pp. 141–66.

Peers, L., and A.K. Brown (eds). 2003. *Museums and Source Communities: A Reader*. London: Routledge.

Pennartz, P.J. 1999. 'Home: The Experience of Atmosphere', in I. Cierraad (ed.), *At Home: An Anthropology of Domestic Space*. New York: Syracuse University Press, pp. 95–106.

Pinney, C. 2001. 'Piercing the Skin of the Idol', in C. Pinney and N. Thomas (eds), *Beyond Aesthetics: Art and Technologies of Enchantment*. Oxford: Berg, pp. 157–80.

Pinney, C., and N. Thomas (eds). 2001. *Beyond Aesthetics: Art and Technologies of Enchantment*. Oxford: Berg.

Pook, S. 2006. 'I Won't Bow to Poppy Fascists, Says Jon Snow', *Daily Telegraph*, 10 November. Retrieved 29 November 2010 from: http://www.telegraph.co.uk/news/uknews/1533751/I-wont-bow-to-poppy-fascists-says-Jon-Snow.html.

Price, S. 1989. *Primitive Art in Civilised Places*. Chicago: University of Chicago Press.

Radford, K. 'Unkind Cuts': Health Policy and Practice versus the Health and Emotional Well-Being of Asylum-Seekers and Refugees in Ireland', *Journal of Ethnic and Migration Studies* 36(6): 899–916.

Roberts, R. 2003. *Emotions: An Essay in Aid of Moral Psychology*. Cambridge: Cambridge University Press.

Ryan, L. 2008. 'Navigating the Emotional Terrain of Families "Here" and "There": Women, Migration and the Management of Emotions', *Journal of Intercultural Studies* 29(3): 299–314.

Schneider, A. 2003. 'On "Appropriation": A Reappraisal of the Concept and its Application in Global Art Practices', *Social Anthropology* 11(2): 75–89.

_____ 2004. 'Rooting Hybridity: Globalisation and the Challenge of *mestizaje* and *cresol de razas* for Contemporary Artists in Ecuador and Argentina', *Indiana* 21: 95–112.

Sherwin, A. 2006. 'BBC Clears Fiona Bruce to Wear a Crucifix', *Times Online*, 18 October. Retrieved 09/08/2006from: http://www.timesonline.co.uk/tol/news/uk/article604643.ece.

Solomon, R. 1983. *The Passions.* Notre Dame, IN: University of Notre Dame Press.

Sommers, M. 2001. *Fear in Bongoland: Burundi Refugees in Urban Tanzania.* New York: Berghahn.

Steedman, C. 1982. *The Tidy House.* London: Virago.

Steiner, C.B. 1994. *African Art in Transit.* Cambridge: Cambridge University Press.

———— 1995. 'On the Creation of Value and Authenticity in the African Art Market', in G.E. Marcus and F.R. Myers (eds), *The Traffic in Culture: Refiguring Art and Anthropology.* Berkeley: University of California Press.

Stocking, G.W. (ed.). 1985. *Objects and Others: Essays on Museums and Material Culture.* Madison: University of Wisconsin Press.

Svašek, M. 2005a. 'Emotions in Anthropology', in K. Milton and M. Svašek (eds), *Mixed Emotions: Anthropological Studies of Feeling.* Oxford: Berg, pp. 1–24.

———— 2005b. 'The Politics of Chosen Trauma: Expellee Memories, Emotions and Identities', in K. Milton and M. Svašek (eds), *Mixed Emotions: Anthropological Studies of Feeling.* Oxford: Berg, pp. 195–214.

———— 2007a. 'Moving Corpses: Emotions and Subject–Object Ambiguity', in H. Wulff (ed.), *Emotions: A Cultural Reader.* Oxford: Berg.

———— 2007b. *Anthropology, Art and Cultural Production.* London: Pluto.

———— 2008. 'Who Cares? Families and Feelings in Movement', *Journal of Intercultural Studies* 29(3): 213–30.

———— 2009. 'Improvising in a World of Movement: Transit, Transition and Transformation', in H.K. Anheier and Y.R. Isar (eds), *Cultural Expression, Creativity and Innovation.* London: Sage, pp. 62–77.

———— 2010. 'On the Move: Emotions and Human Mobility', *Journal of Ethnic and Migration Studies* 36(6): 865–80.

Svašek, M., and Z. Skrbiš. 2007. 'Passions and Powers: Emotions and Globalisation', *Identities* 14(4): 367–85.

Thomas, N. 2001. 'Introduction', in C. Pinney and N. Thomas (eds), *Beyond Aesthetics: Art and the Technologies of Enchantment.* Oxford: Berg, pp. 1–12.

Turkle, S. 2007. *Evocative Objects: Things We Think With.* Cambridge, MA: MIT Press.

Verrips, J. 2008. 'Offending Art and the Sense of Touch', *Material Religion* 4(2): 204–25.

Vertovec, S. 2004. 'Migrant Transnationalism and Modes of Transformation', *International Migration Review* 38: 970–1001.

Walker, J.A. 1999. *Art and Outrage: Provocation, Controversy and the Visual Arts*. London: Pluto.

Walsh, K. 2006. 'British Expatriate Belongings: Mobile Homes and Transnationalism', *Home Cultures* 3(2): 123–44.

Weiner, J.F. 2001. 'Romanticism, from Foi Site Poetry to Schubert's *Winterreise*', in C. Pinney and N. Thomas (eds), *Beyond Aesthetics: Art and the Technologies of Enchantment*. Oxford: Berg, pp. 13–30.

Wierzbicka, A. 2004. 'Emotion and Culture: Arguing with Martha Nussbaum', *Ethos* 31(4): 577–600.

Wikan, U. 1992. 'Beyond the Words|: The Power of Resonance', *American Ethnologist* 19(3): 460–82.

Wilding, R. 2006. 'Virtual Intimacies? Families Communicating Across Transnational Contexts', *Global Networks* 6(2): 125–42.

Wise, A. 2010. 'Sensuous Multiculturalism: Emotional Landscapes of Inter-ethnic Living in Australian Suburbia', *Journal of Ethnic and Migration Studies* 36(6): 917–38.

Wise, A., and A. Chapman. 2005. 'Introduction: Migration, Affect and the Senses', *Journal of Intercultural Studies* 26(1/2): 1–3.

Wolf, D.L. 2002. '"There's No Place Like 'Home'"': Emotional Transnationalism and the Struggles of Second-generation Filipinos', in P. Levitt and M.C. Waters (eds), *The Changing Face of Home: The Transnational Lives of the Second Generation*. New York: Russell Sage Foundation, pp. 255–94.

Wolff, J. 1981. *The Social Production of Art*. London: MacMillan.

Woodward, I. 2007. *Understanding Material Culture*. London: Sage.

Wulff, H. (ed.) 2007. *The Emotions: A Cultural Reader*. Oxford: Berg.

Zarembka, J.M. 2003. 'America's Dirty Work. Migrant Maids and Modern-Day Slavery', in B. Ehrenreich and A.R. Hochschild (eds), *Global Women: Nannies, Maids, and Sex Workers in the New Economy*. New York: Metropolitan and Own, pp. 142–53.

Zolberg, V. 1990. *Constructing a Sociology of Art*. Cambridge: Cambridge University Press.

Zolberg, V., and J.M. Cherbo. 1997. *Outsider Art: Contesting Boundaries in Contemporary Culture*. Cambridge: Cambridge University Press.

1

MATERIALITY, MEMORIES AND EMOTIONS:
A VIEW ON MIGRATION FROM A STREET IN SOUTH LONDON

Fiona R. Parrott

Introduction

This chapter explores how memories and emotions evoked by mundane possessions such as photographs, furniture, music and clothing can illuminate 'the complex forms of subjectivity and feeling that emerge through geographical mobility' (Conradson and McKay 2007: 167; see also Rapport and Dawson 1998). I draw on recent approaches to materiality, which emphasize how sensation and emotion need to be thought about together as responses to objects (Dudley 2010; Edwards 2010), and use this approach to develop the study of migratory life histories that have become central to anthropological accounts of the complexity of migrant identities (Gardner 2002; Chamberlain and Leydesdorff 2004; Burrell 2006).

The data for this chapter are taken from an eighteen-month long ethnographic study of loss and change among eighty households on a street in South London, carried out in collaboration with Daniel Miller (Miller and Parrott 2007; Parrott 2007; Miller 2008). A street of terraced houses was selected that led between two high streets with differing class and ethnic characters. Individuals and households were invited to participate through a process of door-to-door recruitment, with 90 per cent agreeing to participate once the project was explained. This was complemented by weekly attendance at the church and pub, and my sublet of a bedroom in a shared house, which enabled me to live on the street for three months. Of the people from the eighty households who agreed to participate, less than a third had grown up in London, over a third had migrated from within the UK and a further third had moved internationally. In addition, one needs to also consider migration in previous generations, visiting patterns and second or family homes in other countries: elderly Caribbean and Irish migrants, resident for thirty years or more, were some of the most 'local' residents. A quarter of younger participants had moved off the street a year after fieldwork was completed suggesting that mobility in the job and housing market was the majority rule (Cameron 1998).

From the perspective of the researcher entering the different houses on this street, simple definitions of migration, return, community, transience and localism broke down. What emerged from this street-based ethnography was a sense of the impact and experience of international mobility, transnationalism and migration. Mobility did not merely influence peoples' relationships to objects; this sense of movement was experienced bodily and conceptually through my interactions with people, their things and their itineraries. As Hastrup says of her work with Arctic peoples, 'Itineraries make people; they emerge along the way of their dwellings' (Hastrup 2010: 197).

The emotions have been marginalized in fieldwork, yet attention to the interlocutory nature of emotions in fieldwork may provide sources of insight and critical reflection (Davies 2010). Engaging with peoples' domestic objects and the memories and stories associated with those things did not immerse me more strongly in the space of the street, it made me more aware that the spatial parameters of peoples' social life were to be found as part of composite worlds. These dialogues with people about their things variously left me with a sense of peoples' feelings of possibility, disjuncture and contradiction. It is these three aspects of participants' responses to their possessions and their experience of mobility that I focus on in this chapter. Such feelings emerged from what Hastrup has described as the structuring of peoples' 'emotional topographies' (Hastrup 2010: 197).

My sense of the street as a place, generated through fieldwork relationships with over a hundred people living so close together, diverged more and more completely from most of my participants own sense or indeed my own experience of living elsewhere in London. Elsewhere I rarely knew more than a few neighbours. In this respect, immersion did not lead to integration but generated a peculiar vantage point from which to grasp a small part of the entity 'London', and its mix of inhabitants often taken as evidence of its growing character (Wallman 1984; Hall 2000; Reed 2008). Moving between households led me to move between accounts of migratory trends – such as post-war Southern European and Commonwealth migration, recent Australasian professional migration or high gay mobility – which I note in this chapter to help illuminate the lives of those living in this small part of South London over the course of the field research.

Meaning, Feeling and Sensation

Leavitt has argued that what Western social scientists call emotions, and what tends to be 'recognized' as emotions in other cultures, consists of 'experiences that involve both meaning and feeling, both mind and body, and that therefore cross-cut divisions that continue to mark theoretical thought' (Leavitt 1996: 516). Leavitt acknowledged that the experience and expression of emotion does not always take place in explicit categories and vocabularies, as work on the cultural explication of emotion concepts has sometimes implied (e.g., Lutz and White 1986). As Edwards suggests, this less linguistically orientated approach offers a useful starting point from which to examine the emotional impact of objects (Edwards 2010).

Accounts of sensory perception, experienced as part of encounters with objects and places, parallel this discussion of the interlocutory nature of emotions (see Pink 2009). Dudley, in her account of museum objects, emphasizes that emotion, affect, memory and sensation are all part of the experience of objects (Dudley 2010: 8). Edwards, drawing on Leavitt's work, argues that sensation and emotion, feeling as well as meaning, need to be thought about together when exploring the role of photographs in museums (Edwards 2010). Following these authors, the domestic keepsakes and photographs described in this chapter are approached as part of what Leavitt calls 'recurrent situations intended to call forth certain meaning/feeling responses we recognize as emotions' (Leavitt 1996: 524). Objects and their sensory character are involved in the transaction of feelings and emotions with others. This includes fieldwork encounters. By making these exchanges explicit, these can be read as more than the 'naive' description of the emotional (and sensory impacts) of objects on others, or the projection of the authors' responses (ibid.: 518).

This work on bridging the division of meaning and feeling, emotion and sensation, would suggest that it is not enough to theorize artefacts as 'carriers' of personal or collective significance, identity markers that offer the possibility of objectifying a stable self in the face of destabilizing movement (e.g., Mehta and Belk 1991; Belk 1992; Parkin 1999). The advantage of a more developed material-culture approach should be that the contradictions of gain and loss, dissolving, retaining and gaining of affective ties and emotional states are evident in the experience and encounters with objects through which they are differentially expressed.

Possibility

One of the dimensions commented upon in accounts of migrant experience is the sense of possibility that movement has the potential to grant, whether by learning new things (Bravo-Moreno 2006), or in the expectation of new modes of feeling and being relating to the encounter with new lifestyles and the transformation of kin relations that accompanies geographical separation (Conradson and Latham 2007). Although it was part of many people's experience of moving to London, these feelings were emphasized among the skilled, young Antipodean and gay migrants of diverse backgrounds who participated in the research in their relationships to their possessions. It was most extreme when these two identities converged. The fieldwork area was known for its gay community fostered through migration (Kelley, Peabody and Scott 1996), and as one of the various locations favored by Antipodean migrants (Conradson and Latham 2007), but it was nevertheless the case that those scattered among the street's households rarely knew of each other's existence.

James, who was renting a room in a friend's house, had moved to London from Christchurch, New Zealand, when he was twenty-one years old. He was anticipating his return when we met. James made sense of the reasons for his move almost entirely through the feeling of personal transformation that he sought to retain, in part, through mementos of his experience. His tone of voice was soft but forceful when he said he wanted to talk about what he would take with him, not what he had brought from New Zealand:

> As much as I can fit in! You're better off asking me about what I would take with me here in England and not about New Zealand. This is where my life began as far as I'm concerned, in England not New Zealand. So everything I can fit in I will.

He emphasized how he would keep objects which were not usually classified as items of emotional attachment, such as a chequebook. Having only ever perceived my chequebook as a financial instrument, I looked afresh at James's, whose crisp pages and black printed name and bank address seemed, under his touch and vision, part of a pattern of experience and memory of where 'life began'.

James described his home town as 'too small'. He valued these beginnings as the point of transformation. His relationship to the things he had gathered during his time in London had much in common with Conradson and Latham's study of the practice of young New Zealanders and other Antipodean transnationals who spent time in Britain during their twenties and thirties to seek out a sense of energy, happiness and experiential attractions they associated with London (Conradson and Latham 2007). James's experience also involved changes in how he saw himself and how others responded to him as a gay man. Finding some measure of geographical distance helped him renegotiate the terms of his relationships with family and friends in his hometown.

Manalansan (2005) emphasizes the importance of accessing quotidian gay migrant experience in his writing on aspects such as dress and apartment interiors among Philippine gay migrants in New York. Similarly, a focus on mobile possessions not only gives insight into the dynamics of these affective attachments but also the shape that future modes of remembrance will take (see Marcoux 2001). James sought ways to make his experiences in London last through things that materialized his intention to remember. Some things were also display objects, such as ornaments and photographs. By displaying and talking, with words and the sound of emotions, gestures of pride and worldliness, James may have anticipated that he could use these 'objects incarnating remembrance and feeling' on his return in 'the exchange of sensory memories and emotions' with others (Seremetakis 1996: 37).

James's expectation of return to a New Zealand lifestyle – 'going to the beach', 'space' and opening his own hairdressing salon – allows him to reorientate his belongings and his feelings to the respective places with the sense that it is the right time to go back. As Conradson and Latham comment, the degree of possibility of self-invention and cosmopolitanism is also linked to the relatively short-term nature of most Australasian sojourns (Conradson and Latham 2007: 238). James contrasts himself with his sister, whose stay was made more permanent by marriage and having children with a man she met in the UK, and relates this to her sentimentality towards goods sent over from New Zealand:

> I think she doesn't particularly like it here. I want to go now too. But she's got kids. She's trapped here. She has a lot of stuff from New Zealand sent over from the parents and grandparents but I'm not sentimental like that.

James's experience may be briefly compared with interviews with other gay male migrants. Craig, for example, illustrated how a pattern of continual movement and accompanying divestment and ordering of one's things can become central to a person's lifestyle. Over the last ten years he has regularly moved between Europe – mainly London, where he rents a room in a friend's flat – and various parts of Australia. Movement seemed to provide Craig with a catalyst for a degree of self-invention and a selective return or search for new forms of authenticity. Facilitated by his dual citizenship – he has an English father and an Australian Aboriginal mother – he oscillated between the lifestyle of London, including its permissive gay scene, and his work with remote Aboriginal communities.

The weight of Craig's possessions connected his freedom to move and his commitment to remain mobile with the sensory character of his possessions. Every object was assessed; every unnecessary part was jettisoned. With music, first the CDs were separated from their cases and covers, the CDs themselves were given away as he digitized the collection: 'Whoosh, out they go!' He aimed to minimize his accumulation in every way: 'All the time, I'm constantly – why do I need this? Is it important to the future?' Craig gave away his father and grandmother's 'heavy' furniture and decorative objects but continuously archived his digital photographs, documents and e-mails, just as he cared for his mother's family archives, a process that selectively linked the different facets of his personal and family history.

For Jean-Pierre and Ian, one of three gay couples who participated in the research, the sense of possibility and new modes of feeling and being was found through their relationship with each other, as much as with their respective mobility. James grew up in Manchester with his evangelist mother and Jean-Pierre, of French origin, grew up in the Ivory Coast. Their case illustrates how the exchange of sensory memories and emotions associated with music can be part of the establishment of shared origins or destiny.

The process of establishing a shared story of a relationship is an important part of couple formation (Halbwachs 1992; Parrott 2007). Part of their story was the sound of the music of Manchester in the late 1980s, involving bands such as New Order. They took great pleasure in describing how, while Ian was working as a teenager at the bar at the Hacienda (the club at the centre of the music movement in Manchester), Jean Pierre was 'dancing to the same music on the beach'. The mass-produced and distributed nature of this music helped shape its impact as a shared memory that reached back into the past to give their relationship a unique or pre-ordained path and commitment opposed to the quality of an everyday random encounter free from emotional obligations (see Shokeid 2007). Each seemed to draw a different kind of embodied authenticity from this, bringing it to the relationship: Jean Pierre a sense of cosmopolitanism; Ian his first-hand experience of the metropolis and its permissive scene.

It is not always the case that the meaning and emotional effects of objects may be as controlled as the previous examples of migration and mobility as a route into new forms of selfhood, including the selective appropriation of personal or shared origins, imply. As I discuss in the following section, things may come to provoke acute feelings concerning the difference between one's ideal and one's actual situation (Parrott 2005).

Disjuncture

For some migrants who participated in the study, possessions brought with them to bring comfort become the site of the experience of disjuncture in their new surroundings. This was particularly so for Mai, a graduate from Singapore, who we met soon after she moved to a flat on the street with her English boyfriend. They had met in Singapore where many Britons migrate for short-term work opportunities and lived together for two years, but Mai's partner became homesick and took a job in London and Mai enrolled on an MA. It was possible to obtain a student visa but this position only provided Mai with a temporary measure of security and she was uncertain about the future.

Mai found her circumstances isolating. Those who attended her course lived in different parts of London and she found it frustrating that those who she heard speaking Malay or Mandarin on the street would not reply to her when she tried to talk to them there. In contrast, most of Mai's possessions that she brought with her were associated with her sociability. Yet in these circumstances, these things doubly draw attention to feelings of strangeness, loneliness and isolation. It is not only their memories and associations that provoke an emotive response but even their material and sensory character felt out of place. For example, she brought clothes and dresses with her that she would wear to go out with her friends in Singapore. She recalled her boyfriend telling her that 'you could wear thin layers underneath and a thicker layer on top', but she cries indignantly: 'It wasn't true!' Almost all of these clothes are unworn in drawers. One pair of high-heeled brown boots survived. Mai had had them for twelve years: 'They have travelled everywhere with me. I had to get them polished and reheeled and the cost was more than the original but they said they don't make them like that anymore'. She tried to wear them infrequently to preserve them, picking the epitome of English sociality – the pub – as the deserved venue for their outing. Mai has kept other things – such as the cooking pots belonging to her grandmother – but she is only just now learning to cook the soups her grandmother used to make and she has to wait till her boyfriend is away as he doesn't like the taste. It was so cheap to eat out and so varied in Singapore that Mai says she never cooked these dishes herself.

The displayed photographs of her dogs struck me as the most poignant example of the cultural adjustments and movements Mai made both in Singapore and in the UK. These photographs were placed on the couple's living-room shelves. As Mai explained, the dogs were explicitly bought as a counter to the overly quiet home Mai and her boyfriend had made in Singapore. In the first place, their noise and companionship substituted for the populated family household, in which she grew up:

> In Singapore what we do is live with our parents until we get married, and for the guys, if they are the only boy they will marry and live with their parents still. So we're very used to big families, maybe more than two generations living in the same house. I don't have my mum or anyone else, so I thought it would be really good to have my dogs, it's more noise and life. At least I can shout at my dogs! So when I came here it was very different because it's just me and my boyfriend.

The pictures and story of the dogs helped Mai convey her everyday experience of this cross-cultural relationship, reminding one of the way in which migrant related identities may be subject to transformation (Benmayor and Skotnes 2005). Here the photographs of the dogs operated at another remove, a reminder of the idea of having more life in the house, reflecting the double loss of that companionship and family. Their emotional and sensory qualities shaped the sense of alienation Mai may have been feeling; the photographs may be touched but not heard. Lastly, Mai described the impossibility of having pets in London. This seemed to convey with some finality the uncertainty she felt and the constraints of mobility: 'When I left

Singapore I had to leave my dogs behind. If I left London I would have to leave the new pets behind. Then it's the same thing'.

Ho (2008) describes the significance of family ties in shaping London Singaporean migrants' sense of flexible citizenship, but frequent communication with family is subject to mixed feelings. When Mai received e-mailed photographs from a large family outing involving a fishing trip with the extended family, Mai explained: 'I'm so jealous'. Mai's expression of envy conveyed her sense of missing out on these highly valued family experiences. E-mails and photographs sustain transnational family relationships, but they are equally capable of stimulating homesickness and loneliness when coupled with feelings of disjuncture and uncertainty.

Another overseas student who had a serious relationship in the UK made a pact with herself to return home by carrying an American quarter in her purse, just as she had carried an old English 50 pence piece to promise herself that she would come to London:

> I keep them in my bag all the time and when I'm travelling I get quite anxious about making sure that they're there … At the back of my head, if I have them I will make it back to the US because it started with the 50p piece. I was meant to come back here.

But the objects themselves in turn prompted anxiety around their loss. As exemplified by Mai's relationships to things, such a lack of control over the feelings evoked by things may be part of migratory experience, particularly where there are high levels of uncertainty and a greater ambivalence towards one's circumstances.

Contradiction

Contradictory feelings of attachment and investment were particularly evident among some of the older, retiring or retired migrants on the street, especially if they held on to the idea of return. Ageing postwar migrants – such as elderly Caribbean migrants (Plaza 2001; Owen 2001) but equally the less noted and studied Southern European postwar migrants (Holmes 1991) – were to be found among the research households. Certain objects and images could become a means of transforming the myth of return and acceding to the desire to remain in London. They could be part of practices which sustained such contradictions or their resolution. For example, as Ganga (2006) notes for older Italian migrants in Nottingham, the conflict can become one of reconciling the need to be geographically close to children and the need to create an enduring pilgrimage home. This conflict was evident in the life of Javier, a Spanish migrant who moved to London thirty years ago after meeting and marrying an English woman in his hometown of Madrid and divorcing after they had had two children.

The front room of Javier's small flat expressed this contradiction in its two forms of decoration – family photographs of his two daughters, from 'little devils' to serious university graduation portraits, for example – and touristic posters of Madrid. The latter images were mass-produced pictures which helped Javier to feel nostalgia for his homeland: 'They make me homesick for Madrid … Who doesn't miss Spain, you tell me that?' He would continue: 'You might think what the hell I am doing here? I'm here because of my daughters, although they are not children anymore. They used to ask me, "why don't you go back?" but now they know not to ask'. The photographs and posters are positioned to have effects on others as well as himself (Edwards 1999; Attan 2006).

Bravo-Moreno (2006) in her study of Spanish female migrants to London has suggested how national identities are closely linked with family emotional work among Spanish migrants. Men such as Javier also used the representation of family and family practices as a core for their national identities and a means to differentiate themselves. Similarly, Javier thought of Spanish as the language of emotions and intimacy (cf. ibid.):

> We're different mentalities: Spanish, English, you know, different cultures … We don't have the same way of thinking. We are more closer to the family than English people are. Correct me if I'm wrong but I'm not wrong from what I have seen. Well, in Spain, we visit family relations, we gather together all the time, we find any excuse to have the little family party.

Javier called his daughters every day. This repetitive day-to-day interaction was highly valued by him but less so by his daughters. They did not call or visit often enough for Javier. On a day when he was particularly unhappy he described them as:

> Very much English mentality. Sorry. I'm sorry for them. I say, 'you don't come to see me as much as I would like to'. They say, oh well, they have their careers too. They are English not Spanish. They have been born here. They have been brought up by the mother. I call them brainwashed.

Bravo-Moreno notes the strength of certain cultural and family norms among Spanish migrants in London, such as creating a 'Spanish atmosphere' at home: '[Women] produced identifications associated emotionally with memories of their youth in Spain such as smells, sounds, house decoration and frequent visits to Spain' (Bravo-Moreno 2006: 223). Javier, meanwhile, measured his daughters' response to his creation of a Spanish atmosphere in the home as an emotional response to him. Javier told me he drank eight cups of coffee a day and tried to give his daughters 'good coffee'. Big, carefully oiled paella pans hung in the kitchen in the flat: 'I must have paella on Sunday, ever since I can remember'. He loved being asked for instructions to cook Spanish dishes from his daughters:

> She rings me and say 'how do I do that'. Two weeks ago my elder daughter did, she kept me on the phone for over ten minutes. They don't go to ask to the mum either, they ask me.

Javier's personal identifications as they emerged in our conversations seemed to be shaped by the emotional dynamics of pride and shame, love and loss. When he reflected on his close friend who retired to Spain he acknowledged the difficulty of relocation and return, of making a new life again. Staying remained an expression of love and care and a commitment to the values he grew up with, of family closeness. He is his daughters' 'guardian angel', even if 'they know it not'. In this way, staying could be a display of love even if it provokes contradictory feelings of loss, and return can be talked of nostalgically through objects and images in a way which brings shame not pride.

Discussion

This chapter has focused on understanding how the emotional and sensory effects of objects and images are entangled with the dynamics of identification with cultural and personal values that emerge through geographical mobility. Three possible dimensions of migrant experience and the role material culture were discussed through selected illustrations from my interviews with a diverse group of residents from a street in South London. Fieldwork encounters with people and their domestic possessions suggested ways in which their lives and relationships were shaped by migration and mobility and in turn how objects could be key to people's feelings about their circumstances.

First, objects and images were described as part of the possibility for controlled self-invention through travel and mobility. More broadly, 'choice' was exercised according to the practice of divestment and retention of things. Marcoux has described this as the 'refurbishment of memory' (Marcoux 2001). This could involve the selection of objects associated with particular feelings, or a life in which the whole weight of one's possessions materialized the feeling and practice of mobility and renewal. As we saw, however, these processes involve many layers of sensory significance and emotional meaning. Archiving cheque books and digital photographs recalled selective returns to origins and new beginnings, and music was used to fashion a shared destiny.

Second, I considered the uncontrolled emotional effects of possessions and their sensory forms. For instance, things intended to bring comfort – such as clothing that used to be worn out with friends that were only suitable for a warm climate, or the silence of photographs of pets and family – provoked and affirmed feelings of loneliness and isolation.

Third, I described objects and images that evoked contradictory feelings or paradoxical attachments, namely the family photographs and posters of Spanish architecture and landscapes displayed by a Spanish divorcee in his small London flat. In the process of maintaining cultural and personal values, portable objects and images in particular may become the means of sustaining feelings of attachment to a homeland. However, in the process of trying to maintain tradition and attachments they also were subject to transformation, such as the gendering of practices which establish a Spanish atmosphere in the home.

In material culture studies, the anthropology of domestic consumption in industrial settings has focused on the home as an important site of emotive engagement with past, present and imagined futures and projected aspirations (e.g., Clarke 2001; Hecht 2001), and a site that expresses processes of negotiation of conflict and constraint (e.g., Miller 1988; Parrott 2005). Similarly, migration scholars show how the dilemmas of living at home while abroad or abroad at home are played out through material forms in the home in urban consumer settings (e.g., Manalansan 2005; Attan 2006; Burrell 2008).

This chapter aimed to show how personal possessions in the home are not simply identity markers that offer the possibility of objectifying a stable self in the face of destabilizing movement. This picture of stability in the face of loss is split by an understanding of how artefacts are engaged in multiple processes of sensory and emotional identification, with controlled and uncontrolled effects. In each case, processes of emotional and sensory identification also depended on productive structures of visual and material consumption. This understanding develops findings of previous work on migration and belonging. For example, Basu's work on roots tourism in Scotland drew attention to the way North Americans encountered the 'solidity' of heritage landscapes and noted the portability of tourist objects, from jewellery that could be worn everyday on return to photographs displayed or circulated, that literally and metaphorically gave substance to feelings connected with diasporic identities (Basu 2006). Similarly, Wulff's work has examined how people look back to Ireland for identity and belonging from the diaspora using mass-reproduced landscape paintings that repeat links between Irish land, emotion, memory and nature (Wulff 2007). The portability of possessions, their sensory character and their sensory limitations, the global distribution of popular music, the atmosphere established in the home through utensils, food and cooking aromas – all these articulate multiple scales of material and social identifications that change over time and space.

By putting together the stories of residents encountered on a street in South London side by side, I aimed to provide insights into the way migration and mobility is part of the constitution of ordinary residential locations in a global city. Certain trends were particularly in evidence, such as a mobile, international, gay male population and ageing postwar Caribbean migrants, but in other respects the street is a kaleidoscope of migratory experiences. The people and things represented in this chapter were selected through a process of emotional reasoning, that process of translation and 'resonance' (Wikan 1992) where these people and events impacted upon me, the researcher, for their striking reinventions of authenticity, disjuncture between sociality and loneliness and paradoxical social attachments. This chapter is an artefact of those dialogues with people and their things, those moments of encounter and fluxes of interrelation in place.

References

Attan, C. 2006. 'Hidden Objects in the World of Cultural Migrants: Significant Objects used by European Migrants to Layer Thoughts and Memories', in K. Burrell and P. Panayi (eds), *Histories and Memories: Migrants and their History in Britain*. London: Taurus Academic Studies, pp. 171–90.

Basu, P. 2006. 'My Own Island Home: The Orkney Homecoming', *Journal of Material Culture* 9(1): 27–43.

Benmayor, R., and A. Skotnes. 2005. 'Some Reflections on Migration and Identity', in R. Benmayor and A. Skotnes (eds), *Migration and Identity*. New Brunswick, NJ: Transaction, pp. 1–18

Belk, R. 1992 'Moving Possessions: An Analysis Based on Personal Documents from the 1847–1869 Mormon Migration', *Journal of Consumer Research* 19: 339–61.

Bravo-Moreno, A. 2006. *Migration, Gender and National Identity: Spanish Migrant Women in London*. New York: Peter Lang.

Burrell, K. 2006. *Moving Lives: Narratives of Nation and Migration among Europeans in Post-War Britain*. Aldershot: Ashgate.

———— 2008. 'Managing, Learning and Sending: The Material Lives and Journeys of Polish Women in Britain', *Journal of Material Culture* 13(1): 63–83.

Cameron, G., and J. Muellbauer. 1998. 'The Housing Market and Regional Commuting and Migration Choices', *Scottish Journal of Political Economy* 45: 420–46.

Chamberlain, M., and S. Leydesdorff. 2004. 'Transnational Families: Memories and Narratives', *Global Networks* 4(3): 227–41

Clarke, A. 2001. 'The Aesthetics of Social Aspiration', in D. Miller (ed.), *Home Possessions: Material Culture behind Closed Doors*. Oxford: Berg, pp. 23–45.

Conradson, D., and A. Latham 2007. 'The Affective Possibilities of London: Antipodean Transnationals and the Overseas Experience', *Mobilities* 2(2): 231–54.

Conradson, D., and D. McKay. 2007. 'Translocal Subjectivities: Mobility, Connection, Emotion', *Mobilities* 2(2): 167–74.

Davies, J. 2010. 'Introduction: Emotions in the Field', in J. Davies and D. Spencer (eds), *Emotions in the Field: The Psychology and Anthropology of Fieldwork Experience*. Stanford, CA: Stanford University Press, pp. 1–34.

Dudley, S. 2010. 'Museum Materialities: Objects, Sense and Feeling', in S. Dudley (ed.), *Museum Materialities: Objects, Engagements, Interpretations*. London: Routledge, pp. 1–18.

Edwards, E. 1999. 'Photographs as Objects of Memory', in M. Kwint, C. Breward and J. Aynsley (eds), *Material Memories*. Oxford: Berg, pp. 221–36.

―――― 2010. 'Photographs and History: Emotion and Materiality', in S. Dudley (ed.), *Museum Materialities: Objects, Engagements, Interpretations*. London: Routledge, pp. 21–38.

Ganga, D. 2006. 'Reinventing the Myth of Return: Older Italians in Nottingham', in K. Burrell and P. Panayi (eds), *Histories and Memories: Migrants and their History in Britain*. London: Taurus Academic Studies, pp. 114–32.

Gardner, K. 2002. *Age, Narrative and Migration: The Life Course and Life Histories of Bengali Elders in London*. Oxford: Berg.

Hall, S. 2000. 'Conclusion: The Multicultural Question', in B. Hesse (ed.), *Un/Settled Multiculturalisms: Diasporas, Entanglements, Transruptures*. London: Zed Books.

Halbwachs, M. 1992. On Collective Memory. London, University of Chicago Press.

Hastrup, K. 2010. 'Emotional Topographies: The Sense of Place in the Far North', in J. Davies and D. Spencer (eds), *Emotions in the Field: The Psychology and Anthropology of Fieldwork Experience*. Stanford, CA: Stanford University Press, pp. 191–212.

Hecht, A. 2001. 'Home Sweet Home: Tangible Memories of an Uprooted Childhood', in D. Miller (ed.), *Home Possessions: Material Culture behind Closed Doors*. Oxford: Berg, pp. 123–45.

Ho, E. 2008. '"Flexible Citizenship" or Familial Ties that Bind? Singaporean Transmigrants in London', *International Migration* 46(4): 145–75.

Holmes, C. 1991. *A Tolerant Country? Immigrants, Refugees and Minorities in Britain*. London: Faber and Faber.

Kelley, P., R. Peabody and P. Scott. 1996. *How Far Will You Go? A Survey of London Gay Men's Migration and Mobility*. London: Gay Men Fighting AIDS.

Leavitt, J. 1996. 'Meaning and Feeling in the Anthropology of Emotions', *American Ethnologist* 23(3): 514–39.

Lutz, C.A., and G.M. White. 1986 'The Anthropology of Emotions', *Annual Review of Anthropology* 15: 405–36.

Manalansan, M.F. 2005. 'Migrancy, Modernity, Mobility: Quotidian Struggles and Queer Diasporic Intimacy', in L. Eithne and C. Luibheid (eds), *Queer Migrations: Sexuality, US Citizenship, and Border Crossings*. Minneapolis: University of Minnesota Press, pp. 146–60.

Marcoux, J.S. 2001. 'The Refurbishment of Memory', in D. Miller (ed.), *Home Possessions: Material Culture behind Closed Doors*. Oxford: Berg, pp. 69–86.

Mehta, R., and R.W. Belk. 1991. 'Artefacts, Identity and Transition: Favourite Possessions of Indians and Indian Immigrants to the United States', *Journal of Consumer Research* 17: 398–411.

Miller, D. 1988. 'Appropriating the State on the Council Estate', *Man* 23: 353–72.

———— 2008. *The Comfort of Things*. Cambridge: Polity Press.

Miller, D., and F.R. Parrott. 2007. 'Death, Ritual and Material Culture in South London', in B. Brooks-Gordon et al. (eds), *Death Rites and Rights*. Oxford: Hart Publishing/Cambridge Socio-legal Group, pp. 147–62.

Owen, D. 2001. 'A Demographic Profile of Caribbean Households and Families in Great Britain', in H. Goulbourne and M. Chamberlain (eds), *Caribbean Families in Britain and the Trans-Atlantic World*. London: MacMillan, pp. 64–91.

Parkin, D. 1999. 'Mementos as Transitional Objects in Human Displacement', *Journal of Material Culture* 4: 303–20.

Parrott, F.R. 2005 '"It's Not Forever": The Material Culture of Hope', *Journal of Material Culture* 10(3): 245–62.

———— 2007. 'Mais où a-t-on donc rangé ces souvenirs?' *Ethnologie française* 37(2): 305–12.

Pink, S. 2009. *Doing Sensory Ethnography*. London: Sage.

Plaza, D. 2001. 'Aging in Babylon: Elderly Caribbeans in Britain', in H. Goulbourne and M. Chamberlain (eds), *Caribbean Families in Britain and the Trans-Atlantic World*. London: MacMillan, pp. 219–32.

Rapport, N., and A. Dawson (eds). 1998. *Migrants of Identity: Perceptions of Home in a World of Movement*. Oxford: Berg.

Reed, A. 2008. '"Blog This": Surfing the Metropolis and the Method of London', *Journal of the Royal Anthropological Institute* 14: 391–406.

Seremetakis, N. 1996. The Senses Still: Perception and Memory as Material Culture in Modernity. Chicago: University of Chicago Press.

Shokeid, M. 2007. 'The Emotional Life of Gay Men: Observations from New York', in H. Wulff (ed.), *The Emotions: A Cultural Reader*. Oxford: Berg, pp. 299–320.

Wallman, S. 1984. *Eight London Households*. London: Tavistock.

Wikan, U. 1992. 'Beyond the Words: The Power of Resonance', *American Ethnologist* 19(3): 460–82.

Wulff, H. 2007. 'Longing for the Land: Emotions, Memory and Nature in Irish Travel Advertisements', Identities 14: 1–18.

2

THE OBJECTS OF CHRISTMAS:
THE POLITICS OF FESTIVE MATERIALITY IN THE
LIVES OF POLISH IMMIGRANTS

————•◆•————

Kathy Burrell

The Significance of Christmas

This chapter will consider the varying experiences of Christmas among
Polish immigrants in Britain, analysing the changing importance of key
foodstuffs and artefacts in constructions of the festival in the different
geographic contexts of Poland and Britain. For cultures which celebrate
it, Christmas is evidently a focal point in the annual calendar. While the
religious significance of the Christmas celebration is obviously fundamental,
the relevance of Christmas reaches beyond spiritual meaning. As Miller
has argued, Christmas is firmly embedded in, and reflective of, the social,
economic and cultural contexts of the worlds within which it is observed.
The rituals surrounding Christmas are 'key components of contemporary
life' (Miller 1993: 35).

Christmas is a particularly interesting case study for the consideration
of objects and material culture. As a highly ritualized celebration, specific
objects and artefacts are necessarily at the core of the production and
performance of Christmas. On the one hand, the ritualized usage and
reverence of certain artefacts enables the contemporary celebration to
echo former festivals, reaching back to mimic the activities of previous
generations (see Connerton 1989). Through the regular upholding of
Christmas traditions, societies are able to continually form and reform
strong collective bonds, rooted in usable recognized pasts. The materiality

of contemporary Christmases, on the other hand, is one of the festival's most readily identifiable characteristics. Public and private spaces are decorated elaborately to anticipate the arrival of the holiday, filling homes, offices, shopping streets and media outlets with the signs, smells and sounds of the celebration. Christmas is created through key foods and adornments, and of course through elaborate protocols of card sending and gift giving; Christmas shopping, as Carrier describes, is 'an annual ritual through which we convert commodities into gifts' (Carrier 1993: 63). The different rituals of Christmas therefore not only resonate with the past but also service personal relationships in the present. As is now widely acknowledged, gift giving is a material embodiment of social relationships. Christmas is, therefore, a resolutely social construction, orientated around family in particular, and structured, as Kuper (1993: 168) argues, around the moral economy of family and home, as well as the social dynamics of friendship and acquaintance.

Emotions, Migration and Christmas

Christmas is also, evidently, an extremely important occasion with regard to emotions. Much has been written about the emotional components of human life, and especially on debates about the biological versus the cultural nature of emotions. Here, Milton's call for a holistic, ecological approach to understanding emotional responses (Milton 2005), Hochschild's influential assertion about the 'managed' nature of emotions (Hochschild 1983), and the growing recognition of the specific importance of place in emotional dynamics (Davidson, Bondi and Smith 2005) particularly stand out. Emotions are now widely understood as a subjective interaction (Lutz 1986) between the inner self and the outside world, and Svašek (2009) suggests that there are three different ways this process is manifested: through discourse, practice and embodied experience. Baldassar (2008) also includes a further category in her work: that of imagination and ideas. This differentiation of emotional interaction is important for this chapter, where a range of emotional situations which are triggered by Christmas and its associated imagery are considered.

The fact that this chapter focuses on migration also has important emotional implications. More attention is now being paid to the particular emotional strains that migrants face in their lives. Ryan (2008), for example, has used Hochschild's observations on emotional labour to analyse how Irish women in Britain cope with the heavy emotional burden of pleasing their relatives still in Ireland. Similarly, the emotional weight of transnational caregiving has also been noted in several migration studies (e.g., Baldassar, Baldock and Wilding 2007), predominantly from the point of view of female migrants. Women migrants certainly seem to be exposed to particular emotional tensions as a result of their migration, mainly through their familial roles and positions. However, perhaps the most recognized emotional consequence of migration has to be homesickness, and, in many cases, a strong need to feel connected to the original homeland in some way, whether physically through visits home (see, e.g., Baldassar 2001), through other communicative means, or simply psychologically, as an emotional transnationalism (Burrell 2003). As Skrbiš (2008) reminds us, it is the issue of presence, or co-presence, and absence, which is at the heart of experiences of migration. As will be seen, this matter especially has been dominant in the emotional experiences of different Polish migrants.

With all this in mind, it follows that the migrant Christmas carries heavy emotional baggage. Christmas, generally, with its strong emphasis on home, family, friends and familiarity, already brings with it considerable emotional pressure. It is supposed to be a time which is rewarding and exciting, but also comforting, and not the isolating and stressful experience that many struggle through. For migrants especially, Christmas can be a very difficult point in the year, introducing many pressure points within the migration experience during an intense period of time, and can involve homesickness, nostalgia, the desire to uphold certain traditions and rituals, and the need to keep in contact with family and friends. Christmas, furthermore, cannot be organized and observed in just one place but has to be performed transnationally. The spatial scales of the Christmas experience are not only inward/domestic and outward/social, as observed by Bodenhorn (1993), but are reconfigured over national borders. This may have important practical ramifications, but as Davidson, Bondi and Smith (2005) would suggest, the placing of Christmas is an explicitly emotional matter. All the big questions of space and place, therefore, have to be revisited for the migrant Christmas.

The Materiality of the Transnational Christmas: Objects and Emotions

These questions are addressed in part by the materiality of the migrant Christmas. For migrants, the emotional pull of the homeland has to be balanced with the need to invest in a new life in a new place. Just as emotional attachments to various physical embodiments of Christmas in the homeland have to be confronted, the ability to feel comfortable in the new environment is tested. A key part of this is embodied in the movement of goods relating to Christmas. The places where Christmas is being observed may be separated, with considerable distance between them, but they are linked by the goods which are transported between them, moving alongside the migrants. As Rojek and Urry remind us, 'cultures travel as well as people' (Rojek and Urry 1997: 11). For this chapter, there are two important ramifications of this process: First is the emotional significance of objects generally, and Christmas related objects specifically. Svašek (2007), following Gell's arguments about the 'secondary agency' of objects (Gell 1998: 20) – that is, their ability to act as social agents through their roles as vehicles or channels of agency – has highlighted the emotional agency of objects. As she explains, people 'construct the things that surround them as subject-like phenomena' (Svašek 2007: 230). Our emotional lives are intricately bound with the material matter with which we live, and objects have the power to move people to feel and to act. This phenomenon is very clear in the Polish case study presented here, where key objects, by their presence or absence, are shown to trigger specific emotions in different respondents, whether related to a longing for Poland or feeling more settled in the UK.

This last point links to the second significant aspect of the power of objects in the migrant Christmas: the ability of objects to not only affect individuals, but also transform places and place-specific contexts. For all the reverence of tradition, for example, homeland Christmases will change over time, open to different outside influences as new material cultures flow in. The Christmases celebrated in the new environment will also develop in different ways, absorbing elements of old and new forms of celebration, and using particular objects to sustain them. It is the mobility of objects, alongside human mobility, which largely makes this possible. Of course, just as places alter, the meaning of objects is subject to change as they move (Lury 1997), the original contextual specificity of their values and meaning (Appadurai 1986: 4) destabilized, or perhaps even reinforced, through migration, with their subjective, emotional components similarly changed in the process. This chapter will concentrate on these aspects of the materiality of Christmas, exploring how specific, seasonal objects affect the people and places around them.

The Polish Case Study

This empirical focus of this chapter is a case study of Polish–British migration from the immediate postwar era to the post-2004 European Union accession period. At the end of the Second World War approximately 120,000 Polish refuges settled across Britain, with the Polish Resettlement Act of 1948 allowing ex-servicemen and women (who had been fighting with British forces) and their families to demobilize in Britain, and the European Volunteer Workers programmes bringing in displaced Polish people to fill labour shortages (see Zubrzycki 1956; Tannahill 1958). The sense of exile among this cohort has been very strong; not only did most endure traumatic wartime experiences, but the establishment of the socialist regime in Poland after the war sealed their physical and emotional distance from their homeland (see Burrell 2006). The socialist years in Poland also saw considerable movement abroad: despite the state's attempt to prevent the emigration of citizens, millions of people still left, heading predominantly for Germany and the US, but with several thousand migrating to Britain for reasons ranging from marriage and family reunification to professional and economic prospects, and political protection (see Sword 1996). After 1989, steady but small-scale streams of migration continued to Britain until the accession of Poland to the EU in 2004 established Britain, Ireland and Sweden (the only countries initially allowing unrestricted post EU enlargement or 'Accession 8' migration) as major destinations for Polish migrants. The 2007 Home Office Accession Monitoring Report recorded that more than 470,000 Polish migrants had registered to work across Britain since 2004, two thirds of the total number of new migrants registered in this way.[1]

This chapter is based on the combined findings of two studies, bringing together in-depth interviews undertaken with approximately fifty Polish migrants living in the Midlands region of Britain: firstly, postwar refugees in Leicester (Burrell 2006), and then a more recent project on socialist-era, postsocialist and post-accession migrants.[2] Methodologically, both of these studies utilized a life-history approach in the interviews to begin with; respondents were asked about their lives in general first, and the migration aspects of their experiences were discussed more closely later on. This allowed for the whole biography of the migrants interviewed to be considered, placing their migrations in a wider chronological context and capturing important narratives about life in Poland. Importantly, neither emotions nor materiality were initially chosen as issues for special consideration in the research projects. Materiality, however, quickly became a key theme in the different narratives which were created. People's stories about life in Poland and migration to Britain had a very strong material component (see Burrell 2008a, 2008b), highlighting how important it was going to be to pay attention to the material dynamics of the interviews. Emotions came into the interview process much more subtly. Again, there was no overt attempt to focus on emotions during the research. The nature of the interviews, however, and the rapport between myself and the respondents, meant that the emotional journey of migration was always at the forefront of the discussion. I did not have to ask direct questions about emotions; homesickness, excitement, anxiety, exile – all these experiences were talked about in depth throughout the interviews. By paying attention to the human element of these people's experiences and by letting them talk freely about their lives, the interviews produced testimonies rich in emotion. Life-history and in-depth interviews clearly lend themselves to emotion research.

Polish migration to Britain across this time span offers a fascinating example of the complexity of the emotional and material journeys that accompany international migration (see also Burrell 2008b). While moving for different reasons, at different times and under different circumstances, all of these migrations took place in the wider context of the Cold War and the post-Cold War world. Personal and material migrations had to first cross the political and economic divides of Cold War Europe, and then navigate the changing terrains of postsocialism. The migrants' stories and experiences overlap in time, with the contexts of socialism and postsocialism in Poland central to their pre- and/or post-migration lives. This is exemplified especially through the commitment, both during times of shortages in Poland and far away from Poland in Britain, to celebrate Christmas properly, upholding the traditions of *Wigilia* (Christmas Eve) as faithfully as possible – the family meal of twelve non-meat dishes, the giving and receiving of gifts after the appearance of the first star in the sky, and the taking of mass at midnight (see Hodorowicz Knab 1993).

Pulling all the different arguments together, and offering an in-depth insight into Polish migration, this chapter will focus on three key material components of this modern Polish Christmas which demonstrate the depth of penetration of the large-scale geopolitical boundaries of Europe into the everyday material and emotional lives of migrants and their families: oranges, wafers and carp.

Oranges for a Socialist Christmas

As previously explained, all of the people interviewed for this study are international migrants; at some point in their lives they left Poland to live, more or less permanently, in Britain. Even before migrating, however, those who left Poland during the socialist era were already experiencing highly internationalized Christmases. Alongside the traditional and purportedly intrinsically national, and certainly religious, rituals of Christmas, during the socialist era key festivities also came to be imbued with other meanings and associated with other rituals and practices. The realities of living in a shortage economy especially dictated the practical planning of Christmas. Key foodstuffs regarded as integral to Christmas continued to be consumed, but the acquisition of these goods constituted, particularly during the more difficult economic periods of the 1970s and 1980s, another tradition in itself (see, e.g., Wedel 1986; Burrell 2008a). When remembering Christmas from these periods, respondents spoke far more about how mothers and wives had to queue for even longer than usual at this time of year to get the necessary foodstuffs, and how the entire family became involved in the Christmas project, than they did about the actual celebration itself. A new narrative of Christmas was constructed around the highly gendered but usually shared responsibility of locating and securing its most important components, rather than the performances they subsequently enabled. Prominent among these components, and of particular relevance here, were international shipments of oranges.

Due to their scarce nature, high price and foreign origin, oranges in socialist Poland, and in other socialist countries, were powerful symbols of luxury and the exotic, in many ways a continuation of the status that they had held in the interwar period when they had also been considered a luxury, but also important for their health-giving properties (Zion-Gold 2007: 110). Just as Wedel (1986) notes how expensive they were in Poland, usually priced for foreigners, Gronow (2003: 71) observes the high status oranges commanded in Stalin's Russia, with shipments being important enough to warrant reporting in the press. Accentuating their special value, these luxury goods would be made available to citizens at key times of the year: New Year in Russia (ibid.: 36) and Christmas in Poland. Preparations for Christmas, therefore, not only involved more traditional foodstuffs, but also included queuing for oranges, with the fruit becoming closely associated with the Christmas season. When most of the interviewees recalled their memories of Christmas they spoke about oranges. Jacek, for example, was born in the early 1950s and remembered always receiving a box of special food at Christmas-time as a child: 'I remember till now the scent of the orange, because when you open this box – it was usually the size of a shoebox – it was like chocolate there, an orange, some nuts, some biscuits, all different things that you really just didn't have during the year'.[3] Adriana, born over twenty years later, had similar recollections: 'Probably for the rest of my life I will associate oranges with Christmas because this was the only time that you could actually buy them and have them and eat them … I remember Christmas. I will always associate Christmas with oranges'.[4]

The emotional power of these oranges works on several different levels. Perhaps most obviously, the fruit represented the outside world, a world beyond the communist bloc, and although the oranges were not exactly from 'the West' (they were often from socialist Cuba), they conjured similar images of exciting places, just out of reach. The mere promise of oranges could move people to feel excitement and anticipation, a clear case of the emotional agency embodied in the imagined (Baldassar 2008) presence of the fruit. Sylwia's testimony demonstrates this very well:

> Oranges were not really available, exotic fruit wasn't really available. So again one of the Christmas symbols would be these oranges, the smell of oranges around the Christmas tree and all that. So again my mum would make sure that we would have oranges for Christmas, and bananas as well, the ultimate exotic fruit. And there would be every night on the news, they would broadcast, they would show this ship, this ship has departed from Cuba, this huge ship, this ship has departed from Cuba to bring oranges from Cuba to Poland, to Gdynia or Gdansk, in time for Christmas in the Polish shops. So we would watch the news and watch this ship with oranges coming. And they were not really the best oranges in the world, but for some reason – well, obvious reason – they would be coming from Cuba. So you would know, you would be getting ready, the expectation growing, when these oranges will finally appear in the shops so that you can join the queue and get the amount you were entitled to.[5]

The spectacle of these huge, steel ships coming into Gdansk and Gdynia was proof that Poland was connected beyond the rest of socialist Europe, and the oranges they carried, highly distinctive in taste and smell, brought a piece of this world into people's homes – thus temporarily altering their domestic spaces – to be shared and enjoyed with family and friends. As noted, this image of oranges as exotic strongly resonates with the broader phenomenon of the popularity and 'evocative power' (McCracken 1988: 110) or 'enchantment' (Bennett 2001) of Western goods, something which has been observed of most of the communist bloc countries. Blum and Veenis, for example, both analyse the prestigious nature of Western things in the GDR, not only the power of brands such as Coca Cola (Blum 2006: 144), but also the superior aesthetic qualities of more colourful, better feeling, nicer smelling Western products (Veenis 1999: 106). In Poland, Western goods were held in similarly high esteem, available only through the state-run pewex shops for dollars, on the black market, at street markets (see Crowley 2003: 122), or from contacts abroad (Burrell 2008a). As the above also suggests, the powerful, imaginative, emotional agency located within these goods was clearly enhanced by their physical characteristics. It is worth emphasizing the point that these oranges and Western products were valued as much for their taste, smell, colour and feel as for their political status, and as such were resolutely interactive objects, prompting emotion through their consumption and close physical presence.

Christmas was, of course, an especially important time for the procurement and enjoyment of Western goods generally. While the whole experience of shopping for gifts and goods in a shortage economy could push people deeper into the realms of the black market and, for those who could pay, into the *pewex* shops, those who did have families abroad would be more likely to receive parcels at this time of year. In the GDR too, according to Veenis, 'Christmas parcels that East Germans received from their Western relatives were always anxiously awaited because they usually contained some popular Western consumer goods, such as cheap brands of soap, eau de toilette, after-shave and face cream' (Veenis 1997: 126). The social context and emotional consequences of receiving such parcels were not necessarily unproblematic, however. Western gifts highlighted the divisions between those who had contacts and those who did not, sometimes fuelling envy and even resentment. Alina's childhood memories of the 1980s centre quite strongly on her relationship with a school friend who had family connections with West Germany, and received 'better' gifts, particularly at Christmas:

> The worst thing was that my close friend at primary school had all Barbies and Fleur, German one, as she had family in Germany. She is the one who also had Father Christmas chocolate figurines. So she had those Barbies, real ones, their legs bent and that really was the important thing. I once got a fake one and it had plastic legs and they did not bend. I would rather not have had one at all.[6]

As Veenis (1997) further notes, parcels such as these could be uncomfortable reminders of another, inaccessible, world, and signifiers of the overarching political and economic divisions across Europe (see also Burrell 2008a). Cold War politics was played out in many different ways in the everyday lives of Europeans, and all of these foreign and Western products embodied political meanings alongside their more usually recognized social ones.

Oranges also denoted the politicization of consumption and material culture in socialist Poland in another way too. Just by being imported at all, oranges represented the power of the planned economy and the political regime which orchestrated the timing of their availability, using the oranges as agents to try to promote feelings of loyalty and gratitude in its citizens. Once in the homes of Polish citizens, therefore, the oranges also exemplified the political reach of the state. Crowley (2002) has argued that under the regime home spaces cannot be considered as exclusively private spaces, so widespread was the saturation of officially sanctioned domestic imagery, policies and design. The private consumption of oranges was therefore imbued with the public dynamics of the regime.

It is interesting that these oranges and Western things are so deeply embedded in the biographies of my respondents. While these types of products were important in the lives of non-migrants too, they do feel particularly significant for the life-histories of the migrants, who in the structure of their narratives give Western things a prominent position – not exactly as a justification for later emigration but as evidence that they had already been thinking beyond Poland. Through the movement of objects and a type of 'imaginative travel' (Larson, Urry and Axhausen 2006: 13), the outside world had already been envisioned, encountered and consumed at an earlier stage in their lives, with the iconic, aspirational but also uncomfortable position of Western things foreshadowing the actual westward migration movements of respondents. The relationship between exotic/exciting/unsettling and foreign/ abroad/West had already been established through travelling foodstuffs and objects.

Wigilia Wafers in Exile

As already mentioned, Polish Christmas, and in particular the Christmas Eve celebration *Wigilia*, is highly ritualized, requiring specific dishes and practices. Postwar Polish settlers in Britain took pride in reproducing *Wigilia* traditions they had experienced in Poland as closely as possible, using what they could from local Polish-run delicatessens (see also Burrell 2006). Some aspects of Christmas did change to reflect the new environment they found themselves in – like celebrating Christmas Day and eating turkey with friends and family – but the emotional commitment to maintaining an 'authentic' Polish Christmas was clear in the interviews. Jolanta's views were typical: 'Christmas must be celebrated as normal in Poland, fasting on Christmas Eve, the evening is family dinner, and the family dinner is without any meat'.[7] Among these traditions, the significance of *Wigilia* wafers (*opłatek*) stood out (see Hodorowicz Knab 1993: 39). These unconsecrated bread wafers, intricately decorated with nativity scenes, had to be sent from Poland and blessed by Polish priests in Britain, and were always shared at the start of the meal. All of the respondents from this migration movement spoke about the wafers when discussing *Wigilia*; as with the twelve dishes, these wafers were presented as an integral part of the tradition, although interestingly their religious significance was never discussed, suggesting that the emotional importance of the wafers lies elsewhere. In the words of Agata:

> At Christmas we make the Christmas tree on the day of the twenty-fourth, not before. We celebrate Christmas Eve, when the first star, the children look and they see the star, we sit at the table and then we start celebrating. And we have wafers, sent over from Poland, from the Church, and we give them to each other, and we say 'I wish you all the best' and so on. And then we sit at the table and we have twelve dishes that day.[8]

Much has been written about the power of specific objects to connect migrants with their past lives and homelands (e.g., Parkin 1999; Tolia-Kelly 2004; Attan 2006; Walsh 2006). They can offer a tangible continuity with a time and place which would otherwise be lost, something that is especially important for refugees. The personal, emotional resonance of specific objects and artefacts, even things which may appear inconsequential to others, is therefore enormous. Certain objects also work on a much wider level, reaching beyond individual significance to tap into large-scale social and political identities; in the case of the wafers, Polish religious and national identity. These wafers, and the bodily movements and rituals surrounding them, connect to a shared national past (see Connerton 1989) which celebrates Catholicism and the resilience of culture in the face of partition and occupation (see Davies 1981). They also help to keep Poles abroad in touch with Polish customs, allowing a relatively simultaneous diasporic consumption of national traditions. Once again, these sentiments have the potential to chime particularly loudly with an exiled population who feel protective of their original homeland and want to be closer to it.

These strong associations surrounding the wafers were laid bare in the run-up to Christmas in 1980. Although not yet under martial law, the tense situation in Poland had affected communications with friends and family so much that the wafers were either not sent or just not delivered. As the local press reported: 'usually the wafers are sent from Poland, but because of censorship, no communication has been made with families in Poland, and the wafers never arrived'.[9] The local population was deeply concerned, and in a mark of respect the scheduled Christmas folk dancing was also cancelled. Now, in their absence, the wafers reinforced the frustration and anxiety of exile, accentuating the distance between Poland and Britain, rather than bringing the two closer as they had done before. Not receiving the wafers, moreover, was just one particularly pertinent episode within a much longer-term preoccupation with Poland's stability. At least for the older immigrants, what was happening in Poland was as important as what was happening in Leicester. Again, the local press illustrated this very clearly, carrying a story in 1980 about fears that visits between the two countries would be stopped due to the ongoing strikes, and, at the start of martial law, running several pieces on two Leicester-based Polish drivers who had taken vans full of provisions to Poland but had not been heard from since arriving there.[10] Most of the respondents spoke about feeling uncomfortable when visiting Poland, of family members not being able to speak freely, and of working hard to send money, and food and medicine parcels (Burrell 2006: 114). The political character of the communist regime in Poland loomed large over their imaginations of the country, dominating their perceptions of life there, and somehow physically widening the divide. It is interesting to juxtapose these Christmas preparations in Leicester with those in Poland itself. As the Poles in Leicester waited for wafers to arrive from Poland, Poles in Poland waited in queues for oranges from Cuba. And while the non-arrival of the wafers in 1980 was event enough to be reported in the press and necessitate the cancellation of community activities, Wedel (1986: 169) notes the efforts in Poland during martial law to carry on as normal as possible for Christmas.

The *Wigilia* wafers raise some interesting issues with regards to mobility and the integral meanings of objects. Lury has written about the changing values attributed to objects as they move, identifying different types, notably 'traveller-objects', which hold their authentic meaning and travel well, keeping their original denotations in different locations; and 'tripper-objects', which are 'continually reconstituted by their dwellings as they travel, especially by their final dwelling' (Lury 1997: 79). In the first analysis, the wafers seem to fit the former group of 'traveller objects' comfortably: they are a standardized commodity, their function is very well defined, and their usage uniform among those who use them for *Wigilia* festivities. Their integral meaning and purpose is not lost when they travel. However, they are of course also 'tripper-objects' because their political and emotional connotations are obviously affected enormously by their location: while they keep a fundamental ritualistic role wherever they are, they have a notably altered emotional impact outside Poland. They are also affected by temporal contexts: times of crisis in Poland enhance their diasporic association with loss, fear and distance. The wafers are an important reminder that all objects, no matter how 'fixed', are recontextualized to some extent when they move. The oranges, in fact, are another good example of this: the physical function of the fruit is constant, but their emotional impact changes over time and space.

Importantly, the meanings associated with the wafers also have a very strong social component: just as important as the wafers themselves are the relationships which are serviced through their breaking and sharing. Although an overtly religious gesture, this practice is arguably far more about strengthening bonds with family and upholding a long standing societal tradition (see Hodorowicz Knab 1993: 39). The sharing of the wafers offers an opportunity to thank family members for their support during the previous year, and to wish them well for the next one. It is the issues of co-presence and place which are particularly important here. When this practice takes place in Britain it also confirms that it is here that the family is based; it roots the family more firmly in their British environment, and reinforces the emotional closeness of different family members to each other. If the political, exilic significance of the wafers seemed most important for the postwar generation, the social importance appears to have greater relevance to more recent migrants. Maja, for example, spoke about what Christmas means to her emotionally, and the chance it gives her to reach out to her British-born teenage son:

> We do keep our Christmas traditions – Christmas Eve, Wigilia, the most important day in the year, Wigilia. And we have always done, my children. I always cook the twelve dishes there should be on the table. We always try a little of each, we always say the prayers, and that's called the last supper, and you have to eat your last supper when the first clouds appear in the sky. We share the wafer, and then we wish each other, we have a little conversation with each other. I go to my son and I say, 'You have done very well this year, I am very proud of you', and what I wish for you next year, and how our relationship could be, and we always shed a tear. It is a very emotional time.[11]

The social and emotional meanings triggered by the wafers change from family to family and person to person, and are deeply subjective. Alina, a more recent migrant again, even called into question the physical integrity of the wafers, instead privileging the performing of rituals and strengthening of bonds that take place around them. It did not matter to her that the wafers used were the proper ones, as long as the practice still took place: 'No, I had forgotten to ask them in the shop about it, and I just used some of those Italian finger things that you use for tiramisu. I don't have to have the Polish thing, I just pick things, whatever suits'.[12] The Wigilia opłatek, therefore, demonstrate how the essential values of objects can both endure and transform when they migrate, showcasing the complexity and mutability of the meanings attached to, and emotions triggered by, even the most apparently ritualized, standardized artefact.

Carp and Constructions of Home among Recent Polish Migrants

Alongside oranges and wafers, carp also has a special place in Polish Christmas, in this case as one of the main components of the fish-based *Wigilia* meal. As with oranges, carp had to be queued for extensively in Poland during the socialist era. Requiring more than just the hard work and logistics of queuing, timing was also crucial to carp acquisition. Since getting carp just in time for Christmas Eve was practically impossible in a shortage economy, the fish had to be bought several days before and kept alive at home. Sylwia's testimony illustrates how embedded carp became in the run up to Christmas in domestic life, and how synonymous this particular fish has become with a Polish Christmas:

And another period of queuing was the pre-Christmas queuing, to make sure you get everything. Mum would make sure we had a traditional Christmas, so we would queue to get the carp. The carp had to be live. The carp season started in early December, so you ended up buying this carp when the carp was available, so you would buy this fish, live fish, ten days before Christmas, a week before Christmas, and then you would keep it at home. Some people would keep the carp in the bathtub, and then there was the whole family logistics of how to take a bath in the morning because of the carp. My mum wouldn't do that, we would have our carp swimming about in a large bowl, like a laundry bowl. Feeding the carp, by the time Christmas had come, us children we would have formed emotional bonds with the carp. Then of course the carp had to be slaughtered. But there was this double thing, the carp had to be there, and it had to be fresh. It couldn't be one like you buy nearly dead and then you freeze it, nothing like that. And of course there was no certainty that you would get the carp. I mean, it was almost certain that you wouldn't get the carp on Christmas Eve, so you made sure you got one when you found it in the shop. It was a big thing. In some old comedies, Polish comedies from the eighties, there would be the carp motif. Pre-Christmas, the Christmas tree, children running about, the carp in the bathtub, very Polish, very Polish the carp in the bathtub.[13]

The Christmas carp, therefore, triggers many emotions. It elicits pride in the triumph of managing to find something so important in times of shortages; satisfaction in the successful reproduction of traditional meals for *Wigilia*; and excitement within family home spaces for the arrival of Christmas, as the intrusive presence and smell of the fish, like the oranges before but more pronounced, alters the domestic setting for a short period of time. The entrenchment of carp in seasonal television programmes also illustrates the national recognition of these emotional associations, further reinforced by their prominent position in the public discourse of Christmas in Poland. If any ingredient of Christmas has come to signify Polishness, and generate feelings of national identification, then the carp surely must be it.

It is interesting, then, to consider what role carp has been playing among the British-based Christmases of the most recent Polish migrants. Firstly, carp has become, in British public discourse, a potent symbol of post-accession migration generally, and of the different cultural practices of the migrants specifically. Tensions have arisen over the supposed unauthorized fishing and taking home of carp from British rivers by new migrants, who perhaps unaware of British regulations covering fishing, catch carp themselves in order to get hold of the popular and culturally important food. In November 2007 the Fisheries and Angling Conservation Trust issued new posters urging people not to 'Steal, Cook, Kill' fish from rivers, canals and lakes. The use of pictures in the posters was designed to communicate with non-English-speaking East European migrants.[14] The national press followed these developments with widespread coverage of the fishing and eating practices of East European migrants, cementing the image of the newcomers as strange and 'other', and potentially damaging to the British environment, arguably encouraging fear and anxiety in their readership. The *Daily Mail* even carried a story about East Europeans trying to catch swans: 'There are few sights so serene as a swan sailing majestically along the Grand Union Canal. Except, that is, when it is being chased by a gang of hungry, knife-wielding Eastern Europeans'.[15] This type of coverage is reminiscent of earlier hysteria in the *Sun* and the *Daily Express* about asylum seekers 'barbequing the Queen's swans', headlining the frightening prospect that 'refugees eat swans' (Kushner 2006: 23–24). Unfortunately, in its post-accession British environment, carp presents a rather negative public connotation of Polish migration.

Carp, however, is still integral to the Christmases of the newer incomers, and still promotes positive feelings among the migrants themselves. In fact, one of the most important factors here is that carp is now readily available in Britain in the plethora of shops selling Polish products which have sprung up since Poland's EU accession in 2004 (see Pollard, Latorre and Sriskandarajah 2008: 22; Rabikowska and Burrell 2009). Even mainstream supermarkets now sell seasonal Polish products, with most of them stocking carp ready for Christmas in December 2007 (Rabikowska and Burrell 2009). If carp has been used to feed into hostility to A8 migration, and highlights the outsider status of many of the new migrants, it has also helped to initiate a wider process of homemaking in Britain. The importance of the ability to buy Polish food in Britain cannot be overstated, particularly at Christmas time. Before this enhanced availability of Polish food, preparing for a Polish Christmas was a stressful experience for newly arrived migrants. Just as the postwar-era refugees had struggled to find all the components they needed for the *Wigilia* dishes, those arriving in the 1990s and early 2000s found that Polish food was still difficult to get hold of, and that many of the original delicatessens on which the earlier Poles had relied had since closed. In her testimony, Julia spoke about how expensive and time consuming it was to reproduce an authentic Christmas, but she also disclosed more generally how hard she found staying in Britain for Christmas:

> I am very, very much for Polish Christmas. Christmas is a very sensitive subject in our household ... I am a very tough person, but I always cry at Christmas if I am here because it is so different ... I have to find all these Polish products which are not available. I keep my Christmas traditions, the ones that are easy to do ... But I have to say that I think the tradition has to be that we go to Poland, because to do Christmas here you have to have lots of stamina, motivation to go around and buy all these products which are really expensive in the Polish shops. I went to buy a few things and I paid £12 almost for nothing.[16]

As with the wafers, it is the absence of key foodstuffs, and in this case suitable shops, which has a strong emotional impact, simultaneously serving as a reminder of life in Poland and illustrating the seemingly insurmountable differences between the two places, at least at Christmas time. Not surprisingly, many of the more recent arrivals also spoke about the emotional difficulties of this time of year, and the desire to be back in Poland for Christmas. Christmas is a peak time for return visits, and most of the respondents spoke about going home for Christmas every year. Those who had to stay in Britain shared their fears about feeling homesick: Adriana told me that 'I'm not looking forward to Christmas, I don't know what I'll do', and Arleta said that she was 'afraid of Christmas' and that the run up to Christmas was making her miss Poland and her family more.[17] They were both sorry to be absent for the preparations for the twelve dishes, a tiring but special time of the year that, as women, they would normally spend with their mothers, helping to get everything ready. Being away from Poland for Christmas, therefore, has a direct impact on these close family relationships and the traditional sharing of festive responsibilities. It is not just the consumption of the *Wigilia* dishes that is lost, but the atmosphere and structured time of the creation of them.

The phenomenon of being able to buy Polish food in Britain, however, has enabled contemporary Christmas festivities to be celebrated away from Poland more easily. Admittedly, this is a poor substitute for the family relationships which have to be reconfigured on a transnational scale, but Magdalena demonstrated that an important process is happening among at least some of these post-accession migrants. She stayed in Derby for Christmas in 2007, and, although she missed her family, she and her friends managed to recreate a Christmas in Britain that captured a similar social, cultural and gastronomic experience:

> The shops selling Polish food, it is very important because we've got our Polish culture and traditions closely connected with food. For example, Christmas, I've spoken to many people at the agency, Polish people, and they think that now it is not difficult to spend Christmas time here, when they have got their relatives around them it is not difficult to organize traditional dishes. And I also, I and my friends, we spent last Christmas here and we didn't see any difference, apart from being without our parents, our sisters or brothers, our cousins. In terms of food dishes, no difference. We didn't make twelve dishes, we made five or six. We had carp.[18]

The void left by missing family members was partly filled by the comfort of being able to celebrate in a similar style and at the same time, but, more importantly, by an emotional investment in new constructions of the Christmas tradition in Derby, with friends rather than immediate family as the fellow protagonists of Christmas.

The ability to buy carp in Britain for Christmas therefore signifies different scales of homemaking practices (see Blunt and Dowling 2006). Consuming traditional foods in domestic spaces helps to imbue the new environment with the familiar tastes and smells of home, making them feel more homely. While important on a personal scale, this also supports the social and non-familial bonding surrounding Christmas, crucially strengthening the social ties of the migrants in their new lives, and imparting a closer emotional understanding between them. The shops themselves alter the places inhabited by the migrants, both rendering the new local landscapes more familiar to them and asserting the presence of a wider Polish population, one growing in confidence (see Rabikowska and Burrell 2009). Unwittingly, then, carp epitomizes the experiences of post-accession migrants: the endurance of their emotional ties to Poland and Polish traditions, the hostility they have faced in the media and public discourse, and the roots they are establishing through their visibility and activity in the commercial spaces of Britain, and through their new domestic rituals.

Conclusions

This chapter has shown, for Polish migrants, how closely the complex emotions produced by migration are entwined with the material components of Christmas: the hope and appeal of the outside world embodied in oranges; the exilic feelings triggered by the absence of the *Wigilia* wafers; and the role of carp in aiding homemaking processes, but also positioning new migrants as outsiders. Christmas is a deeply emotional festival for those who invest in it; it is about the past, about home, about family, and about friends. For migrants it also intensifies the flashpoints of migration, forcing confrontations with place, belonging and identity that may be easier to ignore at other points in the year.

This study has also illustrated the subjectivity of the emotional value of objects and foodstuffs. It is already accepted that objects are embedded in specific social, political and cultural contexts, but these examples show that they are also entrenched in particular emotional settings, and do indeed prompt strong emotional reactions in people in different ways, changing the emotional dynamics of places – homes and local landscapes particularly. The outward meanings of objects do not necessarily match the emotions they elicit in – or the values attributed to them by – individuals, especially when they are in different countries. Carp in Poland has, among others, comical associations. As has been shown, the connotations in Britain are quite different, with the fish arguably being utilized in media discourse to create hostile reactions towards the new migrants, but cooked and eaten at home by the migrants to feel more settled, and purchased in local shops perhaps as a way of marking some sort of claim over a small part of the neighbourhood. The availability of *Wigilia* wafers may be taken for granted to some extent in Poland, but in Britain they are a cherished product, able to move migrants to feelings of loss, fear and homesickness. Conversely, migrants in Britain may have undervalued their plentiful supply of oranges, as their friends and families in Poland queued for them for hours, excited by the exoticism of their imminent presence, and their enchanting smells and tastes. The varying meanings embodied in the *Wigilia* wafers and carp especially symbolize the emotional challenges of international migration, the political and physical divide between Poland and Britain, and also how these challenges and divisions have changed over time.

The emotional dimension of migration, then, can be best understood through the material contexts which surround it. People do not move in a material vacuum, but furnish their post-migration lives partly with objects and food from their original homelands. The analysis of this practice, and of migrants' interactions with their material worlds more generally, allows a deeper appreciation of what international migration really feels like.

Notes

1. See the 'Accession Monitoring Report' of the Home Office, Department for Work and Pensions, HM Revenue and Customs and the Department for Communities and Local Government (2007), p. 8.
2. All but one of the interviews were undertaken in English (one used a translator) and all names have been changed.
3. Interview with Jacek, 5 February 2003; migrated to Britain in 1987 aged 35.
4. Interview with Adriana, 24 November 2005; migrated to Britain in 2005 aged 31.
5. Interview with Sylwia, 15 May 2007; migrated to Britain in 1999 aged 23.
6. Interview with Alina, 4 May 2005; migrated to Britain in 1998 aged 20.
7. Interview with Jolanta, 26 August 1999; migrated to Britain in 1948 aged 39.
8. Interview with Agata, 2 February 2001; migrated to Britain in 1946 aged 26.
9. *Leicester Mercury*, 14 January 1981.
10. *Leicester Mercury*, 22 August 1980; 15 December 1981.
11. Interview with Maja, 14 November 2005; migrated to Britain in 1985 aged 24.
12. Interview with Alina, 4 May 2005.
13. Interview with Sylwia, 15 May 2007.
14. Fisheries and Angling Conservation Trust (FACT). Retrieved 3 May 2008 from: http://factuk.co.uk/asp_pages/news.asp?type=5.
15. *Daily Mail*, 7 August 2007.
16. Interview with Julia, 5 May 2005; migrated to Britain in 1999 aged 19.
17. Interview with Adriana, 24 November 2005. Interview with Arleta, 10 December 2005; migrated to Britain in 2005 aged 29.
18. Interview with Magdalena, 16 February 2008; migrated to Britain in 2006 aged 26.

References

Appadurai, A. 1986. 'Introduction: Commodities and the Politics of Value', in A. Appadurai (ed.), *The Social Life of Things: Commodities in Cultural Perspective*. Cambridge: Cambridge University Press, pp. 3–63.

Attan, C. 2006. 'Hidden Objects in the World of Cultural Migrants: Significant Objects used by European Migrants to Layer Thoughts and Memories', in K. Burrell and P. Panayi (eds), *Histories and Memories: Migrants and their History in Britain*. London: I. B. Tauris, pp. 171–88.

Baldassar, L. 2001. *Visits Home: Migration Experiences between Italy and Australia*. Melbourne: Melbourne University Press.

———— 2008. 'Missing Kin and Longing to be Together: Emotions and the Construction of Co-presence in Transnational Relationships', *Journal of Intercultural Studies* 29(3): 247–66.

Baldassar, L., C. Baldock and R. Wilding. 2007. *Families Caring Across Borders: Migration, Ageing and Transnational Caregiving*. Basingstoke: Palgrave Macmillan.

Bennett, J. 2001. *The Enchantment of Modern Life: Attachments, Crossings, and Ethics*. Princeton, NJ: Princeton University Press.

Blum, M. 2006. 'Club Cola and Co.: Ostalgie, Material Culture and Identity', in R.A. Starkman (ed.), *Transformations of the New Germany*. New York: Palgrave Macmillan, pp. 131–53.

Blunt A., and R. Dowling. 2006. *Home*. London: Routledge.

Bodenhorn, B. 1993. 'Christmas Present: Christmas Public', in D. Miller (ed.), *Unwrapping Christmas*. Oxford: Oxford University Press, pp. 193–261.

Burrell, K. 2003. 'Small-scale Transnationalism: Homeland Connections and the Polish "Community" in Leicester', *International Journal of Population Geography* 9(4): 323–35.

_____ 2006. *Moving Lives: Narratives of Nation and Migration among Europeans in Post-war Britain*. Aldershot: Ashgate.

_____ 2008a. 'Managing, Learning and Sending: The Material Lives and Journeys of Polish Women in Britain', *Journal of Material Culture* 13(1): 63–83.

_____ 2008b. 'Materialising the Border: Spaces of Mobility and Material Culture in Migration from Post-socialist Poland', *Mobilities* 3(3): 353–73.

Carrier, J. 1993. 'The Rituals of Christmas Giving', in D. Miller (ed.), *Unwrapping Christmas*. Oxford: Oxford University Press, pp. 55–74.

Connerton, P. 1989. *How Societies Remember*. Cambridge: Cambridge University Press.

Crowley, D. 2002. 'Warsaw Interiors: The Public Life of Private Spaces, 1949–65', in D. Crowley and S. Reid (eds), *Socialist Spaces: Sites of Everyday Life in the Eastern Bloc*. Oxford: Berg, pp. 181–206.

_____ 2003. *Warsaw*. London: Reaktion Books.

Davidson, J., L. Bondi and M. Smith (eds). 2005. *Emotional Geographies*. Aldershot: Ashgate.

Davies, N. 1981. *God's Playground: A History of Poland, Volume II: 1795 to the Present*. Oxford: Oxford University Press.

Fisheries and Angling Conservation Trust (FACT) website: http://factuk. co.uk/asp_pages/news.asp?type=5 (accessed 3 May 2008).

Gell, A. 1998. *Art and Agency: An Anthropological Theory*. Oxford: Oxford University Press.

Gronow, J. 2003. *Caviar with Champagne: Common Luxury and the Ideals of the Good Life in Stalin's Russia*. Oxford: Berg.

Hochschild, A.R. 1983. *The Managed Heart: Commercialization of Human Feeling*. Berkeley: University of California Press.

Hodorowicz Knab, S. 1993. *Polish Customs, Traditions and Folklore*. New York: Hippocrene Books.

Kuper, A. 1993. 'The English Christmas and the Family: Time Out and Alternative Realities', in D. Miller (ed.), *Unwrapping Christmas*. Oxford: Oxford University Press, pp. 151–75.

Kushner, T. 2006. 'Great Britons: Immigration, History and Memory', in K. Burrell and P. Panayi (eds), *Histories and Memories: Migrants and their History in Britain*. London: I. B. Tauris, pp. 18–34.

Larson, J., J. Urry and K. Axhausen. 2006. 'Report to the UK Department for Transport: Social Networks and Future Mobilities'. Lancaster/Zurich: Institute for Transport Planning and Systems, University of Lancaster/Swiss Federal Institute of Technology.

Lury, C. 1997. 'The Objects of Travel', in C. Rojek and J. Urry (eds), *Touring Cultures: Transformations of Travel and Theory*. London: Routledge, pp. 75–95.

Lutz, C. 1986. 'Emotion, Thought, and Estrangement: Emotion as a Cultural Category', *Cultural Anthropology* 1(3): 287–309.

McCracken, G. 1988. *Culture and Consumption: New Approaches to the Symbolic Character of Consumer Goods and Activities*. Bloomington: Indiana University Press.

Miller, D. 1993. 'A Theory of Christmas', in D. Miller (ed.), *Unwrapping Christmas*. Oxford: Oxford University Press, pp. 3–37.

Milton, K. 2005. 'Emotion (or Life, the Universe, Everything)', *Australian Journal of Anthropology* 16(2): 198–211.

Parkin, D. 1999. 'Mementoes as Transitional Objects in Human Displacement', *Journal of Material Culture* 4(3): 303–20.

Pollard, N., M. Latorre and D. Sriskandarajah. 2008. 'Floodgates or Turnstiles? Post-EU enlargement Migration: Flows to (and from) the UK'. London: Institute for Public Policy Research.

Rabikowska, M., and K. Burrell. 2009. 'The Material Worlds of Recent Polish Migrants: Transnationalism, Food, Shops and Home', in K. Burrell (ed.), *Polish Migration to the UK in the 'New' European Union: After 2004*. Farnham: Ashgate.

Rojek, C., and J. Urry. 1997. 'Transformations of Travel and Theory', in C. Rojek and J. Urry (eds), *Touring Cultures: Transformations of Travel and Theory*. London: Routledge, pp. 1–20.

Ryan, L. 2008. 'Navigating the Emotional Terrain of Families "Here" and "There": Women, Migration and the Management of Emotions', *Journal of Intercultural Studies* 29(3): 299–313.

Skrbiš, Z. 2008. 'Transnational Families: Theorising Migration, Emotions and Belonging', *Journal of Intercultural Studies* 29(3): 231–46.

Svašek, M. 2007. 'Moving Corpses: Emotions and Subject–Object Ambiguity', in H. Wulff (ed.), *The Emotions: A Cultural Reader*. Oxford: Berg, pp. 229–48.

———— 2009. 'Shared History? Polish Migrant Experiences and the Politics of Display in Northern Ireland', in K. Burrell (ed.), *Polish Migration to the UK in the 'New' European Union: After 2004*. Aldershot: Ashgate, pp. 129–48.

Sword, K. 1996. *Identity in Flux: The Polish Community in Britain.* London: SSEES, University of London.

Tanhahill, J.A. 1958. *European Volunteer Workers in Britain.* Manchester: Manchester University Press.

Tolia-Kelly, D. 2004. 'Locating Processes of Identification: Studying the Precipitates of Re-memory through Artefacts in the British Asian Home', *Transactions of the Institute of British Geographers* 29(3): 319–24.

Veenis, M. 1997. 'Fantastic Things', in S.M. Pearce (ed.), *Experiencing Material Culture in the Western World.* London: Leicester University Press, pp. 151–74.

———— 1999. 'Consumption in East Germany: The Seduction and Betrayal of Things', *Journal of Material Culture* 4(1): 79–112.

Walsh, K. 2006. 'British Expatriate Belongings: Mobile Homes and Transnationalism', *Home Cultures* 3(2): 123–44.

Wedel, J. 1986. *The Private Poland: An Anthropological Look at Everyday Life.* New York: Facts on File.

Wulff, H. (ed.) 2007. *The Emotions: A Cultural Reader.* Oxford: Berg.

Zion-Gold, B. 2007. *The Life of Jews in Poland before the Holocaust: A Memoir.* Lincoln: University of Nebraska Press.

Zubrzycki, J. 1956. *Polish Immigrants in Britain: A Study of Adjustment.* The Hague: Martinus Nijhoff.

3

From Shop to Chapel:
The Changing Emotional Efficacy of the Statue of the Virgin Mary of El Rocío within a Spanish Community in Belgium

————◆•◆•◆————

Eddy Plasquy

Introduction

In 1990, six Spanish migrant youngsters, all members of a local cultural club, launched the idea of organizing an outdoor feast (*romería*) in the Flemish town of Vilvoorde. They knew that, in order to do this in a proper Andalusian way, it would have to be done in honour of a Virgin Mary, and they chose the Virgin Mary of El Rocío (*Virgen del Rocío*) because they had heard she was well-known in Andalusia. None of them, nor their parents, had a special devotion towards this image. Lacking a statue, they went to Brussels to buy one in a specialized shop. But, as the fame of that specific Virgin had not yet reached the capital of Belgium, they bought a statue of the Virgin Mary of Lourdes instead. Five years later, a statue of the 'real' Andalusian *Virgen del Rocío* replaced the one from Lourdes. In the meantime, the colourful outdoor feast not only attracted curious local town folk but also a large number of Spanish migrants from all over Belgium and even from abroad. Today, the *romería* has evolved into a highly elaborate and respected tradition during which the Virgin Mary of El Rocío is honoured as the protector of the local Spanish community in a chapel that is built for the occasion.

According to the Spanish anthropologist Celeste Jiménez (1999), this kind of celebration basically consists of the continuation or imitation of a ritual in order to recreate the dominant symbols of people's Andalusian cultural identity. However, Anne Marie Fortier (2000) has convincingly argued against such an essentialist approach. Informed by Probyn (1996) and relying on her fieldwork among Italian migrants in London, she claims that institutional narratives of identity, rather than surfacing from an already constituted identity, are better viewed as part of the longing to belong. 'Belongings', in Fortier's view, refers not only to people's possessions, but also to their sense of inclusion. In her perspective, practices of group identity are about manufacturing cultural and historical belongings that mark out terrains of commonality, through which the social dynamics and politics of 'fitting in' are delineated. (Fortier 2000: 2).

This approach implies that migrant belongings are constituted both through movement and attachment, suggesting that identity will always be a momentary position of becoming (Fortier 2000: 2). While Fortier focuses on the way in which differences (gendered, ethnic, generational) are constructed to support the formation of a stable and unified 'community', Svašek and Skrbiš (2007) direct their attention to the specific position that objects and images can have in such a process. They argue that the emotional efficacy, as well as the specific meaning that migrants attribute to objects or images, are not given, but are rather the outcome of a transformative process within the diasporic context. In doing so, they rely on the analytic difference that Svašek (2007) makes between the transit and transition of an object or image: the former refers to the locations or its movement over time and across social or geographical boundaries, while the latter relates to the changes in the meaning, value and efficacy of this object or image.

That such a transformative process is also relevant to religious images is often overlooked. While it is true that the meaning and emotional efficacy of an idol is embedded within a specific cultural context, this by itself does not imply that people from or related to a specific cultural context are immediately and fully susceptible to it. Especially when images have been constructed and are perceived as the materialized and territorialized expression of local identities, caution against oversimplification and overgeneralization is warranted (Canépa 2007). When dealing with collective emotional experiences, as is for example the case during a local *romería*, the ritual context comes to the fore as a crucial space which can take up, alter, express, and produce these emotions in a special way (Kapferer 1979; Lüddeckens 2006). Recognizing that most of the emotional efficacy of images is generated within a specific ritual context implies that attention has to be given to how these celebrations are organized, structured and altered. Instead of seeing a ritual as a 'stage' for existing emotions, it makes more sense to approach them in a more dynamic way, one in which interactions with present emotions are brought to the fore.

In the context of ritual events, emotions neither simply pre-exist nor simply result. They are both inherent in the ritual from the very start and at the same time constantly recreated or even strengthened in the ritual process (Lüddeckens 2006: 553). Understanding how an unknown replica became imbued with a specific agency up to the point that it attained the status of a local protector is thus bound to an insight in the way how this local ritual came into existence and further evolved into a major collective celebration. Both seemed to be dialectically connected, and both seems to operate 'through similar experience[s] among members of a group living in similar conditions, through cultural stereotyping of experience, and through shared expectations, memories and fantasies' (Leavitt 1996: 527).

The main goal of this contribution is to document how this transformative process took shape in Vilvoorde, a town in Flemish Belgium. In order to do so, I rely on visual material collected since the early years of the celebrations, and on personal observations and interviews since 1997. From 2001 onwards, extended fieldwork during the *romería* held in the Andalusian hamlet of El Rocío provided additional background information. Based on these experiences, I will argue that the *romería* in Vilvoorde is not so much an exact copy of an existing Spanish example but rather the outcome of a creative process that has its locus within the specific context of this Spanish migrant community in Belgium. The ethnographic data relating to this case further stimulates a reflection on the work of David Freedberg (1989) and Alfred Gell (1998). Both scholars tackle the problem of the agency of images, although in a slightly different way. Freedberg, as an art historian, keeps the focus on the aesthetic qualities of an object, while Gell, as an anthropologist, relates the nature of an object to a specific function of the social-relational matrix in which it is embedded. It will be argued that in the case of Vilvoorde, these approaches do not contradict or exclude each other, as long as the dynamic aspects of the transition do not disappear from sight. However, before tackling both topics, some background is needed. Firstly, I shall explain what is meant by a *romería* and what it is that makes the *Virgen del Rocío* so special; secondly, I shall introduce theoretical reflections on the complex relation between identity, religion and the agency of images.

Romerías and the Devotion towards the Virgen del Rocío

A *romería* is an annual celebration, mostly held during the spring, of the patron saint or the Virgin Mary of a village, and a collective pilgrimage is organized to the chapel where the image of the saint or Virgin Mary is kept. This chapel is usually situated at the periphery of the village, which means that the march (*el camino*) towards it normally does not take more than one day. Before leaving the village, a special mass is celebrated by the parish priest and a procession is held through the village. During the *romería*, a banner (*simpecado*) of the brotherhood that organizes the *romería* is proudly carried around, while the members (*hermanos*) of the brotherhood proudly carry a special medal round their necks. When the fame of the venerated image extends to a regional level, a more complex organization is established to manage the different brotherhoods (*hermandades*) that participate in the *romería* (Moreno 1999).

Romerías are probably one of the most colourful and emblematic expressions of popular religion in southern Spain.[1] Due to their unique blend of festivity, joy and devotion, Spanish anthropologists are even inclined to approach *romerías* as *fiestas*: moments of sensorial and emotional enthrallment inextricably linked to the exaltation of family sentiments, friendship and camaraderie. An occasion to sing and dance unboundedly, to drink and dance lavishly, and a moment where social norms become blurred and sexual transgression tolerated (Cantero 2002; Rodríguez Becerra 2007). At the same time, masses are celebrated in the chapel, and rosaries and processions take place. But here too, excitement and ebullience stands out. The services are accompanied by festive flamenco music, and the rosary is, apart from its explicit devotional meaning, also a moment to show one's most beautiful dress. In sharp contrast with this thrilling atmosphere stand the quiet moments when the pilgrims visit the image of the Virgin Mary to pray and to offer flowers and candles. At these moments, the Mother of God is thanked for the support people have received over the past year, while new favours are asked and new vows are made for the coming one. It is this mixture of the jocular and the devotional, of feasting and religious rituals, of the profane and the sacred, which gives the *romería* its unique character.

The *romería* in honour of the *Virgen del Rocío* is by far the best known in Spain (Moreno 1993; Murphy and Gonzáles Faraco 1996, 2002; Cantero 2002; Rodríguez Becerra 2007).[2] It honours the patron saint of Almonte, a village in the province of Huelva situated 60 kilometres southwest of Seville. The celebration takes place in El Rocío, a settlement which is part of Almonte and situated about 15 kilometres from the historical village. Every year, in the week that precedes Pentecost, this peculiar and idyllic site at the border of the national park of Doñana converts itself from a sleepy hamlet into a vivid town, where tens of thousands of pilgrims, tourists and locals come together to enjoy *la romería del Rocío*. The collective pilgrimage in El Rocío is not restricted to the host village, but instead carried out by an extended network of more than a hundred official brotherhoods. The oldest of these claims to have existed in the sixteenth century, but the majority were founded in the last 30 years, and nine out of ten are from the eastern provinces of Andalusia (namely Seville, Huelva and Cadiz). Thus far, only one brotherhood has been recognized outside Spain: la Hermandad de Bruselas (Cháves Flores 2004). This brotherhood was founded in Brussels in 2000 by a mix of Spaniards and an amalgam of hispanophiles from more than ten countries, all of them working in the European institutions situated there.[3]

The fame of the *romería* in El Rocío not only moved a lot of devotees to strive for the foundation of a brotherhood or an association in their villages, but it also inspired Andalusian migrant communities to start a similar celebration in their new locality, and an impressive number of these exist. According to a 1954 article in a local newspaper, such a celebration had already taken place in Havana, Cuba, in 1944,[4] organized by a society whose name clearly reveals its origins: 'The Benevolence Society of Andalusians and their Descendants' (*La Sociedad de Benificencia de Naturales de Andalucía y sus Descendientes*). However, little more is known about this association. In 1964, a Spanish club in the German town of Bocholt organized a *romerito*, or small *romería* (Martínez 2003). Three years later, a *romería* is mentioned in Columbia.[5] In the late 1960s, the first attempts were made to install a proper Rocío tradition in Catalonia, though it would take until 1980 before this came together and all the logistical problems were overcome. From then on, a yearly *romería* was organized and soon after a whole network of official and unofficial brotherhoods came into existence (Pulido 2006). Around the same time, a similar process was initiated in the southern suburbs of Madrid (Jiménez 1997), Vitoria (in the Basque Country) and Valencia (Padilla Díaz de la Serna 2007). In 1990, the youngsters of a Spanish cultural club in Vilvoorde organized the first *romería* in Belgium, while in Adelaide a reunion of migrant Spaniards started a peculiar *camino annex romería* in 1991.

Identity, Religion and the Agency of Images

Celeste Jiménez (1997, 1999) is convinced that in these aforementioned recreations, the migrants select those elements that in a symbolic way best condense the fiesta. This implicates a conscious election of its components, which, according to Jiménez, in its turn provokes an awakening of their proper identity. As an inevitable consequence, two images come to the fore: The first is an original, situated in a concrete location in Andalusia and known as a legitimate signifier of this symbolic identity. The second image is a replica, void in itself and thus needing to be filled with symbolic meaning before it can actuate as the original. According to Jiménez, the best way to do so consists in striving to get a copy as close as possible to the original, in order to evoke the same interpretations, reactions and sensations.

The way in which Jiménez connects the study of rituals with an unconcealed identity discourse is quite problematic, not only because of its exclusive focus on the recovery of existing cultural elements but also because it neglects the multidimensionality of the agency with which the replica becomes imbued in its new context. By reducing the efficacy of the image to its general status as an identity marker, the emotional impact which is generated by this specific image in this specific context becomes restricted to diffuse nostalgic feelings towards a 'homeland'. Inevitably, such a culturalist and essentializing frame obscures and simplifies the creative processes by which migrants use these elements to redefine their place in exile.

Linking the field of migration studies with the study of religion, Vasquez and Marquardt argue that instead of viewing religion as reinforcing the original culture it is more fruitful to conceptualize it as a protagonist which not only unbinds culture from its traditional referents and boundaries but also its reattachment in new space–time configurations (Vasquez and Marquardt 2003: 35). As such, they plead 'for the development of "thicker", empirically richer approaches to religion and globalization in order to specify the concrete instances where global processes intersect with local lived experience' (ibid.: 51). A growing number of studies match these conditions and confirm that these processes are also at play within a Catholic and Mediterranean-linked migration context (Orsi 1985; DeMaria Harney 1999; Fortier 2000). The work of Fortier in particular is revealing in this respect, as it underlines how hard subjects had to work 'to create communal spaces of belonging based on the perceived reproduction of traditions' (Fortier 2000: 1). All the aforementioned studies deal at one moment or another with a procession in which an image of a saint or the Virgin Mary of the community is venerated. Besides the obvious fact that these manifestations clearly trace the migrant community on the urban map, more underlying motives are brought to the fore to link these Marian devotions to the communities under study. Orsi (1985), for example, connects these traditions to the family and family roles, while Fortier (2000) sees them first and foremost as the construction of an ideal of femininity that relates back to the creation of a local particularity. Yet, regardless of these interpretations, both studies implicitly assume that the images and statues used are embedded within a specific emotional dynamic which ultimately creates their efficacy. This is understandable given the longstanding tradition of most of these celebrations. On the other hand, the process and transformation in which these images are imbued with emotional efficacy is worth an analysis in itself.

Focusing on the efficacy of the images during these celebrations leads inevitably to the underlying question of how images in general become endowed with agency. For theologians, this problem poses too many difficulties: the efficacy of an image stems from the fact that it is the Virgin or saint which is represented by the image that makes miracles happen and arouses veneration. This explanation is founded on pure belief and dogma. Social scientists who do not adhere to these sources, but nevertheless observe and recognize that images can indeed make something happen, approach the issue in a quite different way. According to Freedberg, the response to an image depends firstly on the perception of its aesthetic qualities and only secondly on apparently supernatural ones (Freedberg 1989: 98).[6] This argument is criticized by Gell, who argued that art historians seek to 'distinguish the "power of images" from the power of mere unformed things, however sacred and scarifying their origins' (Gell 1998: 150). Gell, by contrast, argues that (art) objects have no 'intrinsic' nature independent of the relational context (ibid.: 7); the social agency of an object is situated in the effects it causes in its social vicinity (ibid.: 20–21).

The problematic character of Freedberg's argument also shows in the difficulties he encounters when directing his attention to copies of original works, and to secondary imagery inspired by unique originals. After passing over an amount of famous historical cases which illustrate that copies can indeed have a purposive function that approximates that of the represented image, things becomes fuzzier when dealing with cheap reproductions. On these occasions, the efficacy is very quickly reduced to an individualized and merely amulet-like function, serving to cure or ward off hostility and evil (Freedberg 1989: 124–28). However, it remains unclear when this line is crossed, and even Freedberg admits that 'the study of copies and transformations remains one of the great tasks of the history of images' (ibid.: 121).

To conclude this brief theoretical reflection, I believe that when it comes to bringing the emotional efficacy of an image to the fore, and especially when dealing with such a dynamic transitory processes, Gell's position – with its emphasis on sociological, religious and psychological agency – promises a far better starting point. So, adopting Gell's viewpoint, let us look at how the transit and transition of the image in the *romería* in Vilvoorde took place.

The Spanish Migrant Community in Vilvoorde and its *Romería*

The Flemish industrial town of Vilvoorde, situated about 15 kilometres north of Brussels, is home to about 35,000 inhabitants, 10 per cent of whom are of foreign origin. The Spaniards represent the largest community, totalling 29 per cent of the registered migrants. The majority of them have origins in Peñarroya-Pueblo Nuevo, an ore mining town situated in the mountainous region about 70 kilometres west of Cordoba. The existence, growth and decline of this typical frontier town is closely linked to the regional industry which was, for almost more than a hundred years, completely dominated and controlled by a French mining company, the Société Mineur y Metallurgie Peñarroya (García and Fernández 2003). Spanish migrants came to Vilvoorde in three subsequent waves. The first took place in the 1920s when a French engineer saw an opportunity to start his own chemical business in Vilvoorde, and he contracted Spanish workers from his former workplace with higher wages and better working conditions. In 1936, at the outbreak of the Spanish Civil War, the presence of this small group of Spaniards attracted political refugees fleeing the harsh repression of Franco's nationalist forces. During the 'golden sixties', the third and largest wave of immigration took place from Peñarroya to Vilvoorde: more than a thousand workers fled the systematic closing down of the mines in Peñarroya due to a recession in Spain and left for Belgium, attracted by the high demand for manpower in the Belgian mining and refining industry. This meant that the Spanish community in Vilvoorde is now not only the largest in Belgium, but also one with a long-term presence of more than three generations. Most of the migrants are bi- or trilingual, but continue to speak Spanish as their main language at home. From the 1960s on there has been a strong internal social and cultural dynamic within this community, which boasts several football teams, cultural clubs, Spanish bars and a local radio station. At the beginning of the 1980s, the government of Andalusia officially recognized one of these clubs as a cultural centre, the CACD Peñarroya. From then on, it became the most prominent club in town. It is here that the peculiar story of the *romería* of Vilvoorde begins.

From Absence to Presence: Transit

As was previously mentioned, the youngsters who launched the idea of the *romería* had no special affiliation with the *Virgen del Rocío*. One of them suggested the name because he had heard that this Virgin Mary was quite famous, and the others simply agreed. They neither had a clear idea of what was going on in El Rocío, nor had there ever been an adoration of this particular Virgin Mary in their parental town. Besides the fact that strong anticlerical feelings in the town were notorious, the local saint in Peñarroya has always been *la Santa Maria de los Remedios*, complemented with a cult of the Holy Barbara, the patron saint of miners, whose statue was introduced by a German company in the early years of mining in the town (García and Fernández 2003). Besides their ignorance relating to the Virgin Mary of El Rocío, the youngsters had neither planned nor intended to found a brotherhood in the near future, let alone to become officially recognized by the ecclesiastical authorities. As such, it is clear that their initial intentions in organizing the *romería* diverged quite strongly from those who had initiated similar celebrations in Madrid and Barcelona.

A couple of weeks before the first *romería*, the organizers went to a shop in Brussels that specialized in devotional statues to buy a statue of this particular Virgin Mary. They were truly convinced that, as they already knew about her existence, purchasing a copy of her image would not be a problem. However, it turned out they were wrong, and confronted with the risk of having no statue at all for the upcoming celebration they decided instead to buy a statue of the Virgin Mary of Lourdes. According to the organizers, the fact that the *romería* was organized in honour of the Virgin Mary of El Rocío but celebrated with a statue of another Marian incarnation did not really bother them or the participants. When they carried the statue around, people shouted enthusiastically *Viva la Virgen del Rocío!* and to the organizers' surprise they even placed flowers on the improvised stretcher.

The first *romería* took place during a weekend in the month of May. On Saturday morning, the statue was first taken to the club, where it was fixed on a wooded stretcher and placed on a small cart. From there a modest procession took off to accompany the statue to a church in one of the peripheral neighbourhoods of the town, and the majority of the people followed on foot. There were no flags or banners of the club in evidence nor other items that referred in one way or another to a brotherhood. However, an inevitable consequence of organizing a *romería* in honour of a Virgin Mary is the celebration of a mass. Quite conscious of this, the organizers had contacted the priest of one of the smaller churches in town, close to the site where the outdoor feast would take place. The good father agreed, but as it also needed to be a Spanish mass, they made an arrangement with a Spanish priest from Brussels to help celebrate the mass. In order to give it even more of an Andalusian atmosphere, a Spanish choir from Brussels was invited to participate.

After the mass, the procession moved to a nearby football field where a large dance floor had been installed for the occasion, with tents around it to accommodate the crowd. The cart with the statue was placed next to these installations and protected by a canvas in case it started to rain. The official activities of the *romería* consisted mainly in a dance contest and the election of a beauty queen of the *romería*. This rather unusual element was introduced by the youngsters to keep the feast going. As a matter of fact, it has much more in common with a Flemish neighbourhood feast where a beauty contest is often organized as part of the official programme. Meanwhile, the members of the club served typical Spanish food and drinks, while distinctive flamenco tunes filled the air. No other religious activity – such as a rosary – was organized during the *romería*. When the festivities ended on Sunday evening, the statue was taken to the house of one of the Spanish families. There it was guarded till the following year.

Concluding that the introduction of the image was rather atypical sounds like something of an understatement. The image was not related to the migrants' hometown, they did not have a copy of the intended Virgin, and the image that finally acted as 'a stand-in' was not even Spanish but French. Nevertheless, the introduced statue fitted the 'slot' provided for a devotional object by the participating public (see Gell 1998: 7). Fifteen years later, the organizers reflected in the course of an interview on this first performance. It was striking how vividly they recalled their surprise when seeing people offering flowers to the statue. After all, their main goal was the organization of a proper 'Spanish' outdoor feast and not the organization of a religious celebration as such. However, once they saw this devotional attitude of at least a part of the participating crowd, they suddenly realized that something was happening beyond their expectation and control.[7] On the other hand, by organizing a mass, because 'this is the way it is done in the homeland', and their search for a Spanish choir, illustrates how their 'longing to belong' (Fortier 2000: 2) is part and parcel of the celebration. Finally, it is noteworthy that, with the beauty contest, local elements of the hosts' practices became spontaneously intertwined with the imagined framework of the *romería*.

The Following Years: Transition at Work

The success of the *romería* was confirmed in the following years. Despite the fact that on some occasions the Belgian weather fairly messed up the outdoor celebration, more and more people started to participate. Most of them were members of the local Spanish community, but there were also an increasing number of locals who were attracted by the joyful atmosphere. With every year, the *romería* became more elaborated, and while in the beginning the typical flamenco dresses were only worn by the participants of the dance contest, they rapidly became the dominant dress code. This growing success, together with the unpredictability of the weather, meant that after five years, a new location was sought for the event. With the collaboration of the municipality, the next *romería* took place in an impressive historic building, situated in an extended park on the outskirts of town. The square construction of the edifice meant that its four sides enclosed a huge plaza of almost 1,500 square metres, on to which rooms in the wings opened. As such, the feast could continue outdoors while nobody had to fear the rain anymore. However, this move implicated a serious rethinking of the organization of the event. Because the park was situated in a completely different part of town to the former site, the procession and the mass in the neighbourhood church needed to be cancelled. The alternative consisted in holding a so-called outdoor mass in one of the annexes of the new building. The growing number of people attending the festivities also meant that more time needed to be invested in the preparing for the event and cleaning up afterwards. In order to do so, the date of the *romería* was set on the weekend of Pentecost. This guaranteed that on Whit Monday, which is an official holiday in Belgium, everybody could be present to clean up the place. Ironically, this meant that, though those organizing it did not know, the *romería* came to be fixed on the same day as the one in El Rocío. But more surprises were yet to come.

When the women arrived with the statue of the Virgin Mary at the new site in order to prepare for the outdoor service, the other members of the organization were stunned. Not only had they painted her lips cherry red, they had also dressed her with a mantle and a straw hat. Their intention was to imitate as far as possible an image of the *Virgen del Rocío* they had seen in a Spanish magazine, but this was not received very enthusiastically. Some women present even took the hat off before the mass started and replaced it with a corona of wildflowers from the park to make it at least a little more decent. Not until the women went home to get the article and the pictures did things cool down.[8] It is clear that the availability of photographs of the 'real statue' gave them direct access to more information about the ritual in El Rocío. However, this 'transit' of images also disrupted the way things were done in Vilvoorde. In order to avoid similar discussions in the future, the club members decided they needed to inform themselves about what was really going on in El Rocío.

In the following months a letter was sent to the municipality of Almonte. Soon after, the mayor of Almonte kindly replied with some brief information about the history of the *romería* and even included a small statue of the Virgin Mary in the package. In the meantime, the Spaniards in Vilvoorde were also convinced that it was about time they started to use a representation of the real Virgin of El Rocío instead of the one of Lourdes. However, the small replica they received from the mayor was too small to be of use in a respectable procession. Finally, a solution was found when one of the board members suggested that they would contact a relative in Seville and ask him to purchase the biggest statue available. This was easily done; given the popularity of the Virgin del Rocío in Seville, a statue was quickly purchased by the board member's uncle in one of the shops in the city. A couple of weeks later, a plaster figurine about 60 centimetres tall arrived by train in Vilvoorde. The next year, the statue was proudly taken out for the first time as a more 'proper' representation of the Virgin. Not only was it regarded as a 'correct copy' of the original statue; it had also been acquired from the homeland. A few years later, a new and grander stretcher replaced the earlier improvised one. It carried the inscription 'Vilvoorde' on the front, symbolizing the close link between this peculiar statue and people's place of residence. More recently, a fine lace mantle has been hung over the back part of the statue in order to give it an even more elegant appearance. In this way, the image has gained bit by bit some unique characteristics which ultimately make it quite distinct from any other representation.

As if the commotion around the statue mentioned above was not enough, it also became clear that the outdoor mass was not the best solution because it did not really fit well with the overall organization. So, the idea was abandoned for a more prestigious project, namely the organization of a mass in the town's main church. However, this option meant that at the same time not one but two processions came into existence: one bringing the statue from the club house to the church, and a second one taking the statue from the church to the park. After reaching an agreement with the pastor of the main church, this ambitious project took concrete form the next year and has been basically unchanged since then.

The extended description of what happened in the years following the introduction of the ritual demonstrates that the appearance of the religious image, the ritual context and the impact of the event all underwent a profound change. The hilarious restyling episode, during which the women intended to transform the representation of the venerated Virgin Mary, illustrates the pragmatic attitude some migrants have towards the re-enactment of homeland rituals.[9]

The emergent desire to replace the 'stand-in copy' with a 'correct copy' from Spain, together with the increasing need to know more about the specifics of devotion in El Rocío, further illustrates how the increasing importance of the celebration activated a new sense of belonging to a transnational Spanish community. At the same time, the adornment of the stretcher, and especially the addition of the inscription 'Vilvoorde' on the new statue, changed its status from an 'indifferent copy' to a 'unique copy'. This transition not only imbued the image with an additional social and emotional agency, but it also facilitated the re-embedding of the *Virgen del Rocío* as protector of the Spanish community within the larger societal context of Vilvoorde.[10]

Figure 3.1: The statue of the *Virgen del Rocío* carried inside the church of Vilvoorde by members of the local Andalusian social club. Photograph by Eddy Plasquy.

A Re-embedded Image

Its status as protector was not only confirmed by an elaborate and impressive procession,[11] but also by the active support of Vilvoorde's civil and ecclesiastical authorities. In 2005, the city invited a delegation from Peñarroya to participate in the *romería*. On that occasion, the Spanish guests paid their respect to the *Virgen del Rocío* by offering a golden ornament which was fastened to the mantle during the ceremony in the church. From then onwards, it became tradition to bring the procession to a stop in front of the city hall. Inside, the mayor receives a delegation from the Spanish club. After a small reception, the mayor and several aldermen join the procession and participate in the service. When the parade arrives at the church, the stretcher is taken off the cart, and amid great public interest, brought inside. There it is placed on the side of the altar, next to the statue of the *Virgen de la Asuncíon*, the local patroness of Vilvoorde. As always, the congregation is lead in prayer by a Flemish and a Spanish priest. During the mass, a mixed Spanish choir from the local cultural club performs songs which are typical of the *romería* in El Rocío as well as others that they have written themselves. In 2002, the mass was co-celebrated by the vice-archbishop of Brussels-Mechelen.

After the mass, an impressive parade starts towards the park. A highlight of the *romería* is undoubtedly the moment when the stretcher with the Virgin Mary is brought into the central square and shown to the waiting crowd. Festive music, fervently sung by a local band and accompanied by the spectators, praises the *Virgen del Rocío* when the stretcher comes in sight. Then, after a stop at the centre of the plaza, where she is turned to greet the public, the statue is taken to her 'chapel'. This 'chapel' is a structure some 15 metres high and represents the façade of the chapel in El Rocío. It is placed in such a way that the door gives entrance to an area in the building surrounding the plaza. The interior of this space, from floor to ceiling, is entirely covered to distinguish it from the rest of the structure. The walls of the room are decorated with paintings of the provinces of Andalucía. No ornaments or crucifix are present which might refer to the interior of a classic chapel, and neither has an altar been installed. Instead, the stretcher with the statue is simply placed in the middle of the room.

Once the image is put inside, a large queue is formed of people waiting to enter the 'chapel'. There, a couple of women arrange the flowers which are offered to the Virgin Mary, and it does not take long before the statue is surrounded by colourful floral bundles. During the two days of the *romería* the 'chapel' is rarely without a visitor. Many of these, a lot of whom are locals, enter out of sheer curiosity, commenting on the statue, the flowers and the painted decoration. Pictures are taken of the statue and of relatives and friends, posing in front or beside it. Others, however, act as true pilgrims, paying their respect in tranquillity, crossing themselves after praying. Still others touch the cloak, in a spontaneous gesture to make contact with the holiness of the image. The agency of the image becomes even more eminent when small children are brought in and firmly held against the statue.

In the meantime, the feast continues outside. For those who did not bring their own food, stands offer beer, wine, and sherry, as well as sardines, Spanish ham and plates of paella at a reasonable price. Over the years an animated programme has been established, which includes performances of flamenco dancing and demonstrations of the art of Spanish horseback

Figure 3.2: Visitors to the statue in the temporary 'chapel' during the Pentecostal *romería*. Photograph by Eddy Plasquy.

riding in the park. When night falls, the music slowly changes from popular flamenco songs to mainstream pop and dance music, ultimately turning into a huge party with the heavy beats of house music and people dancing everywhere. The next morning everything is cleaned up and prepared for the second day of feasting and dancing. The animated ambiance not only attracts the local Spanish community but also a lot of Flemish townspeople and even delegations from neighbouring countries. I would estimate that several thousand people visit the *romería*.

By now it is hopefully clear that the re-embedding of the *romería* is manifested in different ways: the acknowledgment of the importance of the celebration and the participation of the civil authorities; the placing of the Virgin of El Rocío alongside the image of the local patroness during the mass; the respect shown by the delegation from the Spanish home town; the participation of a huge number of local Flemish people and the presence of foreign delegations of Spanish cultural clubs – all of these elements contribute to this process. The construction of the 'chapel' even make this re-embedding visible in a straightforward, material way: it creates a temporal space in which the emotional efficacy of the image can be all the more present. At the same time, the collective sense of belonging of the Spanish community is powerfully activated by the growing success of the celebration.

Belonging and Emotional Efficacy

Reflecting on how this peculiar *romería* started, evolved and transformed, it is reasonable to claim that the celebration has precipitated an emotional shift among the Spanish community in Vilvoorde. This is first of all apparent in the way that the celebration marks out a field of commonality among the participating migrants. When Cele, one of the collaborators of the first hour, commented that 'When the Virgin Mary is brought out, the sun comes out too!' (*¡Cuando sale la Virgen, sale el sol!*) he pointedly captured the link between the statue, the migrant community and a longing towards a homeland. With the *romería*, a ritual space is created in which a profound and genuine relation with their representation of the Virgin Mary becomes possible. Without the intervention of the Church, the *Virgen del Rocío* evolved, almost spontaneously, to become the individual protector of many Spanish migrants in Vilvoorde as well as the patron saint of the local Spanish community. The extent of this becomes obvious when one enters the living rooms of Vilvoorde's Spanish families. There, pictures, statues and images of their Virgin are overwhelmingly present, while strong feelings of exclusiveness are eminent when probing about the meanings of the Virgin Mary: 'she is ours' (*es la nuestra*) people say.

The coming into being of the *romería* also established a link between the Spanish community and an imaginary Spain in which the site of El Rocío came to play a central role. When the Spanish club moved to new premises, an entire wall was decorated with a huge picture of the chapel of El Rocío, while images of the *Virgen* and paintings with scenes of the *camino* during the *romería* in El Rocío were hung all over the place. Ten years ago, neither the *romería* nor the site was known to the majority of Vilvoorde's Spanish migrants, but today most of them have visited El Rocío during their holidays at least once. Participating in El Rocío's own *romería* is difficult, given that celebrations here and in Vilvoorde take place at the same time. However, creativity was never lacking in Vilvoorde: in March 2009, a group of eleven women from the Spanish community participated in the yearly pilgrimage of the brotherhood of Sanlucar de Barrameda to the shrine in El Rocío, whom they came into contact with through the internet.[12] The connection between the Spanish community and the homeland clearly goes both ways, reinforcing an idealistic image of the homeland on the one hand and an increasing need to know and to experience how things are done 'back home'.

From the start, the *romería* in Vilvoorde was clearly a project of collective pride and was treated as such. At the same time, the statue of the Virgin Mary came prominently to the fore. Today it is no longer guarded in a private house during the year but is instead housed in a chapel in the centre of the city where, every Sunday, a Spanish mass is celebrated. As such, they have very little in common with the kind of celebrations that exist in Barcelona and Madrid, let alone in El Rocío; instead, it is has more in common with the way that an everyday village in southern Spain celebrates its saint, far away from the excitement that surrounds the actual *romería* in El Rocío. One of the most sincere expressions of this consists of the offering of flowers from the *romería* at the municipal cemetery on Whit Monday.

The day after the *romería*, dozens of volunteers clean up the place and start to dismantle the 'chapel'. During that day, a group of women collect the bundles of flowers which were offered in the 'chapel' and take them to the city's cemetery. There, the women redistribute the flowers on the tombs, one by one, in order to cover as many graves as possible. No explicit preference is given to Spaniards, and all categories of deceased, including soldiers from the Second World War, are honoured with flowers. It is an act that, according to them, not only expresses their gratitude to all those who have offered flowers to the Virgin Mary, but also enables them to transmit with these flowers the presence and power of their venerated Virgin Mary to those who could not be with them. It is an act that takes place in an intimate circle, involving five or six women, and is done in a straightforward manner. Without external ceremonial necessities, it is efficiently organized to make sure that no row of graves is missed, nor is the grass field where the ashes are spread overlooked. It is an act that impresses, as it transcends every possible cultural difference and connects a centuries-old Spanish local tradition with the memories of our globalizing way of life. But most of all, it is an act in which the agency of their Virgin Mary, all of a sudden, becomes visible.

Figure 3.3: The day after the *romería* the flowers offered are redistributed at the local cemetery. Photograph by Eddy Plasquy.

Conclusions

The main goal of this contribution has been to contextualize how the statue of the Virgin Mary of El Rocío has gained social and emotional agency among the Spanish migrant community in Vilvoorde. No longer limited to the moment of the *romería*, it has come to imbue the Spanish community with a very profound, authentic sense of pride and belonging. As such, the *romería* in Vilvoorde was never and never will be an exact copy of an existing Spanish example; instead, it needs to be approached as the outcome of a creative process that has its primary locus within the specific context of this Spanish migrant community. A focus on the materiality of the statue proved to be very rewarding in this respect. Its transformation from a 'stand-in copy' to a 'unique copy' – accompanied with increased embellishments (cloak, jewels, stretcher, chapel) and its more elaborate movement through space (procession, *camino*, entrance) – all contributed to the fact that it became imbued with an emotional agency which is prominent on a collective as well as on an individual level. As such, the arguments of Freedberg appear to be confirmed. But this could only happen after the image fitted the 'slot' which was created in its social vicinity. This occurred in the very first performance, in a way that surprised even the organizers. As a consequence, the generation of its initial agency is better approached in the way Gell proposes: 'as a factor of the ambience as a whole ... rather than as an attribute of the human psyche, exclusively' (Gell 1998: 20). From there on, both perspectives (historical and anthropological) are perfectly suitable to document the transition the image underwent.

Vasquez and Marquardt (2003) state that religion is one of the main protagonists in the unbinding of culture from its traditional referents and boundaries, and in its reattachment in new space–time configurations. The case of the *romería* in Vilvoorde clearly illustrates the importance of the creation of an atmosphere of ritual and the impact of an image. At the same time, the image transcends this context as it has come to be seen as the 'informal' patron saint of the community. In this capacity, its emotional efficacy has changed drastically. The statue made the immigrants visible as a social body within the wider society and started to act as their proper divine protector. However, insight into this transition reveals that the impact of globalizing factors within this process must not be underestimated. After all, it is not the local Virgin Mary of their town of origin that is being venerated but the popular *Virgen del Rocío*. The intriguing observation that the introduction of this Virgin as a patron saint stems from her popularity and the highly emblematic character of the *romería* in Spain highlights once again the complex interplay of local and global realities that underlie the emergence of religious festivities within a transnational context and the emotions that are generated by them.

Notes

1. *Romerías* are not restricted to Spain. As a matter of fact they are widely known throughout the Latin world with famous examples in Portugal (Viana do Aletejo, Terena), Argentina (Luján), Mexico (Guadalajara) and Costa Rica (Cartago). On the other hand, it is recognized that their prominence in Andalusian villages is overwhelming. Some 90 per cent of Andalusians see them as an essential element of their culture, placing them after flamenco music but before speaking the Andalusian dialect in order of cultural importance (Cazorla Pérez et al. 1991).
2. How to explain the reputation of the *romería* in El Rocío is another story. The festival has been performed since at least the seventeenth century, involving brotherhoods from neighbouring villages and, from the nineteenth century onwards, ones from Seville and Huelva, but it is nevertheless clear that its contemporary status stems from the 1950s (Murphy and Gonzáles Faraco 2002). At that time, the bishop of the recently founded diocese of Huelva backed the proposals of the brotherhood of Almonte to drastically redesign El Rocío's *romería*. In accordance with local and regional authorities, it was decided to replace the old chapel with an impressive church. This fitted with a more ambitious plan to open up the region economically, including tourism, resulting in a boost to Marian devotion. The new chapel was inaugurated in 1969, since which El Rocío itself has grown, as have the brotherhoods and the number of participants attending the *romería*. Besides these structural and organizational changes, it stands without doubt that the spectacular character of the procession (see Plasquy 2006), as well as its unique location (Murphy and Gonzáles 2002), all contribute to the actual popularity of the *romería*.
3. Discussion of this peculiar initiative in Brussels falls outside the scope of this article, but is included in Plasquy 2010. Let it suffice here to mention that there are no organizational bonds between what happens in Vilvoorde and this 'European' brotherhood.

4. *Odiel*, 8 June 1956, numero extraordinario.
5. *Odiel*, 9 February 1967.
6. By assigning primacy to representation, instead of linking agency to the power of the deities they represent, Freedberg reduces the act of consecration to the moment in which the potentiality of an image becomes activated and realized. In doing so, he takes a stand against those anthropologists who in his view underestimate the relation between how images look and why they work (see Freedberg 1989: 134–35).
7. This reaction illustrates exactly what Gell means when he states that the agency of an image cannot be detected in advance but only recognized '*ex post facto*, in the anomalous configuration of the causal milieu' (Gell 1998: 20).
8. Further confusion was added, according to some, because the women had used a quite unusual picture of the Virgin Mary of El Rocío, namely one taken at the moment when she is dressed *a la Pastora*, or in her so-called traveller's dress. This happens only on the occasions that she is brought from El Rocío to Almonte, something that normally takes place every seven years. This outfit varies significantly from the usual one, in which she is dressed as a queen (*a la Reina*).
9. The involvement of the women mirrors in a striking way the traditional and highly respected role of the *camaristas*, those who dress up the statues before their procession (Albert-Lorca 2002).
10. Following Eriksen, re-embedding is used here to mean 'a widespread family of responses to the disembedding tendencies of globalization' (Eriksen 2007: 9), and whose aim is to retain or recreate a sense of continuity, security and trust (ibid.: 141–54).
11. The celebration begins on Saturday with a procession which starts at the club house and from there winds through the inner city. The cart with the stretcher is pulled by two impressive horses, while an excited crowd of several hundred people follows. In 1998, a group of horsemen was contracted by the club to head the parade, thereby adding another aspect of southern Spanish flavour to the already colourful and joyful event. The size of the parade means that the streets it passes along have to be closed to traffic.
12. One of the obligations of the officially recognized brotherhoods of El Rocío is the yearly celebration of a mass in the chapel in El Rocío. Although it is not stipulated that the brotherhood has to organize a pilgrimage for that reason, many of them do. Participating with the brotherhood of Sanlucar de Barrameda is significant for at least two other reasons: it is not only one of the oldest and most respected ones, but also one of the few which may pass through the national park that lies between the town and El Rocío. The beauty of this *camino* has become one of the hallmarks of the *romería* in El Rocío.

References

Albert-Lorca, M. 2002. *Les Vierges miraculeuses*. Paris: Gallimard.

Canépa, G. 2007. 'Redefining Andean Sacred Landscapes and Identities: Authenticity, Migration and Visual Reproduction in Andean Religious Rituals', in A. Gálves (ed.), *Performing Religion in the Americas: Media, Politics and Devotional Practices of the Twenty-first Century*. Oxford: Seagull Books, pp. 15–34.

Cantero, P. 2002. *Tras el Rocío*. Almonte: Cuadernos de Almonte.

Cazorla Pérez, J., et al. 1991. *La dinámica cultural en la sociedad andaluza*. 2 vols. Seville: Consejería de Cultura y Medio Ambiente.

Cháves Flores, F.J. 2004. *Hermandades del Rocío*. Madrid: Cháves Flores.

DeMaria Harney, N. 1999. *Eh, Paesan! Being Italian in Toronto*. Toronto: University of Toronto Press.

Eriksen, T.H. 2007. *Globalization: The Key Concepts*. Oxford: Berg.

Fortier, A. 2000. *Migrant Belongings: Memory, Space, Identity*. Oxford: Berg.

Freedberg, D. 1989. *The Power of Images: Studies in the History and Theory of Response*. Chicago: University of Chicago Press.

García, E., and S. Fernández. 2003. *Peñarroya-Pueblonuevo: A cielo abierto*. Cordoba: CajaSur.

Gell, A. 1998. *Art and Agency. An Anthropological Theory*. Oxford: Clarendon Press.

Jiménez, C. 1997. *Más allá de Andalucía: reproducción de devociones Andaluzas en Madrid*. Seville: Fundación Blas Infante.

——— 1999. 'Andalucía: identificaciones colectivos en la distancia', *Cuadernos de etnología y etnografía de Navarra* 73: 83–92.

Kapferer, B. 1979. 'Emotion and Feeling in Sinhalese Healing Rites', *Social Analysis* 1: 153–76.

Leavitt, J. 1996. 'Meaning and Feeling in the Anthropology of Emotions', *American Ethnologist* 23: 514–39.

Lüddeckens, D. 2006. 'Emotion', in J. Kreinath, J. Snoek and M. Stausberg (eds), *Theorizing Ritual: Issues, Topics, Approaches, Concepts*. Leiden: Brill, pp. 545–70.

Martínez, A.J. 2003. *Raíces de la Hermandad Emigrantes*. Huelva: Imprenta Jiménez.

Moreno, I. 1993. 'El Roció: de Romería de las Marismas a fiesta de identidad andaluza', in A. Fraguas et al. (eds), *Romerías y Peregrinacions: Simposio de Antropoloxia X*. Santiago de Compostela: Consello de Cultura Galega.

——— 1999. *Las Hermandades Andaluzas: Una aproximación desde la Antropología*, 2nd edn. Seville: Universidad de Sevilla.

Murphy, M.D., and J.C. Gonzáles Faraco. 1996. 'Masificación ritual, identidad local y toponimia en El Rocío', *Demófilo* 20: 101–20.

——— 2002. *El Rocío: Análisis culturales e históricos*. Huelva: Diputación de Huelva.

Orsi, R. 1985. *The Madonna of 115th Street: Faith and Community in Italian Harlem, 1880–1950*. New Haven, CT: Yale University Press.

Padilla Díaz de la Serna, S. 2007. *Rocío: la explosion de la Gran Devoción del Sur en el Siglo XX*. Cordoba: Almuzara.

Plasquy, E. 2006. '¡El Salto a las 02.45! ¿Un ritual establecido o atemporal? cambios rituals durante el inicio de la procession en honor a la Virgen del Rocío', *Anduli: Revista Andaluza de Ciencias Sociales* 6: 133–46.

——— 2010. 'El Camino Europeo del Roció: A Pilgrimage towards Europe?' *Journal of Religion in Europe* 3: 256–84.

Probyn, E. 1996. *Outside Belongings*. New York: Routledge.

Pulido, J.M. 2006. *Rocío, Tiempos de María: Historia Fotográfica del Rocío en Catalunya*. Barcelona: Grupo Área 96.

Rodríguez Becerra, S. 2007. *La religión de los andaluces*. Malaga: Sarría.

Svašek, M. 2007. *Anthropology, Art and Cultural Production*. London: Pluto Press.

Svašek, M., and Z. Skrbiš. 2007. 'Passions and Powers: Emotions and Globalization', *Identities* 14: 367–83.

Vásquez, M.A., and M.F. Marquardt. 2003. *Globalizing the Sacred: Religion across the Americas*. New Brunswick, NJ: Rutgers University Press.

4

SWEATER BUSINESS:
COMMODITY EXCHANGE AND THE MEDIATION OF AGENCY IN THE TIBETAN ITINERANT SWEATER TRADE IN INDIA

—◆◆◆—

Timm Lau

Introduction

Let us say you were in an Indian town at the onset of winter, and you had forgotten to pack a warm sweater. In all likelihood, all you would need to do was to get a taxi or rickshaw and ask the driver to take you to the 'Tibetan sweater market'. Most drivers would immediately know where to go: to a market or a bunch of market stalls, built by Tibetan itinerant traders, where you would be able to choose from a wide range of sweaters to keep you warm. Since the 1980s, Tibetans in India have very successfully filled the economic niche of selling sweaters during the winter months. Their market stalls have become a fixture of the winter scenery in many towns all over India. For the Tibetan traders, this involves buying sweaters wholesale from Indian manufacturers and merchants in industrial centres such as Ludhiana and Delhi, and reselling them during the winter season on temporary markets in Indian cities and towns across the subcontinent. The traders themselves call this activity *tshong*, Tibetan for 'business'.

The sweater business necessitates that Tibetan traders spend a significant part of the year outside their refugee settlements and in intensive engagement with the Indian host society. As the traders buy and sell sweaters, they operate inside Indian local economies and engage with Indian merchants and customers. In this chapter, I will examine how Tibetans build relationships and boundaries between themselves and Indians through trade interactions.[1] The material objects of the trade – the sweaters bought, transported, stored, displayed, haggled over and sold – will take prominent place in the ethnographic narrative I will develop. In other words, this chapter traces the exchange and significance of sweaters in the Tibetan itinerant trade. It follows a commodity through various kinds of exchange to produce a social analysis, and could therefore be seen to follow in the analytic style of *The Social Life of Things* (Appadurai 1986). Similar to the contributions in that seminal volume, the value of the objects in question will be highly significant for my argument. In the present study, this value will appear mainly in the guise of risk and the techniques of its management. However, the sweaters as material objects are not merely placeholders of value and risk. They are also, and very importantly, things through which persons engage in social relations with each other. This perspective will allow me to discuss how Tibetan traders relate to Indians through the objects exchanged between them. I will show that, while the traders evaluate their relationships with merchants and customers in both positive and negative terms, the risk-management techniques employed in the trade are simultaneously based on and give rise to notions of trust. In a social field of marked ambivalence in which Tibetan traders may perceive themselves to be exploited, they nonetheless establish and express personal trust-based relationships with Indians through the exchange of sweaters. In the course of my argument, I will draw out the theoretical implications of this for our understanding of the social aspects of commodity exchange, and suggest that we may view the sweaters traded as objects which mediate agency. In conclusion, I will show that the idioms of trust and distrust connect exchange and belonging as two central concerns of Tibetan traders in the Indian diaspora.

The Sweater Business and the Tibetan Diaspora

Since the 1950s Tibetans have come to India as refugees, and today their number is estimated at over one hundred thousand. Of the first tens of thousands of Tibetans who came to India, the vast majority had been farmers who had relied on livestock and agriculture in Tibet. Since they had to leave land and animals behind, they lost the basis for their subsistence and lacked economic skills matching their new circumstances. Tibetan refugees arriving in India initially found homelessness and poverty, and the absence of economic opportunities which accorded with their skills and knowledge. The first economic foothold they gained was working on road construction sites in the northern states of India, where over twenty thousand Tibetan refugees were employed by the Indian government in just under a hundred road construction sites. Although Indians thought of Tibetans as physically suited to working in high-altitude mountainous terrain (Kharat 2003: 288), many of the Tibetans working in harsh conditions died of diseases or in landslides.

In this context, the business of selling sweaters during the colder winter months as street vendors outside Indian shops, or roaming through Indian villages, was initially discovered as an economic niche in the 1960s by a handful of Tibetan refugees from the province of Amdo (Lau 2007). As the practice proved to be lucrative, it spread among the Tibetan refugee population. From its humble beginnings, itinerant trade involving sweaters had by the late 1980s evolved into the main economic activity of Tibetans in India. In the estimation of my Tibetan informants, including officials of the Dalai Lama's Central Tibetan Administration (CTA), most Tibetan households in India are today involved in the trade through one or more of their members. In many cases, the market stalls have been passed on from the original traders to their children, who are themselves now adults and continue the trade their parents first engaged in. Some of these second-generation traders bring their own children along in the school holidays, providing them with some first-hand trade experience and early insight into the functioning of the sweater market.

For a significant proportion of the Tibetan refugee population in India, then, the itinerant sweater trade takes central place in the annual calendar. The Tibetan traders leave their home settlements in October to start the trading season, selling sweaters on more or less makeshift markets or from roadside stalls in Indian towns, and most do not return home again until February or March the following year. They form transient communities, disbanding and reforming anew every year at their trade destination, where they are organized in market associations. These associations count the Tibetan traders of a particular market as their members and fulfil a number of functions, both as trade associations within Indian local economic contexts, and as new and democratic institutions regulating Tibetan sociality in the market (ibid.).

The particularity of the traders is clearly reflected in both Indian and Tibetan perceptions of Tibetans as sweater sellers. In India, the distinctive identification of named groups associated with a certain professional activity has long-standing roots. This idea is, of course, basic to the social ideology of caste. Although the particular idea of caste does not readily apply to Tibetan traders, Indian local economies have incorporated them as a named group of traders. For Tibetans themselves, however, the label of being sweater sellers has become intrinsically connected to their own understanding of their refugee identity. Although some Tibetans do work in a range of professions in India, from call-centre operators to academics, most of them stay in refugee settlements where economic opportunities are far and few between. They sell sweaters during the winter, and many are either involved in other petty trading activities or remain economically inactive for the rest of the year. Very often, this goes hand in hand with the assumption that they cannot choose another profession. In spite of evidence to the contrary, many of my informants would say: 'We are refugees, therefore we have to do sweater business'. At first, this may seem like Tibetans exist in isolation from the Indian economy and larger society. But, as sweater sellers, Tibetans are in fact interacting closely with their Indian host society.

In the literature on Tibetans in exile, near-exclusive refugee spaces such as settlements and monasteries take centre stage. There is a predominant tendency in the anthropology of Tibetans in exile to focus exclusively on Tibetan social and cultural practice. Whether this occurs out of methodological pragmatism or a sense of what constitutes the 'proper' object of study, the anthropological record so far has served to minimize or obscure the importance of the Indian social environment for the Tibetans living there. In this context, the continuing symbolic significance of Tibet as a lost and remote 'homeland' is generally emphasized.[2] Some existing studies pay attention to questions of Tibetan adaptation, raising the issue of assimilation into the host country (e.g., Saklani 1984; Grunfeld 1987: 202). However, they do so without presenting ethnographic descriptions of Indo–Tibetan relationships and the consequences for the Tibetan diaspora. Social interaction across the division between the diasporic community and host society is in fact common in India, and highly significant for the understanding Tibetans have developed of their own position in the Indian context.[3] The sweater business is one of the prime examples of Tibetan social interaction with the Indian host society. Although it is the backbone of the Tibetan diasporic economy in India, itinerant trade has been noted only by a few authors, none of whom provide an ethnographic inquiry into the social relationships it entails.[4] The present chapter therefore fills an important gap in the ethnographic literature on Tibetans in exile.

Sweater Business is Risky Business

From October 2004 until February 2005, I accompanied a trade party of four Tibetans – three siblings and one sister-in-law – on their itinerant trade in the desert city of Bundpur in Rajasthan.[5] The first stage involved travelling to Ludhiana in the Punjab to buy sweaters. During the trade season, central Ludhiana appears to the untrained eye as a crowded, dusty and polluted maze of main roads and small alleys. The roads are busy with traders and locals, and teeming with all kinds of transport. As the local merchants sell their goods to the traders pouring into the city, every now and then one sees rickshaw drivers steering cycle-rickshaws loaded implausibly high with bundles of knitwear – and their new owners sometimes perilously perched on top. The merchants' outlets are invariably rooms and backrooms located in the central area, with their walls lined head-high with samples of this year's garments waiting to be inspected and discussed by customers. The Tibetan traders navigate their network of merchants, whom they call *lala*, undertaking the purchase of stock in their individual trading parties. Upon approaching a merchant's shop, they are welcomed and offered cushions next to the *lala* with their samples and account books, surrounded by more sweater samples which sometimes double as extra cushions. Immediately, a *chai-wallah* is called for an order of the hot sweet tea aptly described by Mark Falzon as 'the nectar of the traders' (Falzon 2004: 170).

The traders live in rented accommodation in this industrial environment, sleeping on thin cotton mattresses on the dusty floors of dark, empty commercial spaces. Within a week or two, each individual trade party buys hundreds of sweaters in bulk from local wholesalers. The stay in Ludhiana, before the sweaters are bundled up by Indian labourers and transported by road or railway to their respective market destinations, is a tense but action-filled time for the traders. As the stacks of sweaters pile up in barely secured spaces, the risk attached to them grows ever heavier on the traders' minds. The biggest risk is, of course, that the sweaters will not sell. Tibetan traders are fully aware that not every trade season is successful, and that they can incur very substantial economic losses if their investment in sweaters does not pay off. Because Tibetan traders are usually not wealthy, and because the acquisition of large stocks of sweaters represents the acquisition of large risks, this moment represents a very existential economic crisis. The main subsequent areas of risk involved in the buying of sweaters are storage and transport. Both of these necessary moments of the trade are recognized as inherently risky by the traders. Tibetans need to find the safest places possible for their sweater stocks and they need to be vigilant at all times, both during buying in Ludhiana and at their later destination, to prevent the ever-present risk of theft occurring. Transporting the sweaters from Ludhiana to the market destination is also perceived as riddled with risks. There is the considerable question of whether or not the sweaters will actually arrive at their destination, as they could be lost or stolen. Because the traders need to receive the sweaters on time to begin trading, the risk of a delay in transport is also highly dreaded. The sweaters could, for example, be held up at the hands of an unsatisfied official at a state border, necessitating a costly journey. On the other hand, the sweaters could get sent to a completely different location altogether. Transport and storage thus represent two continuous arenas of risk in the sweater trade as they are ongoing until the sweater-trade season has finished and no more sweaters are to be stored or moved anywhere.

We can see that from the traders' perspective the sweaters are inherently risky as well as valuable throughout the trading season. The risks inherent in the sweaters are managed by Tibetan traders in a number of ways. As we will see, trust is central to their techniques of risk management.

Managing Risk: The Importance of Trust

The relationships between Tibetan traders and Indian wholesale merchants, who are often also the manufacturers of the sweaters, are clearly business relationships and as such based on the interdependent interests of those acting in them. As Tsering, a young man in his early twenties and one of my closest trading informants, put it: 'We have good relationships with the traders, because they don't have a business without us, and we don't without them. They need us and we need them'. The garment merchants in Ludhiana have in part specialized in supplying Tibetans – so much so that shop signs in Tibetan script are common. An example of this is the Indian merchant Solkar Industries in Ludhiana, whose proprietor had a bilingual shop sign installed and also encouraged Tibetan traders to leave graffiti in Tibetan script on the shop's wall, describing the quality of the goods on sale (see Figure 4.1). The business card of this merchant was also directed at Tibetan clients, with the greeting 'Solkar wishes Tashi Delek to the Tibetan sweater sellers' in Tibetan script (see Figure 4.2). One of the merchants told me that the reason for this specialization was that the Tibetans are 'good people to do business with'. This interdependency of interests has led to an arrangement where wholesalers enable Tibetan traders to purchase large amounts of sweaters on credit.

The wholesalers trust the Tibetan traders to pay back their loans, given out in the form of sweaters. It is crucial for the Tibetan traders that the

Figure 4.1: Bilingual sign, in Roman and Tibetan script, of Indian garment merchant Solkar Industries in Ludhiana. Photograph by Timm Lau.

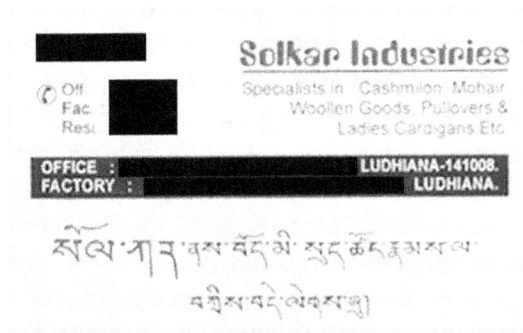

Figure 4.2: Solkar Industries business card. Every effort has been made to trace the copyright holder and to obtain permission for the use of this image.

merchants should place trust in them, as the resulting credit allows them a higher volume of trade on limited funds. In the long-term relationships sought out by both Tibetan traders and their merchants, trust in the Tibetan traders is incrementally built up over time through paying the balance in a timely manner. Some, though not all, of the Tibetan sweater sellers therefore endeavour to pay back the loan incurred as soon as possible. Dorje, who as the eldest brother controlled the finances of the trading group I accompanied, made a point of this when he explained to me why he was well-liked by Ludhiana *lala*: 'When I come to Ludhiana the *lala* smile and say "Welcome, welcome, come in." They like me, because I always pay them full balance at the end of the business, or when I return to Ludhiana. You see how much they like me? That is because I pay my balance on time'.

As the economist Lapavitsas points out, credit trust can be augmented by the debtor's participation in commercial groups, significant social and familial connections, and political contacts, since these can guarantee the repayment of the sum owed (Lapavitsas 2003: 74). The Tibetan traders demonstrate aspects of all of these elements to their merchants. As Tibetans, they appear connected to the recognized nexus of Tibetan Buddhist monasteries. Many Indians know that Tibetan monastic circles attract substantial aid and donations from overseas and perceive these institutions as centres of power and accumulated wealth. And as traders, the Tibetans have organized in market associations which have managed to lobby local governments into permitting the opening of a regular local market and renewing this privilege every year. This represents an impressive political feat for a set of itinerant traders in India. In brief, Tibetan traders manage to distinguish themselves from Indian petty traders and appear as sufficiently trustworthy to Indian merchants. The information about the social determinants of trust is obtained by the merchants over time and through the interdependence of the parties involved in their long-term economic relationships.

The following statistics, based on a random sampling by the CTA's Department of Finance in October 2004 of 1288 Tibetan traders, illustrate

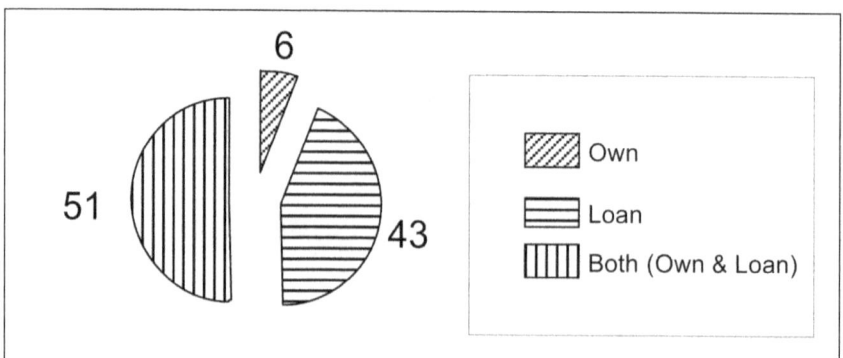

Figure 4.3: Figures on sources of capital (taken from CTA 2005a).

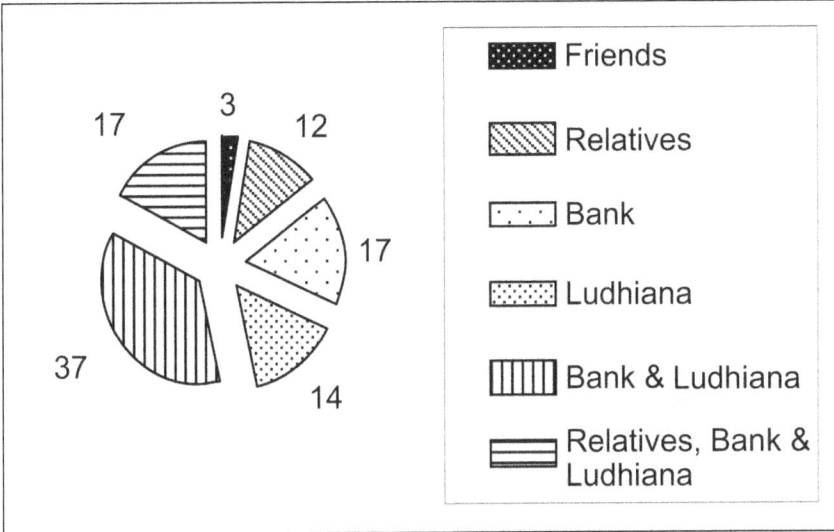

Figure 4.4: Figures on sources of loans (taken from CTA 2005b).

the extent to which Tibetan traders rely on loans from Indian merchants: in order to undertake their trade, nearly all Tibetan traders depend completely or in part on loans (Figure 4.3), and a 68 per cent majority of these depend to some extent on loans from Ludhiana merchants (Figure 4.4).[6]

In this interdependent relationship, trust is mutual: the Tibetan traders also trust the merchants. On the one hand, it is essential that sweaters are given as loans. As the figures cited above bear out, a high proportion of Tibetan traders depend on this practice in order to be able to undertake their business, and place a vast amount of trust on its reoccurrence every year. On the other hand, it is highly significant for traders that some sweaters are taken back as part-payment at the end of the annual trade cycle. Merchants who are in long-term relationships with traders will give assurances that at the end of the trading season they will literally buy back some of the sweaters sold earlier. Traders on the market fretted over sweaters they could not sell, telling me that they 'could not eat them back home'. Therefore, this common risk-management technique was equally important for their trading practice, effectively allowing them to turn a proportion of unsold sweaters into cash. Willingness to take back sweaters is seen as an essential part of 'good practice' on behalf of suppliers, and acts as a determinant of the trust Tibetan traders have in them.

In merchant–trader interactions, and in both parties' management of risk, trust is expressed directly through the objects at the centre of their relationship: first when sweaters are provided on credit at the point of purchase, and then again when they are given back as part-payment at the end of the trade season. In these interactions, the sweaters appear as proof of the trustworthiness of the Tibetan traders' partners, the merchants. This dynamic was very clearly illustrated one day towards the end of our stay in Ludhiana, when a junior employee of a merchant came round to our accommodation with a small number of sweaters bundled together. These sweaters had been left accidentally at the shop by our trade party. The fact that the merchant took such care to have them brought to us was gladly acknowledged by the traders. They proceeded to tell me about similar occasions over the past few years when a certain *lala* had brought such lost items to them, or when another had stored them safely until their next visit the following year. In these narratives, it was not value alone that mattered, since such small bundles of sweaters were not worth very much compared to the total volume of sweaters traded. Yet the sweaters at the centre of these stories were presented as excellent proof that the merchants were trustworthy people.

The Emotional Importance of Religious Objects and Practices

As I accompanied the group of Tibetan traders I had joined on their expedition, I was struck by the important ways in which Buddhist practices represent risk-management techniques for them, enabling stability and security. Even before the start of the trade expedition, adepts are paid by traders to perform divinatory rituals (*mo*) in order to determine the auspicious or inauspicious elements of the forthcoming trading season. The hope is, of course, to avoid risks and thus ensure success. In order to manage the immediate risks associated with the transport and selling of sweaters, practices extend into the realm of protection, one of the most important aspects of popular religious practice for Tibetans (see, e.g., Epstein and Lichter 1983; Ortner 1989: 78–79; Powers 1995: 137). Many of the individual trade parties' families pay for the performance of stabilizing *zhabs brtan* rituals in their homes by local monks and lamas before the start of the business season. Protective objects used during the trading season include ritual implements which have received a blessing (*byin rlabs*) and protective amulets and charms (*srung ba* or *srung ma*), as well as blessed grains from Nechung monastery in Dharamsala. The latter were placed in large bundles of sweaters that were packed in Ludhiana in order to protect them during their risky transport from there to their trade destination (see the foreground of Figure 4.5). I was told that they would guard the sweaters from being stolen, damaged or diverted on their journey to market. When the consignment of sweaters arrived in Bundpur, Tsering pulled out the small bag of blessed grains, raised it over his head and called out in delight. The grains were then hung inside the trade stall alongside pictures of the Dalai Lama and other reincarnated lamas. In sum, popular Tibetan Buddhist practices of protection represent a significant means through which Tibetan traders affectively manage the risk inherent in the sweater trade.

Trustworthy Merchants Are Also Exploiters

Exchanges between certain Ludhiana merchants and Tibetan traders were characterized by an especially jovial nature. With these merchants, business appeared to be on equal footing with banter and joking, and physical expressions of positive feelings were overabundant when the trade party I accompanied visited such merchants. They were explicitly perceived as 'good people' (*mi yagpo*). In my informants' evaluation of merchants, an emotional basis of interaction was interwoven with business practice. 'Good' businesses were those perceived as run by people who developed trust through both business and personal practices. The existing emphasis on trust in the relationship with merchants makes certain relationships appear for Tibetans in India as one of equals, enabling joking relationships and the perception of 'good people'. However, both Tibetan traders and Indian wholesalers share the underlying idea of economic profit. Both sides know 'what the deal is': to make money. Tsering clearly expressed this to me when he said: 'We are looking for good sweaters, not for good people', thus curtly ending a discussion of an Indian *lala*'s positive qualities which had lasted too long for his liking.

Indeed, the 'good people' story about merchants was at times revealed as a myth by my informants. On such occasions, I was told that the *lala* were very bad people, exploiting the Tibetans as their kuli or servants. The Tibetans themselves did all the work of selling the sweaters, with no guarantee of success. The *lala*, I was told, were more insulated from the insecurities and woes of the sweater markets and had little risk. They simply provided the sweaters and made a good profit through them. This parallel, yet conflicting social analysis of the merchant–trader relationship, which traders communicated to me equally freely, offers very distinct characteristics. The business risk is here understood to be distributed very unevenly in the hierarchical relationship between the owner of an enterprise and their dependent customer. The objects (and the embodied risks)

Figure 4.5: Indian customers at a Tibetan market stall in Bundpur, Rajasthan. Photograph by Timm Lau.

exchanged are again central to the analysis, but the sweaters sold by the merchants are now seen to mediate their self-interest: through the sweaters, merchants exploit their own economic advantages and, by extension, the Tibetan traders. When Tibetan traders analyse their exchanges in this way they express the idea that when they buy sweaters in bulk the risk embodied by the sweaters is transferred onto themselves. Therefore, the emotional attitude with which the sweaters are perceived in this evaluation is decidedly one of distrust – the exact opposite of the trust we have earlier found to be developed. This co-presence of opposite evaluations stands in relationship to other hardships experienced by traders on the market, to which we shall now turn.

Good Customers Are Also Thieves

Selling sweaters on the market is, of course, the central interaction of the trading season. No matter what else occurs before the market stalls are open for business, only selling sweaters will generate income. And just as the exchange of sweaters between merchants and traders simultaneously invoked the merchants' trustworthiness and their exploitative agency for the Tibetan traders, the sweaters exchanged between traders and customers transmit ambivalent meanings. On the one hand, friendly and trusting relationships are established on the market. As noted earlier, for the development of trust between traders and merchants, the progression of interactions over many years leads to social relations with Indian customers characterized by amicability. Long-term customers keep returning to the same sweater sellers year after year and become friendly. During my fieldwork in Rajasthan, I witnessed invitations to weddings and celebrations of the Muslim festival of *eid*, and a friendly visit by Tibetan traders to an Indian customer's house. Some years previously, Dorje had become the 'brother' of an Indian woman through the local ritual of *raksha bandhan*, in which an armband tied around the wrist establishes a fictive sibling relationship between two individuals. This relationship engenders supportive behaviour by those who engage in it: the woman and some of her relatives visited the stall on the market and on occasion brought lunch meals for the Tibetans and their helpers working there, as well as providing a familiar and friendly Indian household in Bundpur; Dorje sold them sweaters for the cold winter season.

Tibetan sellers at times also recognize 'good people' among their one-off customers, who then benefit from healthy doses of Tibetan humour and a willingness to sell at a reduced rate. This is often understood as supporting them. In one of the cases I witnessed, a local Marwari man bought an item from Tsering. This customer was a man of particularly striking visual appearance, whose clothes and weathered face betrayed his rural origin in the deserts of Rajasthan. Tsering sold him the items he asked for at cost, foregoing the chance of making a profit. When I asked him why he had done so, he answered that this had been a 'good person' (*mi yag po*), and that he wanted to help him a little by selling for less. In another striking example of this type of interaction, Tsering's sister Dolma sold the most expensive sweaters in the Tibetan traders' stock to four male Indian customers from Kashmir, who were themselves sweater sellers on market stalls Indians had set up outside the fenced Tibetan market. These stalls were normally viewed as representing stiff competition by the Tibetan traders, and their existence was seen as a threat to the Tibetans' business. Dolma, however, had come to know these particular individuals before, and practised her Kashmiri language skills with them. She effectively supported the Kashmiris by selling them the most expensive items in the stock at a wholesale rate, items which provided the Tibetans with highest potential profit margin. It is noteworthy that the four men were traders and far away from their homes (located in a troubled geopolitical space); in effect, they were much like her. During both this and the sale previously described, the trade interactions were characterized by friendly banter, joking and laughter. Like all of the positive relationships I have mentioned in this section, they indicate degrees of familiarity and friendliness, and thus imply a certain level of trust. As we have already seen in the case of merchant–trader interactions, sweaters and their exchange are again central to establishing and maintaining these relationships.

The risk of a 'bad year' with financial losses due to a lack of sales causes great anxiety in all Tibetan traders, and their customers have a central place in this anxiety. Indians were generally characterized as 'hard' (*mkhregs po*) in their haggling, and the grinding routine of haggling – often unsuccessfully – every day visibly took its toll on the traders' spirits. This was frequently expressed in lamentations about Indian customers: hardly a day would pass in which they would not be described as tightfisted, unfriendly, cunning and thieving. Most of these antagonistic representations were based by my informants' experiences of haggling. The intensive haggling between Tibetan sweater sellers and Indian customers stands in stark contrast to the exchange modalities in refugee settlements, where no haggling over prices takes place and interactions are normally calm and friendly. Typical bargaining interactions on the sweater market lasted between five and thirty minutes, including the many interactions that failed to produce a sale. While traders might try to steer conversation into friendly waters through joking and/or the use of Indian languages, many bargaining exchanges were dominated by a more brusque tone. Some customers routinely offered amounts well below the Tibetan traders' expectations of a minimum rate, such that some Tibetans called them 'crazy' (*smyo ba*). They often did not move up more than 10 or 15 per cent from their initial offer, while the Tibetan traders most often cumbersomely tried to keep the rate somewhat higher before giving up on or giving in to a customer. Traders in this rather powerless position were reduced to asking the customers for 'ten rupees more', a sure sign for the customer that they had been successful. This was added to by the Tibetans' important perception that their Indian customers lacked respect towards them as traders, ordering them about in abrasive tones, often without buying anything.

Market relationships and interactions could, therefore, become fraught with frustration. This was sometimes vented by calling the customer names in Tibetan, which, of course, the customer could not understand. In rare cases, interactions even involved aggression. The market association had placed an injunction on fighting with customers for good reason, and incidents resulted in fines. A telling illustration of how irate and frustrated Tibetan sellers could get is the example of a seller in Bundpur who, after a prolonged bout of sometimes heated haggling in which the item to be sold was tossed back and forth, screamed in anger at the Indian customer to watch as he set the sweater on fire and burned it. This symbolic act, ridding the trader of a 'damned' item he could not sell, brings home the point that in the midst of all the ambivalent relationships forged through sweaters, traders also develop intense negative feelings towards the material objects of their trade. The trader who burned the sweater ultimately displayed his utter distrust by destroying the very nodal point of all trade relationships.

It is important to note at this point that, in general, Tibetans in India very rarely had a good word to say about Indians, who were often routinely and categorically described as 'bad' people. Indians were depicted as cowardly and always ganging up on individuals in situations of physical conflict, as well as being described as fanatical and easily brainwashed. Indian officials, meanwhile, were invariably described as corrupt. Such negative characterizations of Indians were often embellished and backed up empirically, so to speak, through elements relating to Tibetan experiences of trade with Indians. Descriptions of Indians as a group would often refer to trade experiences for 'proof' of negative evaluations and antagonistic relationships. Along with the exploitative merchant, they evoked images of Indian customers as stingy and unwilling to pay reasonable amounts for the sweaters they wanted, or even as thieves. A typical statement made at home in the settlements would be: 'Indians are so tight-fisted, they never give you what you ask for on the market'. Such statements often ended in the commonly uttered sentence: 'These Indians, they are very bad'. All of these narratives and statements strongly evaluate Indians negatively in a moral sense, condensed in the Tibetan idiom of being 'bad' (*sdug chags*).

I have argued elsewhere that the categorically negative evaluation of Indians is a discursive process through which a strong sense of difference, and therefore an Indian 'other', is created (Lau 2009). 'Becoming Indian' was decidedly portrayed as the worst thing that could happen to a Tibetan by many of my Tibetan informants. The negative evaluations existing in general discourse about Indians prevail because Tibetans in India have a particular object of fear: not the Indian 'other' per se, but the possibility of turning into that 'other'. The antagonistic construction of morally 'bad' Indians through discourse, then, manifests Tibetan fears of cultural extinction in exile. This fear is best understood as a continuously present, emotive context, rather than a momentary emotional experience. Occasions when my informants voiced fears of their group identity 'disappearing' in India were salient points of discursive expression of this emotive context, which accompanies their lives in exile (ibid.).

This general background of antagonistic representations makes it all the more remarkable that the positive and trust-based relationships I have described are established and maintained during the sweater trade. On the one hand, most of these relationships are primarily business ones, and all of them are established through trade. On the other hand, my description has shown that in this context, positive emotional action such as joking and banter (leading to shared laughter, a powerful expression of shared emotion), the perception of 'goodness' and the willingness to give support, and the perception and embodiment of trust, are key elements in the establishment of these relationships. And as my focus on the objects exchanged has demonstrated, sweaters are central as the material objects through which Tibetan traders and their Indian merchants and customers engage in social relations with each other. The present material, then, supports the arguments of those who challenge the ideological separation of a solely economic, quantitative sphere from other areas of social life characterized by personal, qualitative relationships (see, e.g., Parry and Bloch 1989; Humphrey and Hugh-Jones 1992). The specific focus on material objects, both in my informants' building of relationships and in my resulting ethnography, contributes to our understanding of the role objects may play in pivotal emotional processes of building and maintaining relationships.

Social Aspects of Commodity Exchange

The ethnography presented above shows that sweaters are exchanged between Indians and Tibetans in different ways during the trading season: they are sold and given on credit by the Indian merchants to Tibetan traders; they are given back to the merchant as part-payment of debt at the end of the trading season; and they are sold, sometimes at reduced rates, by the traders to Indian customers. All these transactions are commodity exchanges as opposed to gift exchanges. Even in the case of fictive kinship (*raksha bandhan*), sweaters are not openly exchanged as gifts. The only occasion known to me when sweaters were given as gifts was when our trade party departed from the house we stayed at in Bundpur, the ground floor of which had been our rented accommodation during the trading season, and sweaters were presented as gifts to members of the Indian household. However, the specific event was described to me in very negative terms, as my informants grumbled about the Indian household members' 'greed', which had led them to be not only 'unthankful' for their gifts but to demand better, more expensive ones. This particular giving of gifts did not lead to mutual reciprocity or obligation. On the contrary, my informants were determined to leave without creating such ties.

This turn of events, combined with the fact that the exchange of sweaters in trade interactions can lead to the establishment of trust-based relationships between Tibetan traders and Indian merchants, as well as express the former's benevolence towards 'good people', almost seems to present an inversion of C.A. Gregory's classification of gift exchange and commodity exchange (see Gregory 1980, 1982, 1997). The dichotomy proposed by Gregory between inalienable gifts, which create personal, qualitative relationships on the one hand, and alienable commodities, which create impersonal, quantitative relationships on the other, suggests that the establishment of trust-based relationships should typically be the work of gifts, not commodities. Gregory's classification has, of course, been questioned by anthropologists concerned with exchange theory. Jonathan Parry has pointed out that a 'neat opposition' between commodity exchange and gift exchange does scant justice to continuities between the two in Melanesian societies, leading him to state that Gregory had 'greatly over-drawn' the contrast (Parry 1989: 86–87). Elsewhere, Parry argues that culturally specific ideologies of purely disinterested gift-giving are best understood as standing in direct relationship to the development of spheres of self-interested exchange (Parry 1986: 468–69). James Carrier, discussing gift exchange in North America, has argued that an American ideology of the 'perfect gift' came into existence in conjunction with the rise of industrial capitalism's 'world of commodities' (Carrier 1990). James Laidlaw has shown that Jain gifts to renouncers in India approximate pure gifts, which in their impersonality are similar to commodities (Laidlaw 2000). Laidlaw argues that Gregory's influential reading of Mauss negates the latter's central insight that gift exchange 'is located on the logical and phenomenological trajectory between pure gift and commodity, which are therefore shown to be genetically related and mutually constitutive' (ibid.: 628). Laidlaw's argument about Jain gifts is supported by James Carrier's discussion of commodity exchange. Carrier uses the examples of design, art and craft items to show that not all commodities are equally interchangeable, maintaining that 'not everything that we buy and sell is a pure commodity' (Carrier 1995: 29; cf. Laidlaw 2000: 632). While this allows him to demonstrate that commodities are therefore not totally different in kind from gifts, the logic of this particular example does not apply to the sweaters sold by Tibetan traders in India. The fact that the sweaters are mass-produced in Indian factories is obvious to buyers and sellers in the trade; hence, they are not imbued with special attributes which would make them any less interchangeable than any other commodity.

The scope of Carrier's argument, however, is much more extensive. It is concerned with exchange, capitalism and the effects of abstract conceptual opposites such as 'society' and 'economy', and 'the modern West' and 'non-

Western societies', on our understanding of the relationship between people and objects in industrial societies. In the course of his argument, Carrier cites examples of economic transactions being part of 'the development and maintenance of durable social relations with others' – for example, in the trade with stolen goods in London's East End, as well as examples of the 'overlap of economic and social relations' in retail trade (Carrier 1995: 192, 194; see also Davis 1973; Mars 1982; Williams 1988). The present ethnography, showing that Tibetan traders build trust-based relationships and express goodwill through commodity exchange, adds to that small body of literature critiquing the analytic dichotomy between gift exchange and commodity exchange, while being concerned ethnographically not with gifts but commodities.

Objects and the Mediation of Agency

It may be interesting to contemplate whether there are any particular concepts at work in the Tibetan perception of sweaters as things which would explain their role in establishing relationships. In the introduction to a recent volume on the ethnographic study of artefacts, Henare et al. (2007) outline an analytic methodology that avoids an automatic dualism between things and concepts. This hinges on a kind of 'ontological turn' which allows the researcher to take at face value their informants' ontological assertions about a thing. The study of Cuban diviners by Martin Holbraad (2007), in which their powder *is* their power, is a particularly clear example of this. But this kind of thing (in the strict meaning of the word) differs significantly from the kind of thing the sweaters traded by Tibetans in India are. The traders do not think of the sweaters as holding any particular or extraordinary qualities, other than their hoped-for desirability for customers and hence their potential to attract buyers and make money. The Tibetan traders first and foremost view sweaters as commodities. Hence, an ontological turn in this ethnographic case does not result in a radically different analytic outcome, nor shed any more light on the sweaters' role in establishing relationships between Tibetans and Indians.

Let us instead turn to a closer examination of the way in which the sweaters prompt Tibetans and Indians to relate to each other in their exchange. My ethnography of the Tibetan traders' statements and actions indicates that sweaters as commodities are thought to mediate, at different times, benevolence and exploitation. This is why the idioms of trust and distrust are so prevalent in the sweater trade. Together with risk and value, the sweaters are thought to transport something of the exchange partner's intention between Tibetans and Indians, be it to help or to exploit. Therefore, it seems that one could describe the sweaters as repositories of agency.

That material objects can be agents, in the sense that social agency can be disseminated through objects and act towards others in this way, is an idea that has been argued by Alfred Gell (1998). Gell developed an anthropological theory of art, in which objects as distributed extensions of human agents are called 'indexes' and the process by which indexes act towards others 'abduction'. The recipients, those being acted upon, are active in this process as they abduct meaning from indexes. Gell's theoretical construct, and especially his use of a theory of the abduction of creativity, has come under some critical scrutiny (Leach 2007; see also Bowden 2004, Layton 2003). The objects discussed by Gell are mainly art objects and idols; unlike ordinary sweaters, they very directly stand for an agent and disseminate agency in powerful ways. The commodities traded by Tibetans in India do not typically invite the abduction of creativity (for example, in terms such as design or craft) or other aspects of their makers,[7] and Gell's theory of the abduction of creativity is therefore not relevant to my analysis. But the present ethnography does demonstrate that commodities may be interpreted as mediators of agency. Departing from Gell at this point, however, I suggest that they invite the abduction of intentionality.

This insight may help explain how personal, trust-based relationships are established through commodity exchange. In the Tibetan traders' case, participation in the sweater trade entails the dependence and interdependence typical of long-term trade and credit relations, as well as spontaneous and informal acts of benevolence in the market. In this commercial context, as in other retail and business contexts, trust and therefore the establishment and maintenance of personal relationships become central concerns. These interactions and relationships necessarily revolve around the exchange of commodities, and the participants' personal agency and intentions are most clearly recognized and communicated, or in other words mediated, through the material objects exchanged. Therefore, in some contexts of exchange, commodities may quite simply be equally or more important than gifts in indicating, expressing and recognizing the participants' intentions.

Conclusion

The co-presence of positively charged, trust-based evaluation and its negatively charged, distrust-based opposite in Tibetan traders' assessments of their merchants is highly remarkable. Similarly, the relationships with Indian customers centred around the exchange of sweaters are also highly ambiguous. The same Tibetan traders may interpret the same type of object (sweaters) in the diametrically opposed terms of trust and distrust. This co-presence of opposite evaluations needs to be understood in relation to the overall hardships experienced by traders on the market, as well as the problem of Tibetan identity maintenance in the diaspora in India. The traders' interpretations of sweater exchanges in terms of trust and distrust are highly significant in their discursive construction of belonging and non-belonging in India. The central idioms of trust and distrust in fact connect the two themes of exchange and belonging. Thus, the exchange of sweaters in the Tibetan itinerant trade encompasses an emotional dimension which is highly significant for the ways in which Tibetans in India define themselves, the Indian 'other', and their ambivalent relationships. Tibetans do not want to belong in India, if such belonging entails change in terms of identity and related politics. The whole of the Tibetan diaspora is pervaded by a strong sense of purpose surrounding Tibetan cultural preservation and, thus, non-belonging in India. As traders, however, Tibetans in India have to belong in Indian local economies. This involves trust relationships, emotional ties, as well as social changes which may impact on their identities. The relationships which enable Tibetan traders' belonging as trusted members of Indian local economies are mediated through sweaters. At the same time, the sweaters also mediate the co-present strong ambiguities, negative emotions and distrust felt by Tibetans. Hence, Tsering stated that he was interested in 'good sweaters, not good people'. But this statement displaces the fact that the Tibetan traders are, by necessity as much as by human compulsion, looking for and acting as 'good people' as they go about their business. As mediators of agency, then, the sweaters at the centre of this business are important to the construction of both belonging and non-belonging of Tibetans in India.

Notes

1. This chapter is based on fieldwork with Tibetans in the diaspora in India, carried out from March 2004 until July 2005. It developed out of a paper presented at the LSE Central Asia Seminar on 23 October 2008. I am grateful for the comments provided by participants at the seminar. Research was supported by a Dissertation Research Grant of the Wenner-Gren Foundation; a Research Studentship of the Economic and Social Research Council, UK; a Reginal Smith Studentship of King's College, Cambridge; a Cambridge European Trust Bursary; a Wyse Trust Grant of Trinity College, Cambridge; and a Ling Roth Scholarship of the Department of Social Anthropology, Cambridge University. Writing was supported by the AXA Postdoctoral Research Fellowship I held at University of Calgary from 2010 to 2011.
2. See, e.g., Nowak (1984), Forbes (1989), Fürer-Haimendorf (1990), Ström (1994, 1997), Kolås (1996), Korom (1997), Anand (2000) and Diemberger (2002).
3. See Lau (2010) on the Tibetan consumption of Hindi film.
4. See, e.g., Nowak (1984: 120–21), Subba (1990: 94), Ström (1994: 838–39) and Arakeri (1998: 177, 194).
5. In the interest of their anonymity, I have changed the names of my Tibetan informants as well as the town in which their market was located.
6. I have no information on the sums of money involved in the loans illustrated here. There is thus the possibility of many small loans apparently outweighing fewer much larger ones. But my fieldwork data indicate that although trade volume may differ somewhat between Tibetan trade parties, the vast majority of them trade within a middling range. Only a few traders have a much larger business volume, and are more likely to lend money to several small traders themselves than to use their capital to secure much larger loans.
7. Tibetan traders are of course concerned about the quality of the sweaters they buy, but if this were to be a kind of abduction it would be one of resale value rather than creativity or meaning. Indian customers are, if anything, more concerned with the

identity of the sellers as Tibetan refugees in their country, and hence as people deserving of support through business transactions, than they are with the attributes of the sweaters' makers (see Lau 2007: 157).

References

Anand, D. 2000. '(Re)imagining Nationalism, Identity and Representation in the Tibetan Diaspora of South Asia', *Contemporary South Asia* 9(3): 271–87.

Appadurai, A. (ed.) 1986. *The Social Life of Things: Commodities in Cultural Perspective*. Cambridge: Cambridge University Press.

Arakeri, A.V. 1998. *Tibetans in India: The Uprooted People and their Cultural Transplantation*. New Delhi: Reliance Publishing House.

Bowden, R. 2004. 'A Critique of Alfred Gell on Art and Agency', *Oceania* 74(4): 309–24.

Carrier, J.G. 1990. 'Gifts in a World of Commodities: The Ideology of the Perfect Gift in American Society', *Social Analysis* 29: 19–37.

———— 1995. *Gifts and Commodities: Exchange and Western Capitalism since 1700*. London: Routledge.

CTA. 2005a. 'Source of Capital'. Dharamsala: Department of Finance, Central Tibetan Administration.

———— 2005b. 'Loan Source'. Dharamsala: Department of Finance, Central Tibetan Administration.

Davis, John. 1973. 'Forms and Norms: The Economy of Social Relations'. *Man* 18: 159–76.

Diemberger, H. 2002. 'The People of Porong and Concepts of Territory', in K. Buffetrille and H. Diemberger (eds), *Territory and Identity in Tibet and the Himalayas*. Leiden: Brill, pp. 33–55.

Epstein, L., and D. Lichter. 1983. 'Irony in Tibetan Notions of the Good Life', in C.F. Keyes and E.V. Daniels (eds), *Karma: An Anthropological Inquiry*. Berkeley: University of California Press, pp. 223–60.

Falzon, M.A. 2004. *Cosmopolitan Connections: The Sindhi Diaspora, 1860–2000*. Leiden: Brill.

Forbes, A.A. 1989. *Settlements of Hope: An Account of Tibetan Refugees in Nepal*. Cambridge, MA: Cultural Survival.

Fürer-Haimendorf, C. von. 1990. *The Renaissance of Tibetan Civilization*. Oracle, AZ: Synergetic Press.

Gell, A. 1998. *Art and Agency: An Anthropological Theory*. Oxford: Clarendon Press.

Gregory, C.A. 1980. 'Gifts to Men and Gifts to God: Gift Exchange and Capital Accumulation in Contemporary Papua', *Man* 15: 626–52.

———— 1982. *Gifts and Commodities*. London: Academic Press.

———— 1997. *Savage Money: The Anthropology and Politics of Commodity Exchange*. Chur, Switzerland: Harwood Academic.

Grunfeld, T. 1987. *The Making of Modern Tibet*. London: Zed Books.

Henare, A., et al. (eds). 2007. *Thinking Through Things: Theorising Artefacts Ethnographically*. New York: Routledge.

Holbraad, M. 2007. 'The Power of Powder: Multiplicity and Motion in the Divinatory Cosmology of Cuban Ifá (or *mana*, again)', in A. Henare et al. (eds), *Thinking Through Things: Theorising Artefacts Ethnographically*. New York: Routledge, pp. 189–225.

Humphrey, C., and S. Hugh-Jones (eds). 1992. *Barter, Exchange and Value: An Anthropological Approach*. Cambridge: Cambridge University Press.

Kharat, R. 2003. 'Gainers of a Stalemate: The Tibetans in India', in R. Samaddar (ed.), *Refugees and the State: Practices of Asylum and Care in India, 1947–2000*. New Delhi: Sage Publications, pp. 281–320.

Kolås, Å. 1996. 'Tibetan Nationalism: The Politics of Religion', *Journal of Peace Research* 35(1): 51–66.

Korom, F.J. 1997. 'Place, Space and Identity: The Cultural, Economic and Aesthetic Politics of Tibetan Diaspora', in *Tibetan Culture in the Diaspora*. Wien: Verlag der Österreichischen Akademie der Wissenschaften, pp. 1–8.

Laidlaw, J.A. 2000. 'A Free Gift Makes No Friends', *Journal of the Royal Anthropological Institute* 6(4): 617–34.

Lapavitsas, C. 2003. *Social Foundations of Markets, Money and Credit*. London: Routledge.

Lau, Timm. 2007. 'The Tibetan Diaspora in India: Approaching Itinerant Trade, Popular Cultural Consumption and Diasporic Sociality', PhD dissertation. Cambridge: Cambridge University.

―――― 2009. 'Tibetan Fears and Indian Foes: Fears of Cultural Extinction and Antagonism as Discursive Strategy', *Vis-à-vis: Explorations in Anthropology* 9(1): 81–90.

―――― 2010. 'The Hindi Film's Romance and Tibetan Notions of Harmony: Emotional Attachments and Personal Identity in the Tibetan Diaspora in India', *Journal of Ethnic and Migration Studies* 36(6): 967–87.

Layton, R. 2003. 'Art and Agency: A Reassessment', *Journal of the Royal Anthropological Institute* 9(3): 447–64.

Leach, J. 2007. 'Differentiation and Encompassment: A Critique of Alfred Gell's Theory of the Abduction of Creativity', in A. Henare et al. (eds), *Thinking Through Things: Theorising Artefacts Ethnographically*. New York: Routledge, pp. 167–88.

Mars, Gerald. 1982. *Cheats at Work: An Anthropology of Workplace Crime*. London: George Allen & Unwin.

Nowak, M. 1984. *Tibetan Refugees: Youth and the New Generation of Meaning*. New Brunswick, NJ: Rutgers University Press.

Ortner, S.B. 1989. *High Religion: A Cultural and Political History of Sherpa Buddhism*. Princeton, NJ: Princeton University Press.

Parry, J.P. 1986. 'The Gift, the Indian Gift and the "Indian Gift"', *Man* (N.S.) 21: 453–73.

_____ 1989. 'On the Moral Perils of Exchange', in J.P. Parry and M. Bloch (eds), *Money and the Morality of Exchange*. Cambridge: Cambridge University Press, pp. 64–93.

Parry, J.P., and M. Bloch (eds). 1989. *Money and the Morality of Exchange*. Cambridge: Cambridge University Press.

Powers, J. 1995. *Introduction to Tibetan Buddhism*. Ithaca, NY: Snow Lion.

Saklani, G. 1984. *The Uprooted Tibetans in India: A Sociological Study of Continuity and Change*. New Delhi: Cosmo Publications.

Ström, A.K. 1994. 'Tibetan Refugees in India: Aspects of Socio-cultural Change', in P. Kvaerne (ed.), *Tibetan Studies*. Oslo: Institute for Comparative Research in Human Culture, pp. 837-47.

_____ 1997. 'Between Tibet and the West: On Traditionality, Modernity and the Development of Monastic Institutions in the Tibetan Diaspora', in F.J. Korom (ed.), *Tibetan Culture in the Diaspora*. Wien: Verlag der Österreichischen Akademie der Wissenschaften, pp. 33–50.

Subba, T.B. 1990. *Flight and Adaptation: Tibetan Refugees in the Darjeeling-Sikkim Himalaya*. Dharamsala: Library of Tibetan Works and Archives.

Williams, Brett. 1988. *Upscaling Downtown: Stalled Gentrification in Washington, D.C.* Ithaca: Cornell University Press.

5

MOVING TAMILS, MOVING AMULETS:
CREATING SELF-IDENTITY, BELONGING AND EMOTIONAL WELL-BEING

————•◆•————

Anne Sigfrid Grønseth

Introduction

This chapter explores relations between Tamil refugees in northern Norway and objects such as blessed amulets and strings of cotton threads, leather or similar materials, images of Hindu deities and ritual entities. My original study focused on illness and well-being among Tamil refugees, employing a phenomenological approach to the study of the body inspired by Merleau-Ponty (1962) and Bourdieu (1977). Revisiting the material for this chapter to explore relations between Tamils in exile and certain artefacts expands on how Tamil refugees experience their everyday life as part of active transnational relations, and relations with kin, deities and Tamil Eelam, the Tamil homeland in Sri Lanka. The chapter suggests that such objects do not only preserve a warming sense of nostalgia but also enable and motivate Tamils to deal with emotional issues of social and moral hierarchy, identity and belonging as they face everyday challenges in radically different environments in northern Norway. The exploration of diasporic relations highlights how feelings, emotions and sensations are intersubjective and occur in social contexts (Jackson 1989). As people move and migrate, objects in transit are taken to new locations and take on new values and meanings, informing new identities (Svašek and Skrbiš 2004). Emotions experienced when interacting with artefacts from the homeland may trigger distinct feelings, such as loss, longing, trauma and confusion as well as pleasures, passions and affluence.

Being deprived of traditional social and religious relations to kin and deities, the objects help individual Tamils to mediate and direct such relations from a distance because of their emotional potential. Being separated from kin and temples, Tamils often experience an immense sense of uncertainty and loneliness, or *tanimai tosam* (Daniel 1989). Traditionally, Tamil individuals seek a sense of inclusion and belonging by taking part in relations with family, caste, neighbours, village and land, as well as deities and the cosmos (Banks 1957; Daniel 1984). Being part of these relations creates the ideal of inclusion, or *akam*, whereas separation from these produces *tanimai tosam* as well as disorder and chaos, or *puram*. Not being able to experience confidence and trust in relations with Norwegians and other Tamil refugees in their neighbourhood, certain objects appear to supply Tamils with a minimum of comfort in the present and hope for the future. The items are linked to religion but also to kin as family members are associated with the objects. The chapter demonstrates how these objects have the power to link Tamils to significant relations from the familiar past, to provide precarious feelings of protection, well-being, and 'peace at heart', and to offer hope for a prosperous future.

The Tamils I interacted with during my research tied blessed amulets and strings around their neck, wrist, ankle, waist or other places of their body. Many kept pictures of their gods in household shrines or tucked them under their pillows. Most households singled out a set of kitchen drawers and shelves for utensils used only for preparing ritual foods. Relating to these different kinds of object, Tamils sought emotional and sensational support and relief, as well as protection from what they tended to experience as unfamiliar and threatening surroundings during their exile in the far north of Norway. Being with and sensing the objects, I argue, they experienced a space and moment of security, comfort and hope in which memories, desires and imaginations were felt to come (as if) true in the present, giving hope and promises of fulfilled wishes for the future.

In the following I briefly introduce the methodological and theoretical viewpoint taken in this chapter. Then, I present a short background with reference to the Sri Lankan conflict and Tamil migration to Norway, and the context of fieldwork in Arctic Harbour, one of the fishing villages in Finnmark, the northernmost county of Norway. This is followed by two case studies that in various ways illustrate my main argument. The cases are narrated so as to secure informants' anonymity; any similarities to specific persons are coincidental. The citations presented are condensed and put together from pieces of information gathered during a conversation. As such, the cases serve as illustrations based on engaged interaction and talks with specific persons. During everyday talks we spoke in Norwegian. In addition I conducted open-ended interviews assisted by a local interpreter on various occasions, often recording life histories or specific issues of concern such as illnesses. Discussing the cases, I introduce two analytic sections. First, I address how objects, in a context of globalization and diasporic belonging, hold subjectivity and evoke feelings of identity and community. Second, I attend to how human bodies intentionally interact with objects to ensure well-being and comfort. Lastly, I conclude by stressing the particular force of objects when migrants and refugees are separated from other significant persons and relations.

Methodological and Theoretical Viewpoint: Sharing Experiences with Things

To capture Tamil experiences of illness and well-being as these are constituted in social and cultural processes, my original study took a client-centred approach. Employing participant observation with an emphasis on empathic engagement and sharing experiences, the data generated included information from realms of the tacit and bodily senses and feelings (see Grønseth 2010b).

Experiences of personhood and self are constantly reconstituted by bodily sensory perceptions of social relations and the environment. I draw inspiration from theories of 'embodiment' (Csordas 1994) and 'being-in-the-world' (Merleau-Ponty 1962) that emphasize that emotions and feelings do not originate in a biological and precultural domain, but arise in an existential experience that transcends the dichotomies of mind/body and culture/nature. Thus feelings and emotions are seen to originate in the interplay between bodily perceptions and sensations, and cognitive processes of language and discourses. From this perspective it becomes crucial to recognize that emotions are formed by and contribute to the formation of local, national and international politics and structures.

Paying attention to the tacit as it is expressed in bodily senses and emotions, I propose, enables me to explore how objects and items interplay with Tamil senses of illness, well-being and identity. 'Things' are not defined or categorized beforehand by the researcher but present themselves heuristically within a particular field of identified phenomena (Henare, Holbraad and Wastell 2007). Thus, things are not only 'matters of fact' but 'matters of concern' (Latour 2004). The aim of looking at things as a 'matter of concern' is to transcend the dualism of objects and subjects. Rather than pursuing a dialectic approach between the poles of subject and object, it addresses the nature of agency (Strathern 1988; Gell 1998; Latour 1999; see also Miller 2005). What matters is not human bodies or material forms, but rather the relations between them (Miller 2005). This view fits with Merleau-Ponty's phenomenological understanding of the human body as not only perceptive but also active and intentionally creating meaning, a view that contributes to an understanding of many

Tamil refugees' experiences of illness and stigma as well as well-being and comfort (Grønseth 2010a).

Rather than involving itself in the metaphysical and philosophical debate on agency and materiality, this chapter aspires to contribute to an approach that treats things as their meanings dictate (Henare, Holbraad and Wastell 2007). This is in accordance with the anthropological position of the empathic encounter with peoples' engaged practices. While critically linking people's practices and views to beliefs and philosophies, we need to be aware of in whose interest we present our research findings, producing an empathic and humanistic ethnography (Miller 2005; Grønseth and Oakley 2007). I suggest that including a focus on people's embodied interaction with material culture offers crucial meanings and apprehensions about social life. Exploring things as they appear in social life challenges how the social sciences tend to search for meaning in language, through discourse analysis and the analysis of interview material. As Tim Ingold has observed, we have to go beyond a perspective in which 'culture is conceived to hover over the material world but not to permeate it' (Ingold 2000: 340). From this perspective things are inserted into social, cultural and historical systems from which they gain their meaning and significance, reduced to mere illustrations and reflections of meaning created elsewhere (see also Strathern 1990: 38).

In the human quest of creating meaning and well-being in lived lives and surrounding worlds, materiality offers a vital potential. As things cannot be inferred as axiomatic, they must be sensed, experienced and believed (Simmel 1979: 61). Simultaneously, it is the same material world which constitutes human beings with a sense of self-identity, social personhood and as cultural agents. Such an understanding comes from recognizing that objects can evoke feelings and generate social action in users and viewers (Gell 1998; Svašek 2007a). This does not imply that objects in themselves hold intentions, but rather refers to a potential to generate agency when in interplay with human subjects. Because things are open to human interpretation they have the ability to contain both predefined and familiar significance and new and unfamiliar meaning. Latour's actor–network theory is relevant as it also proposes collapsing the dichotomy of object and subject, a distinction that prevents us from understanding artefacts as actors that together with humans create society (Latour and Woolgar 1979; Latour 1999). Things interact in human relations, and thus hold the potential of subjectivity. They motivate, direct and influence human social life.

Considering the theme of this chapter, it should be noted that objects and artefacts, being active players in processes of disembedding and re-embedding (Eriksen 2003), can shape human experience in different ways, triggering feelings of well-being, happiness and belonging, as well as illness, anger, alienation, uncertainty and so on. This will become clear in the discussion of the case studies.

The Sri Lankan Conflict and Tamil Migration to Norway

Before introducing the two case studies I briefly present a background to the Sri Lankan conflict and Tamil migration to Norway. The complexities of inter-ethnic conflict and civil war in Sri Lanka are as vast as they are soul-shaking and horrific for those who have experienced it as part of their everyday life. Since Sri Lankan independence in 1948 the Tamil minority situation has been a political issue. One can understand the population of Sri Lanka as being divided into three ethnic communities: the Sinhalese majority make up about 74 per cent, the Tamils about 18.2 per cent, and Muslims about 7.4 per cent.[1] Traditionally the Tamil population has been in the majority in the north and east of Sri Lanka, but is represented in smaller numbers in every district throughout the country (outside the north and east). After independence, the Tamil population experienced a policy of increasing discrimination by the Sinhalese majority and a polarized ethnic climate.

In 1956 Sinhalese became the official language of Sri Lanka, which led to increased political tension and discrimination against the Tamil population. In June 1983 there were upheavals, and many were killed and had to flee their homes. Among different political and guerrilla movements, the LTTE (Liberation Tigers of Tamil Eelam) were the most aggressive, leading opposition fighting for an independent state of Tamil Eelam. The civil war has continued for more than twenty years and thousands of people have been killed on both sides. The traditional Tamil majority areas of Jaffna in the north and east of Sri Lanka have been declared war zones, and most Tamil people live in exile or as refugees in their own country. As the majority live in exile and uphold a wish to return to their homeland, Tamils have become a people living in diaspora. They have built communities in almost every corner of the world and have developed a sophisticated global network struggling for the creation of Tamil Eelam. In May 2009 the government took control of the entire area previously controlled by the Tamil Tigers, leading the LTTE to admit defeat. Following the end of the war the pro-LTTE Tamil National Alliance dropped its demand for a separate state in favour of a federal solution. After the civil war ended, the diaspora has continued protests, urging governments to undertake war crimes inspections in Sri Lanka.

When Tamils sought refuge from the upheavals of the early 1980s, there was already a small group of Tamils who had migrated to Norway as part of a Cey-Nor fishing project established in Jaffna in the late 1960s. These migrants managed to arrange for their relatives to be employed in the fishing industry of northern Norway, as well as using another important passage to Norway, enrolment in the Norwegian system of *Folkehøyskoler* (Folk Colleges). A *Folkehøyskole* is a type of private boarding school that offers a variety of subjects. Third World students had admission to these schools, and this served as a loophole for circumventing the immigration ban of 1975 when Norway closed its borders to immigration. After 1983 and the outbreak of the civil war in Sri Lanka, many Tamils found that if they dropped out of one of these schools it was difficult for the Norwegian immigration authorities to force them to return to Sri Lanka. Obtaining a visa as a *Folkehøyskole* student was a possibility until 1989. From then on, many thousands have chosen a different path, illegally crossing international borders and breaking international regulations. The states that are generally favoured by Tamils – Canada, England and New Zealand, followed by Denmark, Norway, Switzerland, and then Germany, Italy and Greece – all have strict immigration policies (Fuglerud 1999). The countries mostly desired for resettlement are often not easily accessible, and Norway is not an exception.

According to Statistics Norway, in 2008, 9.7 per cent of Norway's total population consisted of around 460,000 immigrants and their descendants from 213 different countries and self-governed regions (Daugstad 2008). In 2008, 99,343 immigrants were refugees themselves and 34,424 had arrived as family members to be reunited with them. This total, some 132,400 persons, represents about 2.8 per cent of Norway's total population. Of this refugee population, 13,063 individuals were from Sri Lanka, of which 8,264 were first generation immigrants and 4,799 were born in Norway with both parents from Sri Lanka (ibid.). Virtually all the Sri Lankans are Tamils.

Since the immigration ban of 1975, both Norway's immigration laws and refugee policy have become ever more restrictive. In addition to the UN yearly quota of 700 to 1,000 refugees, individual asylum seekers also arrive. In Norway, asylum seekers are the responsibility of the government. While waiting for their case to be concluded, they live in special refugee reception centers (*asylmottak*), which are spread around in the country. The few asylum seekers that are either granted refugee status or residency on humanitarian grounds are relocated to municipal settlements (*kommunal bosetting*). The time spent in reception centers may vary from a few months to more than a year (see Lauritzen and Berg 1999). Norwegian refugee policy shows little sensitivity to the difficult and often urgent situation of many asylum seekers. As a consequence there is a steady increase in people that avoid applying for asylum, or disappear from refugee centers and become illegal residents.

As one can see, the process of applying for asylum or residence is time consuming and strenuous, as Norwegian authorities are steadily becoming sterner in their acceptance of refugees. Upon arrival in Norway, Tamil refugees feel they are treated with suspicion and mistrust and find that they occupy the lower end of the Norwegian social hierarchy. These experiences influence how many refugees and Tamils perceive being part of or maybe excluded from Norwegian social life (Grønseth 2011).

Context of Fieldwork: Place and Arrival of Tamil Refugees

My research is based on several short term field visits (between 1996 and 1999) among Tamils in Finnmark and a one-year period of in-depth fieldwork in 1999/2000 among Tamils who had sought refuge from the civil war in Sri Lanka, and who had re-established themselves in the fishing village of Arctic Harbour.[2] The Tamil population in Arctic Harbour was offered safety, well-paid jobs and good housing. They were all employed as 'cutters' (*kuttere*) in the fishing industry, filleting and gutting fish. A low-status job traditionally associated with women, it requires skill, speed and efficiency.

Arctic Harbour lies in a small fjord opening onto the Barents Sea. The buildings and houses of Arctic Harbour surround the interior of the fjord and are mainly stretched along one main road and several side streets. The village extends approximately three kilometres. The great, flat, windswept mountains rise along the shore behind the settlement, leading to the Finnmarksvidda plateau.[3] There is not a tree in sight, only a few bushes firmly secured between cracks providing shelter from the storms which sweep the area. Between November and February, the sun sinks below the horizon, disappearing altogether and plunging the village into its polar winter. During winter blizzards, the roads are closed and covered by snow and ice. After the months of darkness the sun returns, finally coming in midsummer to shine both day and night, never dipping below the horizon from May until July. On a lovely summer's day the temperature remains below twenty degrees Celsius, and the air may be thick with swarms of mosquitoes.

The community of Arctic Harbour prepared itself for the arrival of the Tamils. The municipality wanted to introduce them to Norwegian values and local traditions through six 'friendship families' who would take special care of and introduce their designated Tamil family to the ways of life that were considered essential for establishing a sense of well-being by the residents of Arctic Harbour. The Tamils were invited for dinners of typical local foods, and were taken on drives to see the landscape. They were also introduced to the Norwegian custom of hiking and cross-country skiing. The Norwegians took pride in introducing the newcomers to the local 'good life', introduced them to local food customs and encouraged an appreciation of the area and its physical environment.

This initial hosting of the Tamils was meant to integrate them into Arctic Harbour social life. This did not succeed. Although the Tamil population was well integrated into the local (and national) economy, they faced social and cultural segregation. The Tamils did not respond by incorporating Norwegian and Arctic Harbour traditions and values into their lives, nor did they forge ties of friendship and other kinds of social relationship with Norwegians. In general, they politely withdrew from contact with Norwegians and sought relations with other Tamils in Arctic Harbour. The

Tamils established a well-functioning local Tamil Association that arranged a broad spectrum of activities including sports, religious ceremonies, a Saturday Tamil school that offered culture and language education to the children, as well as other social gatherings. In spite of a well organized local Tamil Association, the Tamils generally lacked confidence and trust in each other. Lacking the familiar elements of traditional social organization – kin, caste, temple and neighbourhood – the Tamils experienced a lack of order and struggled to build trust and confidence in each other. Torn from their home village and kin (*akam*) and thrown together with others in a radically different new place produced a strong sense of chaos (*puram*), insecurity and aloneness (*tanimai tosam*). Talk of illness (particularly mental illness), politics and caste was carefully avoided so that the refugees did not expose themselves to the additional social and emotional tensions of gossip, shame and stigmatization.

Following a focus on Tamils' frequent visits to local health centres, where they reported pains and aches that health personnel could not diagnose, my research moved on to look at how Tamils felt and dealt with experiences of illness, health and well-being (Grønseth 2006a, 2006b; Grønseth and Oakley 2007). Whilst being with and sharing everyday life experiences with the Tamils of Arctic Harbour (see Grønseth 2010b) I became aware of specific entities which were of vital importance to how Tamils handled issues of sickness, health and prosperity. While living in the village, most Tamils expressed a deep insecurity and longing relating to the lack of a Tamil Hindu temple and priests. The closest Tamil Hindu temple was in Oslo, which could only be visited by taking a three-day drive or an expensive flight with stops and transfers. Given the lack of a temple, priests or any place or persons that could heal or cure the refugees' pains and aches, the Tamils sought to ease their condition with small objects such as amulets, strings and threads, pictures of Hindu deities and a few specific kitchen utensils used to prepare and serve ritual foods. These things seemed to become of pivotal concern for the Tamils in dealing with issues of identity, community, illness and well-being. Such themes and issues are illustrated in the following two cases.

Nila: 'The Blessed Strings from My Sister Connect Me to My Gods and My Family'

Nila came to Norway in 1989 by way of family reunification. She had married her husband two years earlier in Colombo, Sri Lanka. They remembered each other vaguely from a few family visits during their childhood. At a large family gathering in Chennai, India, their eyes and hearts had met. Since Bala, her future husband, lived in Norway at the time, they exchanged letters, and with their parents' consent they married a few months later. Nila felt very lucky to escape the dreadful situation in Sri Lanka, but was also terribly insecure living in her new surroundings. She said she felt afraid and uncertain of how to deal with her everyday life and family. However, she did well as a cutter at the fish plant, and in spite of many (unspoken) differences she got along with the Tamil women in Arctic Harbour. She was proud of her ability to help family who were left in Sri Lanka with money, and she also sent videos and pictures of her prospering family in Norway. After giving birth to her son Darshan and moving into a better house, she felt a certain relief but also a growing discomfort and loss of selfhood (see also Grønseth 2006a). She longed for kin, and longed for a temple to seek comfort by. She said she felt terribly alone.

It was a Friday morning and Nila got up in the early morning. She prepared a lunch box for her husband who went off early to work at the fish plant. Usually Nila would go with him, but today she was going to stay at home to look after their son Darshan, who was ill. He had a skin rash and slight fever, and had also lost his appetite, so she decided not to send him to the day-care centre. Nila had been concerned about her son's health for some time. She called me the evening before, and asked if I would come and help her the following day. When I arrived she had a ritually purifying shower before visiting the household shrine, made on a shelf in Darshan's bedroom. She lit some incense and offered a small bowl of sweet rice porridge and fruits. She did her puja and prayed to the gods for good health and prosperity for her family. She particularly asked the gods to keep her son sound and healthy. While Darshan slept, Nila and I shared a light breakfast. Then she got out the utensils for making a ritual meal and we cleaned them so as to be ready for making Friday dinner. Nila put on the stove and warmed the steel of the utensils to make sure they were purified properly, and then we washed them thoroughly in hot water and soap. When all was ready, she went to wake up Darshan. She washed him carefully, dressed him and offered him some sweet rice and a drink of water, but he hardly ate any. We then visited the local health centre, as Nila felt a strong urge to have Darshan checked. She felt very uncertain and explained to me:

> Darshan is very vulnerable. I am all alone. I have no one to consult. There is no kin here and no temples I can visit. I sent money to my sister and asked her to send me blessed strings from the local priest and temple back home in Sri Lanka. I have knitted the threads around Darshan. It protects him from evil forces, from sickness and misfortune. My husband has one around his neck too. I have one around my arm. I feel safer. I need to protect my family. I prey to the gods, but I feel uncertain of my prayer's force. I am so far away and alone. I need my family. When preparing ritual meals, purifying the utensils, lighting the incense, I often have a feeling of being close to my mother. It gives me a sense of belonging. I feel very anxious. I visit the local health centre. Sometimes they give medication. It reduces fevers and colds, but it does not help me. They say I should remove the strings. They say the strings are uncomfortable, can cause itching and become dirty. They do not understand my concerns. I need my family.

When preparing dinner together with Nila later the same day she told me about her younger sister. They used to be very close. Together with their mother they used to visit the local temple. Nila told me how she used to feel a certain peace, but also thrill, when visiting the temple. Nila told me about all the sounds, smells, tastes, songs and colours that used to be part of her life; the sounds of her village and the voices of her kin, the smell of people's cooking, the taste of her mother's vegetable curries, the colours of the saris and flower decorations at the temple. It made her feel like she was immersed in a sense of 'togetherness' and 'community'. As Nila pointed out, 'there was always someone to confide in and someone to offer guidance and comfort'. When her father was sick, kin and neighbours had offered their help on the land and brought food for the family. The local priest had carried out puja and healing rituals. Fortunately, her father recovered. Nila and her family felt a deep gratitude, and as she explained it enforced their sense of belonging to villagers, neighbours, kin and attachment to the temple and deities.

Living in Arctic Harbour, Nila experienced the scenery as 'dead and empty silence', and the villagers and neighbours as 'threatening relations'. The people, both Tamil and Norwegians, left her feeling insecure and uncertain, and she felt that her identity was threatened. She felt lost and alone, but explained that she felt more whole when she engaged with her religion and family: 'I pray to the gods. I talk on the phone [with relatives]. I need their support. The blessed strings from my sister connect me to my gods and my family. When I prepare ritual foods, I bond with my mother. I feel more of myself'.

Segar: 'I Feel the Amulets, and I Am Reminded of Who I Am'

Segar had planned to study engineering in Jaffna, but because of the civil war his plans had to be abandoned. When his father was sent to prison and his younger brother joined the LTTE he felt responsible as the eldest for taking care of his family. He found work as a teacher. The LTTE contacted him and in secret he did some work for them. When his mother found out, she was terrified and afraid of losing him to the war. She brought him to the temple and made vows (promises) to the gods in exchange for her son's safe escape from Sri Lanka. The extended family raised enough money for his travel and his mother tucked an amulet in his pocket just before he took off from Colombo on his journey. While his mother cried and waved, and with a small bundle of clothes and a picture of the local god Pillear in his pack, he departed.

After a few stops elsewhere he arrived a few months later in Norway and applied for asylum. He still recalled the trembling sensation when he entered Norway, where he was questioned by the police and escorted to the asylum reception centre. He clenched his hand around his amulet in search for support and comfort. After almost half a year he was granted a residence permit on humanitarian grounds and offered the opportunity of well-paid work in the fishing industry in Finnmark. Together with another

Figure 5.1: Ritual foods offered to the Hindu gods on a home altar. The offering bonds things, humans and gods together and affects people's sense of identity and well-being. Photograph by Anne Sigfrid Grønseth.

Tamil young man, he first stayed in one fishing village and then moved on to Arctic Harbour were there was a greater demand for labour. In Arctic Harbour he sought the close company of a group of Tamil young single men. They never spoke of their misery, but sharing the sensation of being lost and alone they offered each other support and friendship.

Segar and I sat in his one-room apartment drinking soda water, talking and glancing at a Tamil TV programme broadcast from London. It was a Saturday afternoon. Segar felt low and lonely. His body was a bit restless; his feet and hands made constant small movements. Every once in a while his hands went to his throat and touched an amulet attached to a string around his neck. He also fiddled with some strings around his wrist. Segar said he had only lived alone in his apartment for the last six months. Earlier, he did not feel alone since he shared most of his time with other Tamil young single men. They used to share meals and sleep at each other's places. Now, one friend had moved to Oslo and the others had married and settled with their new families. Segar now felt terribly alone.

I asked him about the items his hands were touching every now and then, the amulets and strings around his wrist, and he said:

> They give me a sense of security, of peace and hope. I feel a kind of companionship, a connection to my family. It reminds me of good days. My father gave me this amulet [touching the one on his chest] before he went to prison. One year later he died. He was a hero. He said his life was in the hands of the gods and our people. He fought for Tamil Eelam. The amulet gives me hope that this dream will come true. This amulet [touching the one on his wrist] is from my mother. She had it blessed at the local temple by the priest before I escaped. It gives me support and protection. I need guidance. It is difficult to fall asleep. I keep a picture of Pillear under my pillow. It helps give me rest. Every night I look at it and pray my family will be okay and that I will unite with them again. Sometimes I feel like suffocating and then that I might explode. I look at Pillear, and it helps me breathe. I feel the amulets, and I am reminded of who I am.

Segar explained that his parents were looking for a bride for him. Segar had contributed to his two younger sisters' dowry and they were now safely married. One lived in India, and one in Germany. Now, it was Segar's turn. He had received letters with pictures of possible brides. So far, they had not succeeded in finding a suitable candidate. Segar had recently sent a letter to his parents suggesting one of his cousins whom he remembered as 'very delicate, but quite outspoken'. He told me that they had played as children. Segar had a clear memory of her. When he had said his farewell to his family, just before he had escaped, he had seen her at a distance from the corner of his eye. Somehow, Segar said, the amulet from his mother did not only give him a sense of safety and protection, but also evoked the thrill of excitement he had felt when exchanging a glance with his cousin. He knew that, only a few years ago, she had moved to live with family in Malaysia. He hoped that his parents might contact her family and propose that the two of them marry. Segar went on, touching his amulet as he spoke: 'As time has passed, I have come to believe that the amulet from my mother holds a promise of a good marriage. I think my cousin is the right wife for me. The thought of her brings me good memories of play and laughter. I touch the amulet, and I can recall her glance and a sense of peace'.

Things and Persons as a Whole: Creating a Sense of Belonging and Well-being

The cases above demonstrate that Tamils in Norway do not simply reproduce a Tamil home world outside their home country, but rather use items to create a sense of a diasporic belonging. The changes in bodily engagement with the artefacts are not characterized by radical and dramatic shifts but rather by small additions to or accentuations of already familiar features. Considering how the objects interplay with Tamil experiences of diasporic identity and belonging, the cases cited above also illustrate how things and feelings are deeply connected. In Nila's case, objects such as kitchen utensils used for preparing ritual foodstuffs were immersed in a practice that evoked emotionally powerful memories. By cleaning and purifying utensils and preparing ritual dishes, Nila sensed togetherness with her mother and felt 'more like herself'. When tying strings around her son and herself, she experienced protection and safety. These experiences arose particularly out of her interaction with things related to her relatives and the deities they shared. Through the strings, Nila felt closeness to her sister, kin and the Tamil community. The blessed strings further connected Nila to the gods and the temple which together supplied her with a promise of her family's future well-being and comfort.

In interactive relation, the objects themselves turn into subjective entities as they supply content and direction, producing feelings and meanings and framing action. Social life, in other words, cannot be distinguished from what Latour calls 'non-human actants' (Latour 1999: 141, 180). Thus, things play an active and powerful part in generating identity, morality, sensations, feelings and meanings. The creation of new feelings, practices and meanings cannot be fully understood without acknowledging the mediating role of artefactual actants. Objects, in other words, hold in themselves a disposition for subjectivity which comes into play when interacting with humans. They do not hold a fixed essence that can be disclosed, but are open for various interpretations and interactions that create meaning and practices for people in distinct and shifting social, political and cultural contexts. For Tamil refugees, as for refugees and migrants in general, this open-ended and flexible feature of material culture makes it a precarious vital instrument in an existential struggle for meaningful relations and practices in new and unfamiliar environments. Artefacts can confirm old meanings, attachments, relations and practices, while simultaneously being ready to create new ones. From this perspective, it is the interaction, or rather the process taking place between subjects and objects, that generate emotions, sensations and agency. Thus, when Tamils interact and engage with significant entities they can experience a relation that provides agency and the creation of new meanings and practices.

The perspective of object agency, I suggest, highlights how entities such as blessed strings and kitchen utensils used for rituals supply individuals such as Nila with a feeling of belonging. They make her feel more in control, actively 'protecting' her family. By interacting with significant mediating items, Nila upholds and revitalizes relations with her family, kin and gods. Furthermore, she experiences how things inform her sense of self (Bateson 1972). Objects are thus classified as part of the self in an active systemic relation. Seeing Nila's everyday interactions with things as they stimulate relations, feelings and meanings shows us how Nila, together with these things, is part of a processual and interactive systemic cluster. This questions the distinction between objects and subjects, and highlights their dialectic relationship. When Nila interacts with things she engages in practices that attend to and negotiate cultural specific meanings, while also experiencing feelings in her body (Leavitt 1996: 530). Objects can thus be regarded as mediators in a relational, emotional, interpretive and agentive process.

This is also illustrated in the case of Segar when he engaged in touching the amulets given to him by his family. Feeling alone and insecure, he touched the amulets and experienced a 'sense of security, of peace and hope'. He felt 'companionship and connection to family', and the action increased his hope that the 'dream of Tamil Eelam will come true'. By 'feeling the amulets', Segar said, 'I am reminded of whom I am'. As in the case of Nila, the interaction gave direction to his sense of self. Segar's experiences confirmed vital features of amulets' predefined cultural meanings, mediating relations with deities, kin and Tamil Eelam.

Living in exile and separated from these relations, the cases of Nila and Segar demonstrate how things, such as amulets and strings, hold the power to transmit such relations and generate feelings across time and space. Not only do the amulets transmit collective cultural meanings but they also create individually specific meanings and feelings, as seen in the example of Segar's 'thrill of excitement'. Interacting with the amulet, Segar not only reproduced cultural meanings and familiar sensations, he also created new ones, such as the promise of a good marriage.

In sum, this section has focused on how the study of diasporic belonging provides an opportunity to explore relations between objects and humans, which are crucial in migrants' feelings and experiences of belonging and well-being. By exploring the case studies it emerged that the process in which persons and things interact should be considered as an analytic whole, and not as separate 'human' and 'non-human' phenomena. The objects hold subjectivity that comes into play and gives direction to feelings and experiences of Tamil exiles in Arctic Harbour.

The Interplay of Things and Bodies: Multi-sensorial Perception

The power of things to affect human feelings and meanings comes not only from their potential for subjectivity but also stems from their ability to interact directly with the human body, shaping multi-sensorial perception. Mobile artefacts can be experienced as 'subject-like agent[s], and an extension of one's body', like a bag which is always carried along, filled, emptied and refilled with possessions, thrown away and picked up, and in time become a companion (Svašek 2007b: 231). In the Tamil case, strings, amulets, kitchen utensils and pictures of deities, as well as other entities such as chairs, beds and foodstuffs, were all experienced and handled by the human body. Things involved in bodily practices make up a crucial aspect of the production of feelings and meanings.

Without touching, seeing, smelling, listening to or tasting things, the human body has little left through which it can come to know and perceive its changing subjectivity. This acknowledgment rests on an understanding of a body that intentionally perceives the entities surrounding it, engaging in interaction and experiencing distinct sensations, feelings and meanings (Merleau-Ponty 1962; Jackson 1989; Csordas 1994). Recognizing the human body not only as the locus for experiences of feelings but as an active perceptive and intentional unit (Merleau-Ponty 1962; Csordas 1994), it further appears that bodily practices and the handling of objects make a crucial contribution to the interactive process of creating feelings, meanings and practices. There is, of course, a crucial distinction between objects and humans when it comes to intentionality. While items hold subjectivity that may motivate and direct feelings and agentive processes, items do not act with intention.

For Nila and Segar, the bodily interplay with things gave a sense of contact with home and of belonging to a diaspora of kin and deities. Through the entities' ability to activate the senses, Nila and Segar felt a belonging to their Norwegian home environment. From touching and perceiving the objects' presence, they derived strength and agency to live their life in the present and plan for the future.

When Tamils, such as Nila and Segar are separated from kin and deities they usually relate and interact with, and their body intentionally seeks out, things that direct them toward a sense of togetherness, peace, comfort and hope. Nila experienced protection and comfort when tying the blessed strings around her son's, her husband's and her own body. Watching the images of her gods and feeling their gaze while doing puja, Nila experienced security and 'peace at heart'. Segar's hand touched the amulets and this helped him feel connected to his kin, to Tamil Eelam and a promise of a good marriage. When he had difficulties falling asleep, feeling that he might suffocate and possibly explode, Segar touched the picture of his god Pillear and brought it into his sight. By exchanging touch and sight, he was again able to breathe. Being in the presence of Pillear, he was reassured that he would one day be reunited with his family. The cases demonstrate how an engagement with artefacts offered bodily sensations and feelings to Nila and Segar, supplying them with experiences of well-being. Recognizing the interaction between the human body's intentional subjectivity and the object's (non-intentional) subjectivity, it became possible to see how Tamil refugees sought relations with specific objects that supplied them with a minimum of comfort and hope for a prosperous life. Nila's and Segar's bodies sought contact with items that offered religious as well as social connections, thus increasing emotional well-being and comfort.

The quest for togetherness and belonging takes place in partially overlapping social, religious and spiritual spheres (Fuller 1992; Kakar 1997). Specific religious artefacts trigger hope and promises of a future in union with god; nirvana or *moksha*, which is understood to be the final realization of self (*atman*). Recognizing the far away future of fulfilling this goal, I suggest that Nila and Segar linked the religious items they held dear to the domain of social relations. In Hindu philosophy, religion does not, *pace* Dumont (1980), pertain to a separate realm, but is rather part of everyday social life (Wadley 1977). This may be seen to fit with how Marriot and Inden (1977) refer to a non-duality between action and substance. Understanding how substance in a Tamil and South Asian context includes not only substances contained within the body but also that which passes between bodies (ibid.) highlights how objects are part of an (embodied) social and religious wholeness. Thus, actions, substances, objects, power and purity are inseparable elements in Hindu ideas of being and action.

Living in exile in Arctic Harbour and being cut off and separated from ordinary Tamil social and religious relations in Sri Lanka, certain items became pivotal for Nila's and Segar's sense of self, well-being, comfort and peace. Experiencing their new surroundings as partly 'insecure', 'threatening', and 'empty', Nila and Segar searched for ways to find 'protection', 'safety' and 'certainty'. Not being able to make sense of their new environment, their bodies turned towards things that increased positive self experience as members of a connected transnational family, and held out the promise of a future that they hoped would be fulfilled. Nila bonded with her mother and her gods and felt 'more of herself'; Segar bonded with his gods, his kin, and Tamil Eelam, and strengthened his belief that his wish for a future wife would be fulfilled. These feelings of being close, of belonging, of hope, I suggest, arose from the interactive process between perceptual, intentional and active engagement with objects as mediators that interfered and directed human experiences and interpretations.

Concluding Remarks: Objects as Mediating New Identities and Senses of Belonging

Exploring the interplay between Tamil refugees and certain objects that they brought with them in the context of being resettled in a fishing village within the Arctic Circle has provided an opportunity to look at senses of identity, belonging and well-being and how they are deeply affected by transnational social relations, cultural production and emotions. The amulets, strings, images of gods and ritual utensils all served and mediated in an agentive process of recreating crucial social relations, cultural values and practices to maintain a sense of identity, belonging and emotional well-being.

This chapter has sought to highlight how objects not only confirmed and repeated the habitual and expected, but also contributed as powerful interactors, linking spaces and times, and thus opening up new and unexpected senses of self, togetherness and comfort. The ability of objects to mediate between past, present and future meant that they supported and stimulated the Tamils to handle emotional and social issues in the new and unfamiliar surroundings of Arctic Harbour. Engaging with specific artefacts, the Tamils felt 'more of themselves', closer to kin and closer to other diasporic Tamils. Objects, open to human perception and interpretation, turned into subjective entities that interfered with and affected individual's actions, feelings and values.

Things make different persons as much as persons make things different. When Tamils moved and escaped the war in Sri Lanka, the amulets, strings and ritual utensils they carried with them became objects that increased their sense of self and belonging in exile. At the same time, the objects also inspired new ways of engaging with their new homes. But it remains an open question how, while continually living their everyday life in Norway and interacting with familiar and unfamiliar material surroundings, Tamils such as Nila and Segar will create other new senses of self, belonging and emotional well-being in the future.

Notes

1. These figures are taken from Tambiah (1991: 4), citing the 1981 census.
2. Arctic Harbour is one of several fishing communities along the northern coast of Norway where there is a substantial settlement of Tamils. There were about 200 Tamils in a population of approximately 2,500 inhabitants during 1999/2000. The numbers vary over time as the population as a whole is shifting, mostly due to fluctuations in the need for labour in the fishing industry.
3. The inhabitants of Finnmarksvidda are mostly indigenous Sami who traditionally make a living as reindeer herders. Along the coast there is a more mixed population, consisting of Sami, who combine fishing and reindeer herding, and non-Sami Norwegian inhabitants.

References

Abu-Lughod, L., and C.A. Lutz (eds). 1990. *Language and the Politics of Emotion*. Cambridge: Cambridge University Press.

Banks, M.Y. 1957. 'The Social Organization of the Jaffna Tamils of North Ceylon, with Special Reference to Kinship, Marriage and Inheritance', Ph.D. dissertation. Cambridge: Cambridge University.

Bateson, G. 1972. *Steps to an Ecology of Mind*. New York: Ballantine Books.

Bourdieu, P. 1977. *Outline of a Theory of Practice*. Cambridge: Cambridge University Press.

Csordas, T. (ed.) 1994. *Embodiment and Experience: The Existential Ground of Culture and Self*. Cambridge: Cambridge University Press.

Daniel, E.V. 1984. *Fluid Signs: Being a Person the Tamil Way*. Berkeley: University of California Press.

_____ 1989 'The Semiotics of Suicide in Sri Lanka', in B. Lee and G. Urban (eds), *Semiotics, Self and Society*. Berlin: Mouton de Gruyter, pp. 67–100.

Daugstad, G. 2008. Innvandring og innvandrere 2008. [Immigration and Immigrants 2008]. *Statistiske analyser 103*. Oslo: Statistics Norway.

Dumont, L.1980. *Homo Hierarchicus: The Caste System and its Implications*, rev. edn. Chicago: University of Chicago Press.

Eriksen, T.H. 2003. *Globalisation: Studies in Anthropology*. London: Pluto Press.

Fuglerud, Ø. 1999. *Life on the Outside. The Tamil Diaspora and Long Distance Nationalism*. London: Pluto Press.

Fuller, C.J. 1992. *The Camphor Flame: Popular Hinduism and Society in India*. Princeton, NJ: Princeton University Press.

Gell, A. 1998. *Art and Agency: An Anthropological Theory*. Oxford: Clarendon Press.

Grønseth, A.S. 2001. 'In Search of Community: A Quest for Well Being among Tamil Refugees in Northern Norway', *Medical Anthropology Quarterly* 15(4): 493–541.

_____ 2006a. 'Experiences of Illness: Tamil Refugees in Norway Seeking Medical Advise', in H. Johannessen and I. Làzàr (eds), *Multiple Medical Realities: Patients and Healers in Biomedical, Alternative and Traditional Medicine*. Oxford: Berghahn, pp. 148–62.

_____ 2006b. 'Experiences of Tensions in Re-orienting Selves: Tamil Refugees in Northern Norway Seeking Medical Advice', *Anthropology and Medicine* 13(1): 77–98.

_____ 2010a. *Lost Selves and Lonely Persons. Experiences of Illness and Well-being among Tamil Refugees in Norway*. Chapel Hill, NC: Carolina Academic Press.

_____ 2010b. 'Sharing Experiences with Tamil Refugees in Northern Norway: Body and Emotion as Methodological Tools', in A.S. Grønseth and D.L. Davis (eds), *Mutuality and Empathy: Self and Other in the Ethnographic Encounter*. Wantage, Oxon: Sean Kingston Publications.

_____ 2011. 'Tamil Refugees in Pain: Challenging Solidarity in the Norwegian Welfare State', *Journal of Ethnic and Minority Studies* 37(2): 315–32.

Grønseth, A.S., and R. Oakley. 2007. 'Ethnographic Humanism: Migrant Experiences in the Quest for Well-being', *Anthropology in Action*, special issue 14(1/2): 1–11.

Henare, A., M. Holbraad and S. Wastell (eds). 2007. *Thinking through Things: Theorising Artefacts Ethnographically*. London: Routledge.

Ingold, T. 2000. *The Perception of the Environment: Essays in Livelihood, Dwelling and Skill*. London: Routledge.

Jackson, M. 1989. *Paths toward a Clearing: Radical Empiricism and Ethnographic Inquiry*. Bloomington: Indiana University Press.

Kakar, S. 1997. *The Inner World: A Psychoanalytic Study of Childhood and Society in India*. Oxford: Oxford University Press.

Latour, B. 1999. *Pandora's Hope: Essays on the Reality of Science Studies*. Cambridge, MA: Harvard University Press.

_____ 2004. 'Why Has Critique Run Out of Steam? From Matters of Fact to Matters of Concern', *Critical Enquiry* 30(2): 25–48.

Latour, B., and S. Woolgar. 1979. *Laboratory Life: The Social Construction of Scientific Facts*. Beverly Hills, CA: Sage.

Lauritzen, K., and B. Berg 1999. *Mellom håp og lengsel. Å leve i asylmottak* [Between Hope and Longing. Living in an Asylum Center Reception Center]. Trondheim: SINTEF.

Leavitt, J. 1996. 'Meaning and Feeling in the Anthropology of Emotions', *American Ethnologist* 23(3): 514–39.

Marriott, M., and R.B. Inden. 1977. 'Toward an Ethnosociology of South Asian Caste Systems', in K. David (ed.), *The New Wind: Changing Identities in South Asia*. The Hague: Mouton, pp. 227–38.

Merleau-Ponty, M. 1962[1945]. *Phenomenology of Perception*. London: Routledge and Kegan Paul.

Miller, D. 2005. *Materiality*. Durham, NC: Duke University Press.

Simmel, G. 1979[1900]. *The Philosophy of Money*. Boston: Routledge and Kegan Paul.

Strathern, M. 1988. *The Gender of the Gift*. Berkeley: University of California Press.

_____ 1990. 'Artefacts of History: Events and the Interpretation of Images', in J. Siikala (ed.), *Culture and History in the Pacific*. Helsinki: Finnish Anthropology Society, pp. 25–44.

Svašek, M. 2007a. *Anthropology, Art and Cultural Production*. London: Pluto.

_____ 2007b. 'Moving Corpses: Emotions and Subject–Object Ambiguity', in H. Wulff (ed.), *The Emotions: A Cultural Reader*. Oxford: Berg, pp. 229–48.

Svašek, M., and S. Skrbiš. 2004. 'Passions and Powers: Emotions and Globalisation', *Identities* 14(4): 367–83.

Tambiah, S.J. 1991. *Sri Lanka: Ethnic Fratricide and the Dismantling of Democracy*. Chicago: University of Chicago Press.

Wadley, S. 1977. 'Power in Hindu Ideology and Practice', in K. David (ed.), *The New Wind: Changing Identities in South Asia*. The Hague: Mouton, pp. 133–57.

6

THE PRICE OF PROGRESS:
'DYING ARTS' AMONG THE KAREN OF THE ANDAMAN ISLANDS, INDIA

Sameera Maiti

It was around late afternoon in Webi (Mayabunder, North Andaman Island) while I was returning to where I was staying after a day-long interview session that I saw a group of shy yet chirpy young Karen girls and boys going towards the local church.[1] When asked, they informed me that they were going to practice the *taka*, their traditional dance form, with Father Saw Setha and his wife. I found this interesting because although I was collecting information about Karen arts and crafts I was also interested in other ethnographic details, which I felt would be important in the light of their demand to be granted the status of a 'scheduled tribe'.

In India, 'scheduled tribe' is a status which would give the Karen special privileges, funds and concessions, and is granted to underdeveloped groups across different parts of India. In India the term 'tribe' is not used pejoratively and in opposition to a notion of a 'more cultured' type of social organization; by contrast, it is a highly sought after status. The Indian Constitution vaguely defines 'scheduled tribe' as a 'tribe or tribal community or parts or groups within tribes or tribal communities', which may be declared so through public notification by the president of India in accordance with Article 342 of the Constitution. As Dash Sharma states, a 'scheduled tribe' in the Indian context is 'an administrative and legal term whose purpose is to label specific groups – based on their socioeconomic status, religious and cultural customs – in order to provide them with special attention as mandated by the country's constitution' (Dash Sharma 2006: xi).

During the early days of my field work, I had heard about Saw Setha, a well-established and respected member of the community, the priest of the local church and general secretary of the Karen Youth Organization (KYO). The KYO is a non-governmental organization, established in 1994 with the aim of putting forward, in an organized manner, the demands and grievances of the Karen; recently it has taken up the initiative of demanding, from the Indian government, the status of 'scheduled tribe' for the Karen community. Finding it a good opportunity to gather information about traditional arts in the community, as these were central to their demand for tribal status, I approached Saw Setha, who proved more than willing and helpful to provide information. After allowing me to sit and watch the youngsters rehearse in their traditional Karen attire, we started discussing what he saw as the sad state of traditional Karen arts and crafts.

I was informed that Saw Setha and his wife were making an effort to revive the *taka*, or bamboo dance, which had nearly died out a decade and a half ago. They were training a group of twenty-five young boys and girls in the dance, and there were several others eager to be part of the group since those who are part of the dance troupe get the opportunity of visiting the mainland when the group goes off to put on shows. Saw Setha and his wife were not the only ones who were upset about the pitiable conditions of traditional Karen arts and crafts. The passion felt by the older members of the community for the traditional arts and crafts, which the community members had brought when they migrated from Burma, and their present plight, can be gauged by the fact that my 82-year-old key informant, Saw Thabadoo, tirelessly spoke to me for six hours at a stretch on the topic. Before discussing the condition of Karen arts and artistic activities, it would be beneficial to know the community a little better.

Karen Migration to the Andamans

The Andaman and Nicobar Islands are an archipelago of more than three thousand islands – some big and some small, some inhabited and some not – off the southeast coast of India in the southern part of the Bay of Bengal. Often described as 'green islands', because of their natural beauty and blue-green water, the Andamans have long been called *kalapani* (black water) in India because of their history as a penal settlement under British rule, a place from where one never returned to the mainland. This, however, is a reputation which the islands have now shed. Immortalized by Radcliffe-Brown (1922) in his landmark book *The Andaman Islanders*, the islands are home to several groups, one of them being the Karen.

The Karen are a Burmese migrant community residing in the Mayabunder and Diglipur administrative units (*tehsil*) of the North Andaman district of the Andamans. Believed to have originally been inhabitants of Mongolia, according to Karen legend, the despotic and cruel nature of the Mongolian kings forced the Karen to move southwards to east Turkistan and China around the third millennium BC.[2] From here the 'peace-loving' Karen moved to Tibet in the early second millennium BC.[3] However, the ill treatment meted out to them by the Chinese king, Ghaw Hsin, forced them once again to migrate in the first millennium BC, and they settled in various parts of Thailand, Burma, Cambodia and Vietnam. Gradually, migrating over the time, most of them had settled in the eastern hilly tracts of Burma (now Myanmar) by 800 BC.

Some two-and-a-half millennia later, British colonial expansion led to the establishment of Burma as a province of British India in 1886. In 1924, H.I. Marshall, principal of the Karen theological seminary in Rangoon, stopped off at Port Blair in the Andamans on his way back from the US to see his cousin Colonel Ferrar, Chief Commissioner of the Andaman and Nicobar Islands. Ferrar informed Marshall of the shortage of labour in the islands and of the administration's generous settlement scheme –which included several benefits, like free land and a year's rations – which was being used to attract settlers to undertake forestry work and work in the islands' timber mills.[4] Marshall took this as an opportunity to help the hard-working and honest Baptist Karen of Burma, many of whom were in a pitiable condition. On his return to Rangoon, he published details of the generous settlement offer in a Karen newspaper, *Hsah Tu Gaw* (Morning Star). On reading the news and later visiting the Andamans, Reverend Lugyi, a Karen priest, decided that it was an excellent opportunity to improve the conditions of some of his people. Since the entire migration process was arranged by missionaries of the American Baptist Church, only poor, landless, Christian Karen were selected for relocation, although there were also Karen belonging to other faiths who were interested in taking advantage of the scheme. In April 1925, the first batch of twelve families, under the leadership of Reverend Lugyi, reached the Andaman Island as settlers. Impressed by the benefits received by the first batch, in 1926 a second batch of fifty families came to settle on the island, and the first Karen village, Webi, was established. Several small batches of migrants continued to arrive in the Andamans over the next few years. In 1947, when India gained independence, the migrants made Andaman their permanent home by opting for Indian citizenship. Until 1947, the Karen had maintained close contact with relatives in Burma.[5] However, with the passage of time, this contact has declined to the infrequent exchange of letters with distant relatives in Myanmar today.

Mrs Kane, one of the two surviving migrants of the first batch, came to the Andamans with her family when she was eight years old. She remembers how the elders used to discuss the difficult life they had led in Burma and the uncertain future they faced in the Andamans, about which they had great hope. They also talked about the happiness they felt about their improved conditions and life style, but also about their occasional longing for the place where they were born and had spent most of their life. She concluded her recollections by saying: 'But ultimately we were all very happy with our condition here [pause] especially after the coming of the second batch and the setting up of Webi [pause]. All were very happy because many of our close relatives and friends joined us'. This statement clearly indicates that the feeling of disembeddedness did not last long for the Karen, since the conditions and experiences of the migrants in their homeland had not been very good.

Experiences of disembeddedness depend, to a great extent, on the factors that lead to a decision to migrate. In the case of the Karen, the decision to migrate was neither forced on them nor one taken under any kind of pressure; rather, it was motivated by them opting for a better life, one free from economic deprivation and ethnic persecution. The conditions in the Andamans also proved very conducive to the Karen. The area where the Karen settled was huge, secluded and uninhabited. Thus, they did not have to adjust, adapt or integrate themselves into a previously existing community or dominant culture. They were free to live and start their lives as they wished, and this helped them create a world of their own and embed themselves in their new surroundings.

A Brief Ethnographic Profile of the Karen

Recent demographic analysis reveals that the Karen population of the Andamans stands at over 2,000 (Maiti and Agarwal 2007), whereas according to the 1951 census their number was merely 384 (Ghosh 1955), and in 1978 it stood at 815 (Roy 1998). The Karen speak their own language belonging to the Sino-Tibetan family and use the Burmese script. Coomar (1994) and Singh (1994) state that, on the basis of language differences, the Karen of Andaman are divided into two sub-groups, the Sgaw and Pwo. However, my own research revealed that neither are the Karen aware of, nor do they accept, any such division (Maiti 2004). According to them, all the Karen residing in the Andamans belong to the Sgaw group and there are no longer any Pwo to be found living in the Andamans.

The Karen of Andaman belong to the Baptist Church and in accordance with its rules practice monogamy. Traditionally, endogamy is the prescribed form of marriage, but cases of exogamous marriage with locals from other caste and religious groups is on the rise. Nuclear families are the preferred form, though quite a few extended families exist. The Karen are mainly a uxorilocal but patriarchal community. Inheritance is bilateral since both sons and daughters inherit an equal share. However, it is the men who actually control and take decisions regarding how to use the inheritance. This rule of inheritance, however, is not binding since those who have steady employment or are economically well-off will sometimes give their share to others. The entire community is very close-knit, with every member ready to help one another in times of need.

Today, the Karen inhabit six villages in the Mayabunder administrative unit – Deopur, Kamatang-9, Karmatang-10, Latau, Lucknow and Webi –

and two villages in the Diglipur administrative unit – Borang and Chipong. Most of these villages have at least a few people from other religious and caste groups residing with the Karen and as such contacts with them have resulted in greater interaction between the two. Further, this interaction has led to several changes in Karen lifestyle apart from inter-community marriages. While some Karen are totally opposed to this interaction and express their dissent openly, others take it as a necessary part of surviving in a changing world.

The Study

Researchers from different disciplines have analysed the dynamic relationship between art and emotion from various perspectives.[6] Matravers, for example, writes: 'Great art provides some of the most valuable experiences it is possible for us to have. Such experiences engage many aspects of our mental life simultaneously: filling our senses whilst at the same time making demands on our intelligence, our sympathies, and our emotions' (Matravers 1998: 1). Mistretta has similarly noted that 'art, in its ever-vital role in society, helps to create and stabilize/reinforce our emotional makeup, on both an individual and societal level' (Mistretta 2001: 1). Focusing on the potential use of art practice for patients who are unable or unwilling to express themselves through language, Silver (2001) demonstrated that drawing techniques can be used as a from of treatment as they stimulate patients' cognitive and emotional development. Commenting on contemporary psychoanalytic approaches to emotions, Jurist (2006) suggests that such theories should include a focus on subjective art experiences as these throw light on complex emotional processes.

In line with these views, this chapter attempts to critically analyse the position of traditional arts and crafts among the Karen, unravelling the emotional dynamics that inform the debate about 'dying cultures' and 'the protection of cultural heritage'. Here it would be pertinent to point out that by 'arts and crafts', I do not mean only the fine arts but also what several scholars have called the applied or liberal arts. Personally, I prefer not to make a distinction between the two. This is because archaeological excavations worldwide have proved, time and again, that from a very early stage of the evolutionary development of humans, people have created works of art. Even today, beauty and symmetry are added to function in an attempt to make things more appealing. Moreover, the so called fine arts perform several functions, although they are not obviously visible.

This chapter is based mainly on data collected via in-depth, unstructured and sometimes directed interviews, observations, discussions and case studies. Furthermore, although most socio-cultural anthropologists tend to dislike and ignore the use of statistical analysis, I attempted to substantiate the information I gathered by collecting additional data using a simple house-to-house survey. Fieldwork was carried out in all six Karen villages of Mayabunder in November and December 2003 in an attempt to analyse the position of traditional arts and crafts in the community, and the diverse attitude of the older and younger generations towards these.

The analysis presents the contradictory views and conflicts that exist in the Karen community today with regard to arts and crafts. Undoubtedly change is an evident phenomenon and one cannot, and does not, expect any culture to freeze in time. As an outsider, I neither have the right, nor the will, to judge whose perspective is right. Selfishly, however, as an appreciator of handicrafts and artefacts, I wish every diverse form and style to stay alive so that we may be in a position to admire and enjoy these varied products which are unique examples of humanity's ingenuity and creativity. This will be possible if every local example of human creativity is at least given a chance to survive.

Karen Arts and Crafts: A Sense of Home

Faced with difficult conditions in Burma, the Karen migrants had hardly anything to bring with them when they left for India. Moreover, sea journeys were not considered very safe and everyone was asked to travel with the minimum amount of luggage. Consequently, the migrants arrived with very few artefacts; instead, what they brought were the embodied memories of skills that could be used to manipulate raw materials freely available in the area in which they settled, without disturbing the ecosystem, for fulfilling a majority of their requirements. Thus, along with the migrant community came a distinct and unique culture in which even the simplest items of daily use reflected their appreciation for craftsmanship and natural materials. Fortunately for them, the natural environment and climatic conditions in the Andamans were similar to that in Burma, and so were nearly all the raw materials available. Thus, they had no problem acquiring the raw materials needed for making various items and they hardly had to adapt or improvise any manufacturing techniques.

The British administration gave the Karen a month to settle down, and after that only the young men were called off to work in the forests. The elderly members, women and children stayed at home or worked on the land given to them by the administration. This gave them ample time and opportunity to create an environment similar to that in which they had lived in Burma, with similar material surroundings. Under these circumstances, the material culture and artefacts the first settlers crafted in the Andamans acquired a new meaning and emotional efficacy. The artefacts helped recreate the ambience of their old village and home. Being surrounded by things that were typical of their homeland not only made them feel comfortable, it also helped them feel connected to the culture and traditions of their homeland. In a way, the process of reproducing material items was a way of reconnecting with their past, creating a sense of continuity for the first generation of migrants. As Mrs Kane put it: 'There was no difference in Webi or any Karen village in Burma apart from the distance. We had reconstructed nearly everything just as it was in Natchaung village [in Burma], were we came from'. Thus they were 'at home' in more than one way in the Andamans.

The broad range of Karen functional items which can also be considered to have artistic dimensions include architecture and the products of weaving (mats, basketry, cloth), woodworking and metalworking. In addition, there are various performing arts which include dancing, singing and dramatics. The traditional Karen *shee* is a two-storey pile dwelling, constructed by family members with the help of close relatives, situated in the middle of sprawling fields and gardens, far from the sight of those on the metalled road. It rests on a framework of wooden and bamboo poles and has a wooden floor. The walls are made of bamboo mats, while the roof is made of a bamboo frame which is thatched with palm leaves. The ground floor is used to house domestic animals and as a granary, while the upper storey is used as the living quarters. The mat walls stand out as the most attractive part of the *shee* by adding to its beauty.

Mats are made of bamboo and various other locally available leaves, most notable among them being palm (*tal*) and tavoo leaves. Mats used as walls may either be 'rough' and made of crushed bamboo, or 'fine' which are made of finely split and polished bamboo. These are woven using the check or twilled plaiting techniques. Extra care is taken, however, with finer mats by weaving in various patterns or by mixing light and dark tints and different shades of the bamboo or leaves used. Fine mats upon which people sit or lie may have exceptional patterns, which are specially woven using kewra (a sweet-smelling flower) and palm leaves.

Among the traditional crafts, the Karen are adept at manipulating bamboo and cane in various artistic ways. Thus, baskets (*chey*) of various attractive shapes and sizes are found in most Karen houses. These are made using all the known techniques of basketry. Most common and eye-catching among these are the grain storage bin (*fossey*), medicine basket (*nabyadao, ta na my chey*), egg basket (*saathey*), clothes basket (*kandi*), winnowing tray (*koley*) and hat (*khoki*). Karen efficiency in bamboo and cane work can easily be seen in the beautifully crafted furniture which includes sofa sets, tables, chairs and stools. Bamboo and reeds are also used to make fishing traps (*buh*) for shallow-water fishing. Besides traps, nets (*pwa*) of various thicknesses are also woven for fishing in both shallow and deep water.

The art of weaving cloth with the help of a small portable handloom was brought by the migrants from Burma, and in the past all women wove their traditional garments – the blouse (*ochiyebo*) and wraparound skirt (*nee*) – on it. Apart from traditional attire, the Karen bag is also woven in a similar way with fine, colourful geometric patterns and tassels hanging down. The most popular colours used for weaving were red, black, white and blue.

Wood is used to fulfil several of the community's requirements and therefore woodwork is another area where the Karen traditionally display their expertise. Special mention must be made here of the indigenous canoe (*khlee*), boat (*dungi*), mortar (*sekhwo norito*) and various show pieces, besides the usual furniture, agricultural implements and household objects. All the items mentioned are examples of Karen craftsmanship and can be considered artefacts in their own right. The constant need for hunting, chopping and skinning knives (*dao*) of various shapes and sizes, fishing hooks, harpoons and other similar implements make it necessary for a few community members to learn the art of blacksmithing. This art was, however, never known to all, but only to two or three members of the community.

Lastly, there are the performing arts. The traditional Karen dance, *taka*, or 'bamboo dance' – since it involves the use of bamboo – is jointly performed by men and women. I found in the Karen *taka* certain similarities with the bamboo dance performed in the state of Nagaland in north-east India. It is possible this was due to Saw Setha's close contact with the Church in Nagaland, which he often visited. This, however, was my own observation and was brushed aside by Saw Setha, saying that the proximity of Burma to Nagaland was probably the reason for the similarities in the dance form. Traditional folk songs relate mainly to sowing, harvesting and fishing, besides which there are devotional songs praising Christ and other hymns that are sung in the church. A few traditional comedy skits and fables (plays with a moral) are performed on Christmas Eve and Good Friday. Only men take part in these plays, in which they disguise themselves as women and animals if the script so demands.

Social and Material Change: Becoming 'Modern'

Until the early 1980s, when members of other ethnic and caste groups started coming to and settling in the Andamans, the Karen had maintained many of their cultural practices, both material and non-material. Few changes had been introduced since their arrival. However, the gradual contact and interaction with other communities that began in the 1980s led to considerable transformations. The new non-Karen settlers – mainly from Ranchi, Madras and Bengal – brought their own cultural practices. Most of them had lived close to the urban mainland population and were influenced by urban consumer culture, where almost all items are bought from the market. The new settlers thus did not have the skills of crafting artefacts for themselves.

An increase in the number of settlers in the area led to the setting up of a larger market that catered for the needs and demands of this new population. Contact with the newcomers led to the Karen gradually developing a desire to own similar products. They regarded the use of such commodities to be an important part of being 'modern and developed', and hoped that consuming mass-produced goods would bring them closer to the mainstream population of the country. As a result, traditional Karen artefacts were gradually replaced by easily available market products. The sudden increase in the means of transport and communication, and exposure to new things through growing media facilities, also fed the wish of many Karen to be like what they saw as the more 'developed' mainstream population.[7] The result was a drastic change in Karen material culture.

Houses made of reinforced cement concrete and asbestos sheet are fast replacing traditional pile-built dwellings. In place of beautifully and finely woven mats and baskets, plastic furniture and aluminium vessels are being used at an increasing rate. Similarly, woodworking is no longer practised with the kind of zeal that it was earlier. A change in the traditional dress style is also evident: nearly 60 per cent of women have taken to the *salwar-kurta*, the dress form common in most parts of India. It is now mainly the elderly and a few middle-aged women who continue to wear traditional attire, which youngsters only wear while performing traditional dances and occasionally at festivals in an attempt to look 'fashionably ethnic'. Similarly, traditional songs are fast being lost to the latest Bollywood numbers among the youngsters in an attempt to show themselves up to date with the latest happenings on the mainland.

Thus, although the Karen have managed to maintain many aspects of their traditional lifestyle for years, in an attempt to 'progress' and 'become modern' they are gradually giving up much of their heritage, including their various arts and artistic activities. This is not surprising, since notions of progress and development promoted by discourses of 'modernity' have long been opposed to specific ideas associated with 'tradition'. It is a well-established and accepted fact that the entire discourse of 'tradition' versus 'modernity' was part of the colonial project itself, which presented so-called 'tribal' and 'eastern' cultures as static traditions and Western civilization as their modern, dynamic and innovative opposite. This opposition thus forms a part of the idea of 'the modern' itself, and has informed the social sciences. It remains a fact that for many years, numerous sociologists and anthropologists defined 'development' – itself a form of 'modernization' – in terms of contemporary Western models, presenting it as an improvement on situations in non-Western settings. It is only since the 1980s that scholars have started to question the entire discourse of 'tradition versus modernity', regarding various 'local' or 'vernacular' models of modernity, as an alternative perspective. Clifford, for example, 'does not see the world as populated by endangered authenticities ... rather [he] makes space for specific paths through modernity' (Clifford 1988: 7). Another important contribution is Knauft's edited volume, promoting an understanding of modernity along divergent lines and patterns. Knauft and his contributors agree that '[m]odernity as a concept is fraught with difficulties, especially in the singular' (Knauft 2002: 22).

It must be emphasized that there can be a vast variety of ways in which individuals respond to the introduction of new ideas and technology. While some vehemently oppose these, others gladly accept them while others try to create a kind of synthesis, amalgamating the best of both pre-existing and novel elements of culture. In any situation of change, individuals justify the different ways in which they evaluate change. Our task as social scientists is then to explore why particular people have specific views, and how their attitudes are shaped by wider structural processes.

In the case discussed in this chapter, while on the one hand the older generation opposed the change and lamented the disappearance of knowledge and certain skills, on the other hand the younger generation seemed to be blindly attracted to things that they perceived to be 'modern' and 'developed'. Karen youth are, however, not the only ones who seem to be influenced by, and indirectly support, the discourse of tradition and modernity. Years of considering Western societies as the most 'progressive' and 'developed' has affected numerous societies, especially those in the developing world. Thus, a substantial percentage of Indian citizens seem to blindly follow Western lifestyles. While a section of the educated urban masses tries to copy what they see as the 'Western culture model' in its totality – views, attitudes, behaviour and technical advancement – the rural masses copy local 'modern' populations in an attempt to be progressive and developed. Their attempt, however, only involves the adoption of the outward signs of modernity – the material culture, advanced technology and the use of consumer items. This attempt is almost always accompanied with the idea that to show oneself as being 'modern' and 'developed' one must also discard all traditional artefacts and material items, the possession of which indicate one to be 'traditional', 'old-fashioned' and 'un-' or 'underdeveloped'. The situation of Karen youth is similar, where in an attempt to join the mainstream many young Karen desire to possess the outward signs of modernity and progress – that is, a modern house (a permanent construction of RCC, bricks, stone and so on, and which does not need regular repairs), a motorcycle, an office job, satellite and cable TV, a music system, the latest clothes, and so on.

Decreasing Knowledge of Art and Craft Production Skills

The points made above are further strengthened by the quantitative data presented in Tables 6.1 and 6.2. As mentioned earlier, a few simple questions were put to the members of 298 families regarding their level of skill and knowledge relating to the main traditional art and craft activities. The data clearly indicates a decline in skills and output. Karen families specified that they considered a person deft in an art and/or craft if their products could be appreciated for certain qualities: *safai* (neatness, finesse), *khubsurati* (beauty and perfection) and *barabar ka kaam* (evenness, symmetry). Other indicators of deftness were being a fast worker, being able to produce innovative designs, being frequently asked by others for help and guidance in making similar artefacts, and being asked to produce an artefact for a token payment. One is believed to have 'basic skill' when one can produce an artefact without anyone's help, and an expert when all the above requirements are met.

Table 6.1 reveals that the art and craft practice in which most people are either deft in or possess the basic skills of is mat making, since the number of such families stands at 220. This is followed by basic woodwork (which includes the making of various implements, vessels and household furniture) and the construction of *shee*, which are known to 166 and 117 families respectively. The least well-known crafts seem to be handloom weaving, blacksmithing and the making of decorative wooden furniture and show pieces, which are known to members of one or two families only – that is, less than 1 per cent of the 298 families sampled. Meanwhile, a total of 71 families (nearly 24 per cent) reported that no one among them possessed any knowledge of a traditional art or craft. A point to note here is that, although members of a few of these families did have basic skills of some crafts, they asked me to count them out since they had either not attempted to make an artefact for a long time or needed constant guidance from others. Thus, although in percentage terms it may seem that a large

Table 6.1: Skill levels of traditional arts and crafts among Karen families in the villages under study.

Sl. No.	Art / Craft	Families (Total : 298)			
		Deft	Basic	Total	Percentage
1.	Construction of shee	52	63	115	39.59
2.	Basketry	11	49	60	20.13
3.	Mat making	98	122	220	73.82
4.	Basic woodwork	66	100	166	55.70
5.	Dungi and Khlee	5	2	7	2.34
6.	Wooden show pieces/ decorative furniture	2	—	2	0.67
7.	Black smith	1	—	1	0.33
8.	Weaving cloth	1	1	2	0.67
9.	Weaving of fishing nets	15	10	25	8.38
10.	Dancing / Singing	20	27	47	15.77
11.	Drama	5	2	7	2.34
12.	None of the above			71	23.82

Note: a family is categorized as deft in a specified art/craft if one or more members of the family are considered deft by the community members.

number of families have no knowledge relating to traditional arts and crafts, in fact it is not completely so.

Tables 6.1 and 6.2 merely support the qualitative analysis that reveals the complex situation which has arisen in the community in relation to art and craft activities. It is easily observed from Table 6.2 that traditional art and craft skills are unevenly distributed among the sample. It can be seen that skill in traditional arts and crafts is more common among those over 40 years of age, to whom it is considered an important part of their life, whereas the younger generation either have no knowledge pertaining to these at all or have only some basic knowledge. This reveals a casual and disinterested attitude among youths towards an important aspect of their culture. In fact, the tables clearly indicate that most of the skilled artists and craft producers are aged 50 years and over. And it is this very group whose members passionately propagate the production of traditional art forms, arguing that the slow production process not only results in valuable products but also increases makers' personal well-being and stimulates harmonious sociality.

Case Studies

We can better understand the situation and emotions involved by considering the views of a few individuals. The cases also indicate the emotional impact of different artefacts on different people.

Naw Lalachi

Forty-nine-year-old Naw Lalachi of Deopur is one of the three women to have kept alive the art of weaving traditional Karen cloth on the handloom. Laughingly, in a soft and modulated voice which did not, however, camouflage the sarcasm and dejection she felt, she asked me: 'Why are you so interested in this? Are you trying to make fun of me? My children feel quite embarrassed to tell outsiders that their mother weaves cloth on a handloom. They feel it is a sign of being uneducated and rustic'. Showing me a piece she was weaving, she asked:

> It is not that bad, eh? I learnt it from my mother and she did from her mother who had come from Burma as one of the first settlers here. But today none of my two daughters are interested in learning this ... But still, there are some people among us who like to use the traditional Karen bag and so I manage to sell three to four bags for 80–90 rupees each in a year.

The clashing views of individuals relating to the same art can be gauged from this case. While most of the youngsters consider traditional items to be a source of embarrassment, being a sign of backwardness for them, a majority of the elderly still feel attracted to such things, which are a part of their culture and tradition.

Table 6.2: Distribution of knowledge by age and sex of traditional art and craft production skills.

Sl. No.	Art / Craft	0-14 years		15-39 years		40-49 years		50 years & above		Total having knowledge of the art/craft
		Male	Female	Male	Female	Male	Female	Male	Female	
1.	Construction of shee	—	—	161 (43.4)	123 (33.5)	59 (72.0)	36 (52.2)	74 (97.4)	69 (97.2)	522 (31.4)
2.	Basketry	—	—	30 (8.1)	72 (19.6)	30 (36.6)	50 (72.5)	52 (68.4)	66 (93)	300 (179.3)
3.	Mat making	—	1 (0.3)	101 (27.2)	221 (60.2)	76 (92.7)	61 (88.4)	70 (92.1)	71 (100)	601 (36.0)
4.	Basic woodwork	—	—	45 (12.1)	—	64 (78.0)	—	71 (93.4)	—	180 (10.8)
5.	Dungi and Khlee	—	—	1 (0.3)	—	3 (3.7)	—	5 (6.6)	—	8 (0.5)
6.	Wooden show pieces/ decorative furniture	—	—	—	—	1 (1.2)	—	2 (2.6)	—	3 (0.2)
7.	Black smith	—	—	—	—	—	—	1 (1.3)	—	1 (0.05)
8.	Weaving cloth	—	—	—	—	—	1 (1.4)	—	2 (2.8)	3 (0.2)
9.	Weaving of fishing nets	—	—	7 (1.9)	4 (1.1)	56 (68.3)	45 (65.2)	66 (86.8)	58 (81.7)	236 (14.1)
10.	Dancing / Singing	—	2 (0.7)	25 (6.7)	25 (6.8)	11 (13.4)	17 (24.6)	37 (48.7)	23 (32.4)	140 (8.4)
11.	Drama	—	—	2 (0.5)	—	5 (6.1)	1 (1.4)	7 (9.2)	1 (1.4)	16 (0.9)
	Total population	336	299	371	367	82	69	76	71	1671
	Total population	635 (38.0%)		738 (44.1%)		298 (17.8%)				1671 (100%)

Note: Percentage in parentheses

Saw Moses

Fifty-six-year-old Saw Moses from Lucknow is an expert in fabricating the traditional knife (*dao*) as well as a variety of fishing hooks and barbs for harpoons. At the time of my fieldwork he was the only blacksmith left in the community. When praised for his efficiency and fine work, instead of seeing pleasure what I got was a sad look that made his plight quite evident. He replied, 'This skill will die with me. None of the youngsters is interested in learning such a laborious art'. Then, in a strange, strangled voice he added, 'but it is fine ... that way I have no competition. Everyone comes to me to buy iron implements'. On the other hand, Saw Joseph, his nephew, pointed out:

> Hunting is banned so no one needs the *dao* for it. For fishing also, the latest equipment is easily available in the market, and nowadays with Chinese products being so very cheap to buy this is no longer a skill worth learning. I want to learn computers [he smiles]. That way I can get a well-paid job.

Here one easily gets an indication of how discussions regarding particular art and craft skills can trigger grief and dejection among some about what they see as a dying tradition, while the same generates a totally different feeling among others. Adopting a practical and indifferent attitude, such individuals justify not learning a craft skill since the demand for its end products is in rapid decline.

Saw Pantha and Saw Yudatha

Saw Pantha and Saw Yudatha from Karmatang-9, both in their late forties, were the only ones who could make the beautiful carved wooden showpieces and decorative furniture which are bought by well-off locals and tourists. Both were of the view that youngsters were not attracted to take the art up as a profession, since there is a lot of hard work and patience involved in the creation of every single piece, while the monetary return is low. In a very matter of fact manner, Saw Yudatha stated: 'The children of our community are now only interested in becoming "sir" and "madam" [by which he implied having office jobs]. Traditional occupations do not attract them'. Many youngsters see the learning of traditional crafts as a waste of time. This view reflects to a great extent the impact of the monetary economy on the community.

Saw Thompson and Saw Lashi

Thirty-seven-year-old Saw Thompson and 33-year-old Saw Lashi were residents of Latau. Both were doing very well in their fishing business, and belonged to one of the richest Karen families in Mayabunder. Although both had been trained as children in several of the traditional Karen arts, they noted that it was pointless to devote time and energy to them. They questioned me politely: 'Do you do such things? Then why do you want us to carry on with it? If we were to indulge in such things, we wouldn't be so well off today. Instead we too would be sitting in a corner satisfied weaving baskets and making cane furniture'.

Their comments reaffirmed the conclusions drawn from the previous case, and represented the thinking of the majority today. It can clearly be seen that many Karen strongly believe that to progress and develop one must leave the outward signs of being traditional or rural behind. Furthermore, many displayed the latest electronic gadgets in their houses – TVs, satellite dishes, DVD players and other items – demonstrating their interest in 'things modern'. Further discussions with most of the youth yielded almost identical views. A few sharper ones amongst them justified their stand, pointing to the strict government ban on cutting wood and use of forest products, most of which are the essential raw materials for traditional crafts.

Saw Thabadoo and Saw Thandey

Eighty-two-year-old Saw Thabadoo and 58-year-old Saw Thandey, both residing in Lucknow, were experts and ardent lovers of Karen arts and artefacts. Saw Thabadoo was the only one in the community who could make the traditional Karen winnowing tray and tortoise shell comb. He was also expert in all other wood, bamboo and cane crafts, and sold his products to fellow Karen who were unable to make the articles as skilfully as he did.

Saw Thandey worked as a guard for the Forestry Department, but loved making artefacts of bamboo and wood in his spare time. Both expressed their distress, talking about the future of their beloved arts, pointing out that their own children and grandchildren did not share their feelings. Saw Thabadoo commented sadly, 'Now everything is available in the market and no one needs to have even a basic knowledge for survival'. His statement revealed that for most of the Karen interested in traditional arts and crafts, craft making has become a source of both pleasure and sadness: they enjoy the practice themselves but regret the younger generation's lack of interest.

Art and Emotions: Clashing Views

Over the years, numerous studies have pointed out that arts and crafts do not merely deal with the creation of beautiful things, nor are they just an entertaining hobby for the rich and idle; rather, they have numerous other functions to perform that potentially increase feelings of well-being. Anderson put it effectively when he stated: 'art seems to have several qualities. It expresses as well as communicates. It stimulates the senses, affects emotions, and evokes ideas. It is produced in culturally patterned ways and styles; it has cultural meaning' (Anderson 1989: 11). More recently, psychotherapists and physiotherapists have started recommending art and craft production to people with emotional problems and physical disabilities, also drawing on the positive potential of engagement with material culture production.[8]

For the older generation, Karen art and craft production had a clear emotional meaning. Each piece produced by them had a social history; they attached special memories to them, relating the artefacts to their makers and users. When commenting on their attachment to these items, elderly Karen spoke in terms of 'feelings' (*mehsus karna, lagna*), 'perspectives' and 'thoughts' (*sooch*). They explained these to be individualistic, partly affected by one's upbringing and cultural background, and by specific socio-historical conditions. Lutz (1986) has argued that discourses of 'emotions' vary in different cultural settings, influencing people's outlook and moral judgements. In the case of the Karen, their understanding of 'feelings' explained why several of the older generation admitted that, if they would have been younger, they might have felt and behaved just like the youngsters do.

This insight does not take away their deep sense of regret for seeing their traditional arts slowly dying away. For people like Saw Thabadoo, Saw Thandey and Naw Lalachi, pursuing these arts and crafts kept them connected with their roots and brings back sweet memories of the past. For them their skills and products were an important part of their history, an indicator of their cultural background and an embodiment of their community's identity, which they felt they must keep alive. They felt emotionally attached to the skills they had learnt from their elders, and wished their children to continue with them. Often they would speak nostalgically of the days when they were being trained by their parents, grandparents and other elders. Furthermore, the elders emphatically stated that, while training a child in any art or craft, one is not doing just that. The process lends itself to informing the child of, and making them aware of their ancestors, cultural past and cultural heritage. It does not only teach the child an art or craft that has several uses in daily life, and make them familiar with and proud of the culture of the community, for it also brings about an emotional bonding with the older generation. This bond, they argued, was essential for cross-generational understanding. In a community like that of the Karen, they argued, this was all the more important because parents depended to a great extent on their children in the later part of their life. The closeness created during training helped them communicate effectively with each other, even at a later stage in life. Given the present situation, where children are no longer interested in the traditional arts, the elders also felt that they were missing out on the opportunity the training process would otherwise have given them to understand the younger generation and bond with them.

Criticizing the Effects of 'Modern Life'

All the elders of the community stated that pursuing the arts not only helped increase one's level of patience but also brought about emotional stability, helping one to easily adjust to normal life. Saw Thandey explained: 'We are a very shy and peace-loving community. Our religion and Church tells us not to be aggressive, materialistic and greedy. In fact one should be happy with as little as possible'. To a great extent the elders attributed their calm and peaceful nature to their being involved in some form of art at an early stage in life. They stated that their elders had intentionally taught them to make art and craft objects because to do so was time consuming and required lots of patience. The need to focus kept their materialistic desires and ambitions under check. In addition, the use of naturally available resources for making most of their artefacts helped them develop an intense respect for nature and therefore work towards its conservation as much as possible. Interestingly, their views resonate with an alternative view of ecologically sustainable progress.

During my research I could easily see that the older generation felt more secure and comfortable with their traditional artefacts in and around their living quarters. This was probably why those of forty years and more who were not skilled craft persons preferred to buy traditional artefacts from those in the community who were more adept then they were, while the younger generation preferred to be surrounded by the latest market products which showed them to be 'modern'. The younger generation found it difficult to understand their elders' 'irrational' attachment to the 'old' arts and crafts. According to them these were things of the past and should be left in the past. Most of them felt awkward about the fact that they still used objects which according to them depict their 'poverty' and 'backwardness', revealing them to be *jahil*, 'unaware', 'uneducated', 'of a rustic disposition'. Several of the youngsters confronted me, asking: 'You too consider us backward and undeveloped, don't you? That is why you are here to study us. Why else are you not studying the urban developed people like yourself?' They stated that to progress they needed to change their lifestyle to a more modern one. The easiest way in which this could be done, they said, was by giving up the material signs of their past – their traditional dwellings, attire, bamboo craft, woodworking, and so on. Once the outward signs of belonging to a 'different' and 'migrant culture' were removed, they expected to easily become one with the rest of the country. They felt that to progress they needed the capacity to purchase mass-produced commercial products, and for this it was essential to devote their time to income-generating activities, rather than to arts and crafts. Thus, a situation has arisen in which the younger generation are discarding their traditional arts and crafts, but in the process they are also hurting the feelings of their elders who feel proud of these, objects and skills that to them represent their 'cultural uniqueness'. The indifferent attitude of the youngsters towards the Karen traditional arts and artefacts is further adding to the distress and regret felt by the elders for what they see as their 'dying arts'.

Youth Work and the Politics of Tribal Status

Under these circumstances, the only ray of hope for reviving traditional Karen arts and crafts seems to be the Karen Youth Organization (KYO).[9] In pursuance of its aims, the KYO has started encouraging youngsters to marry within their own ethnic group, and stimulating them to take up traditional arts and crafts, at least as a hobby, to help maintain the community's 'cultural identity and uniqueness'. However, while the organization is encouraging the youngsters to be involved in the production of traditional arts, it neglects involving the older generation of the community in its endeavours. This can be considered one of its drawbacks, since suggestions and guidance from the elders could have proved a great motivator for the community, potentially increasing the pace of revival. The fact that the *taka* dance has been revived due to the earnest attempts of Father Saw Setha and his wife is a clear indication that, if attempted, all the traditional arts and crafts may be revived. I say this despite it being quite evident that the entire discourse of 'dying arts' and 'cultural uniqueness' is being politicized by the KYO in an attempt to support and justify their claims that the Karen are an underdeveloped, homogeneous community with a distinct culture so as to be granted the funds and privileges of being recognized as a 'scheduled tribe'.

In India the politics of 'scheduled tribe' status is very complicated. In recent years, several such attempts have been made by communities at various levels, adopting different means to achieve their goal.[10] In the Andaman Islands too, several communities, including the Karen, have tried to gain 'scheduled tribe' status. An active member of the KYO informed me that the shortage of employment opportunities in the area, and the difficulty of securing employment when opportunities arose, had given rise to the idea that the KYO should put forward a demand that the Karen should be categorized as such. This would be very beneficial, since almost all the posts reserved for 'scheduled tribes' on the Andaman Islands were occupied by the Nicobarese, who constituted 98 per cent of the total 'scheduled tribe' population.[11] If granted the desired status, the Karen would stand a very good chance of acquiring good jobs, besides various other benefits, there being no competition from other tribal groups besides the Nicobarese. The Karen are trying to justify their demand, stating that they were considered and are still considered a tribal group in Myanmar before they came to India, and therefore should be considered one in India too. In conclusion, although the Karen may never be granted tribal status in India, if the KYO seriously takes up the task of reviving other traditional arts and crafts in a manner similar to the *taka*, they might be able to salvage whatever knowledge of these remains before it dies out.

Notes

1. I am grateful to Maruška Svašek, not only for inviting me to the workshop on 'Migrant Art, Artefacts and Emotional Agency' held at Queens University, Belfast, in February 2007, where the first draft of this chapter was presented, but also for her valuable comments and suggestions which have helped develop the chapter tremendously. I would also like to thank the anonymous referees who pointed out areas requiring clarification.
2. This legend is taken from Anon. (2001), a Karen-produced document published as a souvenir of the jubilee celebrations that marked the 75th anniversary of Karen settlement in the Andamans. For more Karen legends, see Marshall (1922).
3. The epithet 'peace loving' is one Karen use to describe themselves, and is to be found in the contributions to Anon. (2001). Saw Thande also informed me that it was because of their very 'shy, peace-loving and timid nature', and their reputation for this, that the community remained unharmed during the Second World War when the Japanese captured the Andamans. As Saw Thande put it to me in 2003: 'Neither the British army nor the Japanese army troubled us. Not one of our men or women were ever captured since we never sided with anyone. We just did our own work. During that time we were new migrants and hardly even spoke to non-Karen. Non-Karen started settling in the nearby area only in the eighties. Till then there was no outsider here to interact with. So we lived a very aloof and secluded life, happy with ourselves here. Even in Burma, our ancestors never fought or revolted against the rulers, they preferred to move to a more peaceful place and that is why the Karen have migrated so much in the past'.
4. The shortage of labour arose because people from the mainland were not ready to relocate to the Andamans. This was mainly due to three reasons. Firstly, traditionally Hindus believe that crossing the sea causes them to lose their caste, and this would lead to expulsion from their caste group. Secondly, the distance of the Andamans from mainland India and hazards of travelling by boat caused many to be too afraid of going there. And lastly, the islands had a reputation of being a dreaded place from where no one ever returned. The latter belief is due to the fact that during the colonial period freedom fighters were sentenced to life imprisonment in the cellular jail of Port Blair, capital of the Andamans, and were not allowed to return to the mainland.
5. I was also informed, in confidence, by some elder Karen that they used to travel illegally between the two countries by boat to meet relatives until the early 1980s. Thereafter, however, travelling became dangerous because of an increase in patrols by the Indian Navy, and so such visits had to be stopped.
6. See, e.g., Matravers (1991, 2001), Hjort and Laver (1997), Mistretta (2001), Silver (2001), Jurist (2006) and Svašek (2007a, 2007b).
7. Post-independence, Indian state policy promoted technical advancement and modernization in a bid to accelerate the pace of overall development in the country.
8. For more details on the use of arts and crafts by psychotherapists and clinical psychologists for curative and therapy purposes, see Coleman and Farris-Dufrene (1996) and Zahavaeva (2005). For a more general idea of art therapy one can visit internet sites such as Art Therapy Blog (http://www.arttherapyblog.com/art-therapy-benefits/, retrieved 15 May 2009) and the art therapy entry in the medical dictionary of Farlex's Free Dictionary site (http://medicaldictionary.thefreedictionary.com/Art+Therapy, retrieved 15 May 2009). As for physiotherapy, in India, as in several other places, physiotherapists are advising people with partial paralysis, including

restricted hand or finger movement, to practice an art or craft which would involve the movement of the hands and fingers. This not only helps exercise without pressurizing the patient too much, but is also believed to have a positive psychological effect on the patient which helps speed up recovery. Surprisingly, I found one such case during fieldwork among the Tharu tribals of Lakhimpur-Kheri (India) where a semi-paralysed man had been advised by a local healer to weave traditional hand fans (a time-consuming involving twilling fine multicoloured woollen strands on to fine cane strips to form various geometric patterns) in an attempt to help him exercise his fingers. According to the patient himself, twilling the fans had not only helped improve his condition and grip to a great extent, but it had also made him feel more worthwhile since he could now manage to do several little tasks himself.

9. The KYO, as mentioned earlier, was established in 1994 by a small group of educated Karen for the improvement of the community and to voice demands in an organized manner. Officially, the KYO has ten aims, three of which are important in the present context: '1) To educate the youth of the Karen community about their culture and traditions, language, folk songs and folk dance. 2) To support and help the youth of the community in setting up facilities for imparting knowledge in the fields of agriculture, fishery, poultry, pig rearing, wood work, cane and bamboo work, weaving and allied subjects which will help in the development of the community ... 6) to conduct seminars, exhibitions and other culture and support activities for the development of the Karen community' (KYO 1994). The other seven aims deal with encouraging education and with the acquisition of loans, grants, donations and so on. Although at present the founding members (all in their mid or late 40s) are the only ones to play an active role in the functioning of the KYO, with Saw Setha (acting as general secretary) looking after a majority of its work and day to day activities, there are a number of teenagers and youngsters also who are now getting involved with the organization following encouragement from its founder members.

10. One of the most recent was the demand for 'scheduled tribe' status by the Gujjar community of Rajasthan in mid 2007. This, however, took on a very ugly and fierce turn involving the heavy destruction of public property, such as railway tracks, trains and buses. To add fuel to the fire, the dominant Meena (who have tribal status) vehemently opposed the Gujjar demand, fearing stiff competition from them if their demand was met. This led to armed clashes between the two groups. The entire episode not only cost the country a great monetary loss but also led to the death of several people and exposed the ugly side of the desire to develop and progress using shortcuts.

11. The Union Territory of Andaman and Nicobar Islands has a total of six 'scheduled tribes': the Sentinelese (who remain to this day hostile and unapproachable), Jarawa (a very primitive tribe; totally uneducated and having only just begun contact with the outside world), the Great Andamanese, Onge and Shompen (all of whom are in a stage of transition from their primitive lifestyle and are numerically very small) and the Nicobarese (who are the most developed, educated and modern among the rest).

References

Anderson, R.L. 1989. *Art in Small-scale Societies*. Englewood Cliffs, NJ: Prentice Hall.

Anon. 2001. 'Karen Settlement in Andaman and Nicobar Islands'. Junglighat: Mahesh Offset.

Clifford, J. 1988. *The Predicament of Culture: Twentieth-Century Ethnography, Literature, and Art*. Cambridge, MA: Harvard University Press.

Coleman, V.D., and P.M. Farris-Dufrene. 1996. *Art Therapy and Psychotherapy*. Bristol: Taylor and Francis.

Coomar, P.C. 1994. 'Karen', in K.S. Singh (ed.), *People of India*, Vol.12: *Andaman and Nicobar Islands*. Madras: Affiliated East-West Press, pp. 87–95.

Dash Sharma, P. 2006. 'Introduction', in P. Dash Sharma (ed.), *Anthropology of Primitive Tribes in India*. New Delhi: Serials Publication, pp. xi–xxx.

Ghosh, A.K. 1955. 'The Andaman and Nicobar Islands', *Census of India, 1951*, Vol. 17, Parts 1 and 2. Delhi: Manager of Publications, Government of India, Annexure C.

Hjort, M., and S. Laver (eds). 1997. *Emotions and Arts*. New York: Oxford University Press.

Jurist, E.L. 2006. 'Art and Emotion in Psychoanalysis', *International Journal of Psychoanalysis* 87: 1315–34.

Knauft, B.M. (ed.). 2002. *Critically Modern: Alternatives, Alterities, Anthropologies*. Bloomington: Indiana University Press.

KYO. 1994. Registration papers of the Karen Youth Organization. Unpublished document.

Lutz, C. 1986 'Emotion, Thought, and Estrangement: Emotions as a Cultural Category', *Cultural Anthropology* 1(3): 287–309.

Maiti, S. 2004. 'The Karen: A Lesser Known Community of Andaman Islands (India)', *Man in India* 90(3/4): 627–42.

Maiti, S., and M.K. Agarwal. 2007. 'Demographic Analysis of a Small Community with Special Reference to Fertility Trends: The Karen of Andaman Islands (India)', *Journal of the Indian Anthropological Society* 42(1): 83–98.

Marshall, H.I. 1922. *The Karen People of Burma: A Study in Anthropology and Ethnology*. Ohio: Ohio State University.

Matravers, D. 1991. 'Art and the Feelings and Emotions', *British Journal of Aesthetics* 31(4): 322–31.

———— 1998. *Art and Emotion*. Oxford: Clarendon Press.

———— 2001. *Art and the Emotions: A Defence of the Arousal Theory*. Oxford: Oxford University Press.

Mistretta, S. 2001. 'Art and Emotions', *Ballet Instructor's Newsletter*. Retrieved 12 January 2007 from: http://www.100megsfree4.com/ballet/newsletter2.html.

Radcliffe-Brown, A.R. 1922. *The Andaman Islanders: A Study in Social Anthropology*. Cambridge: Cambridge University Press.

Roy, S.B. 1998. 'The Karen of Andaman Island: A Demographic Study', in *Anthropology of Small Populations*. Calcutta: Anthropological Survey of India, Ministry of HRD.

Silver, R. 2001. *Art as Language: Access to Emotions and Cognitive Skills through Drawings*. Philadelphia, PA: Brunner-Routledge.

Singh, K.S. (ed.). 1994. *India's Communities: H–M*. New Delhi: Oxford University Press for the Anthropological Survey of India.

Svašek, M. 2007a. *Anthropology, Art and Cultural Production*. London: Pluto.

——— 2007b. 'Moving Corpses: Emotions and Subject–Object Ambiguity', in H. Wulff (ed.), *The Emotions: A Cultural Reader*. Oxford: Berg, pp. 229–48.

Zahavaeva, A. 2005. 'Art as Philosophy of Healing', *The Philosopher*. Retrieved 8 June 2008 from: http://www.the-philosopher.co.uk/healing.htm.

7

ARTEFACTS AS MEDIATORS THROUGH TIME AND SPACE:
THE REPRODUCTION OF ROOTS IN THE DIASPORA OF LUSSIGNANI

———◆◆◆———

Enrico Maria Milič

In 2007, as part of my research on Italians originating from the island of Lussìn (today known by the Croatian name of Lošinj), which lies in the Adriatic Sea between Italy and the Balkans, I looked through a book of old photographs that illustrated the life of Italians on the island before their postwar exile. In the introduction, the editor, an elderly woman from Lussìn, stated:

> I have been the 'curator' of this photographic book about old times, but there is a need to credit the many, so many Lussignani and friends of Lussignani who helped me in so many generous ways. How could I name all of them? But I remember and thank all of them. Flipping through these pages we will feel again united and we will relive our past. (Hreglich Mercanti 2000: 3)

These words reflect the main argument of this chapter: that artefacts that constitute human environments have the potential to alter people's sense of time, space and self.[1] This topic was one of my most important concerns during my research between 2007 and 2009 amongst Italians originating from Lussìn.[2] During this period, I attended several events organized by them, both on the island and in Trieste, where numerous Lussignani have settled. I conducted forty mostly unstructured and semi-structured interviews, paying specific attention to the interviewees' interactions with artefacts and photographs relating to the island.[3] As Elizabeth Edwards has noted, photographs should not just be regarded as unproblematic visual documents of past times, but rather as 'multi-sensory objects, which in turn elicit multi-sensory responses that shape and enhance the emotional engagement with the visual trace of the past' (Edwards 2010).

Emotions are indices of what is important to humans (Oatley and Jenkins 1996: 122). During my fieldwork, I perceived expressions of 'interest' and 'attention' in my informants as emotional engagement (Milton 2005a: 33), taking cues from their 'postures, inflections of the[ir] voice, [and] facial expressions' (Milton 2005b.: 223). These emotional pointers led me to understand that memories of and claims to the island were partially fed through multi-sensorial engagement with publications such as the photographic book. In addition to verbal references to emotion words and evocative stories, they gave me a more complete view of their engagement with their own past and the past of others originating from the island.

Discourse and the Experience of Rootedness

The production of publications containing memories of 'old times' on Lussìn must be analysed against the background of Italy's involvement in the Second World War and postwar Yugoslav politics. During the Second World War, the island formed part of fascist Italy, but – as with other islands in the Kvarner region – it was claimed by Yugoslavia after the war. The new Yugoslav state-socialist regime that supplanted twenty years of fascism was marked by anti-Italian nationalism, which resulted in an exodus of the island's mainly Italian speaking people. According to historians, from 1945 to 1954 between 190,000 and 350,000 left in an often violent context of political turmoil, and ethnic and social revenge (Nemec 1998, 2003; Pupo 2000, 2004; Rumici 2001). The majority of these considered themselves Italians and many relocated to the new Italian Republic, just beyond the new border with Yugoslavia. Others settled in the rest of Italy, moved to other European countries, or migrated to Australia, the United States and elsewhere.

Hreglich Mercanti (quoted above) was one of the many Lussignani who settled in Trieste. Her book of photographs, entitled *Ricordando Lussìno* ('Remembering Lussìn'), contains pictures and text about prewar Lussìn, and the publication is one of many produced by the island's diasporic community. These publications include the main focus of this chapter, the quarterly journal *Lussino: Foglio della Comunità di Lussìnpiccolo*, known as *Foglio Lussino* for short. This journal is published by a Trieste-based formal organization of exiles from Lussìn, the Community of Lussìnpiccolo (*Comunità di Lussìnpiccolo*), founded in 1998. It is an A4-size, full-colour journal, varying between forty and eighty pages per issue, and is freely distributed to about 2,000 addressees, thanks to the voluntary contributions of diasporic Lussignani.

A dominant and emotionally evocative discourse in these various publications centres on notions of 'rootedness' and deserves particular attention. Licia Giadrossi-Gloria Tamaro, president of the Community of Lussìnpiccolo and chief editor of *Foglio Lussino*, has frequently used the term 'roots' to argue that it is crucial to keep the past alive. She has emphasized, for example, the need to 'reconstruct our roots, far-away from home' (*ricostruire le nostre radici lontani*) (Giadrossi-Gloria Tamaro in issue 24 of *Foglio Lussino*, 2007: 1). Roots keep plants and other vegetation firmly in the soil, and are essential to their survival, so the metaphor suggests that staying connected to the island is quite 'natural', and essential for Lussignani well-being and survival.

The call for the reconstruction of roots by some Lussignani has a wide reach; their publications, and in particular *Foglio Lussino*, are distributed all over the world. These textual artefacts are read, looked at and touched by members of a global diaspora who, it will become clear, increase their sense of belonging to Lussìn when engaging with the texts and photographs.

My analysis builds on anthropological studies that have explored diasporic connections to homelands (Malkki 1992; Clifford 1994; Tweed 1997; Rapport and Dawson 1998; Friedman 2002; Ballinger 2003, 2004). I explore the capacity of an object, the diasporic journal, to trigger and transmit memories of the past, providing an artefactual focus for transnational identification.[4] As several scholars have demonstrated, artefacts can express and evoke strong emotions (Miller 1987; Gell 1998; Navaro-Yashin 2007), and emotions may be politicized in specific historical and social contexts (Svašek 2006, 2007). I take inspiration from the analytic framework of Svašek (2005), who has explored emotional processes as discourses, practices and embodied experiences. I will show that the idea of rootedness does not only create knowledge about Lussignani subjectivity but also arises from and reinforces embodied memories and imaginations of loss of and yearning for the island.

In this chapter I argue that it is necessary to move beyond approaches that analyse 'rootedness' as a textual metaphor (Malkki 1992; Ahmed 2004; Ballinger 2004), and add a perspective that takes bodily and sensorial experiences into account (Csordas 1990). I will show that *Foglio Lussino* functions as an emotional agent that has extended the capacity of the Lussignani to communicate beyond the immediacy of a shared time–space framework.

Losing Lussìn

The Yugoslav Census of 1945 recorded 1,989 Italians and 972 Croats in the municipality of Lussìn, named after its main town, Lussìnpiccolo (Mali Lošinj in Croat). Sixteen years later, the number of Italians recorded had declined to 75 while Croat numbers had risen to 3,354 (Argenti

Tremul et al. 2001).[5] After the absorption of Lussìn by Yugoslavia, its Italian schools and the local association representing the Italians of the island were closed by the authorities. The elderly Lussignani I spoke with stressed that the new regime did not welcome any display of attachment to Italy and its languages, Italian and Venetian. The many houses left abandoned by the exiles were taken over by newcomers from the Yugoslav mainland.

The social equilibrium between the two communities that had lasted at least a couple of centuries was overturned. The bourgeois strata of the island, almost entirely made up of old families of sea entrepreneurs and captains speaking Venetian, quickly disappeared. Croats became the leading ethnic group and hid much of the visible evidence of Italian-Venetian presence. They destroyed monuments, and removed Italian road signs, and even today references to the Italian past are often embarrassingly absent in publications by local historians and tourist agencies.[6]

For those Italians who left, the loss of their homeland was a shocking experience. They had to mediate 'a lived tension' and were faced with 'the experiences of separation and entanglement, of living here and remembering/desiring another place' (Clifford 1994: 311).[7] The few Italian Lussignani who decided to stay found themselves destabilized as the changing landscape triggered feelings of homelessness. As Ballinger notes with regard to the wider group of Italians living in Post-Yugoslavia, even today they admit to having 'a sense of an interior displacement, an exile of the heart and mind, if not the body' (Ballinger 2003: 220). Under these new political circumstances, the Lussignani had to reorganize their social life, either away from the homeland or in a completely new context on the island.

After having resettled elsewhere, the diasporic Lussignani made efforts to keep in touch through family and other networks, gathering periodically, often meeting up in Lussìn or in other localities around the world. As I have already indicated, over the last twenty years in particular, publications about Lussìn have started circulating, creating a media-connected transnational community. These books and journals not only serve as a platform for communication, but – in the form of photographs of pre-exile Lussìn – they are also material realities that are added to other material memories of the island. In the homes of most Lussignani, particularly those of the first generation, I saw many objects referring to the past. Ballinger found the same in the homes of Italian exiles from Istria, who 'attempt[ed] to relocate and re-create Istria not just mentally ... but also in their new dwellings' (ibid.: 172). She reports a variety of objects and images – including photographs, paintings, stones taken from the homeland, fragments of the family home's foundation, or vials of seawater. Similar practices have been explored in other studies of exiles, such as Cubans in Miami (Tweed 1997) and Sudeten Germans in Bavaria (Svašck 2002).

The Transgenerational Transmission of Feelings

In the case of the Lussignani, the generation of those who left the island has inevitably entered its last years, which adds a matter of urgency to their cause. The transmission of Italian Lussignani identity to the younger generation has become a key preoccupation for some. When the founder of the Community of Lussìnpiccolo, Giuseppe Favrini, died in 2005, the new president, Licia Giadrossi-Gloria Tamaro, stated in *Foglio Lussino*: 'The life of our Community continues not just because of the will of Giuseppe Favrini who provided [us with a] conscience and urged all of us to research the historical and cultural truth of Lussìn. It is because of all of us: we want to continue, to search for and share knowledge about our roots' (Giadrossi-Gloria Tamaro 2006: 1).

In April 2007, Licia said to me that she actually had no real recollection of her departure from the island: 'This is my experience, but I am already a person that didn't live through the exodus, I lived it through the account of others'. I encouraged her to recall her knowledge of her family's departure from Lussìn, at which time she was two years old. Visibly moved, she stated:

> These are very old memories for me ... I remember the dolphins that went down the side and past the boat ... This is for me an unconscious memory, as now, when I think about it, I can't remember it ... Obviously it has been a pain too big, that of losing both of my parents in an accident, hit [in Trieste] by an army truck driven by a drunk Englishman.

She referred here to the postwar presence of British and American soldiers in Trieste. At the end of April 1945, almost all the north-eastern Balkans became part of Communist Yugoslavia, while the main city of the region, Trieste, and a tiny strip around it, was ruled from 1945 to 1954 by the Anglo-American Allied Military Government. In 1954 Trieste was again incorporated into Italy. Continuing her story, Licia recalled how, at the end of the 1990s, she moved back to Trieste from Cortina, where she had spent a great part of her life. In Trieste she intensified contact with friends of her father, who showed her photographs of him attending the Nautical School in Lussìn. She began meeting a larger group of Lussignani whom she characterized as 'interesting persons, well educated, enterprising'. They kept telling her about life on the island, and the stories helped her to familiarize herself with her deceased parents' past. In 1998, she formalized her engagement, deciding to join the Community of Lussìnpiccolo. She explained: 'I joined and it has been a passion, a really interesting discovery for me as I retrieved my roots'.

Her second-hand knowledge about the island turned into lived experience once Licia began participating in the physical world of the exiles. Emotional interaction was vital. She made new acquaintances, interacted with them, listening to their recollections, and engaged with material objects and images relating to the past on the island. Physical co-presence and interaction with the artefacts thus enabled her to resonate the experiences of others in her own body, finding roots beyond her own past experiences.

Experiencing Roots through *Foglio Lussino*

But what do Lussignani mean when they say they care about their 'roots', and how does the journal give space to individual voices? Konrad Eisenbichler, son of two Italian exiles from Lussìn and an academic working in Canada, was asked by the journal what Lussìnpiccolo (the main town of the island) represented for him:

> It is my roots, the place where I was born, light and heat. After all, I am a Lussignano, independent of the fact that they assign different citizenship to me. Lussìn is my most important point of reference. I was much too young at the time of the exodus and so I didn't experience directly that period and the reasons for our departure as my parents did. I can understand their pain but my perception of the island is completely different from theirs: it is open, engaging and passionate. (Turcinovich Giuricin 2009: 2)

Like Eisenbichler, many Lussignani use the discourse of roots to refer to a sense of belonging to a well-specified place (the island), to identify social roles (for Eisenbichler his relationship with his parents) and identities (his citizenship), to point to a dynamic emotional attachment ('different from theirs', 'light', 'heat', 'engaging', 'passionate') and to the political quality of the latter ('open', which I understand here to mean a sense of being 'inclusive' and 'open to diversity').

Following Safran (1991), Clifford has suggested that a diasporic, 'collective identity' is defined by the relationship between 'a history of dispersal, myths/memories of the homeland, alienation in the host (bad host?) country, desire for eventual return, [and] ongoing support of the homeland' (Clifford 1994: 305). Eisenbichler's words reveal the complex emotional dimensions of diaspora formation where the second generation may have a quite different emotional attachment to the homeland than their parents, creating a new relationship with the place of origin. This makes the notion of 'collective' misleading. Eisenbichler does, however, feel empathy for his parents, and uses the journal as a platform to express feelings for the place where, like his parents, he was born. His words are intended to move younger generations who were born away from the island. Connecting older generations with younger ones, material objects such as *Foglio Lussino* play an important role as what Nora has termed 'places of memory' (*lieux de memoire*), a concept that identifies a history that 'rests upon what it mobilizes' or, better, provides a medium of 'carnal attachment to ... faded symbols' (Nora 1989: 24).

Objects as a Focus of Research

Numerous scholars have demonstrated that artefacts are often mediators of belonging, memory and identification (Nora 1989; Fabian 1996; Forty and Küchler 1999). My own theoretical interest in and methodological preoccupation with objects influenced the dynamics of fieldwork as I systematically encouraged interviewees to give voice to comments about the material reality surrounding them.

In April 2007 I met Gianni Piccini, an exile from Lussìn who was in his seventies. Before the exodus he was a labourer in a shipyard in Lussìn. After his exile, he became an employee in the Italian state-run railway in Trieste and is now retired. I explained I would like to know about his life story and his relation to Lussìn. When I entered his home in Trieste, he and his wife Eleonora Zerial warmly welcomed me, offering coffee, cake and ice-cream. The friendly behaviour of Gianni and Eleonora was partly expressed through several artefacts that were displayed in their living room. All the items related to their life, whether a collection of poems by their son or one of the several books, texts and images relating to people and places of Lussìn. Their friendliness was aimed at making me comfortable and at making me understand what they had gone through. In other words, they extended their selves through the working of artefacts (Gell 1998).

Rather tellingly, the initial attempt to constitute a relationship between us was founded very little on words and much more on objects and displays of feelings. Touching, opening and commenting on the objects in front of me and placing them in my hands lit up Gianni's face. A few minutes later Eleonora took down a picture of a sunny seascape in Lussìn to show to me. Gianni pointed out that this was one of the places where he used to swim with friends when he was young. At times I sensed that Gianni was particularly moved after handing me an object, and that, while watching me interact with it, he seemed to wait for an empathic reaction.

When I asked him directly what *Foglio Lussino* meant to him, he did not really have an answer. This stood in sharp contrast to his passionate handling of the journal as an evocative artefact. He was obviously bothered about his verbal silence because he rang me the next day. With an emotional tone in his voice, he explained that he had thought about it and had come up with a reply: 'The journal ideally deletes the space and the present. It is a *trait d'union*. It permits communication with people, it erases the distances within years, the kilometres'. For him, *Foglio Lussino* was a nexus allowing people to enter an imaginative and sentimental context created by themselves and other members of the diasporic group. As such, it was a space where he could feel and share the embodied presence of the island, something that had already been highlighted the day before through his focused bodily engagement with the journal.

The Island as *Mise en Scène* for the Memories of Lussignani

Analysing the work of the American photographer Shimon Attie, the psychologist Jeanne Wolff Bernstein has demonstrated how photographs can create a potential space in which past and present can suddenly come alive, blurring the relationship between subjects and objects. Producers of photographic representations infuse them with their own subjectivity through selection and approach, creating a 'transitional realm' where 'the spectator is given a wide realm of to-and-fro movements between past and present that permits the creation of an object world that did not exist before' (Bernstein 2000: 347).

In this section, I shall show how photographs published in *Foglio Lussino* provide a transitional experience, aiming to trigger a specific emotional effect. Every issue includes old photographs, such as shots of the school classes of the old Lussìn Nautical School, smiling Lussìn sea captains, and past events such as marriages within the community. Paintings of old ships as well as aged postcards of Lussìn are also recurrent items in the journal. One can find images of documents from the Habsburg era or the period under the Italian government as well as recent photographs covering several themes. The latter category of images includes shots from a summer reunion of exiles and their descendants having fun on some beach or scenic images of the beautiful landscapes and towns on the island.

The representations of present-day island life never show Croatian inhabitants. This is not surprising because, as Bolton has suggested, photographs can be 'methods for producing an alternative reality' (Bolton 1989: xi). The journal is also selective in other ways. The editor of the journal, Licia Giadrossi-Gloria Tamaro, told me she avoids pictures of people on the cover and instead usually chooses reproductions of old postcards or glorious landscapes of today's Lussìn. She explained: 'If you favour one person or another, then you could trigger envy: I'd prefer not to'. Furthermore, she reckoned that avoiding photographs of people on the cover creates a more 'ageless' publication, accessible to various generations.

During an interview in June 2009, I asked Licia to choose three images in the journal that she considered representative of the community she leads. One of these pictures (Figure 7.1) shows a bird's-eye view of the town of Ossero (Osor), placed in between the islands of Lussìn and Cherso (Cres).

Licia found the picture in a book published 'for tourists, and sailors in particular'.[8] She had herself contributed to this book, and stated: 'That's a wonderful, intriguing book, because it has very good quality pictures of wonderful places like Ossero that I have visited … But this picture … moves me, because here [in the journal] I know that there is a story behind it'. It shows, she said, 'Ossero, with its beauties and with its tragedies'.

The photograph offers multiple vantage points on the past, as Licia explained: 'In the text [that accompanies the photograph in the journal] we honour the deceased, and that's it. But the photograph of Ossero implies

LussinO

Foglio della Comunità di Lussinpiccolo
Storia, Cultura, Costumi, Ambiente, Attualità dell'Isola di Lussino

Quadrimestre 27 - Settembre 2008 - Spedizione in a.p. art.2 comma 20/c legge 622/96 - Filiale di Trieste C.P.O. - Via Brigata Casale
Tariffa Associazioni senza fini di lucro: art.1, comma 2, D.L. 353/2003 convertito in Legge 27/2/2004 n°46, DCB Trieste
In caso di mancato recapito inviare all'Ufficio Trieste C.P.O. per la restituzione al mittente che s'impegna a corrispondere il diritto fisso dovuto

Avvenimenti importanti per la nostra Comunità

di Licia Giadrossi-Gloria Tamaro

Nei mesi scorsi un evento di grande rilievo ha interessato la nostra Comunità: la posa della lapide in pietra d'Istria a memoria dei giovani militari italiani fucilati a Ossero il 22 aprile 1945.

È una testimonianza scomoda che finalmente riaffiora e rende onore a quei soldati italiani che lì hanno perso la vita e che da allora giacciono dimenticati in una fossa comune.

Il clima di terrore che si era creato a seguito dell'armistizio dell'8 settembre 1943, delle conseguenti occupazioni delle Isole da parte dei tedeschi e dei partigiani di Tito, della confusione che regnava tra i giovani italiani, arruolati da poco per servire la patria e subito abbandonati al loro destino, lo si sente ancora dai racconti dei testimoni.

A Ossero, nello stesso sito dove vennero fucilati i 21 militari italiani della X-MAS e i 7 del battaglione Tramontana di Cherso, vennero seppellite anche due partigiane di Tito, quasi subito riesumate, mentre, dall'altra parte del muro, all'interno del cimitero, sono sepolti 16 tedeschi e altri si trovano ancora in una fossa comune a Belei.

I 28 militari italiani sono tuttora abbandonati in quel campo ed è merito del capitano Federico Scopinich di aver condotto accurate ricerche in tutta Italia e "in loco" per conoscere le loro identità. Anche Flavio Asta della Comunità di Neresine si è impegnato a far luce su questa vicenda per tanti anni rimossa.

Adesso si può chiedere alle autorità croate e al Ministero della Difesa italiano, Commissariato Onor Caduti di Roma, di accordarsi per la riesumazione, con l'auspicio che non passino altri sessant'anni!

Figure 7.1: The cover of *Foglio Lussino* 27, September 2008: the town of Ossero. Courtesy of *Foglio Lussino*.

a broader story, that of Ossero, an old Roman city of 25,000 inhabitants, then abandoned because of malaria, now with 300 inhabitants'. An explanation of the these deceased is to be found in the article printed next to the picture, which mentions the recent ritual commemoration of twenty-eight Italian soldiers killed in April 1945 in Ossero. These men were killed by partisans and were officially commemorated on the island for the first time in July 2008.[9] The community of exiles made a particular effort to find the names of all those killed, and called for their exhumation in the name of their 'forgotten sacrifice for the country'. But as Licia makes clear, the photograph was intended to imply a 'broader story'. In the view of the editor and of many Lussignani, the history of Ossero, now with a Croatian majority population, should be linked to its Roman origins. Roman culture is seen as strongly connected to that of contemporary Italians, as opposed to the Slavic heritage of Croatian culture. Roman heritage, in other words, indexes the right of Italians to be acknowledged as rooted here.

Some of my informants could read local history into the image, associating Ossero with its Roman past and with the soldiers who were slaughtered as they defended their country. Both the connection to Roman (or pre-Italian) history and an Italian past of suffering reinforced the notion if the island as an 'Italian' space, potentially triggering feelings of sadness and anger about the 'injustice' that precipitated exile. While this was the aim of the journal's editorial board, this does not mean that they necessarily achieved their aim. Many of my informants said they normally skipped the articles, paying attention to the photographs rather than the text, which meant that to some extent they had the freedom to create other fantasies. Without the accompanying text, the pictures steered viewers towards feelings of nostalgia, pride and love for their homeland. Memories evoking sadness and anger about their loss were, however, always potentially present.

Licia's second example (Figure 7.2) was an image of a gentle storm (*neverin*) hitting the seafront of Lussìnpiccolo.

The picture was taken before the war by Mario Lussìn, one of a family that owned a photographic shop on the island. Mario Pfeifer, a descendant of the photographer, and who now lives in Milan, contacted the editor of *Foglio Lussino* via the internet and offered to share the picture with the readers of the journal. When I asked Licia what kind of emotions the picture triggered in her, she replied:

> Memories, I would say. Because it also portrays the house where my grandfather lived [after the war]. I went there several times, and I remember the storms, all the ships jumping because of this weather. When it was sunny, I remember that. Sometimes my cousin and I threw water from the window to people that were passing by on the seafront. We were young...

In Licia's last example (Figure 7.3), she showed me two pictures which showed contrasting conditions of the building of the old Nautical High School of Lussìn.

Figure 7.2: The cover of *Foglio Lussino* 29, April 2009: a gentle storm hitting the seafront of Lussìnpiccolo. Copyright Lošinj Museum.

The school educated many bourgeois Italians on the island who went on to be employed as sailors or in other sea-based activities. The school is thought to have been the cornerstone of the fortunes and culture relating to the sea among the Italians of Lussìn. As the right-hand shows, the current building has become a ruin in recent decades. Again I asked the editor what she and other Lussignani felt, seeing these two images. She replied:

> Anger, because of the [Croatian] wish to disregard all Italian or Venetian memories. In a place like this, such a precious thing ... has been only now been bought by an Austrian company that is going to make a four-star hotel, changing its dimensions. The end of this building marks the end of Italian and Venetian symbology. Nautical culture started [to be taught] here with the fall of the Republic of Venice, in 1797.

Licia's responses clearly indicate that exposure to the images as material realities is intended to feed feelings of rootedness, of belonging to the island.

The *Storia Minima* of Lussignani

The conservation and reproduction of relevant images of the past as a source of identity is a preoccupation for many communities wanting to reproduce their roots. Many communities, aware that social oral memory is vanishing and that '[written] history [will] soon sweep them away' (Nora 1989: 12) are absorbed in the preservation of artefacts triggering perceptions of their

Verso il 1840 si diffuse il convincimento che solo un Istituto Nautico pubblico avrebbe potuto soddisfare le esigenze di un centro marinaro in continuo progresso. Le istanze in merito trovarono accoglimento tre lustri più tardi, nel 1855, 150 anni fa. Il 17 gennaio di quell'anno veniva istituita la Scuola Nautica statale. Condizioni per esservi ammessi erano una sufficiente conoscenza dell'italiano e delle operazioni aritmetiche nonché un biennio di navigazione. La Scuola ebbe sede prima nell'edificio della Scuola Elementare sul piazzale del Duomo, poi nell'edificio del Comune e, infine, dal 1875 e fino alla sua chiusura del 1948, nell'edificio costruito sul piazzale all'angolo fra la Piazza e Prico.

In questa Scuola, prima privata e poi pubblica, si formarono capitani e armatori così preparati e intraprendenti da far crescere la marina libera di Lussino fino a superare, nel decennio 1860-1870, per numero di bastimenti e tonnellaggio, quella di Trieste. Con il nascere e progredire della navigazione a vapore questi capitani e armatori si trasferirono progressivamente a Trieste il cui porto, nel decennio 1930-1940, raggiunse Marsiglia al primo posto nel Mediterraneo. A Trieste le principali Compagnie di Navigazione, i Cantieri di Monfalcone, la prima Compagnia di aviazione civile italiana vennero fondate e appartennero ai Lussignani. Erano dei Lussignani le maggiori partecipazioni azionarie nelle Compagnie di Assicurazioni triestine. Erano pure lussignani gran parte dei più apprezzati Comandanti, Ufficiali e Marinai della Flotta mercantile triestina.

Due anniversari quindi, per noi Lussignani importantissimi: 200 anni dall'inizio a Lussino dell'istruzione nautica e 150 anni dalla fondazione della Nautica statale lussignana. Per ricordarli la nostra Comunità sta predisponendo la ristampa dei volumi pubblicati per due anniversari della Scuola statale, a Lussino nel 1905 per il 50° e a Trieste nel 1955 per il 100°. A Trieste perché nel 1955 si stava completando il nostro Esodo. La nostra Nautica era stata chiusa nel 1948, dopo 140 anni d'insegnamento ininterrotto nella nostra lingua italiana. Da Eroi tanti Suoi allievi sono caduti e tanti hanno combattuto per la Patria Italiana. Tutti hanno scelto con fierezza la via dell'Esodo.

Dal 1960 è stata aperta a Lussino una Scuola che prepara alle professioni marinare secondo l'ordinamento iugoslavo e croato. Scuola di lingua croata condotta da insegnanti croati che, salvo forse per la tecnica nautica, non possono in alcun modo considerarsi i continuatori degli insegnanti italiani che hanno determinato il prestigio della nostra Nautica. Oggi, salvo pochissime unità, insegnanti e alunni della Scuola croata sono figli e nipoti degli occupatori slavi. Tutto ci è stato rubato, la nostra isola, le nostre case, i nostri beni. Volevano anche, intenzione la più grave e offensiva, che rinnegassimo la nostra identità italiana. Ci siamo difesi, alcuni di noi sono stati uccisi, fucilati o annegati, in grandissima maggioranza abbiamo affrontato l'Esodo. Ora vogliono appropriarsi anche delle nostre gloriose tradizioni dicendo che sono anche le loro e sottintendendo così che tutti noi siamo di origine slava. Presentano infatti la loro scuola come la continuazione della nostra che, lo ripetiamo, non aveva niente a che fare con la loro. Solo ed esclusivamente agli allievi che in 140 anni si sono formati nella nostra Nautica italiana è dovuto il prestigio che Lussino ha raggiunto nel campo armatoriale, cantieristico, marittimo e anche sportivo velico. Durante tutto il secolo austriaco lingua d'insegnamento e materia principale era l'italiano. L'Austria rispettava la nostra identità latino-veneta e le nostre lingua e cultura. Durante i trent'anni italiani la nostra Nautica portava il nome dell'eroe istriano Nazario Sauro. Il Suo eroismo è stato d'esempio per

tutti noi. Non vogliamo fare la guerra. Vogliamo solo sia scrupolosamente rispettata la verità storica. Questo è lo scopo della nostra Comunità. Vorremmo non fosse dimenticato.

Figure 7.3: From *Foglio Lussino* 17, February 2005: the left-hand picture shows the Nautical High School of Lussìn, as it was before the Second World War; the right-hand picture, shot recently by staff of the journal, shows the current condition of the building. Courtesy of *Foglio Lussino*.

life world, and for some this becomes a political goal. As noted earlier, this
viewpoint holds true when we look at the text that accompanies cover-page
images in *Foglio Lussino*, for these always involve political statements or
deeply politicized views of history.

The journal also includes articles that give voice to individual memories.
In the words of editor Licia: 'I want the Lussignani to speak, I want to
remain aloof, I wish to print unpublished stories ... I don't want to print
news. I don't want to publish news items. At most, news items should
be a trigger [of memories]. I'm interested in each and everyone's *storia
minima*'. The texts of these *storia minima* (minimal stories) sent in by
readers occupy the vast majority of the pages of the journal. The stories
focus on the personal reminiscences of many, memories of a past that is
revitalized as they are shared through the publication. Usually, the texts
are personal accounts by exiles from Lussìn or their descendants. They
tell anecdotes about specific individuals, families or groups of people from
the island, providing an account of lived experiences or a sequence of life
episodes. The stories include accounts of events during an author's youth
on the island, and narratives about other elderly Lussignani or those who
have just passed away.

These texts usually occupy one page or less and can be read in two or
three minutes.[10] To take one example of a *storia minima*, the following
recalls a secret escape from the island during the years that followed the
Yugoslav take-over. The Yugoslav authorities banned many Italians from
leaving the country in the first decade after the war. Some Lussignani tried
to reach Italy by leaving at night in small boats, a dangerous undertaking as
one risked being shot by Yugoslav patrols. The text is a letter sent to *Foglio
Lussino* by Claudio Delise, an exile now residing in France and published
in issue 21 of the journal:

> I was at my brother's, who shared *Foglio Lussìn* 7, September 2001, with me.
> I am not able to express all my pain in reading the fate of my friend Mario
> Fillinich, one of those killed in Lischi in 1956 when trying to escape to Italy.
> In Lussìn, they all knew that they hadn't been lucky and that, maybe, they had
> been made prisoners, but not that they were killed. I remember an episode: we
> were kids, playing 'guards and thieves' in Cigale (a beach on Lussìn) ... Mario
> Fillinich hid behind a wall ... [All of a sudden] my brother Luciano appeared
> with lion-hearted courage with Mario over his shoulders. He had kind of
> fainted. We brought him to the beach, threw some water over him and then he
> came round. I tell you this without knowing that, later, he would be barbarously
> killed. His mother died from the pain. (Delise 2006: 31)

Once again, we can see that the journal helps people create connections
that go back and forth through time, reminding readers of the existence of
other Lussignani, updating them about their fate and creating a notion of
imagined community through transnationally distributed stories. The style
of the *storia minima* is very personal and gives the sensation of emotional
co-presence and dialogical interaction. This is very different from most

newspaper stories, in which journalists write in the third person and attempt to provide emotionally detached accounts of facts for anonymous readers.

Presenting an Alternative History

Michael Carrithers has identified two main genres in verbal production: narrative thought and paradigmatic thought (Carrithers 1992: 76–117). Paradigmatic thought is characterized by generalizations, where there is only one truth summarizing all experiences. Examples of paradigmatic thought are abstract discourses about religion, the history of historians and other ideological discourses, like those that imply the existence of a nation as a collective entity. By contrast, narrative thought is based on personal stories about individuals that implicitly call for the empathy of readers towards the characters of the story, and an eventual identification with them.

It may be clear that if readers can empathise with other readers and authors through *Foglio Lussino*, this does not happen by chance but by a careful politics of emotions on the side of the journal's editors. In Licia's view, the *storia minima* produce counter-knowledge that undermines official history:

> I remember there was a great lack of communication covering the experiences and the lives of the exiles. They have always been taken for granted by Italian politics and by the winners [of the Second World War]; those are the definitely the Resistance and the Left ... Therefore there was the need to tell ... your own personal stories to others. It is a historical, minimalist claim of lived experience, to also get a moral acknowledgement of a life choice that the Italian Republic almost dismissed.

Licia thus challenged mainstream ideological views of history, using the journal to allow Lussignani to claim personal, concrete connections to the island. It is again important to emphasize that her attempts have been politically motivated. *Foglio Lussino* has supported political interpretations of its *storia minima* on its covers, pushing the narratives closer to a paradigmatic genre of thought, reinforcing a perspective on the past that ignores the voices of Croats on the island. The editors have also defended their position by claiming historical objectivity. The editors have, for example, presented stories of secret escapes and suffering as historical facts that need to be addressed by the Italian and Croat governments. Based on these facts, the leaders of the exile community have demanded economic compensation for the loss of property they and their families incurred as a consequence of the advent of Yugoslavia and its take-over of Lussìn.

Interestingly, however, only a few of my interviewees emphasized their interest in political goals and compensation. Most of the older Lussignani I spoke with used the journal not as a political tool but rather as a medium for gaining access to other Lussignani and exchanging information and feelings about their past on the island.

Conclusion

In this chapter I have analysed the reproduction of the roots of a diasporic community through a specific artefact, the journal published by a Trieste-based group of exiles from the Adriatic island of Lussìn. The analysis has demonstrated that Lussignani discourses and experiences of roots claim emotional attachment to a place where the social life of their community developed before their expulsion from Lussìn. Roots are also seen in the empathic identification of Lussignani with other members of their community, which has strengthened feelings of belonging to a single transnational diaspora.

I described how individual Lussignani have appropriated objects and images that index their connection with their homeland – not just to mark space symbolically but also to create well-being. This behaviour can be understood when one is able to grasp the emotional dimensions of exile as felt by the exiles themselves. While the artefacts act as emotional agents, their effect depends on the emotional dispositions of their owners, who use them to create a nexus through time and space, satisfying an urge to feel united and connected to the past. When this happens, objects create new perceptions of spaces and times and the distinction between subjects and objects become increasingly blurred.

Crucially, the knowledge produced in the *Foglio Lussino* is knowledge based on embodied actions and interactions that contrast with mainstream journalism and history. It is embodied knowledge about past lived experience with which the old Lussignani can easily empathise. Objects like the journal can, in this sense, produce counter-knowledge that undermines official history by giving voice to individual views. Alternatively, the published stories may be used to make claims in the name of an imagined community.

The birth and social life of the journal has depended upon the capacity of younger generations of Lussignani to identify through empathy with the life worlds of the first generation of exiles. The journal has allowed some of their offspring and other sympathisers to make an experiential leap towards altered perceptions of time, space and selves, helping them to understand the Lussignani and their urge to remain linked to their homeland.

Notes

1. Many thanks to Maruška Svašek, who has been more than a guide in the thinking and writing of this chapter. I am also grateful to Paul Tout for his English skills.
2. In this chapter I prefer to employ the Venetian variant of the place name of the island, Lussìn. Although the Italian Lussino is almost always employed in the text of the journal which is the object of my study, I prefer the Venetian Lussìn. The latter is the

name of the island used in everyday oral communication by the islanders still living on the island and by many exiles in the diaspora. Moreover, using Lussìn better safeguards my distance from Italian and Croatian nationalisms using, respectively, Lussino and Lošinj. Besides the name of the island, when using a place name for the first time, I give both the Italian and Croat versions if they are available. I subsequently employ Italian place names as they are those usually used by the people under study. It should be noted that the name Lussìn is used in the 1911 edition of the *Encyclopaedia Britannica.*

3. This chapter is based on fieldwork conducted intermittently between April and August 2008, and examination of the journal *Foglio Lussino* in June 2009. A draft of the chapter was submitted to some of my most important interviewees in summer 2008 for comments and revisions. My interviewees include Lussignani in the diaspora and also several old Lussignani who did not leave the island and go into exile.

4. In interaction with people, objects are invested with meanings that reflect and assert who we are (Fabian 1996; Svašek 1996, 2007; Attfield 2000).

5. I provide these data to give a general idea of the phenomenon. The data of the censuses before, during and after the Yugoslav period contain many ambiguities and are obviously influenced by the political pressures on respondents and on those designing and interpreting the questionnaires. Some of these ambiguities are highlighted by Argenti Tremul et al. (2001).

6. The most blatant misrepresentations in public life overlooking the exile of Italian-Venetians from the island after the Second World War. Other contemporary practices concern the Croatization of history and language. In Lussìn, for example, the baritone Josef Kaschmann (1850–1925) and the naturalist Ambrogio Haracich are referred to (in books, brochures and on statues) as Croats and appear with Croatized names (Josip Kašman, Ambrož Haračić). According to my informants, there is historical evidence that suggests that these scholars could not have identified themselves as Croatian nationals. One-sided interpretations are not confined to the reconstruction of history. To Croatize the names and surnames of families originating in Lussìn, the spelling is changed. For example, on the official website of the public Lussìn Tourist Agency, 'Cosulich', the name of the Venetian family of ship-builders, has become 'Kozulić'. When the island was part of Yugoslavia this practice was widespread, and my interviewees claimed that such practices still occur today.

7. Similarly, the Istrian novelist, Claudio Tomizza, has written about the moment he left his home-town in the early 1950s: 'When the terms of the exodus expired, I made an opposite reasoning: the soul of things, of places, of memories, was transferred over there, on the other side. And I left, knowing or just fearing to locate myself in a space in between, neutral and difficult, and so many times I would have felt being a stranger, even to myself' (Tomizza 2001: 33). Tomizza claimed mixed cultural origins and lived his life between Trieste and his hometown, a place which staged a similar exile to that of Lussignani.

8. The image is taken from Magnabosco (2007).

9. The soldiers killed in Ossero came from all over Italy, and were part of the military unit known as X Mas. Between 1943 and 1945, the unit acted independently of Italian regular forces. After the collapse of fascism in 1943, there were two states ruled in the name of Italians: the monarchy in the south and the Italian Social Republic, governed by Mussolini, in the north. X Mas, formerly a special unit of the Italian army, deserted both and autonomously focused their actions on the north-east borders of the Italian monarchy, fearing the occupation of these territories by Yugoslav troops. X Mas has become historically infamous for its brutal war crimes, carried out in the name of the 'defence of the country'. The stories in *Foglio Lussino* that mention X Mas do not give a broader historical context but make a connection with Italianness and the state of Italy. One of my interviewees provided an interesting reflection on this absence of context (cf. Ballinger 2004). In the last years, the Italian

national debate about the Second World War has in many regards cleared fascism and its supporters. The frequent result is that the partisans and Allied troops are now considered no more worthy of commemoration than those who were considered to be 'on the wrong side'. However, it must be noted that the stories about the X Mas soldiers killed in Ossero do not represent the vast set of stories gathered in the journal that have no direct connection to nationalist discourses.

10. *Storia minima* revives in written form some aspects of 'the art of storytelling' (Benjamin 1968). Benjamin regarded storytelling as a performance, crafted for a community of listeners (cf. Spector 1998). As an editorial policy, the choice to include *storia minima* is reminiscent of the emphasis of much recent social-science literature on the inclusion of the voice of the informant, a reaction against earlier styles of detached scientific writing. As Clifford noted: 'Since the seventeenth century … Western science has excluded certain expressive modes from its legitimate repertoire: rhetoric (in the name of "plain", transparent signification), fiction (in the name of "fact"), and subjectivity (in the name of "objectivity"). The qualities eliminated from science were localized in the category of "literature"' (Clifford 1986: 5). The recent emphasis on alternative modes of writing that counteract more detached mass-media narratives has also occurred in communication studies. There is, for example, a huge debate about the radical difference of narrative approach bloggers take in contrast with much journalism in the mainstream media (Weinberger 2006). In a way, *Foglio Lussino* can be compared to blogs as a comparable reaction to mainstream knowledge broadcast by media and well-established institutions of education. For similar arguments on blogging, see also Milič, Marchetto and Costa (2008). It must be noted, however, that the charge of many exiles against biased mainstream representations of history can be ironically reversed against them. Quite often, Lussignani in the diaspora reinforce alternative readings of history through their personal stories that are similarly biased. According to Ballinger (2003: 44) and Sluga (2001: 176), a memory without shades of grey has been built for decades during the Cold War by the ghettoized work of regional historians, unable to escape from ideological (Western block versus Eastern block), 'ethnic', and national boundaries and perspectives. In Sluga's words, 'Western historians who have uncritically accommodated those representations and narratives' have been partly responsible (ibid.: 176).

References

Ahmed, S. 2004. *The Cultural Politics of Emotion*. New York: Routledge.

Argenti Tremul, A. et al. 2001. *La Comunità Nazionale Italiana nei Censimenti Jugoslavi 1945–1991*. Rovigno and Trieste: Centro di Ricerche Storiche di Rovigno/Unione Italiana-Fiume/Università Popolare di Trieste.

Attfield, J. 2000. *Wild Things: The Material Culture of Everyday Life*. Oxford: Berg.

Ballinger, P. 2003. *History in Exile: Memory and Identity at the Border of the Balkans*. Princeton, NJ: Princeton University Press.

——— 2004. '"Authentic Hybrids" in the Balkan Borderlands', *Current Anthropology* 45(1): 31–60.

Benjamin, W. 1968[1936]. 'The Storyteller', in H. Arendt (ed.) and H. Zohn (trans.), *Illuminations*. New York: Harcourt Brace, pp. 83–107.

Bernstein, J.W. 2000. 'Making a Memorial Place: The Photography of Shimon Attie', *Psychoanalytic Dialogues* 10(3): 347–70.

Bolton, E. 1989. 'Introduction', in E. Bolton, *The Contest of Meaning*. Cambridge, MA: MIT Press.

Carrithers, M. 1992. *Why Humans Have Cultures*. Oxford: Oxford University Press.

Clifford, J. 1986. 'Introduction', in J. Clifford and G.E. Marcus (eds), *Writing Culture*. Berkeley, University of California Press, pp. 1–26.

———— 1994. 'Diasporas', *Cultural Anthropology* 9(3): 302–38.

Csordas, T.J. 1990. 'Embodiment as a Paradigm for Anthropology', *Ethos* 18(1): 5–47.

Delise, F. 2006. 'Lettera', in *Foglio Lussino*, Issue 21. Triesk: Associazione italiana del Lussignani non più residenti a Lussino.

Edwards, E. 2010. 'Photographs and History: Emotions and Materiality', in S. Dudley (ed.), *Museum Materialities: Engagements, Interpretations*. London: Routledge.

Fabian, J. 1996. *Remembering the Present: Painting and Popular History in Zaire*. Berkeley: University of California Press.

Forty, A., and S. Küchler (eds). 1999. *The Art of Forgetting*. Oxford: Berg.

Friedman, J. 2002. 'From Roots to Routes: Tropes for Trippers', *Anthropological Theory* 2(1): 21–36.

Gell, A. 1998. *Art and Agency: An Anthropological Theory*. Oxford: Clarendon Press.

Giadrossi-Gloria Tamaro, L. 2007. 'Editoriale', in *Foglio Lussino*, Issue 24. Triesk: Associazione italiana del Lussignani non più residenti a Lussino.

Hreglich Mercanti, N. 2000. 'Introduction', in P. Budinich and N. Hreglic Mercanti (eds), *Ricordando Lussino*, Vol. 5. Trieste: Rigoni, pp. 1–3.

Magnabosco, P. 2007. *Adriatico*, Vol.2: *L'arcipelago delle Absirtidi: le isole di Cherso e Lussino*. Vicenza: Magnamare.

Malkki, L.H. 1992. 'National Geographic: The Rooting of Peoples and the Territorialization of National Identity among Scholars and Refugees', *Cultural Anthropology* 7(1): 24–44.

Milič, E.M., E. Marchetto and R. Costa. 2008. 'Online Blogging Communities Questioning Real World Politics: An Italian Case Study', *Reconstruction*. Retrieved 12 October 2009 from: http://reconstruction.eserver.org/084/milic.shtml

Miller, D. 1987. *Material Culture and Mass Consumption*. Oxford: Blackwell.

Milton, K. 2005a. 'Meanings and Feelings and Human Ecology', in K. Milton and M. Svašek (eds), *Mixed Emotions*. Oxford: Berg, pp. 25-42.

------- 2005b. 'Afterword', in K. Milton and M. Svašek (eds), *Mixed Emotions*. Oxford: Berg, pp. 215–24.

Navaro-Yashin, Y. 2007. 'Make-believe Papers, Legal Forms and the Counterfeit', *Anthropological Theory* 7(1): 79–98.

Nemec, G. 1998. *Un paese perfetto: Storia e memoria di una comunità in esilio, Grisignana d'Istria 1930–1960*. Gorizia: Leg.

———— 2003. 'Fuori dale mura: Cittadinanza italiana e mondo rurale slavo nell'Istria interna tra Guerra e dopoguerra', in M. Cattaruzza (ed.), *Nazionalismi di Frontiera: Identità contrapposte sull'Adriatico nordorientale 1850–1950*. Catanzaro: Rubbettino.

Nora, P. 1989. 'Between Memory and History: Les Lieux de Mémoire', *Representations* 26: 7–24.

Oatley, K., and Jenkins, J.M. 1996. *Understanding Emotions*. Cambridge, MA and Oxford: Blackwell.

Pupo, R. 2000. 'L'esodo degli Italiani da Zara, da Fiume e dall'Istria: un quadro fattuale', in M. Cattaruzza, M. Dogo and R. Pupo (eds), *Esodi: Trasferimenti forzati di popolazione nel Novecento Europeo*. Naples: Edizioni Scientifiche Italiane.

———— 2004. *Il Lungo Esodo*. Milan: Rizzoli.

Rapport, N., and A. Dawson (eds). 1998. *Migrants of Identity. Perceptions of Home in a World of Movement*. Oxford: Berg.

Rumici, G. 2001. *Fratelli d'Istria, 1945–2000: Italiani Divisi*. Milan: Mursia.

Safran, W. 1991 'Diasporas in Modern Societies: Myths of Homeland and Return', *Diaspora* 1(1): 83–99.

Sluga, G. 2001. *The Problem of Trieste and the Italo-Yugoslav Border: Difference, Identity, and Sovereignty in Twentieth-century Europe*. New York: SUNY Press.

Spector, S. 1998. 'Edith Stein's Passing Gestures: Intimate Histories, Empathic Portraits', *New German Critique* 75: 28–56.

Svašek, M. 1996. 'What's (the) Matter? Objects, Materiality and Interpretability', *Etnofoor* 9(1): 49–70.

———— 2002. 'Narratives of "Home: and "Homeland": The Symbolic Construction and Appropriation of the Sudeten German Heimat', *Identities* 9: 495–518.

———— 2005. 'The Politics of Chosen Trauma: Expellee Memories, Emotions and Identities', in K. Milton and M. Svašek (eds), *Mixed Emotions*. Oxford: Berg, pp. 195–214.

———— 2006. *Postsocialism: Politics and Emotions in Central and Eastern Europe*. Oxford: Berghahn.

———— 2007. *Anthropology, Art and Cultural Production*. London: Pluto.

Tomizza, C. 2001. *Il Sogno Dalmata*. Milan: Mondadori.

Turcinovich Giuricin, R. 2009. 'Lussignani a Roma nel Giorno del Ricordo', in *Foglio Lussino*, Issue 29. Triesk: Associazione italiana del Lussignani non più residenti a Lussino.

Tweed, T. 1997. *Our Lady of Exile: Diasporic Religion at a Catholic Cuban Shrine in Miami*. New York: Oxford University Press.

Weinberger, D. 2006. 'Knowledge and Fallibility (Or: Postmodernism is right)', *Joho the Blog*. Retrieved 12 October 2009 from: http://www.hyperorg.com/blogger/mtarchive/knowledge_and_fallibility_or_p.html.

8

MAKING CONNECTIONS:
BIOGRAPHY, ART, AFFECT AND POLITICS

Maggie O'Neill

One day you feel everything is yours here, it doesn't matter, and another day you don't – and that is my personal experience. And when it comes to art, you can't avoid this 'double consciousness', that one day this belongs to me and another day it does not.

—Gary

This chapter provides an account and analysis of an arts research project that used participatory action research and participatory arts to explore what belonging means to members of four transnational communities living in Derby, Leicester, Loughborough and Nottingham.[1] Those involved were either seeking asylum or had been granted refugee status, and included a group of emerging and professional artists. Our collective research and art making was an outgrowth of previous work that took place as part of a regional network called 'Making the Connections: Arts, Migration and Diaspora'.[2] The network had identified the pivotal role of arts and culture in facilitating processes of belonging and integration, and also stressed the importance of innovative research methodologies in generating knowledge about experiences of migration. In addition, it aimed to challenge myths and stereotypes around the issue of incoming migrants, and intended to produce work that could inform social and cultural policy.

This chapter analyses the genealogy of the 'Sense of Belonging' exhibition, an art event that evolved out of collaborative work. In addition, it focuses on events that took place over one day when I was invigilating the exhibition. I discuss my engagement with the art works and visitors to the gallery, and reflect on my experience of the sensory, relational and emotional dynamics involved.

Emotions and Attachment

People attach to their environments through emotional processes. Sarah Ahmed gets to the heart of the matter when she states that 'emotions are not simply "within" or "without", nor feelings that belong to individuals, but ... define the contours of the multiple worlds that are inhabited by different subjects' (Ahmed 2004: 25). The word 'emotion', she notes, stems from the Latin term *emovere*, which means 'to move, to move out'. In other words, 'emotions are what move us', and are also 'about attachments, about what connects us to this or that ... Emotions, then, are bound up with how we inhabit the world "with" others' (ibid.: 27).

Ahmed argues that 'emotions do things, and work to align individuals with collectives – or bodily space with social space – through the very intensity of their attachments' (ibid.: 26). This implies that 'emotionality – as a responsiveness to and openness towards the worlds of others – involves an interweaving of the personal with the social, and the affective with the mediated' (ibid.: 28). Her approach is useful when exploring the dynamics of belonging and non-belonging in a world of movement, where mobile people like the migrants and refugees who participated in the project respond to and partially shape their changing circumstances.

Ahmed also draws attention to the physicality of emotional interaction, the fact that people can be moved by the proximity of others. This insight is crucial to the approach taken in my research, where the methodology brought researchers and research together as interacting bodies, sharing time and space, and walking and working together over a considerable period as they cooperated to create artistic and academic end products.

Methodology: Exploring (Non)belonging through 'Conversive Way Finding'

The 'Sense of Belonging' arts research project was launched with a series of guided walks in June 2008, followed by a series of participatory arts research workshops led by City Arts, Charnwood Arts, Long Journey Home and Soft Touch community arts organizations. The walks, inspired by the arts practice of Misha Myers,[3] were 'designed to enable a series of relationalities and dialogues between walkers' (O'Neill and Hubbard 2010: 50) about belonging, home and emplacement, revealing what 'it means to be situated in particular places ... [and] the various ways people are attached and attach themselves (affectively) into the world' (Grossberg 1996: 185–86).

Myers's arts practice and methodology, called 'conversive way finding' asks people to draw a map from a place they call 'home' to a special place in their present location of residence; to draw landmarks important to them along the way; to stop at a place that reminds them of home; and to stop at familiar, comforting and unfamiliar places too.[4] She also asks people to trace landmarks they see along the way onto their original map. During the walk, conversations are taped; some are documented using film and photography.

In our project, a performative post-walk discussion, held at a local youth centre and facilitated by Misha Myers, was also included. It involved reflections from all participants.[5] We began to identify shared experiences and themes for the development of the arts research practice and workshops. The arts research workshops took place in each town between June and December 2008, led by the community arts organizations in collaboration with the researchers and participants. The resulting artworks and some of the narratives produced in the workshops were exhibited at the Bonington Gallery at Nottingham Trent University in January 2009.[6] They demonstrated what 'belonging' meant to their makers, as the works expressed feelings about place making, belonging and friendship, and reflected on their experiences of living in Nottingham, Derby, Leicester and Loughborough. Some art works also commented on the perilous journeys individuals had made to seek freedom and safety. The walks, the post-walk discussion and the arts research workshops created an existential space in which the participants could feel, express and share emotions related to their journeys, their 'double consciousness' and their experience of being 'home away from home'. The project also enabled the participants to develop and showcase their specific cultural contributions and skills.

Ethno-mimesis: A Politics of Feeling

Fifteen years ago, I began to develop an approach on the borders of art, ethnography and biographical research that transgresses conventional ways of producing, analysing and representing research data. Using participatory processes, I developed what I called 'ethno-mimesis', an exploration of the sensuousness of ethnography, immersing myself in the life worlds of participants.[7] Valuing their knowledge, experience and expertise, I looked for ways of representing the complexity of psychic processes and social relations experienced in ethnographic contexts, and chose to combine art and ethnography. Working in partnership with artists, community arts organizations and other groups and individuals, my aim was to produce ethnographic knowledge in collaboration, thus undermining the knowledge/power axis between knowledge producing experts and described and analysed informants. Ethno-mimesis – as a methodological and performative praxis – interweaves ethnographic participatory methods and art production (O'Neill et al. 2002, 2005; O'Neill 2008).[8] 'Mimesis' refers not to mimicry or imitation, but to sensuous knowing. Through the mimetic moment of embodied cognition we can develop a critical perspective that includes 'empathy' (O'Neill 2001, 2008, 2009).

Ethno-mimesis involves feeling involved and working with the sensuousness of personal connections between researchers and participants. This approach is in critical tension with a rational, scientistic production of 'objective' data. I have found inspiration in Adorno (1984), who has stated that knowledge involves immersion, identification and subsequent distancing followed by critical reflection – this is a deeply relational process that is also articulated in Witkin's concept of 'subjective-reflexive feeling' (Witkin 1982). There are also traces of this relational dynamic in Margaret Mead and Gregory Bateson's use of 'distanced subjectivity' (Mead 1972; Bateson 1980), in Nieto's discussion of 'subjective-objective observation' (Nieto 1990) and more recently in Geurts and Adikha's discussion of Anlo-Ewe sensorium and the specific concept of *seselelame*, which involves the interrelationship of emotion, sensation, consciousness and knowing (Geurts and Adikha 2006: 37). The importance of 'distanced subjectivity' here expresses the relational and sensate dynamic between subject and object, reflexivity and critical analysis. Moreover, it also involves being aware of the objective mediation of subjects and subjectivity and the vital importance of examining societal conditions in order to read these against appearance, against the grain, to expose conflicts and antagonisms.

In previous projects I have used narrative biographical methods, usually within the context of a participatory action research (PAR) methodology, to explore lived experience.[9] The resulting narratives have been represented in art forms, including photography, performance and poetry, reflecting the fact that narrative storytelling – telling our biographies – is a sensory, sensuous and performative experience (Given 2006; Jones 2006; Roberts 2006).[10] I have described this methodological process as being situated at the intersection of critical, cultural and feminist theory, lived experience (ethnographic and PAR methods) and praxis as purposeful knowledge. Working with life histories, biography, narrativity and the representation or reimagining of people's stories in visual and performative art forms, I am interested in the ways that the knowledge produced in such research can intervene in policy and practice, and how it can be transformative, causing changes and making a difference.

In summary, the methodological contribution of combining ethnography and biographical research with art and mimesis involves the creation of a 'potential space' (Winnicott 1982), a reflective space (between art and ethnography) in which dialogue, listening, narratives and images can emerge. Methodologically, this research was built upon a decade of participatory research in the east Midlands with local communities and community arts organizations on experiences of forced migration. The embeddedness of the research in previous relationships of trust, recognition and learning enabled the coproduction of relatively safe spaces where narratives and visual representations were shared and represented visually and poetically. In the 'Sense of Belonging' project we focused upon the themes of transnational identities, exile, home and belonging. The emotional aspects of people's lives emerged or unfolded in the ethno-mimetic text, and sometimes 'pierced' the public in ways that brought them in touch with the 'intractable reality' of the 'other'. Our work fed into cultural politics and praxis through a radical democratic and cultural imaginary that contributed to processes of social justice via a politics of recognition – as a counter to misrecognition in the east Midlands, and as part of a longer term process of arts research involving networking across the borders between academia, community arts, communities, policy and practice.

A Sense of Belonging: Walking, Talking, Place Making and Creativity

As noted earlier, we launched the arts research project with a performative event replicating the arts practice of Misha Myers.[11] Following Myers's model, walks were led by residents who were seeking asylum or had gained refugee status or humanitarian protection. Their walking partners were local dignitaries, policy makers, community artists or other residents. They started off at a place viewed by individual residents as 'home' and ended at a place they experienced as 'special'. During the walk, the resident talked about their life. The process of narrating aspects of one's past and present biography took place in a dialogic space between walker, co-walker and the environment. What Myers calls 'making place through process' emerged – a performing of emplacement, not as linear process but a dialectical, complex process eliciting multiple modalities of experience –'between here and there and nowhere', not only for the new arrivals but also for the co-walkers.

By way of an example, Figure 8.1 provides an image of James's walk from a place he called home to a special place followed by a fragment from the transcript of the conversation that occurred during the walk. James[12] has refugee status and is a professional artist; the co-walker is a housing officer for the city council.

CO-WALKER: Okay. It is a very interesting project. I have to say I have not come across anything like it before. So this is your home?

JAMES: Yes, this is home. We are in a village in north of Kurdistan on the border with Iran and we are going to our land. And also we get to the point that there is a war there, and we had to leave our village. And now we are going through the village and we will get to my uncle's summer house, which is this part. It reminds me of my first house in [inaudible]. The summer house was really lovely. It was just beautiful, on this mountain, and you go there and they had [a] pond, water in the summer, which is very, very hot in the summer obviously. And we go there as we were children and have a swim, all day, and hang around. The house had a big garden, and in the garden mulberries, walnuts and fruits and this sort of thing. And we go in the garden and pick up fruit and eat and just enjoy them ... every summer. And over there it will be our land; we grow mulberries.

CO-WALKER: Yes, I think I know what they are. 'Here we go round the mulberry bush'. It is a nursery rhyme we say to children over here. I would not know what a mulberry looks like though.

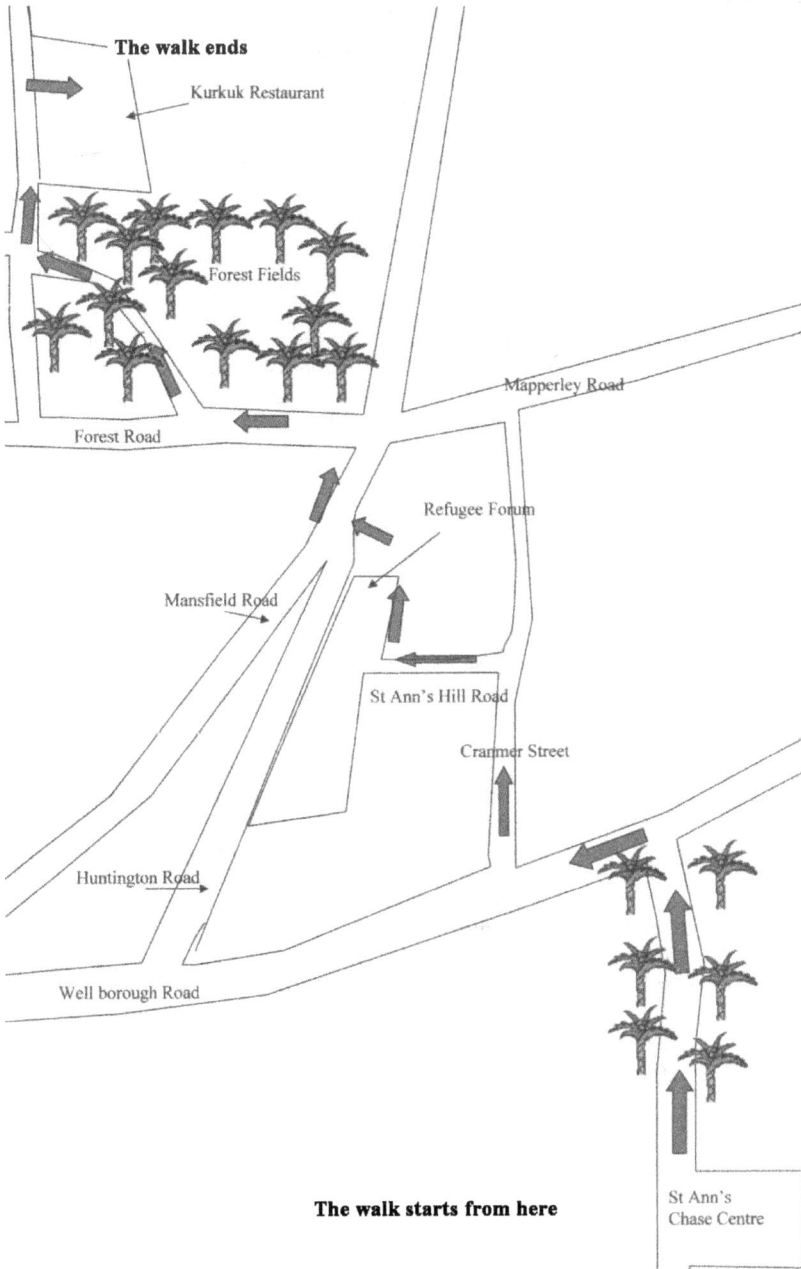

The walk ends

Kurkuk Restaurant

Forest Fields

Forest Road

Mapperley Road

Refugee Forum

Mansfield Road

St Ann's Hill Road

Cranmer Street

Huntington Road

Well borough Road

The walk starts from here

St Ann's
Chase Centre

Figure 8.1: Mapping a walk from a place called home to a special place. Courtesy of Jaism Ghafur.

JAMES: It is a bit like a blackberry, and is white and very sweet. So that
              was before the war started, happy years and nice time. And in the
              summer time we enjoy the food and everything, and other seasons
              we enjoy different things, the season for walnuts. And also we will
              play in the leaves in the autumn, very big trees, and the leaves
              came down and we play in the leaves that are a red colour, and
              hide ourselves and stuff. Yes, it was beautiful, and that was every
              summer. And here that place is close to Iran. As I said, it was
              very close to Iran. Again in the summer, that was 1979 when the
              government of Iran changed.
CO-WALKER: Right. Okay.
JAMES: In that period it was chaotic ... No one had control over that area,
              the mountain area. It was mainly freedom fighters from communist
              party and other Kurdish part [who] were controlling the area. And
              we had the opportunity to, with the Kurdish people of Iran near
              our village, [we] organized a picnic together and we go to this big
              mountain. Of course you have to have a car, for without a car you
              would not be able to go there, and we go and have a nice time
              together.
CO-WALKER: Fine, I see.
JAMES: It is one of the highest mountains there, so we thought: go there in
              the summer for a picnic and nice time. But now this is 1980, when
              the war starts between Iraq and Iran. I don't know if I can say that
              our village was the first area to be affected, one of the first; it was
              right on the border.
CO-WALKER: Okay, one of the first
JAMES: And we had to leave because bombardment started in our village,
              And we had to leave, a lot of houses were...
CO-WALKER: Demolished?
JAMES: Yes. And all sorts of people died, killed, and so we had to move.
              We wanted to go to another city of Kurdistan but Iraq government
              would not let us get out; they said, 'No you can't get out, you have
              to stay there and suffer'. And so we had to leave the village empty,
              and we had to go through mountain, again three months, the same
              route we took to our land. We went to the top of the mountain, [the
              one] that I said we went to for the picnic at the Iranian border, and
              we went to one of the Iranian villages that is next to the mountain.
              And we had to go down again, like when we get to the top of this
              hill – it sort of reminds me of that [sigh]. I was about seven years
              old, and for some reason I can remember that very well, and for
              other things I can't.
CO-WALKER: Okay.
JAMES: I even remember what I am wearing [laughs].
CO-WALKER: So, do all the – you know? Is that what makes you feel more at
              home then, remembering these things and relating to them?
JAMES: Yes. Walking up this hill reminds me of the hill in Kurdistan, a
              mountain, and you have to walk like this [laughs].
CO-WALKER: Indeed.
JAMES: So, yes, that is why it reminds me of that ... So now we go through
              the forest. That place, the refugee forum, down here, [it] reminds
              me of after 1993 – we build an organization, and I was a founding
              member, to protect people and children. I used to work voluntarily
              and I have a similar role here.
CO-WALKER: That makes you feel very much at home doing the same?

JAMES: And here it reminds me of the park, right in the centre of the city. This park has mountains around it, people go there in spring for Kurdish New Year, [they] go there in thousands for picnic.

CO-WALKER: So a big social event.

JAMES: Yes, it reminds me of that. And such a nice view on top of a hill. And look at the mountains in the distance and the sky And it is just beautiful scene – lake and sky meet and you can't tell which part is which, and this reminds me of that.

This excerpt from James's walk enables both the co-walker and reader to understand something about his experiences, particularly in relation to the senses, emotions and attachments involved in 'transit' (Svašek 2007) between here and there. It also creates an insight into his experiences of peace and conflict, and demonstrates the role of memory and remembering in creating a sense of belonging. The co-walker's empathic engagement is illustrated in the connections as well as mirroring back elements of his own reception (and personal experience) of belonging. For example, the mention of mulberries evokes the cultural signifier – or, in Volkan's terms, 'cultural amplifier' (Volkan 2009: 6) – of the nursery rhyme, an aspect of the co-walker's own sense of belonging and identity.

The exchange also reflects how the physical landscape anchors relational ties for James, and the ways that aspects of the landscape can serve as transitional objects – the intermediate space between psychic and external reality. St Anns Hill Road in Nottingham becomes a transitional link or object to the mountains of Kurdistan; Forest Road, and the area known as 'the forest', a large open space of common green land edged by trees, becomes a transitional phenomenon or object related to the park in the centre of Kirkuk.[13] The walks enable the co-walkers to reflect on transnational experiences in a performative way and they see their towns and cities through new eyes.

Incorporating Transitional Objects and Experiences into Art

The arts workshops that followed the walks in Nottingham focused upon particular objects or transitional phenomena that embodied emotional experiences related to 'home', including a coffee pot, landscapes, smells, sounds, fabrics and textiles, Sunday morning football after church, and recipes (see also Fortier 1999: 41). As symbols of 'home', they were incorporated into art works. In Nottingham, Heather Connelly and Rosie Hobbs facilitated workshops with a women's group that was also supported by Refugee Action. In the initial workshops we spoke together about concepts and memories of home, belonging and place making. One woman from Kosovo said:

> Where I lived to begin with there were many British families and they didn't really bother me as they thought I was British. But when I spoke and asked teenagers to be quiet or something, they would say 'Go back to your own country'. It is

difficult everywhere with teenagers. Now I live in an area with lots of refugees and
families from India [and] Pakistan and we can say anything to each other – we
understand each other.

For a Congolese woman it was hard to move from a large house to a
small house with little space. When asked what helps women feel a sense
of belonging, they mentioned photographs, music, cooking, the smells
of spices and coffee, and objects like coffee pots, crockery, colours
and fabrics. As one of the women said, feelings of home were evoked
when consuming 'traditional food, when we meet each other we make
traditional coffee and feel at home'. For a woman from Eritrea, home
was 'here, where my children were born, are with me'; another woman
mentioned 'being able to speak your own language at home'. To feel at
home, women would visit 'parks and green spaces, Nottingham, London,
restaurants with traditional food and churches'.

When asked how they would like to represent themselves in the
exhibition, one woman from Kosovo said that she 'would like to make a
powerful image of a woman and embroider it, to show that women can
be beautiful but also strong'. The women wanted to represent themselves
as individuals and as groups. Objects that made them feel at home and
things they would like to have sent to them in England were coffee, cloth
and coffee pots. Some of the women brought examples of their traditional
cloth, crockery, kettles and pots into the workshops. We also created
felt and worked with *mehndi* patterns, screen printing, and embroidery,
all influenced by the colours and textures, objects and textiles women
brought into the sessions. The women particularly enjoyed felt making
and embroidering patterns onto their felt pieces, and embroidering work
they had made onto large cushions.

It was agreed that a gazebo would be decorated with silk screens for
people attending the exhibition to step into the women's world. The women
made silk drapes with Rosie to decorate the tent and create a sensory
environment, a welcoming space that would also elicit understandings of
women's lives and cultures. We also taped conversations with the women
and created sound files to use as part of the exhibition. This allowed
the public sitting in the installation space to hear female migrants and
refugees' voices and women's stories, physically connecting them with the
makers of the installation.

Bonding through Art

Sitting in the home-made gazebo and listening to the sound files of
the women talking evoked a sensory and sensuous connection to the
makers' sense of being both in Nottingham and their home countries,
and highlighted their transitions and feelings on 'movement in between'.
Audiences also got a sense of the injustices wrought by the asylum and
immigration system as a lived and embodied reality.

Gell's work on the agency of art objects (Gell 1998) and Svašek's focus on artefacts' ability to stir emotions through the embodiment of complex intentionalities and the mediation of social agency is useful here. As Svašek notes, '[s]ocial actors do not just produce and use artefacts, but are also impressed, captivated, motivated and manipulated by them' (Svašek 2007: 67). Referring to Molotoch, De la Fuente discusses the potential of art to mediate emotions and sensorial experience as follows:

> Art entails objects (or situations) that have the capacity to draw upon 'social-psychological associations' which are heavily compressed and give that object (or situation) an air of 'transcendence'. Art transcends mundane and routine perception, by compressing experience in the following manner: the magic of art is in the way complex social and psychological stimuli are made to conjoin, a kind of *lash up* of sensualities. (De La Fuente 2007: 419)

Evaluating the impact of the arts workshops on the participating migrant and refugees, the organizers pointed out that the project had enabled the women to positively attach to each other.

There have been a number of positive comments about both the women's group and the city arts projects, how this has made them feel more positive, belonging. One woman talked about being reminded of her sewing skills and the other about meeting the other women and making friends after moving to Nottingham from London. Making friends for all of the women is something that makes them feel like they belong. Hence a key theme emerging from the workshops with women in Nottingham was how women related to each other through our project. We witnessed the ways that the group bonded in the sessions, and the way they embraced the artistic work and helped each other. They also improved their language skills in the process. As with walking, art making created the necessary space and facilitated connections through the creative process, stimulating movement between women's inner worlds and their social, external reality. As one of the participants noted:

> We are sewing and we are talking together about our problems. We have known each other two years now, but here we sew and talk, we do not need to look and learn. We enjoy sewing, we learn to make felt. For me I learn lots of things; now I am interested in art. I think all the ladies, we have become friends. I make a joke and she understands me, and she can come back with a joke. I feel we are friends.

Figures 8.2 and 8.3 show contributions to the exhibition by the Nottingham women's group.[14] The points expressed above, as well as my own thinking and grappling with the transformative role of arts and creativity in the space between art and ethnography, was experienced in an embodied, relational and also revelatory sense when I invigilated the exhibition one day and connected with the art forms, the visitors and the artists.

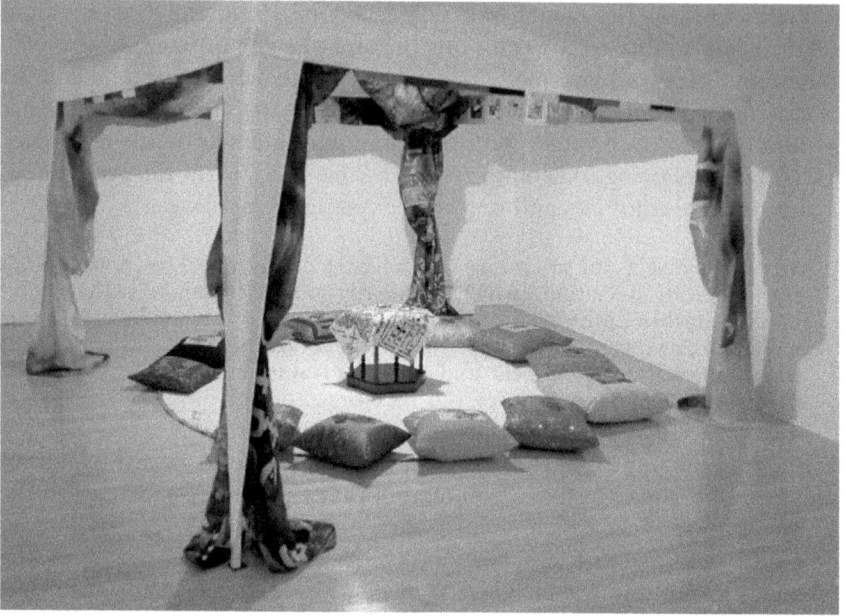

Figure 8.2: 'Home-made', City Arts and the Vine Women's Group. Photograph by Aria Ahmed.

Figure 8.3: 'Home-made'. Photograph by Aria Ahmed.

Observing and Feeling the 'Sense of Belonging' Exhibition: Connections and Mimesis

My day of invigilation was a chance to connect with the different pieces in the exhibition and observe others doing the same. I recount below my engagements with just two of the artforms: the 'Home-made Gazebo' (City Arts) and 'Home away from Home' (Long Journey Home, Derby). Both artworks were created by people who were waiting for a response to their asylum claim, had been refused and had appealed or who had been granted refugee status or humanitarian protection.

'Home-made': The Gazebo

Two female visitors, having spent some time in the exhibition, stopped to talk to me on their way out. They spoke about the gazebo the women's group had developed, the rich colours of the silk screen decorating the walls, the textiles, cushions and table cloth, the comfort and welcome of the space. One of them said that is was 'an emotional experience. It evokes an emotional response'. As we were talking, a large group arrived of what seemed to be international students with two group leaders. The group turned out to be a conversation class of asylum seekers and refugees from the library, and the two group leaders were librarians. They really took hold of the space, moving around and touching the stone and steel sculptures. Two people, one with a video camera, moved to the gazebo and sat down on cushions, talking and filming.

Figure 8.4: Visitors experiencing 'Home-made'. Photograph by Maggie O'Neill.

Figure 8.5: Visitors experiencing 'Home-made'. Photograph by Tove Dalenius (Soft Touch Arts Co-operative).

More people from the group drifted over to the gazebo and soon they were all there, sitting and talking. Two or three people led the conversation. I overheard them speak about injustice and conflict. A woman declared she was very happy to be part of the group and that the group had given those present a chance to reflect on the issue of belonging. They each spoke in turn about how they felt about belonging, what belonging meant to them. One woman asked: 'Why do the English people feel they belong or not?' Another spoke: 'Isn't it important to feel part of society wherever you are from?'

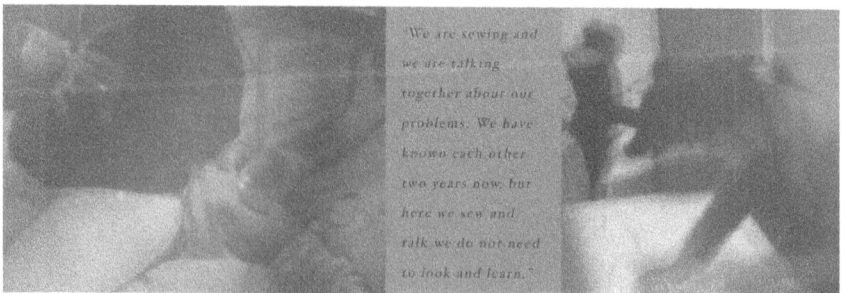

Figure 8.6: 'Home-made' insert. Photograph by Heather Connelly.

The group also talked about the voices of the women audible on the soundscape and the quotes written on cards that Heather Connelly had produced from weekly workshops with women at the Vine Centre. One card said: 'I am happy here I feel safe but I worry about my brothers child I have not seen him for 8 years'. Particular comments by the visitors, such as 'These people have survived' and 'We have survived' demonstrated how the art work brought about a process of empathetic identification.

'Home Away from Home'

'Home away from Home' was an installation made of wood, photographs, textiles, cigarette packets, water bottles and children's clothes. The work was accompanied by an explanatory text that told the reader that the textiles that covered the box-like structure were literally created from the stories of the participants. Pieces of thread, cloth and, in some cases, photographs had been woven into the squares, and the enclosed space depicted the refugees' experience of escaping their countries in containers and lorries. Exhibition visitors were able to climb into the box to feel the confined space. Their senses were engaged by the items the artists had included in the container, including a chocolate wrapper and an empty plastic bottle. The sounds of ports, stations and engines were mixed in with the stories of those who had taken journeys, and included texts such as 'After twenty seven years I breathed in freedom air', and 'My home? It was one and now it is two. I have been divided into two places like two souls in one body'.

Figure 8.7: 'Home away from Home', Derby Long Journey Home. Photograph by Aria Ahmed.

During my time in the gallery, two women were immersed in moving in and out of the installation and called the others to look at and sense the materials. One noted: 'I just about fit in the box, and the smell and the things in there, it really brings it home to you'. One of the young men approached me and said: 'It is great to see people's journey, especially as we are all on a journey'. One of the group leaders pointed out: 'All of the people in the group have had the experience of arriving'.

Evoking Memories and Narratives of Suffering

Leyla, a woman from Iran who took part in the Derby walks and workshops, brought two friends to see the exhibition and her work. Her friends, one younger and one older woman, were clearly moved by the experience of engaging with the artworks. Leyla told me about her feelings: 'I am much moved and feel tearful and upset. I brought my friends here who share this journey. It is important that people understand our journey'. She went on to speak about her experience, and emphasized that it was embedded and embodied in the exhibition piece:

> My husband and I were separated and my brother suggested that I climb onto a moving lorry. My brother did. It was hard, I said 'No'. What if I gave him my daughter and she falls on the floor? My son was eleven and my daughter was five. There were lots of lorries on the journey from Iran to Calais. We waited almost two months at Calais with my two children. Some of the agents, they care for us, they understand. A woman came to see me. She said: 'We feel for you, one month on your own with the children, and we know a way that has not been tried'. We had to lie amongst packing boxes, six people: myself, my son and daughter, and three others. We waited for five hours inside the lorry in the car park in the cold of winter. Then we left. Five hours is like five days. My daughter was sleeping but she was only five years. My son had to pee. I said to do it in the corner; he said, 'I can't Mum'. I said, 'You have to just do it'. In the [Channel] tunnel we were in a queue for four hours. Then we travel to Loughborough; we thought we must be in Scotland! In the police station they bring us pot noodle, but we can't eat that. I said, 'Can we have bread?' The children were crying. I said to the police, 'Which camp are you taking us to?' He said, 'We don't put people in camps in England. You will go to a hotel in Leicester'. We got there very late. I said, 'Can we have bread for the children?' 'No, all the kitchen is closed up until morning'. So we slept. I woke with a start and ran into breakfast place, crying 'Please please can I have breakfast for my children'. An Iraqi man said to me, 'It is okay, everyone is here for breakfast. You can have breakfast'. I had not changed my clothes or washed. The journey was hard, very painful.

I was very moved by Leyla's engagement and sense of pride in the work she was part of, and her sense of the importance of the exhibition for helping people to understand the journeys people make to freedom and safety, coming so far to bring her friends to see it and for them to share her journey, which was also their journey; and in turn I felt privileged that she also shared her experience with me. For Leyla it is important that people in

England understand the reasons for fleeing your home, for making perilous journeys in terrible conditions, for risking the safety of your children.

Evaluating the Project

I reflected upon the positive connections that were forged across the boundaries between professional artist, community artist, the groups who created the works and the individuals and groups who visited the exhibition. Evaluating the project, one member of the team said during a focus-group meeting:

> If you look in the comments book, the impact that the pieces have is great, in forging connections between the communities who produce the art and the communities attending the exhibition. Several comments have specifically said you know that we would like more work like this in spaces like this and we'd like to see more art which is issue-based.

The connections validated the impact and outcomes of the participatory process and partnership that marked our project. This was a genuinely participatory project and the collaborations (between community arts organizations, university researchers and community groups) were developed, enhanced and cemented. Participation in the walks and follow-up discussions led to the themes for the artworks. Narrative and art making came together and were reflexively embedded in the works that were produced from biographical material, conversations and art making. Related to this is the way that the research element had been taken up, so that research was not solely the responsibility of the university researchers but intrinsic to the process of conducting the arts workshops, thus making the community arts process also a research process – we were all researchers on the project. So reflections and evaluation on the arts research process in the community art setting was a strong positive outcome that is now being taken up in follow-on work with the East Midlands Participatory Arts Forum partnership (EMPAF).[15]

Critical Issues

In developing the project the partners hoped that the work we conducted together would have multiple benefits, that it would challenge people to think differently by addressing myths and stereotypes, and be of benefit to community groups and artists by raising their profile, supporting capacity building, providing them with commissions as well as focusing upon and supporting the employability of artists. Hence our hope was that the work would be transformative across many levels. Moreover, this was a project that was part of a decade-long trajectory of participatory action research in the east Midlands, deeply embedded through time in the networks and horizontal and vertical processes and practices of inclusion, and based on relationships built up over some years. At its core was the idea of working together to create change, addressing social injustice and identity issues, improving the lives of new arrivals – whether as migrants, asylum seekers or refugees – as well as reflecting upon the social role of art.

A central tension emerged around concepts of identification and identity thinking regarding the label 'refugee artist' in the 'transit' of work from creation to exhibition, as well as around how we negotiate these categories within the context of funding regimes and structures. One of the professional artists in the project felt that the labels 'asylum seeker' and 'refugee' had negative connotations and fixed his identity. He resisted the transition from 'artist' to 'refugee artist'. Alex Rotas (2004) identifies this issue in a paper exploring the identity of professional artists who are also refugees. He writes of how the categories or labels identifying artists and participants as 'asylum seeker' or 'refugee' can serve to fix their identity as 'other' and 'othered'. These categories have many negative connotations within the public imagination. And, rather like the designating of artists with the monolithic term 'black', they may become contained, differentiated and controlled until the people themselves take hold of the term by which they are designated and make it a site of resistance and source of pride.

Another professional artist was concerned about the politicization of the arts and social research. As he said during a focus-group meeting, art should not be linked with politics: 'Artists want to be valued as artists of their work as well; they don't want just to be valued as social change or political agents of research'. This raises an important point for further discussion and analysis and led to my thinking about the affective dimension of the PAR process and the impact of the exhibition. There seemed to be historical tensions between what might be called 'art' and 'participatory community arts', the latter commonly being less valued within art worlds.[16] It is important to hold on to the points of tension and explore these to make sense of art, affect and emotional agency as well as broader social, political and cultural structures and processes.

The conundrum, identified by Doy (cited in O'Neill and Hubbard 2009), is that on the one hand the government gives funding to arts organizations and universities to support cultural projects involving refugees and asylum seekers; on the other hand, there is a lot of money and state power devoted to the daily harassment of migrants, including policies to keep out, imprison, deport and cause physical and mental damage to them and the populations they come from, such as Iraq or Afghanistan. This is an important issue faced by researchers in the arts and humanities when working with the arts, migration and diaspora.

Conclusion: Transit, Transitional Objects and Emotional Impact

Working in ethno-mimetic ways using participatory methodologies is a useful and ethical way of producing knowledge at the intersections of art and ethnography. Engaging and connecting with the feelings and intellectual and political viewpoints that mediate the tensions between emotion and materiality can help us to understand better the 'micrology' of migrants' lives, and in turn this can help us conceive more fully our own lives within the context of wider socio-political structures and processes, such as the governance of the asylum/migration nexus. In this process we can also access greater understanding of the implications of our own actions and subjective reflections. I am thus in agreement with Gray who states that research is, 'simultaneously an embodied, emotional, mindful and political activity' (Gray 2008: 947). The reflexivity and emotionally mediated process of our research and practice is an example of the process of critical reflexivity in sociological research.

Observing and talking with the visitors, seeing at first-hand the way that people engaged in a feeling-based and physical way with the exhibition, was instructive. The exhibition space at the end of the day looked lived in: cushions were askew, the neatly folded maps containing the cards were left undone, cards lay where the viewer had left them, the flap of the box was left undone so one could peek inside at the objects left there by the makers. It felt very good to have experienced and connected with the work and the visitors through my own embodied and emotional engagement with it. I thought about Svašek's point that 'artefacts "do" things: they reproduce the agency of their commissioners, makers and users; they evoke emotional reactions with and amongst individuals, and urge people to take certain actions and positions' (Svašek 2007: 85–86). Drawing upon Ahmed, we can see that emotionality, 'the responsiveness to and openness towards the worlds of others' (Ahmed 2004), involved movement and connection in the space created by the exhibition, which involved the interweaving of the personal and the social, mediated by and in material things.

The point made by Svašek is also intrinsically related to the value of participatory action research and participatory arts as forms of ethno-mimesis and their attempt to 'make a difference'. Our aim was to raise awareness about the routes people take to reach safety and to subsequently create a sense of belonging, a sense of home in a new situation. Transnational belonging involves mobility and multiple affiliations, as well as loss and dislocation. Lives and roles are transformed in the process, people become 'refugees' or 'asylum seekers', experience downward mobility and often find themselves located at the margins of the margins. Having a voice and a personal and political space in which to tell and share our stories can be facilitated in the process of participatory research. In turn, art based on participatory research is not just a mimetic reflection on someone's origins but brings something new into the world.[17] As Svašek (2007) suggests, when recontextualized into a gallery space, the meaning and emotional agency of such works may change. The 'Sense of Belonging' projects demonstrated that this may generate a dialogical process of reflection and sensorial interaction that links the visual and the imaginary to other sensory registers (Buckley 2006: 62), connecting inner and outer realities.

Notes

1. My thanks to Maruska Svašek for her editorial support and to Aria Ahmed and Heather Connelly for permission to print the photographs. Thanks also to Misha Myers, Tove Dalenius and Heather Connelly for her involvement in the project as consultant, sharing her arts practice with us and for leading post-walk discussions. This chapter derives from the project 'Transnational Communities: Towards a Sense of Belonging', funded by the AHRC Knowledge Transfer Programme. There were three strands to the project: an arts research project called 'Sense of Belonging'; a diversity-pool event to aid the employment of emerging and professional artists in exile; and a web-based resource, 'Beyond Borders, Making Connections', to aid networking, and raise the profile of, and try to ensure the employment of, artists (see www.beyondbordersuk.org). The 'Sense of Belonging' exhibition emerged out of our arts-research-based work. The AHRC-funded project is a partnership between Loughborough University, Charnwood Arts, City Arts, Long Journey Home and Soft Touch Arts, and is an outcome of a successful two-year programme of workshops and seminars entitled 'Making the Connections' (see www.makingconnections.info), also funded by the AHRC, that in turn grew out of previous AHRC-funded participatory research and participatory arts practice led by O'Neill and O'Neill and Tobolewska (2002) in partnership with community arts organizations and two communities of new arrivals in London and the east Midlands.
2. This was undertaken by the partners Charnwood Arts, City Arts, Long Journey Home and Soft Touch community and participatory arts organizations and Loughborough University.
3. Misha Myers, artist and anthropologist, was consultant to the walks and we launched the project using her model and arts practice. Misha also facilitated a performative feedback event after the walks where many of the themes for the workshops and subsequent reflections emerged. Commenting upon her experience of the day she said: 'The project was successfully led by participants' own interests and desires and well structured to facilitate their contributions of knowledge and creative endeavour. For me personally it was a wonderful opportunity to extend my approach to a different context and to develop and test new strategies'.
4. See Myers (2007, 2008, 2010); see also the websites http://www.homingplace.org/ and http://www.wayfromhome.org/.
5. The epigraph to this chapter is taken from one of these post-walk discussions.
6. The exhibition was curated by the photographer John Perivolaris. The press release from the exhibition stated: '"Sense of Belonging" will showcase the work of emerging exiled artists as well as work created out of participatory arts and participatory action research initiatives that explored the concept of "belonging" with refugees and asylum seekers in the East Midlands ... Using film, sculpture, mixed media textiles, painting, photography, music and performance, the artists, both individually and collectively, synthesize issues of cultural identity, displacement, relationships to surroundings, personal reflections on the process of exile and belonging with a celebration of the rich cultural contributions refugees and asylum seekers bring to cities and communities'. Each arts organization developed art works for the exhibition, and there were ten exhibits altogether: three pieces by participants and community arts organizations in Derby (Home Away from Home), Leicester (A Special Place), Loughborough (I Had a Dream ...) and Nottingham (Home-made). Six pieces were also made by established and emerging artists who were part of the artists-in-exile regional art organization.

7. This early work involved collaborations with performance artist Sara Giddens within the context of my ethnographic participatory work with female sex workers. A trilogy of work was produced, including live art, a DVD and a photographic exhibition (see O'Neill 2001; O'Neill and Giddens 2001; O'Neill et al. 2002).

8. Other theorists working at the intersections of art and ethnography and art and anthropology include Gell (1998), Pink (2001, 2006, 2007a, 2007b), Irving (2007), Myers (2007, 2008), Svašek (2007) and Schneider (2008). Svašek's work on art and agency also explores the relationship between art and affect. Work on the sociology of emotions provides important reference points for developing work in this area (e.g., Ahmed 2004). The aforementioned theorists provide important ideas and concepts for thinking through the relationship between art and society and the politics of representation. Moreover, Jones (2006) argues that traditional methodologies do not deal well with the sensory, emotional and kinaesthetic aspects of lived experience; and in considering these aspects in research, interviews and observations could be the locus not just for gathering information but for producing performance texts and performance ethnographies. The ethno-mimetic process represented in this chapter is performative and develops knowledge as praxis.

9. Participatory action research (PAR) is based upon the principles of inclusion and participation, valuing all local voices (not just the loudest) and facilitating sustainable outcomes and interventions. A phenomenological approach, PAR fosters safe spaces for dialogue and reflection, and helps to counter stereotypes. It also offers a form of doing research based upon respect for otherness and difference, and typically involves working with participants as co-researchers (community members as experts) through democratic processes and decision making (Fals Borda 1988). This involves mutual recognition, through what Fréire (1970) calls dialogic techniques. It uses innovative ways of consulting and working with local people, for example through arts workshops, forum theatre methods and stakeholder events.

10. Our stories, our experiences and our histories can also be told through images, poetry and performance, not in the sense of 'encoding meanings in images but the insight that memory and action find articulation in images, that ideas are structured as images' (Weigel 1996: 10). Walter Benjamin (1992) 'argues for the politically emancipatory significance of the image for the way that we develop the capacity to actively intervene in and shape the world around us' (ibid.: x). Adorno (1984) described works of art as rebuses, or picture puzzles, and showed us that what is contained in artworks is the sedimented stuff of society.

11. See also Myers (2010) and O'Neill and Hubbard (2010), which both appeared in a special issue of *Visual Studies* on 'Walking, Art and Ethnography'.

12. All participants in the project are referred to using pseudonyms.

13. Young discusses the role of transitional phenomena as 'the sensuous, comforting quality and the sense of something that is favourite and to which one turns' (Young 2009). Winnicott called the 'in between' space between subjective and objective reality 'potential space' and wrote that creative perception is fostered by a negotiation of the gap between self and other (Winnicott 1982). Indeed 'this area relates to play, as well as to religious and aesthetic experience in adult life – indeed the whole "cultural field"' (Glover 2005: 2).

14. Photographs from the exhibition can be accessed at two websites: http://www.guardian.co.uk/society/gallery/2009/jan/13/sense-of-belonging-exhibition?picture=341562670, and: http://www.qub.ac.uk/cden/NewsandEvents/RelevantExhibitions/SenseofBelonging/.

15. The latter work includes what is the research potential of the community arts movement and what is the difference between sociological research and research conducted by arts workers in the process of their work with groups and communities.

16. In the gallery space, work facilitated by community artists such as 'Home from Home' and 'Home-made' were exhibited alongside the work of professional and emerging artists.
17. Tim Ingold, drawing upon Kandinsky, writes about 'the power of the imagination ... in continually bringing forth the forms we encounter' not as a representation but an 'emanation" (Ingold 2010: 25). In 'ways of mind walking', Ingold refers to the connection between art, music, walking and inner life – 'emotion' (ibid.: 21) – by describing Kandinsky's concept of 'inner necessity', the inner truths or 'abstract content' of the work of art that can 'directly touch the soul and set it in motion' (ibid.: 21).

References

Adorno, T.W. 1984. *Aesthetic Theory*, trans. R. Hullot-Kentor. Minneapolis: University of Minnesota Press.

Ahmed, S. 2003. 'Collective Feelings or, the Impressions Left by Others', *Theory Culture and Society* 21(2): 25–42.

———— 2004. *The Cultural Politics of Emotion*. Edinburgh: Edinburgh University Press.

Bateson, M.C. 1980. 'Continuities in Insight and Innovation: Toward a Biography of Margaret Mead', *American Anthropologist* 82: 270–77.

Benjamin, W. 1992[1936]. 'The Storyteller', in H. Arendt (ed.) and H. Zohn (trans.), *Illuminations*. London: Fontana, pp. 83–107.

Buckley, L. 2006. 'Studio Photography and the Aesthetics of Citizenship in the Gambia, West Africa', in E. Edwards, C. Gosden and R.B. Phillips (eds), *Sensible Objects: Colonialism, Museums and Material Culture*. Oxford: Berg, pp. 61–86.

De la Fuente, E. 2007. 'The "New Sociology of Art": Putting Art Back into Social Science Approaches to the Arts', *Cultural Sociology* 1(3): 409–25.

Fals Borda, O. 1988. *Knowledge and People's Power: Lessons with Peasants in Nicaragua, Mexico and Columbia*. New York: New Horizons Press.

Fortier, A.M. 1999. 'Re-membering Places and the Performance of Belonging(s)', *Theory, Culture and Society* 16: 41–62.

Fréire, P. 1970. *Pedagogy of the Oppressed*. New York: Herder and Herder.

Gell, A. 1998. *Art and Agency: An Anthropological Theory*. Oxford: Oxford University Press.

Geurts, K.L., and E.G. Adikha. 2006. 'Enduring and Endearing Feelings and the Transformation of Material Culture in West Africa', in E. Edwards, C. Gosden and R.B. Phillips (eds), *Sensible Objects: Colonialism, Museums and Material Culture*. Oxford: Berg, pp. 35–60.

Given, J. 2006. 'Narrating the Digital Turn: Data Deluge, Technomethodology, and other Likely Tales', *Qualitative Sociology Review* 2(1): 54–65.

Glover, N. 2005. 'Psychoanalytic Aesthetics: The British School, Chapter Six. Aesthetics, Creativity, and the Potential Space', *Free Associations*. Retrieved 13 September 2007 from: http://www.human-nature.com/free-associations/glover/index.html.

Gray, B. 2008. 'Putting Emotion and Reflexivity to Work in Researching Migration', *Sociology* 42(5): 935–52.

Grossberg, L. 1996. 'The Space of Culture, the Power of Space', in I. Chambers and L. Curtis (eds), *The Post-Colonial Question*. London: Routledge.

Ingold, T. 2010. 'Ways of Mind-walking: Reading, Writing, Painting', *Visual Studies* 25(1): 15–23.

Irving, A. 2007. 'Ethnography, Art and Death', *Journal of the Royal Anthropological Institute* 13: 185–208.

Jones, K. 2006. 'A Biographic Researcher in Pursuit of an Aesthetic: The Use of Arts-based (Re)presentations in "Performative" Dissemination of Life Stories', *Qualitative Sociology Review* 2(1): 66–85.

Lopez, S.L. 1999. 'The Encoding of History: Thinking Art in Constellations', in M. O'Neill (ed.), *Adorno, Culture and Feminism*. London: Sage, pp. 66–74.

Marfleet, P. 2005. *Refugees in a Global Era*. London: Palgrave Macmillan.

Mead, M. 1972. *Blackberry Winter: My Earlier Years*. New York: Kodansha.

Myers, M. 2007. 'Along the Way: Situation-responsive Participation and Education', *International Journal of the Arts in Society* 1(2): 1–6.

——— 2008. 'Situations for Living: Performing Emplacement', *Research in Drama Education* 13(2): 171–80.

——— 2010. 'Walk With Me, Talk With Me: The Art of Conversive Wayfinding', *Visual Studies* 25(1): 59–68.

Nieto, J.A. 1990. 'The Contribution of Anthropology to the Understanding of Sexual Behaviour Changes in the Context of AIDS', in M. Hupert (ed.), *Sexual Behaviour and Risks of HIV Infection*. Brussels: Facultés Universitaires Saint-Louis, pp. 45–58.

O'Neill, M. 2001. *Prostitution and Feminism: Towards a Politics of Feeling*. Cambridge: Polity Press.

——— 2008. 'Transnational Refugees: The Transformative Role of Art?' *Forum for Qualitative Research* 9(2). Available online at http://www.qualitative-research.net/index.php/fqs/article/view/403

O'Neill, M., and S. Giddens. 2001. 'Not All the Time ... but Mostly: Renewed Methodologies for Cultural Analysis', *Feminist Review* 67: n.p.

O'Neill, M., S. Giddens, P. Breatnach, C. Bagley, D. Bourne and T. Judge. 2002. 'Renewed Methodologies for Social Research: Ethno-mimesis as Performative Praxis', *Sociological Review* 50(1): 69–88.

O'Neill, M., and R. Harindranath. 2006. 'Theorising Narratives of Exile and Belonging: The Importance of Biography and Ethno-mimesis in "Understanding" Asylum', *Qualitative Sociological Review* 11(1): 39–53.

O'Neill, M., and P. Hubbard. 2009. 'Transnational Communities: Towards a Sense of Belonging', research report for the AHRC. Loughborough: Loughborough University.

——— 2010. 'Walking, Sensing, and Belonging: Ethno-mimesis as Performative Praxis', *Visual Studies* 25(1): 46–58.

O'Neill, M., and B. Tobolewska. 2002. *Global Refugees, Exile, Displacement and Belonging: Afghans in London*. Nottingham: Exiled Writers Ink and Waterman's Multimedia Centre.

O'Neill, M., P.A. Woods and M. Webster. 2005. 'New Arrivals: Participatory Action Research, Imagined Communities and Social Justice', *Social Justice* 31(1): 75–88.

Pink, S. 2001. *Doing Visual Ethnography*. London: Sage.

———— 2006. *The Future of Visual Anthropology*. London: Routledge.

———— 2007a. 'Walking with Video', *Visual Studies* 22(3): 240–52.

———— (ed.). 2007b. *Visual Interventions: Applied Visual Anthropology*. Oxford: Berghahn.

Roberts, B. 2006. *Micro Social Theory*. London: Palgave Macmillan.

Rotas, A. 2004. 'Is "Refugee Art" Possible?' *Third Text* 18(1): 51–60.

Schneider, A. 2008. 'Three Modes of Experimentation with Art and Ethnography', *Journal of the Royal Anthropological Institute* 14: 171–94.

Svašek, M. 2007. *Anthropology, Art and Cultural Production*. London: Pluto Press.

Volkan, V. (2009) 'Large-group Identity: "Us and Them" Polarizations in the International Arena', *Psychoanalysis, Culture & Society* 14(1): 4–15.

Weigel, S.Z. 1996. *Body and Image Space: Re-reading Walter Benjamin*, trans, G. Paul, R. McNicholl and J. Gaines. New York: Routledge.

Winnicott, D.W. 1982. *Playing and Reality*. London: Routledge.

Witkin, R. 1982. *The Intelligence of Feeling*. London: Heineman.

Young, R.M. 2009. 'Cultural Space' in *Mental Space*. Retrieved 26 June 2010 from Robert. M. Young's home page: http://human-nature.com/mental/chap2.html

9

CROSSING BORDERS:
MIGRATION, MEMORY AND THE ARTIST'S BOOK
————•◆•◆•————

Deborah Schultz

Introduction: Arnold Daghani

During the Cold War, many artists left the communist states of Central
and Eastern Europe due to political persecution. However, many others
emigrated to follow their dreams of success in the 'free world', where artists
were perceived as succeeding according to the merits of their work rather
than as the result of political or other affiliations. For Arnold Daghani
(1909–1985), migration brought with it hopes of recognition and success. He
left communist Romania, not due to persecution but ambition, and finally
settled in the UK in search of his artistic dream. While living in Romania,
he refused to work in the Socialist Realist style or join the Artists' Union
and so was unable to exhibit publicly. A UK newspaper article of 1985
dramatically reported that he was 'hounded from Communist Romania',[1]
but the reality was rather more complex.

As one of the main themes of this chapter is movement across space
and time, it is useful to situate Daghani's movements in the wider political
context of change across Eastern Europe. Arnold Daghani was born into
a German-speaking Jewish family in Suczawa (in Romanian, Suceava) in
the region of Bukovina in the Austro-Hungarian Empire. However, after
the First World War the region was incorporated into the newly expanded
state of Romania. In the 1930s Daghani moved to the capital, Bucharest,
but in 1940, after his home was badly damaged in an earthquake, he and
his wife Anişoara moved back to Bukovina, to the regional capital Cernăuţi

(formerly Czernowitz, now Chernivtsi in Ukraine). At the time Bukovina was in Soviet hands, but in June 1941 German and Romanian troops occupied the region. In June 1942 Daghani and his wife were included in a large deportation from Cernăuţi and taken through Transnistria and across the River Bug to a slave labour camp at Mikhailowka in south-west Ukraine. Through a complex series of events, in July 1943 they managed to escape to the ghetto of Bershad in Romanian Transnistria, and by March 1944 they had made their way back to Bucharest. They remained there until 1958 when they left for Israel.

Daghani's life was structured by a series of displacements and relocations due to political circumstances and changes over which he had little control, brought about by the fall of the Habsburg Austro-Hungarian Empire, the expansion of nation-states and the Second World War. However, leaving Romania in 1958 for the 'free world', at the height of the Cold War, was his own decision. Although it was not possible for him to succeed as an artist while Socialist Realism dominated the cultural arena, he was not forced to migrate but chose to do so to fulfil his artistic ambition. During the rest of his life he spent time in Vence, in the south of France (1960–1970), moving to Jona, near Zurich, in Switzerland (1970–1977) and finally on to England, where he spent the remaining years of his life in Hove, near Brighton (1977–1985).

Although a person may chose to leave a country, it is not necessarily easy to do so. Daghani's motivation for leaving was prompted by suffering, by feeling unable to express himself freely and by his rejection of the political system. However, he left behind the context to which he belonged. While living in Bucharest he had kept apart from public artistic activities but had a wide range of contacts, and it was when he was abroad, when he wanted to fit in, that he experienced what it meant to be an outsider. Struggling between preconceptions and aspirations, like so many others, he 'dreamt of belonging' (Bauman 1988). In crossing artistic borders (by combining word and image in a variety of media) and crossing the geo-political borders of the Cold War, propelled by destiny and aspirations, he ended up in a lonely territory, beyond the margins of what was artistically accepted at the time, experiencing what Edward Said described as 'the loneliness of exile' (Said 1999: 369). In his extensive writings he commented on being in different locations, but he did not make visual works about migration. In fact, he did not want to see himself as a migrant. He wanted to be part of the dominant culture and his works were more about being a Modernist artist alongside Picasso, Matisse, Klee and Chagall than issues of migration.

Daghani's sense of identity had been disrupted and was never fully resolved. Without a present to which he felt a part, away from admirers and supportive critics, he turned to a painful but more familiar past, and past traumas came to dominate the present. The trauma of his time in the slave-labour camp in Ukraine, where most of the other inmates were killed, and his subsequent survivor guilt, came to haunt his drawings and writings.

Figure 9.1: 'Western Wall' in Arnold Daghani's apartment in Jona, Switzerland (1970s), from Arnold Daghani, *A Pictorial Autobiography*, Vol. 3 (1963–1976). Arnold Daghani Collection, University of Sussex. © Arnold Daghani Trust.

He developed his own way of working, combining words with images, art with documentation. Thus, motion and emotion were intimately related, the trauma of the past coupled with the instability of the present. His works crossed physical, conceptual and aesthetic borders and became a safe space around him. Indeed, the walls of his apartments were covered with things that he had made in a wide range of media and formats, from drawings and paintings to books and objects (see Figure 9.1). The latter often took as their starting point existing domestic items: windows, chairs, lamps, coffee grinders, even the bathroom tiles. He became increasingly reclusive, living within his own constructed world. Nothing made by any other artists intruded upon this homogeneity.

Creative Production and Emotional Response

This chapter focuses upon Daghani as a case study to examine how his history of forced labour and exile, both examples of movement across state borders, impacted upon his creative production. It explores the effects of displacement, both through force and choice. Students engaging in the study of works by artists such as Daghani can become more conscious of their emotions and of their knowledge learning than with other subjects. Although they have not had direct experience themselves, students studying subjects such as the Holocaust often respond in emotional ways which form a fundamental part of their learning. But how do students articulate what are usually considered non-academic responses? This essay relates to a recent project at the University of Sussex, 'Creative Responses to the Holocaust: Interacting with Artefacts and Exploring New Assessment Methods', which acknowledged the place for emotional responses to academic subjects and the need to mobilize these responses in creative ways.[2] The project explored the idea that interaction with artefacts deepens student learning. By combining conventional lectures and seminars with hands-on contact with artworks and documentation by Daghani, students were encouraged to reflect creatively both on the artist's, and on their, responses to the Holocaust. Through contact with artefacts, students entered a three-dimensional space of learning and engaged with the subject on a new level.

The Movement of Objects across Time and Space

Daghani's books are of special interest to this discussion and form the basis of this study.[3] They have a particular object-like character, and he took them with him whenever he moved, allowing him to create a sense of home as a displaced person within their pages. Some parts of his books, such as drawings or paintings that were smuggled out of the camp or ghetto, and later in diplomatic bags out of Romania, already had a history of motion before they were incorporated. He worked on his books over many years, adding and modifying parts, using them to continually reflect on his life. They enabled him to combine his dual intentions to document history and create art.

Thus, Daghani's books have complex emotional significance. By operating on a range of senses and combining media, they challenge the experiential limits of conventional art objects. They extend beyond the purely visual domain by engaging the viewer both through words and images in a multitude of ways, from using words as images to creating hieroglyphic visual symbols. Furthermore, through direct interaction with his books, the reader/viewer extends into three-dimensional space and experiences the sense of touch, resulting in a deeper involvement with the object.

As a displaced person with a troubled personal history, Daghani tried to come to terms with his past, creating a verbal and visual life narrative that documented the horrors of the camp and the trauma of survival. Ziva Amishai-Maisels has identified five categories of artistic production in camps and ghettos: 'official art; spiritual resistance through the assertion of individuality; the affirmation and commemoration of life; the function of art as witness; and art as catharsis' (Amishai-Maisels 1993: 3–4). While Daghani produced some official art – instructed, for example, by camp guards and officers to paint their portraits or interiors of their rooms – and although his work broadly asserts individuality and affirms life, it most strongly relates to the category of art as witness. To some extent his practice was comparable to that of other imprisoned artists such as Halina Olomucki and Karol Konieczny: Olomucki felt her 'sole purpose in life was to live so I would be able to testify before the world about the most terrible of all atrocities and the courage of the inmates of Auschwitz', while Konieczny wanted 'the young to know how it was, so that they understand, and will never allow such conditions to ever be repeated in the future' (quoted in ibid.: 6). Their comments express a general wish that their images should help to ensure that such a catastrophe never happens again. Through the publication of his diary and the subsequent legal investigations, Daghani's testimony went one step further, crossing over from the artistic to the legal realm and bringing the horrors of the camps into wider public visibility in order to achieve justice for those who had lost their lives. Thus, his practice extended the effects of artistic production, by combining images with words, and with documentation. He can be seen as a 'knowledge producer', providing specific knowledge about what it meant to have suffered in a historically and individually specific situation.

Through his extensive writings alongside his visual works, he politicized his suffering, trying to take control of his memories of oppression through the political act of asking for wider acknowledgement of the existence of past atrocities. In contrast to the work of survivors such as Zoran Music and Isaac Celnikier, who used expressionist means to graphically portray the horror of the Holocaust, Daghani's drawings and paintings were understated, tending towards a naturalistic style of 'calm, objective reportage' (ibid.: 8). Initially, it would appear that it was through the medium of words that he sought to convey the trauma of the experience. However, while his camp and ghetto images were not formally shocking, he often represented scenes in terms of Christian iconography, thereby drawing on a strong tradition of emotional engagement with the viewer (Freedberg 1989; Gell 1998). When a child was born in the camp accommodation, for example, he referred to the nativity, and when the young poet Selma Meerbaum-Eisinger died and her body was handed down from her bunk, he made visual parallels with Christ's deposition from the cross (Schultz and Timms 2008). While the use of such iconography attests to the artist's spiritual sensitivity and complex religious identity (he may, at some point, have become a Protestant), it also indicates his knowledge of powerful visual forms that communicate to the viewer familiar with Christian culture. Thus, he used emotional responses for political aims, his hope being that his artistic production would not only raise awareness of the camps in Ukraine but would result in justice for their victims.

Diaries and the Layering of Memory

Daghani extended his agency through his books, which were largely based on his memories of the camp and ghetto during his internment in 1942/43. While living in Bucharest his drawings and writings related to his present life, but when abroad he became increasingly haunted by the past. In 1960, the year in which he moved from Israel to France via England and Switzerland in search of a new home, a German translation of his diary (Daghani 1960) led to legal investigations by the German public prosecutor in Lübeck into what had happened in the slave-labour camps in Ukraine.[4] The diary covered the period from August 1942, when he was deported to Mikhailowka, to the eventful summer of 1943 when he and his wife escaped and spent a few months in the ghetto in Bershad before returning to Bucharest. Very little evidence survived from the camps in Ukraine and his diary was considered highly valuable. Many of those who had been at Mikhailowka, including Daghani, gave testimonies. However, after a number of years the proceedings were dropped for lack of hard evidence.

The investigations prompted Daghani to rewrite his diary in a number of versions, adding further details from memory and incorporating new material from copies of the legal documentation. Although he did not live in an anglophone country until 1977, he wrote mainly in English, with the hope of reaching a wider audience. From the 1960s until he died in 1985, he reworked and revised both the original version of his diary and the artworks that he had smuggled out of the camp and ghetto, creating elaborate and extensively detailed versions with further drawings and paintings. From the documents in the Lübeck files, he handwrote and typed lengthy extracts into his revised diaries. These multi-layered works bring together images and writings from various periods, interweaving memories with current events which are presented in relation to the past. They employ a layering of memory and narrative, cumulatively enriched over a period of time. They are fragmented and repetitive; some periods are barely covered, while others are examined in extensive and minute detail, over and over again. Memories continually reappear, making the past a persistent part of the present. Daghani's written and visual works operate in slightly different ways. While his written diaries exemplify the desire and need to recall details both from memory and from external sources, commemorating his fellow inmates and drawing historical attention to the camps in Ukraine, his visual works often demonstrate a lack of control in which images appear to have been more involuntary, arising from his unconscious memory.

Lisa Saltzman and Eric Rosenberg ask: 'What does it mean for a visual object to mediate the relation between a traumatic history to which the object in some sense bears witness but for which it can only account imperfectly?' (Saltzman and Rosenberg 2006: ix). Is the relation mnemonic with 'the representation of an absent subject ... a way of remembering an event whose traumatic nature mandates renewed attention?' (Wallace 2006: 3). Daghani's practice demonstrates these problems of representation: How can the artist represent trauma? Or memories? Through representation or abstraction? His works lie at the intersection of event, experience, memory and representation. These areas overlap while, at the same time, the works highlight the spaces between them. This is why he used both words and images, acknowledging the ultimate void in representation. Neither medium is able to provide a full representation, and ultimately they 'do little more than point to their own limitations, producing as their ultimate subject the insurmountable distance between themselves and the traumatic event they seek to evoke' (ibid.: 3).

The Book as Object

Daghani's books became densely packed containers of emotions and memories, ranging from the pocket-sized to the monumental, some weighing in excess of twelve kilogrammes. Books provided the spaces in which to work and rework experiences and he transported them with him when he migrated around Europe. They are transportable, can be carried across borders and occupy less space than works to be displayed singly. As he became officially stateless, these books effectively became sites of home, offering security within their pages. They are carefully constructed, at times self-conscious, multi-layered documents. Writing about the nomad, Italian artist Pier Paolo Calzolari has commented that he is 'not someone without a home, on the contrary he is someone who always and everywhere has his home with him ... This home that one carries around is the home of memory' (quoted in Malsch and Meyer-Stoll 2003: 8). As containers of memory, Daghani's books became part of his self-constructed home. As he migrated from one disappointing land to another he was able to seek refuge by returning to their familiar pages. It is worth examining some examples in more detail to elucidate how they make visible the effects of their history and of the traumatic history of their producer.

Daghani's books contain some items that already had a complex history of motion. The 1943 watercolour reproduced as Figure 9.2 depicts the interior of the accommodation at Mikhailowka where Daghani and his wife Anişoara were housed. It is painted in soft colours and is small (measuring 20 x 29 centimetres). The figures are carefully depicted and the scene appears remarkably cosy. This item had a long journey rendering it rich with emotional references: hidden inside a metal tube, smuggled out of the camp and ghetto, sewn into the lining of Anişoara's coat and later smuggled out of communist Romania via a diplomatic bag, it was transported across geographical borders and time before reaching its current home. Some years after its making Daghani pasted it onto a sheet of much larger paper on which it sits surrounded by white space, forming part of his folio *1942 1943 and Thereafter (Sporadic Records till 1977).*[5]

In a short concise inscription the artist draws the viewer's attention to the water damage on the top edge of the painting that occurred when he and Anişoara waded across the River Bug in July 1943. Thus, the significant point of crossing in their escape between the danger of Nazi-occupied Ukraine and the relative safety of Romanian Transnistria left its visible

Figure 9.2: Arnold Daghani, Untitled (Mikhailowka accommodation) (1943), from *1942 1943 And Thereafter (Sporadic Records till 1977)* (1942–1977), Arnold Daghani Collection, University of Sussex. © Arnold Daghani Trust.

and irremovable, indexical mark on the image; it is a unique 'watermark', confirming its authenticity. This small sheet with coloured marks on it becomes a meaningful historical item. It is seemingly insignificant, but testifies to the emotional agency of objects, seeming to offer the contemporary viewer direct physical access to another time and place. It indicates how the impact of a historical event can be experienced through the immediacy of artworks.

One of the most striking and monumental examples of Daghani's books is *What a Nice World*, a particularly bulky item formed by roughly stitching together with thick red plastic thread a number of spiral-bound sketchbooks (see Figure 9.3).[6] The rough work on the spine seems to encapsulate the most striking qualities of the book: passion, frustration, anxiety and creativity. Both its subject matter and the process of its making convey intense emotion. Daghani worked on this clumsy and heavy volume for over thirty years, continually adding to its intensely layered pages. Despite its size (it weighs over twelve kilogrammes), he carried it with him to the public prosecutor in Lübeck when he gave his testimony, indicative of its importance to him. He later added notes from the investigations, thereby bringing his individual artistic reflections together with legal enquiry. It is a powerful and intense object, filled with drawings and written reflections as well as quotations from the testimonies. It is both artwork and document.

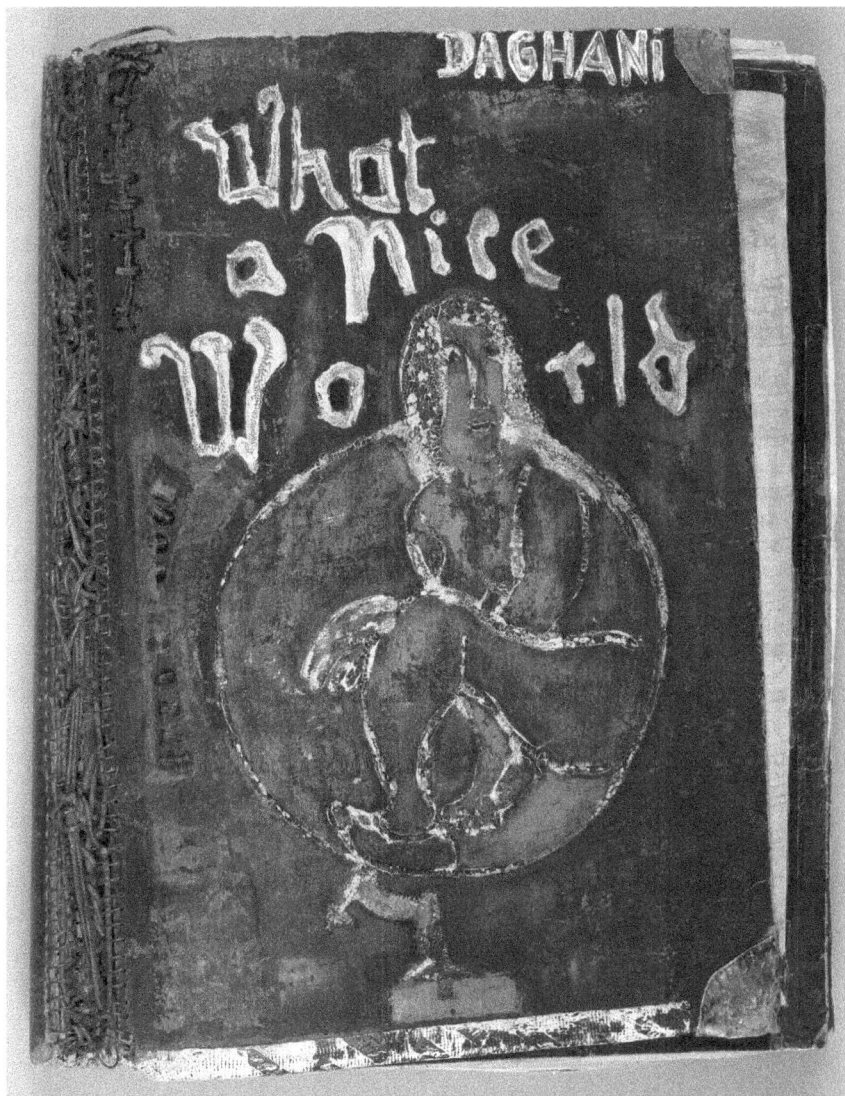

Figure 9.3: Arnold Daghani, *What a Nice World* (1943–1977). Arnold Daghani Collection, University of Sussex. © Arnold Daghani Trust.

Memories and Trauma

The pages of *What a Nice World* combine memories from the past with comments on the present day as Daghani brought together images relating to his wartime experiences with later artistic concerns. This practice produced some unlikely juxtapositions such as a drawing of a female nude combined with social commentary. The title of the book signals the artist's black humour and indicates the double-sided nature of the project:

the world is that within which he lived, which deported him to a slave-labour camp and which did not recognize his artistic abilities. The world is also that of the book, his constructed individual world within which he was able to express freely his memories, fantasies and aspirations.

Each page within the book is covered. These are productive spaces within which to represent thoughts and emotions, and signify 'the battleground of internal conflicts that the artist brings out into the open' (Stross 1991: 26). Many were evidently worked on over an extended period of time, engaging in a permanent dialogue between the past and the present. Although Daghani saw himself as an artist rather than as a writer, he wrote extensively. As has been noted, many artists use 'both visual and verbal means of communicating', and 'explore image and language' to address 'the function of trauma and its apprehension' (Bradley, Brown and Nairne 2001: 7). He combined the two media freely and in overlapping ways, such that images are often very descriptive while verbal inscriptions are rendered highly visual. In his writings he employed a range of styles from a simple freehand to an Old English form. His most dominant style, and that which he mainly used in *What a Nice World*, was Gothic script, which confers on the text an authority reminiscent of sacred manuscripts (Schultz and Timms 2008). Being so obviously time consuming to produce, it signals a work of particular significance, while also attesting to the emotional commitment on the part of the artist. There are pages upon pages of this rather laboured, elaborate writing in *What a Nice World* and other volumes. The sense of a personal endeavour is clear while the use of handwriting seems to confirm the authenticity of the work. At the same time, the aestheticized writing and ornamentation may be seen as a distancing device; rather than write in his own hand, Daghani adopted a stylized form that enhanced his authority. With illuminated first letters, and the cover decorated with metal corners, the book looks as if it could only have been produced before mechanical printing presses were invented, challenging Walter Benjamin's prediction on the effects of mechanical methods. A pencil on a leather string is attached to the book, accentuating the act of writing by hand, and suggestive of the artist's absence.

One of the first openings is covered by a map of Daghani's birth region, Bukovina, pasted over the two pages (Figure 9.4). On the top left hand corner, positioned at the start of the opening and at a right angle to the map, is a photograph of his parents. Dated 1913, it shows a well-dressed couple in their forties, and Daghani dedicated the opening 'To my parents Mina and Viktor'. Both the black and white photograph and the old map of a region that was once an important part of the Austro-Hungarian Empire, but has since become less well known, are richly evocative. On the map he underlined a few place names in red ink and beneath it provided a brief history of the region. The places highlighted are of importance for him and in just a few words he effectively evoked their political, historical

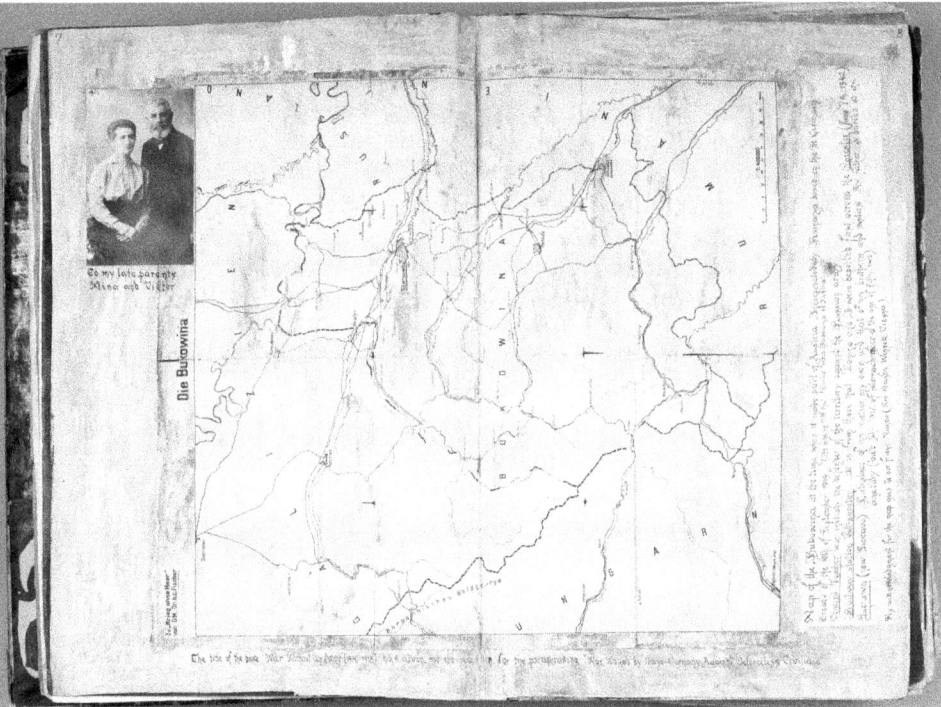

Figure 9.4: Arnold Daghani, Untitled (Die Bukovina) (undated), from *What a Nice World* (1943–1977). Arnold Daghani Collection, University of Sussex. © Arnold Daghani Trust.

and emotional dimensions. He noted the railway station at Volksgarten, near Cernăuți, from where he and Anişoara were deported across the River Dniester on 7 June 1942. He highlighted his birthplace, Suczawa, where his mother and siblings were also born, and noted that his father was buried in its cemetery in 1917, aged 52. Thus the photograph takes on an added poignancy. Not only does it originate from a distant time and place, but it represents a man who, only four years later, would die at a young age. A mass-produced map is thereby transformed into a personal document, the sites of Daghani's traumatic individual and family history marked out on it. His method is succinct yet potent and in only a few words he makes effective connections that resonate beyond what is stated.

These pages were carefully constructed, making a number of references and reflecting Daghani's thoughts over time, whereas others appear to have been made more spontaneously (Figures 9.5 and 9.6). Here are images in loose dark ink wash, often combined with bronze or gold paint. Many feature ghostly, shadowy faces, suggesting those of Daghani's former fellow inmates who did not survive and who haunted his memories. Using ink wash rather than a clear line, recognizable forms turn to pure medium and the density of memories. Silent faces suggest fractured communication of a presence still felt after many years. These faces come to haunt the viewer too as they turns from one to the next. There are page after page of these larger-than-life-size shadowy faces. Each is filled with sadness, creating a powerful bond between viewer and book.

Whereas the right-hand pages appear carefully constructed, these faces on the left seem to emerge from involuntary memory. The notion of 'involuntary memory' is best known from Marcel Proust's famous experience of eating a *madeleine* that returned him directly to his childhood. For Proust, this 'instant' was prompted by the sensation of taste, while for Walter Benjamin it has been suggested that smell had a comparable effect (Leslie 1999: 116). Benjamin argued that 'true' (in contrast to 'intentional') memory is involuntary and provokes a shock effect. For Daghani, involuntary memories did not seem to come as a shock. Nor were they associated with blissful childhood recollections. Rather, they seemed to haunt his mind, remaining with him over many years. They were involuntary because he could not control them, repeating unrequested in parallel to the forced state of exile (Schultz 2004).

Figure 9.5: Arnold Daghani, Untitled (Face) (1966), from *What a Nice World* (1943–1977). Arnold Daghani Collection, University of Sussex. © Arnold Daghani Trust.

Figure 9.6: Arnold Daghani, Untitled (Face) (1964), from *What a Nice World* (1943–1977). Arnold Daghani Collection, University of Sussex. © Arnold Daghani Trust.

Thus Daghani's past traumas remained with him. These images of shadowy faces were produced in the 1960s and 1970s, some twenty to thirty years after the events to which they indirectly refer, and they are numerous, not only in *What a Nice World* but in many other books as well as on loose sheets of paper. For Daghani the process of making such images seems more compulsive than cathartic, repeated over and over again without end. Both image making and writing seem to have been necessary activities and a means of exploring the relationship between language (visual or verbal) and events. Blanchot makes a point that seems to reflect Daghani's activity too: 'Not to write – what a long way there is to go before arriving at that point ... One must just write, in uncertainty and in necessity' (Blanchot 1995: 11).

Trauma and Representation

There has been extensive discussion about the relation between trauma and representation, both from the point of view that the relation is mnemonic – in that the representation returns the viewer/reader to the traumatic event – and from the point of view that it is impossible to represent trauma, that its very nature precludes adequate representation. Daghani's practice seems to provide a dialectic between these viewpoints. Writing, making images and bearing testimony were necessary but ultimately unsatisfying activities, and Daghani's oeuvre speaks through repetition rather than finding a way of working through his experiences to reach another place. For him, the scripting and imaging of his experiences was a circular activity in which writing led to more writing, images to further images. The proliferation of different formats of his diaries, of voices offering different viewpoints on events, of endless shadowy faces, gives a sense of unending circularity that overrides structural chronology. His tireless revisions, in which certain narratives are obsessively recalled and reinscribed again, not only acknowledge but highlight the spaces between event, memory, and verbal and visual representations. For none of these representations are mimetic, all involve different filters. Events are transferred through our subjective responses, to which earlier memories add further layers of interpretation. It is not through decisive images that Daghani communicates and represents trauma, but through his messy, repetitive and unresolved practice. Andrea Liss asks: 'what would it mean to create a representation of the Holocaust that would render it accessible, easily understandable?' (Liss 1995: 118). Neither Daghani's images nor his methods claim to do so. Rather, they acknowledge the need for a problematic rather than a resolved response, that closure is not only impossible but, as has been argued, inappropriate, for it 'would represent an obvious avoidance of what remains indeterminate, elusive and opaque' (Friedlander 1992: 53).

Like Primo Levi and other survivors who wrote of the camps, Daghani had a strong sense of responsibility, and he might well have echoed Levi's words: 'I am at peace with myself because I bore witness' (Agamben 1999: 17). However, neither Levi nor Daghani seems to have really found peace through their activities. Elsewhere Levi wrote: 'We survivors are not only an exiguous but also an anomalous minority: we are those who by their prevarications or abilities or good luck did not touch bottom. Those who did so, those who saw the Gorgon, have not returned to tell about it or have returned mute ... We speak in their stead, by proxy' (Levi 1989: 21). Daghani too wrote of his continuing feelings of disquiet: 'Not to this very day have I been able to get rid of the horrifying thought how our fellow inmates were butchered one after another. By right we should have shared their fate'.[7] But the shame of being a survivor has humanist implications, as indicated by Bruno Bettelheim: 'Only the ability to feel guilty makes us human, particularly if, objectively seen, one is not guilty' (Bettelheim 1979: 313).

Daghani's endless activity suggests both a personal fear of his own forgetting and a broader fear of the inmates and the camps in Ukraine being forgotten by history. As Daghani carefully wrote and rewrote the events of those years, the process of making seems to have become as significant for him as the resulting works. His guilt of surviving when others perished became intertwined with his awareness of the impermanence of memory and the danger of public forgetting. His frustrations were intensified by the lack of interest in the camps in Ukraine, and Daghani believed ever more strongly that his account had to be heard. He referred to himself as a historian, obliged to provide 'A Chapter of Contemporary History' that was still largely unknown, to remind the world of the events in this forgotten part of the Holocaust.[8] Despite his inability to find an artistic home, and a lack of recognition of his work outside Romania, it would be misleading and clichéd to perceive Daghani as living in isolation. Although he seems to have felt very alone, and in some sense 'possessed by the past' (Caruth 1995: 151; cf. Svašek 2005: 200–1), he made both visual and written works for an audience, producing knowledge for, and actively communicating with, the social and political world around him. Indeed, it can be argued that the very act of bearing witness contradicts the notion of isolation. By telling or retelling one's story, whether through words, images, sound, performance or any other medium, the survivor becomes witness to their own history. Furthermore, they are 'no longer isolated within a past event, but ... now placed in the present in the dialogical situation with a listener' (Van Alphen 2006: 227). Testimony confirms that the person has physically survived the events and lives in the present. It not only produces knowledge but also, as Van Alphen argues, acts 'as a humanizing trans-active process ... which enables the survivor to reclaim [their] position as an interrelated subject and as a witness of history' (ibid.: x). By producing, by making things that go out into the world, Daghani confirmed his existence.

Books as Art

In some respects the monumental format of *What a Nice World* anticipates the practices of later artists, for example the even larger and more cumbersome books created by Anselm Kiefer in the late 1980s, not out of ink and paper but lead. These books are so heavy that they can barely be lifted; they too communicate as much from their size and scale as their contents. The pages bear the traces of time, with photographic images combined with other often organic materials and marks derived from their making. While these and other books by Kiefer are grounded in historical reflection, they 'suspend the traditional connection between picture and text and almost completely eliminate the semantic function' (Adriani 1991: 10). Their references are less precisely communicated than in Daghani's books as the artist has less of an emotional need to do so. Kiefer deals more with national trauma than with his own personal experiences. In Daghani's works there is often a discordant tension between word and image, with each fighting for dominance and the space of the page becoming overworked. By contrast, Kiefer's works are aesthetically more coherent.

In Sigrid Sigurdsson's installation *In the Face of Silence* (1989–1993), a permanent project at the Karl Ernst Osthaus-Museum, Hagen, Germany, books are used in more personal ways, engaging with the relationship between the individual and history. Hand-made books combine her sketches with texts, and biographical materials with historical documents. These books are more accessible than Kiefer's lead volumes, since they can be lifted down by visitors from their individual compartments and read at a tabls. The work is extensive, built up over a number of years, and now comprises around 730 books containing 30,000 items arranged on subdivided shelves around a room. The collection is designed to be open and interactive, with visitors invited to participate by adding further entries on blank pages. Aleida Assmann has described the project as a 'storehouse memory', a work that 'gives the impression of a mixture of archive, library and cabinet of relics'. Thus its construction can be seen as an equivalent to the workings of individual and collective memory (cited in Fehr 2000: 42). Sigurdsson's project was consciously planned, whereas Daghani's books largely developed more organically, combining to form the accumulated works of a lifetime. While the works of Kiefer and Sigurdsson may bear some formal resemblance to Daghani's albums, their communicative techniques are very different.

Artists' books are intended as works of art in themselves. They are complete units with a range of media, in which 'form and content are indivisible' (Courtney 1999: 1). What makes Daghani's books particularly distinctive is their additional status as historical documents. They combine visuals with documentary material on war, the experiences of the modern artist, exile and the nature of memory. Unlike artists who use words as aesthetic texture, or whose historical references are suggestive, Daghani's writing is legible and its content is to be communicated. His words are written to be read rather than as pure mark-making, his books representing his combined roles as historian and artist.

Experiencing *What a Nice World*

With over three hundred pages in total, it takes some time for the viewer to examine *What a Nice World*. There is so much to read and so much to look at; the effect is overwhelming as viewers/readers are taken on a journey through the artist's memories and emotions. They play an active role in looking at/reading a book, as opposed to a more passive role before a painting that, for example, hang, out of reach, on the wall. With a book viewers/readers turn the pages at their own pace and feel their texture. Both temporal and textural elements are central to the experience of the book, and a direct sensory connection is made to the artist whose hands worked on the same surfaces. The viewer/reader takes the book into their space, making it part of their life for the viewing duration. With a volume this size, that may be a number of days. It becomes interconnected with the viewer's/reader's other activities, and viewer's correlations are made with events, experiences and people in the viewer's/reader's life.

Between 2007 and 2009 I ran a project at the University of Sussex with my colleague Chana Moshenska entitled 'Three-dimensional learning: Interacting with artefacts and exploring new assessment methods'. Part of the project used works by Daghani to teach about the Holocaust and complement more conventional methods, thereby demonstrating the ways in which artworks contribute to knowledge production. In seminars we offered groups of students hands-on contact with Daghani's artworks and documentation to explore the hypothesis that interaction with artefacts deepens student learning. The project argued that any subject can be enhanced through haptic engagement. Through touch, and by extending into three-dimensional space, learners becoms more conscious of themselves and increasingly self-reflective. Touch extends and enhances sight. By taking the learner into another dimension, haptic engagement encourages and improves learning and creativity. Curiosity and engagement are increased as the learner experiences a deeper involvement with the subject.

In the seminars, following a brief overview of Daghani's life and career, students were given the opportunity to handle a selection of his works. The atmosphere was informal and discussions continued while the items were examined. The students were given worksheets to fill in with questions encouraging them to engage with the items more deeply. The seminars went very well and the students described the material as 'fascinating', 'poignant' and 'very complex'. They felt it gave 'an insight into Daghani's life not just his work'. They found his words were easier to grasp than academic writing and the images, especially photographs, reminded them that the Holocaust did not take place very long ago. They were struck by the range of material, the intensity of it and the ways in which his camp experiences affected his whole life's work. They noted what seemed to be a contradiction in the works: their intimate quality combined with an evidently public intention. They responded to the individual voice Daghani offers, and the connection to the range of individuals he encountered. They were impressed by the way in which he emphasised 'the dignity and humanity' of the camp inmates, and they found that his practice of writing names 'makes their deaths more real' and 'humanises each victim'. In one particular work the names of the other camp inmates were arranged as a face, and they found themselves reading the names which they would be less likely to do with a list. However, one student also noted that, 'Although he gives voice (and faces) to those who have been forgotten, he simultaneously highlights the futility of their deaths and how they have become nameless'. This example alone demonstrates how visual images enabled students to deepen their knowledge and understanding of the Holocaust. The immediacy of the works made the students feel comfortable with offering their own comments and responses in an open way, something that they might have beee less likely to do when presented with an academic text. Their confidence with the works enabled them to reach a deeper level of engagement.In response to the question on whether seeing Daghani's work altered in any way their understanding of the Holocaust, they responded: 'It wasn't anything like I thought it might be. The interaction with the material has made it far more accessible'; 'It brings into focus the enormity of what happened'; 'It has confirmed that it is un-representable'; and 'it reaffirms a belief that the experience never leaves the survivors/victims'. It gave one student 'a closer understanding of an emotional response to the Holocaust'. Another noted: 'Seeing the paintings and drawings has brought a new dimension to the Holocaust as they seem to reflect the survivors' inner state of mind in a way writing does not. The huge amount of work Daghani has produced show that he is possessed by his memories and also his need to express himself'. They found the viewpoint of an individual a valuable way of understanding Holocaust survival, trauma, guilt, relationships and memory. The range of media, words and images made them understand how there are 'many different ways to express the events', and they considered whether words or images are more appropriate forms of representation. They felt that his work conveyed the dehumanizing effects of the Nazis and that it was very important in terms of the experience of a survivor and the lack of a healing process. It personalized the Holocaust, so that 'You can actually start to imagine the people involved rather than thinking of them in terms of statistics'.

The results of the seminars demonstrated that the students were already emotionally engaged in the subject of the Holocaust. The Arnold Daghani Collection provided a forum in which to openly discuss their responses and to address wider issues of Holocaust representation. The interdisciplinary nature of the items enabled students to make connections between different parts of their studies – for example, issues of representation, history and trauma. The opportunity to have direct access to his works brought to life what they had read and discussed in class, confirming our belief that seeing Daghani's work would alter their understanding of the Holocaust. Students felt confident in expressing themselves openly and were able to reach a greater understanding of the Holocaust due to the combination of the material and its hands-on accessibility.

Conclusion

Motion, emotion and memory interact in complex ways in Daghani's work. He was a person in motion who – as a multiple, relational, being in the world – politicized his experiences of suffering through his work. Furthermore, his books, with examples such as *What a Nice World*, have powerful emotional agency. Their history of movement – for example, through smuggling or as support for testimony – and their subsequent indexicality help to shape their emotional impact.

The book format enabled Daghani to express the complexity of his emotions within a densely layered portable unit. Its form conveys its meaning. Within its experimental pages he could combine a range of artistic features and bring together words, images, narrative and documentation. The book crosses stylistic borders, mixing media, materials and forms of representation. It could be taken with him from one country to the next, across time and space, carrying his memories and experiences, a safe space within which to construct his own world, combining the past with the present. It is both private and public; an ostensibly intimate object, it seems to have been made with a hoped-for audience in mind. It connects individual emotional experiences with wider social and political issues. Daghani's habit of revising and amplifying his diaries may complicate the issue of historical authenticity, but the aim was to enrich our understanding both of events in the camps and of the subsequent traumas.

Combining images with words, art with documentation, Daghani's books provide the viewer/reader with specific knowledge about what happened in a particular cultural, historical and political context. They do so not in mimetic terms but through a multitude of means: their indexicality, texture, scale, their layering and repetition, and, perhaps above all, their absence of literal representation and their acknowledgement of the void between experience and interpretation. They not only communicate the artist's individual experiences but speak to the historical legacy of the Holocaust, the effects of displacement, migration and trauma, and the problems of (verbal and visual) representation.

Notes

1. 'Hove turns down "genius"', *Brighton and Hove Leader*, 11 May 1985, p. 11.
2. The project ran from 2007 to 2009 and was funded by the Creativity Development Fund, University of Sussex.
3. The term 'books' is used here to refer to both bound and unbound items, the latter of which might more accurately be referred to as folios.
4. Daghani's diary had first appeared some thirteen years previously in Romanian: Daghani (1947).
5. A. Daghani. 1942–1977. *1942 1943 and Thereafter (Sporadic Records till 1977)*. Arnold Daghani Collection, University of Sussex (hereafter ADC/G2).
6. A. Daghani. 1943–1977. *What a Nice World*. Arnold Daghani Collection, University of Sussex.
7. Daghani, ADC/G2/113v.
8. Daghani, ADC/G2/131r.

References

Adriani, G. (ed.). 1991. *The Books of Anselm Kiefer*, trans. B. Mayor. London: Thames and Hudson.

Agamben, G. 1999. *Remnants of Auschwitz: The Witness and the Archive*, trans. D. Heller-Roazen. New York: Zone Books.

Amishai-Maisels, Z. 1993. *Depiction and Interpretation: The Influence of the Holocaust on the Visual Arts*. Oxford: Pergamon Press.

Bauman, J. 1988. *A Dream of Belonging: My Years in Post-war Poland*. London: Virago.

Bettelheim, B. 1979. *Surviving and Other Essays*. New York: Knopf.

Blanchot, M. 1995. *The Writing of the Disaster*, trans. A. Smock. Lincoln: University of Nebraska Press.

Bradley, F., K. Brown and A. Nairne. 2001. 'Introduction', in *Trauma*. London: Hayward Gallery.

Caruth, C. (ed.). 1995. *Trauma: Explorations in Memory*. Baltimore, MD: Johns Hopkins University Press.

Courtney, C. 1999. *Speaking of Book Art: Interviews with British and American Book Artists*. Los Altos Hills, CA: Anderson-Lovelace Publishers.

Daghani, A. 1947. *Groapa este în livada de viẞini*. Bucharest: Socec.

———— 1960. *Lasst mich Leben!* Tel Aviv: Weg und Ziel Verlag.

———— 1961. 'The Grave is in the Cherry Orchard', *Adam: International Review* 291, 292, 293.

Fehr, M. 2000. 'A Museum and Its Memory: The Art of Recovering History', in Susan A. Crane (ed.), *Museums and Memory*. Stanford, CA: Stanford University Press, pp. 35–59.

Freedberg, D. 1989. *The Power of Images*. Chicago: University of Chicago Press.

Friedlander, S. 1992. 'Trauma, Transference, and "Working through" in Writing the History of the Shoah', *History and Memory* 4: 39–55.

Gell, A. 1998. *Art and Agency: An Anthropological Theory*. Oxford: Clarendon Press.

Leslie, E. 1999. 'Souvenirs and Forgetting: Walter Benjamin's Memory-work', in M. Kwint, C. Breward and J. Aynsley (eds), *Material Memories*. Oxford: Berg, pp. 107–22.

Levi, P. 1989. *The Drowned and the Saved*, trans. R. Rosenthal. New York: Random House.

Leys, R. 2000. *Trauma: A Genealogy*. Chicago: University of Chicago Press.

Liss, A. 1995. *Trespassing through Shadows: Memory, Photography and the Holocaust*. Minneapolis: University of Minnesota Press.

Malsch, F., and C. Meyer-Stoll. 2003. 'Foreword', in *Migration*. Vaduz: Kunstmuseum Liechtenstein, pp. 7–15.

Said, E. 1999. *Out of Place: A Memoir*. London: Granta.

Saltzman, L., and E. Rosenberg (eds). 2006. *Trauma and Visuality in Modernity*. Hanover, NH: University Press of New England.

Schultz, D. 2004. 'Forced Migration and Involuntary Memory: The Work of Arnold Daghani', in P. Wagstaff and W. Everett (eds), *Cultures of Exile: Visual Dimensions of Displacement*. Oxford: Berghahn, pp. 67–86.

———— 2009a. 'The Diaries of Arnold Daghani', in D. Schultz and E. Timms (eds), *Arnold Daghani's Memories of Mikhailowka: The Illustrated Diary of a Slave Labour Camp Survivor*. London: Vallentine Mitchell, pp. 125–32.

———— 2009b. 'Arnold Daghani as an Artist: Life and Representation', in D. Schultz and E. Timms (eds), *Arnold Daghani's Memories of Mikhailowka: The Illustrated Diary of a Slave Labour Camp Survivor*. London: Vallentine Mitchell, pp. 133–56.

Schultz, D., and E. Timms. 2008. 'Survival and Memory: Arnold Daghani's Verbal and Visual Diaries', in D. Schultz and E. Timms (eds), *Politics and Pictorial Narrative in the Nazi Period: Felix Nussbaum, Charlotte Salomon and Arnold Daghani*. London: Routledge, pp. 64–91.

Stross, T. 1991. 'The Painter's Studio', in G. Adriani (ed.), *The Books of Anselm Kiefer*, trans. B. Mayor. London: Thames and Hudson, pp. 22–35.

Svašek, M. 2005. 'The Politics of Chosen Trauma: Expellee Memories, Emotions and Identities', in K. Milton and M. Svašek (eds), *Mixed*

Emotions. Anthropological Studies of Feeling. Oxford: Berg, pp. 195–214.

Van Alphen, E. 2006. 'The Revivifying Artist: Boltanski's Efforts to Close the Gap', in L. Saltzman and E. Rosenberg (eds), *Trauma and Visuality in Modernity.* Hanover, NH: University Press of New England, pp. 222–48.

Wallace, I. 2006. 'Trauma as Representation: A Meditation on Manet and Johns', in L. Saltzman and E. Rosenberg (eds), Trauma and Visuality in Modernity. Hanover, NH: University Press of New England, pp. 3–27.

10

THE EMOTIONS AND ETHNICITY IN THE INDO-CARIBBEAN

Leon Wainwright

The art experience in Trinidad and Tobago is substantially the same as that of any other tropical colony or territory which became independent after long rule by a European country. From the point of view of sophistication, the accepted form or type of art expression is Europeanized, as are the materials and concepts employed in its production. This form, in art and life, is considered as being superior, desirable, right and proper. The trained artists of the country have all been schooled in Europe or Canada or the United States. There also exists a vast amount of art production at the 'folk' level, which is worthy of consideration. These folk arts are preponderantly of African and East Indian origin. The popular arts are American-influenced.

—Alladin (1975: 136)

This opening epithet is from a piece of writing by the Indo-Trinidadian M.P. Alladin (1919–1980), published in 1975 during his tenth year in office as Trinidad and Tobago Director of Culture. It draws a distinction between 'artists and craftsmen' – indeed, this is the title of Alladin's essay – and the notion of 'origins'.

In Trinidad, roughly equal numbers of people identify with South Asian (or 'East Indian') as with African backgrounds, while the remaining population comprises a growing spectrum of ethnic mixes. Trinidad's large community of East Indians are descended from those who came shortly after emancipation as indentured laborers, alongside an equally large number of the descendants of enslaved Africans. This unusual demography is the background to why discourses of Trinidadian nationhood have become the site for the state-sanctioned production of ethnicity. In the mid 1960s, M.P. Alladin and his contemporaries set out to broker art making in particular as the quintessential 'foundation' on which to raise a national cultural consciousness after independence from British rule. The aim was to transform the situation that Alladin described, what remained 'after long rule by a European country'. It became incumbent upon artists to loudly proclaim ethnic differences within an ideological programme of 'unity through diversity'. During the most vigorous moment of anti-colonialism, in an attempt to unlock the country from its colonial past, such interests condensed in the official culture of 'creole nationalism'. This would comprise (and yet maintain as discrete activities) fine art and 'craft', as in Alladin's description, and other fields such as carnival, music, theatre and literature.

Drawing on fieldwork undertaken since 2004, this chapter explores Indo-Trinidadian or 'East Indian' contributions to the aesthetic and emotional dimensions of diaspora experience, focusing on image making, celebration and performance.[1] In general, it looks at the continuing legacy of the expectations outlined by Alladin: the links that were forged between ethnic difference and cultural production. The notion of Trinidadian 'Indianness' featured in the official emphasis on art as a foundation in the process of decolonization. The role assigned to art in building the independent nation can be read in the question of the commercial success of artists who identify themselves as Indian and then compared to how Indianness is being renegotiated in popular contexts. As I argue, this throws light on the matter of the counter-hegemonic ownership of cultural practices within contemporary diasporic communities and the emotional field in which this operates.

Image makers, wedding performers and the singer-songwriters of chutney and other 'East Indian' musicians offer alternatives to the prevailing ideas about 'Indianness' that were instituted in Trinidad during decolonization. In this regard, such artists are makers of knowledge in their role as producers of cultural objects (and by virtue of their ability to speak and to offer accounts of their own experience, as in the interview material I present here). My central concern, therefore, is to examine what these individuals and their cultural productions reveal about the relative and shifting historical landscape of postcolonial emotions, memory and political desire. Much research in anthropology and visual and material culture studies has insisted on framing cultural objects as significations of national places, transnational connection, political position or ethnic 'belonging'. But we have yet to confront the ways in which diaspora culture is commoditized – the way in which its aesthetic forms are taken to be representative of one or other ethnicity or diaspora, and taken as 'signifying' visual media. The alternative is to pay due regard to a broader sense of 'the cultural' beyond this 'representational' status.

A closer discussion of the aesthetic presence of such aesthetic forms in relation to the emotions indicates a more complicated status for the cultural. What results is an understanding of the complex intersections of cultural practices and the emotions. As such, I have taken a specific approach to what Raymond Williams once termed 'structures of feeling', by relating to how my informants engaged with an everyday vocabulary of the emotions and the relation between this and their cultural objects. Williams identified 'characteristic elements of impulse, restraint, and tone; specifically affective elements of consciousness and relationships: not feeling against thought, but thought as felt and feeling as thought: practical consciousness of a present kind, in a living and interrelating continuity' (Williams 1977: 132). I recognize that cultural objects are the conveyors, or media, of political and social meaning. Even so, I would suggest that cultural production is at the same time important for generating various sorts of 'positioned' historical presence that involve an emotional dimension which is itself a structuring agency. Aspects of memory and remembering (evidenced in the testimony gathered through interviews, for instance), and visual, musical and performed elements, offer the basis for extending our existing approaches to the analysis of 'feeling'. Being implicated in this emotional field, I show how the historical and cultural context of the Indo-Caribbean leads us to question the status of the emotions rather than to take them for granted. I ask how the Caribbean setting is responsible for changing the operations of the emotions, and how to arrive at an understanding of the conditions of that setting by way of an analysis of emotion.

Transit, Transition, Transformation

The continually shifting emphasis given to ethnicity – its frequent rearranging in temporary ways – through cultural practices in Trinidad, takes place within a complex emotional economy. The prefix trans- (as in transit, transition and transformation; see Svašek 2010) may be used instructively to emphasize the dynamic status of art and cultural production – and the production of social interactions and political positions – in this setting. Notably, such interest in this prefix extends beyond the paradigm of translation. Translation was once a key element of postcolonial cultural and literary criticism, especially the study of colonizer–colonized relations under conditions of empire (see, e.g., Bhabha 1994). Rather than settle on the theme of translation, however, I would suggest looking further, at the intersecting nature of cultural practices and the emotions. I do not take cultural practices as in any simple way translations of emotional conditions or concerns. Instead, I am interested in the critical transformations that exist across contemporary globalized, diasporic spaces beyond interest in cultural texts as instances and sites of translation. This is an expanded analysis of the production, circulation and reception of cultural phenomena, but one that gives attention to their locations in time and space through their entanglements in the emotions.

Of course, the historical legacy of imperialism may also be seen in the postcolonial Caribbean. The colonial past is entwined with the present inequalities of global power in the twin-island Republic of Trinidad and Tobago. This entwining is suggested by the centrality of continuing attempts to overcome the divisions of colonial rule, such as by appropriating the concept of national identity and a multi-ethnic society, and by working toward an ideal of independence. As I will illustrate, the belief invested in this unfinished project of national freedom, and in particular the yearning for cultural autonomy, is evidenced in the attempted separation of the country's national art market from the international networks of contemporary art works and artists. This operates in tension, however, with the localization of those art discourses which are drawn from contact or experience of the wider world, such as through training overseas. I would suggest that this ought to be taken as an indication of the globalizing processes at work in the Trinidadian context – processes of attempted detachment from the 'outside' and the international that happen under their abiding influence.

This transitory quality of Trinidad can be explored further in the relationship between creativity, ethnicity and the emotions. It is useful to look at how the key trans- concepts interact with one another. For instance, the contemporary transitions and transformations that the island is undergoing can be traced to and understood with a mind turned to its history of transit, the long-standing patterns of the movement of subjects and objects. I often heard during fieldwork some historical narratives of the transit of enslaved Africans and indentured South Asians, as well as the Chinese, Europeans and those from the Middle East who moved to the Caribbean, as well as the indigenous subjects who were displaced and whose lives were disrupted. These accounts were offered largely on the premise of being a useful introduction to the island for any foreigner. However, their deeper significance is that their central theme of cultural origins holds a role in shaping present day social relations. Narratives of geographical movement were relayed to me as if they explained Trinidad's present day ethnic differences. But this rather scripted historical present was coupled with much anxious debate about the need for the country to transform and develop beyond its historical past.

One such transformation is the growing prospect of an emerging national or creole identity which is capable of collapsing and reconciling older ethnic differences. Through fieldwork I gained a better sense of how this has particular consequences for those people historically identified as Indo-Caribbean. It may not be helpful any longer to speak of an Indo-Trinidadian identity as a dynamic cultural category at all. Individuals of this group, particularly of the younger generation, frequently declare themselves more comfortable with a Trinidadian creole identity than an Indian one (Mohammed 2002: 130–47). Despite what we may understand to be the motivations for Indian and Hindu nationalisms, this creole or Trinidadian identity is increasingly assured across ethnic divisions. It is less common to find that the current generation feels marginal or victimized and so less likely to identify with an 'Indian' or 'Indo-Trini' label. This is even the case in parts of the island such as the rural central and southern areas that are widely identified as East Indian. 'Indian' contact and settlement with Afro-Trinidadians has contributed to the overall heterogeneity of the island. During fieldwork I stayed in an Indo-Trinidadian household in Claxton Bay, where all the plots of land along one side of the road (which I will call 'Ramnarine Trace') were distributed among the offspring of my host's grandfather, who gave one to each of his nine children. Despite the fact of their ownership of this land, daily contact with Afro-Trinidadian neighbours, and shared contact points such as the local shops, work, schools and the public transport stand, made for constant mixing. A large ashram sited at the end of Ramnarine Trace had become a place for Hindu, Muslim and Christian prayer. Hindu *satsangh* was held there on Christmas morning and Eid ul-Fitr celebrated. There was also a wide range of places for Christian worship – Seventh-Day Adventist and the New Testament Church of God – described locally as 'new churches'.

Metaphors of transit, transition and transformation have a wide significance in Trinidad and illuminate how creative practices and ethnicity intersect. They show creative practices as having processual qualities which are suited to the dynamic social circumstances that I have outlined. As artists in Trinidad struggle to enter and shape the island's growing contemporary art milieu, the sort of Trinidadian creole that they embrace is very much at odds with the earlier nationalist one, in which creole culture was equated with a Euro-Afro blend (Cozier 1999: 23).[2] In this sense, the creole concept is historical, being subject to change from this earlier manifestation to a more recent one. In recent debates on creativity, the distinction drawn between improvisation and innovation is instructive here and may help to convey the character of certain transformations in Trinidad. For example, Hallam and Ingold state: 'The difference between improvisation and innovation ... is not that the one works within established convention while the other breaks with it, but that the former characterizes creativity by way of its process, the latter by way of its products' (Hallam and Ingold 2007: 2). After the country's independence, the creole concept became an officially mobilized 'improvisation' of sorts in the face of historically imperial attitudes, and in an effort to produce an 'innovative' and distinctive Trinidadian culture. What has yet to be addressed is how the contemporary innovative and improvisatory cultural practices of Indo-Caribbean artists and musicians may be located and assessed. Since Trinidad is both a context for changing improvisatory modes of creative production, as well as innovation, then the task is to show their unfolding present and possible future. Hallam and Ingold's distinction between improvisation and innovation appears to break from that made by Michel de Certeau in the contrast he drew between strategies and tactics (de Certeau 1984), and thereby his emphasis on what is broadly speaking the spatiality of resistance. Even so, it would be worthwhile to ask how analysis of the emotional dimensions of improvisation and innovation might complicate these thinkers' preoccupation with both the material (in the shape of process and product) and the spatial.

Finally, a specific focus on Indo-Caribbean identities is revealing for the contextual study of creative practices in the Caribbean region more broadly. Historically, problems of creativity have largely been aligned along a Euro/Afro axis, such as in the formation of political consciousness and discourses of national belonging. But this only misrecognized creative practices, taking them to be simply instruments of social and political change at the expense of a more transformative conception of culture. It was an outcome perhaps of the Marxism of nation-building discourses and historical revisionism in the postwar Caribbean. I want next to show in the case of a single artist how a creative practitioner has lived with constraints of this political kind (alongside other, largely career-related constraints) and why this experience should be registered through the emotions.

An Emotional Chronology of 'Indian Art' in Trinidad

I came to know the artist Shastri Maharaj (b.1953) in 2004 and began to see his biography and his art as significant for understanding Trinidadian concepts of 'Indianness' (see Wainwright 2007). Maharaj is often referred to as an 'Indian artist', and the 'Indian art' he is known for connects to Trinidad's anti-colonial history and a wider discussion of the Indian diaspora in the Atlantic world. Maharaj's career as an artist illustrates how Trinidad's changing demands for ethnic difference are constructed visually. A surprising detail of his career is that such demands cannot be sustained. Not only has the artist himself struggled to cope with the contextual need to be 'Indian', and to offer 'Indian art', but that need has turned out to be shifting and cannot be relied upon as a source of commercial success or critical acclaim. As such, Maharaj's art and experience show up the alleged rewards of the emphasis on ethnic difference and the incompatibility of an assumed relation between visual creativity and ethnicity.

Shastri Maharaj lives in the town of Chaguanas in central Trinidad, and at the time of my interviews with him he was occupied during the working day with teaching in the visual arts at the nearby Valsayn Teachers' College. In 1972 he went to Canada to study mathematics and physics at the University of Winnipeg, and then went on to achieve a Bachelor of Fine Arts degree at the University of Manitoba. Maharaj told me about his time in Canada, when he was taught by the installation and performance artist Jeff Funnell (b. 1940). Another art teacher made an impression on him once he returned to settle in Trinidad in 1981: Alexander King, who had been taught by Georges Braque. After his education abroad, Maharaj worked to establish himself in Trinidad as an artist, doing, as he put it when I interviewed him in 2004, 'new wave shit, postmodernism, all that'. His aim had been to 'visually assault society', as he put it, 'just like Dubuffet, Schnabel and Miró'.

Figure 10.1: Shastri Maharaj, *Sunday* (1990), acrylic on canvas, 152.4 x 106.7 cm. By permission of the artist.

Subsequently, during the 1980s Maharaj avoided making the sort of visual images that had satisfied political interests in the arts in Trinidad during decolonization (see Figure 10.1). He sought to ignore the officially championed approach that had been taken by M.P. Alladin and artists of a previous generation, as this would in his view have positioned his art as Indo-Trinidadian or as made by a Caribbean 'East Indian'. As Maharaj described in his weekly newspaper column 'Art is Life': 'The themes of his [M.P. Alladin's] paintings documented the cultural and social traits and customs of the East Indians ... elements of design and colour that speak of the presence of the East Indian' (Maharaj 1992). Bravely refusing to emphasize an East Indian 'presence', Maharaj aimed for a contrary position.

The impact of his painterly, figurative practice can be seen in press reviews of the time. These emphasize Maharaj's foreign education and the welcome sophistication that he brought to Trinidad's art scene. A few years earlier, William Gordon, staff writer for the establishment newspaper the *Trinidad Guardian*, wrote a review of a solo exhibition by Maharaj staged in Trinidad's capital Port of Spain in his weekly column, 'On the Art of Life': 'This show reflected those influences rather than the typical concerns of "Third World Art", of art as a vehicle for personal discovery rather than as an applied craft with firm rules and clear basic presumptions ... Shastri has been able to accept the challenge of avant garde art influences in North America' (Gordon 1983). Such high praise – of the local youth whose exploits overseas had earned him the accolade of artist – was not typical of the sort of encouragement that East Indian artists were given in Trinidad after independence (Scher 1999). Indeed, beyond critics such as William Gordon, Maharaj would find that his ambition to 'visually assault society' had a rather limited following. There was pressure from official bodies such as the National Council of Indian Culture to represent 'East Indian life' and pursue an 'applied craft'. In 1983 the Council sponsored a painting competition on the theme 'East Indian Life-Styles: One Face of our Nation', with a first prize of three weeks in India. A call went out for original works 'including subjects such as family life, ceremonies, festivals, work, music, dances, etc., both of past and present times'.[3] Staged to inspire competitors, visitors to the shopping plaza West Mall – in a wealthy north-west suburb of the capital – were invited to view the work of Rajiv Kaushik, an artist brought specially from India, whose 'high standard of traditional painting and batik wall hangings show the fastidious conventions and subtle colour sense of classical Indian Art ... Jewel-like Rajput pieces and all the enchanting plays of Lord Krishna and the gopis, show a whole world in flat stylised spaces of richly patterned charm'.[4]

Maharaj, feeling undervalued and misunderstood, decided his only opportunity for gaining local patronage to lie with a compromise. As he reflected: 'The Indo-Trinidadian amidst a very Eurocentric approach to culture, in terms of music, song, dance and dress, realized that the proliferation of his art forms had to be presented in a form that would be appealing to its followers to ensure their continued support' (Maharaj 1992). By the end of the 1980s, Maharaj's attitude to imaging had changed (Figure 10.2). His pieces began to take on overt indicators of East Indian ethnicity as prescribed by his intended audience. He warmly embraced a creole nationalist formula which involved elaborating on a group of motifs of 'Indianness' and invocations of 'tradition' that were not dissimilar to those being solicited for the competition at West Mall. For much of the 1990s and after, Maharaj's paintings developed in this way, often with

Figure 10.2: Shastri Maharaj, *Symbiosis* (1992), acrylic on canvas, 182.9 x 104.1 cm. By permission of the artist.

Figure 10.3: Shastri Maharaj, *Janeo* (1998), acrylic on canvas, 121.9 x 76.2 cm. By permission of the artist.

Figure 10.4: Shastri Maharaj, *Jour Overt* (2000), acrylic on canvas, 61 x 43.2 cm. By permission of the artist.

recognizable Hindu elements coupled with details drawn from local geography (Figure 10.3).

The result was initially a success in meeting the approval of the island's government. With the coming to power of the mainly Indo-Trinidadian-led United National Congress in 1995, and through support from the ascendant East Indian elite, Maharaj's national status as an artist appeared to be confirmed. However, the assured patronage which favoured Indo-Trinidadian 'culture' suddenly disappeared when political power reverted to the People's National Movement in 2002, which traditionally has an Afro-Trinidadian following. From Maharaj's point of view this led to the demand that he produce images which avoided the 'Indian' references of his works of the mid-1990s. From 2002, his art once more changed track, and he deliberately gave up his earlier treatment of 'Indian' themes.

Art and Ethnicity at their Emotional Limits

When I met Shastri Maharaj he had come to paint images of houses (see Figure 10.4). These capture the common pattern in Trinidad of building two-storey frames for domestic dwellings. At one time these were put up in brick and wood but are now all built with concrete, although they are still recognizable for having only the upper floor enclosed. This leaves a space

Figure 10.5: Shastri Maharaj, *Barracks* (2006), acrylic on canvas, 61 x 43.2 cm.
By permission of the artist.

'under the house', as it is referred to, for storage and eventual completion by
subsequent generations of the household (see Figure 10.5).

While otherwise common throughout the country, for Maharaj these
'stilt-' or as he suggested 'bird-' or 'spirit-houses' are emblematic of the rural
parts of the island. He has produced an open-ended series of these in which
the houses are frequently placed in spare, largely defoliated surroundings,
jutting above smooth horizons of baked earth. By assigning some of these
works titles which indicate place names, like *Somewhere in Fyzabad*, he
has added a further association to more isolated parts of the country where
East Indians have traditionally lived and worked the sugar plantations.[5]
Maharaj told me to look for houses like these in Caroni, a sugar-growing
area not far from his home.

During our first few meetings there was nothing that Maharaj told me
which would suggest that he was uncomfortable with the expectation
placed upon him as an East Indian making 'Indian art'. On the contrary,

the ethnic geography of Trinidad indicated by his painted houses seemed to confirm his desire to identify himself as Indian. He told me of his growing aim to illustrate his Hindu beliefs, while remaining careful to point out that his works should not be regarded as 'Hindu art'. As he told me, his works are intended as a pointer or channel back to himself: 'They get to the source. I am the source'. He recalled a dream in which he found himself in dialogue with a guru, prompting him to paint an image of the goddess Lakshmi.

Maharaj and I talked about the way in which the theme of Indianness has been present throughout his career and is being continually modified through his works. He told me that maintaining an 'Indian art' has required an effort that is difficult to sustain. This is due to the shifting background of interests in ethnicity at the levels of official patronage and the local art market. He complained about feeling disadvantaged by living in Chaguanas, a place which is generally characterized as an East Indian heartland, despite the high degree of ethnic mixing there as in the rest of Trinidad. His tangible hostility toward other artists who make up the urban elite in Trinidad's capital, Port of Spain, was underscored by an ethnic distinction: 'I'm a Hindu artist. I want to be independent of French creole [urban elite] patrimony, and vogue crowd. They prostitute art. The Johnny-come-lately artists haven't gone through the test of time. [They are] upstart artists who have no philosophy behind their work, and paint recreationally'. The growth in newcomers to the vocation is the result, Maharaj explained, of the relatively low commissions demanded by galleries, of around 30 to 33 per cent. A worse problem for him, however, was the coupling of patterns of patronage with ethnicity. Maharaj no longer enjoyed much public interest or could consider his art a viable source of income since, he complained, 'Professional Indians don't buy art'. This has meant him looking to buyers from 'across the board, of other ethnicities – architects, lawyers'.

It might be said that Maharaj's feelings demand nothing more than an orthodox historical analysis of 'decline'. This would focus on the theme of a failing career for an artist curtailed by professional rivalries, a state of saturation in the local art market, and an erosion of opportunities for promotion and display. There is plenty here to confirm what the sociology and anthropology of art have identified as the myth of the free creator, unaffected by outside influences, and they have shown that art producers always operate within professional fields of power, competing for recognition, status and economic gain (Bourdieu 1984; Svašek 2007: 88–92). This is an extension of the critique brought to bear within the history of art by artists and thinkers of the modernist avant-garde, who have extensively problematized the idea of the artist as, in Charles Harrison's terms, an 'authoritative aesthetic spokesman' (Harrison 1983: 12). Harrison has dismantled claims for creative autonomy by taking seriously the idea that 'what a painting expresses or means *must* be a function of what it is made of and from, culturally, socially, technically, historically, psychologically and morally, independently of the mind of the spectator' (ibid.: 12). In the Caribbean case this would lead us to reject the uncritical notion of Maharaj the painter as an 'authoritative ethnic spokesman', to rephrase Harrison (cf. Price 1989; Araeen 1991; Wainwright 2009a, 2009b).

Putting the emotional aspects of Maharaj's experience into the foreground, the limitations of using ethnicity as an analytic category become clearer. Here we are faced simultaneously with the fallacy of creative autonomy and the inadequacy of the art-as-ethnicity paradigm. As such, it makes sense to disentangle the visual from the category of ethnicity, and to explore creativity within a more 'embodied' history. Recent analysis of the emotions has covered the terrain of both 'the vehement passions', such as grief, fear, rapture and so on (see Fisher 2002; Altieri 2003), and affects and emotions such as shame, humiliation, irritation, anxiety, envy, disdain, surprise and so on (see Ngai 2005). Having set out the chronology of his emotional experience, it is Maharaj's sense of disillusion in particular which emerges as the ground for another analytic path. Maharaj lives rather uncomfortably with the idea of 'Indian art' that first emerged during decolonization. It was instituted during independence through the emphasis on art as a signifier of ethnic diversity within the national community. However, the concept of national culture devised in that earlier period has had an effect that is being felt well beyond such anti-colonial beginnings. The founding moment of nationalism amounted to the reifying of ethnic differences, in a widely enacted objectification and 'commodification of ethnicity' (Yelvington 1993: 10). This has had a lasting significance for art practice. One outcome is that commodification is just as capable of working with as against the agency of visual image makers. A commodified ethnicity thereby disavows what transformative potential that difference once promised during decolonization.

With this in view, it is easier to see why Maharaj should feel that his ambitions as an artist have been so curtailed. He is marked by a deep ambivalence about the connotations of Indianness around his dwindling art practice. In his studio he showed me attempts to detach his images from any such connections, with arrangements on canvas of geometrical shapes in space rather like Kandinsky's. Another group of his unsold works included large canvases reminiscent for me of those by the Indian painter Bhupen Khakhar, who has also worked to complicate the matter of identity in post-independent India, namely by emphasizing his homosexuality. Maharaj regards this range of visual interests as testament to his uniqueness, and an indication of his potential for perpetual creative development. As he told me in 2004: 'I'm not playing with people's expectations, I'm just becoming less ignorant daily. I am sacrosanct, there's no Indian man like me, with family, and painting'.

The artist's narrative about his career, told in a vocabulary of the emotions, bears a more complex relationship to difference than is accounted for in the ideology of the multicultural nation. Certainly, he spoke in a way that frequently mixed references to ethnicity and religion, much as the anthropologist Aisha Khan has noted that Trinidad's South Asian diaspora more generally mixes metaphors of race and religious identity in the ideology of the mixed or 'callaloo nation' (Khan 2004). But the horizons of visual creativity and difference have remained at odds in Maharaj's emotional experience. This is despite ambitions to bind them together through the artist's attempts to insert or insinuate his art into Trinidad's hegemonic imaginary of difference.

The notion of 'Indian art' in Trinidad is starkly a historical category. The account I have given here should show up the serious care that is needed to avoid any simple analytic coupling of creativity and ethnic difference. This becomes clearer when tracing out the purposeful adjustments to his practice that Maharaj has made at stages in his career. Some of his works have employed essentialist categories of ethnic difference which he had previously declared as anachronistic from the point of view of his avant-garde training. A leading contradiction of anti-colonial thought was that it often borrowed and restated the official ideologies of ethnic difference that originated during colonization. Maharaj reproduced this pattern at the moment when he embraced visual motifs of Indianness that have a precedent in the visual descriptions of India that circulated throughout the British Empire. By choosing to paint these motifs, Maharaj also replayed the hierarchy deriving from European academic conservatism in which painting presides over other media of visual representation. Maharaj's aim was to put these associations to other uses: they were to furnish his faith in the value of constructing an Indo-Trinidadian identity, the promise of finding a market and achieving national importance. As such, over subsequent years, Maharaj has persevered with the 'Indian art' idea. This is despite his sense of disillusion and the developments in Trinidad whereby ethnicities are commodified and emptied of any transformative value. The artist's emotional experience suggests that there are points when the resource of ethnicity and the connotations of 'Indian art' become circumscribing and reach their limits.

Everyday Emotions beyond Ethnicity

In August 2004 I attended a wedding in Chaguanas, the following description of which is taken from my field notes:

> At about 9 PM I went to Chaguanas, to a large gathering of perhaps 160 people celebrating the night before a Hindu wedding. The ceremony itself was to take place at the Hanuman murti and ashram, but this evening, the bride's parents were hosting 'a night of entertainment' as the master of ceremonies put it at their home, which involved singing, dancing and some comedy. Food was served on large green leaves in a spacious backroom, and with almost the same variety as at that morning's puja. On a brightly lit temporary stage in a large open-plan room, unfurnished save for scores of light plastic chairs and balloons, a

drummer played on an electronic drum pad, whilst another musician handled an electric keyboard. In the course of the evening they accompanied a string of singers, male and female, while pre-recorded music that played through a PA system formed the backdrop for the children and adolescents who danced in the style of sequences from popular Indian films, dressed in brightly coloured costumes. Most of the singers were soloists singing in Hindi or Bhojpuri, which they read from personal notebooks carried with them on stage. The mood of the songs ranged from the melancholy Mr Amar Ali McDougall, to a more jubilant quintet that included the bride's mother, which began a medley of songs at a moment early in the proceedings when a sacred practice, the 'parching of the *lawa* (rice)' (they sang, *Bhuje de lawa, bhuje de lawa*) was taking place over an open fire in front of the domestic shrine. I took a photograph of two women central to the 'parching' engaged in some dancing, 'winding their waists' and 'wining' [rhythmic gyrations of the hips] as they 'parched'. The bride, dressed in sari blouse, skirt and pinned dupatta danced to great appreciation, and my informant let me know that this was an unusual happening at a woman's own wedding celebration. The MC made several reminders between acts that amongst the families of the bride and groom were musicians and singers who formed the majority of the performers that evening. One especially popular singer of chutney songs from outside the family held the stage for about 40 minutes to do a comic set comprising snippets of sung verse in Hindi and Bhojpuri. Their finale was a song with the refrain, in English, 'the cat licked the butter, the cat licked the butter'.

This passage describes a context in which wedding performances, which include those by members of the wedding party, and in this case even the bride herself, carry a persistent identification with East Indianness. The juxtaposition of this private context with that of the art making, display and public reception of Shastri Maharaj is suggestive of how ethnicity is signified in private and public spaces – since these two contexts certainly speak to that division. It also points to how identifications with Indianness are codified in high art as compared to the popular arts, or popular culture. Further, the space of wedding celebration evidences what Maharaj insists upon as a running element in his visual practice: the emotionality surrounding the desire for a grounded, or as he put it, 'grassroots' understanding of his works, evidenced in his treatment of everyday 'East Indian' themes.

Maharaj's images in part demonstrate what David Freedberg has dubbed 'the effectiveness, efficacy and vitality of images themselves' (Freedberg 1989: xvii). Stylistic and iconographic switches in his art are an embodied response to Trinidad's changing political scene. I have tried to make clear how this 'effectiveness' is, however, circumscribed in the everyday context, drawing on Freedberg's suggestion that art-historical study ought to attend simultaneously to everyday forms of material production (which picks up on a similar interest among the earlier art historians Riegl and Wölfflin). It is obvious that there are links between the everydayness of Maharaj's career and the wedding scene. The emotional aspects of the wedding that I attended are crucial to any assessment of this 'popular' identification with an Indo-Trinidadian community. They are uncomfortably positioned by the inscription of Indianness as a cultural component of the Trinidadian national community.

Another way to explore the dynamics of the production of Indianness is to address an area of practice that sits beyond as well as within the national. One such is the field of performances by singers such as Rikki Jai. Through parody and self parody they are a complex reversal of the widely marketable Indo-pop culture of Trinidad, and the apparent attachment to the national suggested by the privacy of wedding spaces. Jai (born Samraj Jaimungal, in Friendship Village, San Fernando) emerged as a singer and songwriter in Trinidad with his song 'Sumintra' in 1988. The more recent 'Boleh Murugwah' focuses on the ritual of parching unpolished rice on the eve of a Hindu wedding, part of the two-day *matti kaur* ceremonies in which women, predominantly, take the lead; and which at other times involves the burying of spices, and suggestive games and role play thought to serve as the sexual initiation of the bride and bridegroom.[6] Much of the song is sung not in English but in Bhojpuri, a language of the Indian state of Bihar from where many of Trinidad's indentured labourers came to the Caribbean after 1843.

Within Jai's career we can trace a move from his initial role as an entertainer for an Indian audience to an expanded field. His concerts and audio and video recordings are widely distributed among national and international listeners, those within the Caribbean region and its diaspora. It is notable that Jai is thereby shedding the status of cultural producer for an audience of any single ethnicity or national space. Even so, it is notable that he has succeeded in retaining each of these publics while reaching out more widely.

The basis for his appeal has been looked at in the style of his performances. Bangalore-based scholar Tejaswini Niranjana notes that Jai performs chutney, chutney-soca, and calypso – labels for a body of music that broadly ranges from folk-derived Bhojpuri lyrics and rhythms to those sung in Trinidadian English using Afro-Caribbean beats. Jai thereby shows an ability to move among genres with melodic lines which are distinct from one another. As Jai suggested to Niranjana in an interview, chutney and Hindi film songs have an 'Indian *gamak*' (musical ornamentation) which distinguishes them from soca or calypso (and which would suggest that for Jai chutney-soca is more like soca than chutney). Jai has explored the relations between these genres by being one of the first singers to hire a dance troupe and a drama troupe to provide the background narrative for his performances – a formula more familiar in soca. As Niranjana writes, 'He felt that the chutney industry was "too dormant" compared with the more interactive performances in the "soca industry". Before he introduced soca performative elements, he said, there were "no hands in the air, no rags, no towels [being waved]"' (Niranjana 2006: 237–38). The younger singer-songwriter Ravi B extends the address to multiple audiences typical of Jai, and yet with a particular appeal to a new Indo-Caribbean constituency who are themselves consumers of diverse music styles.[7]

Returning briefly to Maharaj, when the artist spoke about his time in Canada, he emphasized the international connections in the story of his life and career. This period of transit may be matched with an account of transformation: at one point or another, as I have outlined, Maharaj and Rikki Jai alike had both identified with, and yet de-identified or disavowed, the categories 'creole', 'Indian', and 'Indo-Trinidadian'. The scope for their success in doing so was set by constraints that were beyond their influence. These often prevailed upon them from the past. The overall national theme of transition from colonial subjects to inhabitants of a free and sovereign state would suitably provide a wider historical backdrop to these contemporary shifts.

The suggestion here is that attention to the movement of objects such as works of art and music may usefully extend analyses of emotions and ethnicity. The movement of objects and images valued as fine art – taken to Trinidad from a European context of production and reception – converges in transit with images referring to a notional Hindu identity, such as those painted by Maharaj or promoted by the National Council of Indian Culture. The latter are appropriated by the ideological category of 'European art', as I have shown. This has had mixed results for those seeking to reconcile the otherwise divergent historical antecedents of the art of the colonizer and the artefacts of the colonized.

Such objects have become the fraught site of some further, ensuing transitions. Maharaj's art, as with Rikki Jai's music, has at various moments signified Indianness and, at others, a creole identity that bespeaks an association with nationhood. The meaning of these productions then undergoes transition as their significance shifts with time and location. Maharaj's art is neither 'popular', nor for that matter is it, as he suggests, 'elite' – at least not enough to be embraced by 'French creole', middle- or upper-class art patrons. Equally, to describe Rikki Jai's works as simply 'popular' music would mean foregoing a discussion about which public or audience his music appeals to, and whether this may be delineated easily by social group or nationality. Even more problematic is whether Jai's music may be described according to ethnicity, since an ability to transition any neat category of ethnic difference seems to be its defining feature.

Overall, these patterns suggest a need to open up the theme of ethnicity and to question its suitability as a foundational category for cultural analysis. Performers such as Rikki Jai complicate the easy assumption that musicians of the Indian diaspora stand at the centre of a network of relations between those seeking to forge an East Indian ethnic community through cultural phenomena. Chutney music is contingent with practices of differencing which defy the circumscriptions of Indian nationalism and transnationalism. This music cannot be separated from the more complex production of publics within the Caribbean and its diaspora – in other words, those publics and groupings which run across ethnic boundaries. Wedding music also raises the question of whether these performances reproduce 'folk' traditions of celebration in any significantly different way from how music such as Jai's has renegotiated 'folk' signifiers. In each case we are presented with the issue of how mass-marketed music such as Hindi film scores, chutney and chutney-soca are being consumed through private rituals. There is a parallel here to Maharaj's frequent reconsiderations of such 'ethnic indexicality' – the ostensible visual indication of ethnic or diasporic difference in his art. These reconsiderations are made uncomfortably along the timeline of his career. The changes that he experiences are an embodied locus of the historical conflicts taking place more widely in Trinidad around the mobilization of Indianness.

Understanding the relationship between emotions and ethnicity requires an extended look at various options for understanding cultural practices. On the one hand is the emotional dimension, or the affective elements of cultural practices; and on the other, the field of cultural reception where ethnic and diasporic difference is inscribed onto an otherwise ambiguous phenomenal surface. This is a dimension that critical study of diaspora spaces has been unable to contemplate at any depth, largely because cultural analysis itself has contributed to the inscription of difference. It has also routinely elided aesthetics (a particular area of concern within artistic discourse) with theoretical approaches focused on visual signification and, more specifically, an interpretative model of 'culture as text'. In this way the role of aesthetics has been largely bypassed; there is a tendency to translate the realm of cultural experience into the thematic (and largely poststructuralist) vocabulary of representation.

Adopting a greater interest in the emotionally affective presence of cultural practices might combat this tendency. It would help, for instance, to understand the experience of Maharaj as he busily responds to changes in a local art market heavily imprinted by wider political attitudes to difference. Jai's shifts among musical languages and his growing audience would also become comprehensible. The presence of these cultural processes can be distinguished from the changing relation between representation and ethnicity. However, perceptual and emotional questions, such as those under the heading of an aesthetics of diaspora, are actively foreclosed by a methodological approach which decodes the cultural and treats it as nothing more than a component of diasporic differencing (and is, indeed, a form of semiological reductionism). Notwithstanding critical concerns regarding 'the politics of emotions' (Lutz and Abu-Lughod 1990; see also Ahmed 2004; Svašek 2006), we still know very little about how emotions feature in cultural practices in postcolonial contexts. But this may only arrive with a proper departure from the generic identification of the role of culture in decolonizing and diasporic spaces such as the Caribbean.

Such are the dynamic transformations that works of art and music both undergo and entail when they are caught at a locus of contestations between questions of meaning and emotional efficacy. Works of art and music are in one historical instance the condensation of anti-colonial feeling, nationalist pride and ethnic difference. However, whether they are capable of sustaining that status is uncertain, since they are subject to transit, transition and transformation, and become the object of further change.

Finally, this brings me to another 'trans-' word: transnationalism. This has been the focus of much recent research in anthropology and cultural studies, often with respect to cultural practices. I have outlined cultural practices as having a more complex link to transnationalism than in the current approaches, where culture serves as a signification of transnational connection as well as deriving its efficacy from that ability to signify. In that account, cultural forms move between national locations and make transnational links possible – they are the basis for a shared or transmitted sense of ethnic 'belonging' within one or other diaspora. This maps a cultural geography of transnational connectivity. In the setting of the Indian diaspora emerges a picture of how diverse locations relate to other parts of the global diaspora, as well as to Indians in the Asian sub-continent. Cultural practices – including media such as music, film and television – are vital for forming and continuing such lines of contact. In this sense, otherwise overlooked elements of 'the cultural' are thought to offer a symbolic reach, and enable a thriving economy of relations within diaspora communities.

The material I have offered in this chapter offers in part a response to the usefulness of such paradigms and their understanding of cultural practices in diaspora spaces as being important most of all for their ability to mediate and communicate. By contrast, I have indicated that the cultural refuses to occupy this status alone, and that this needs to be made clear if we are to resist the allure of a commodified aesthetic of diaspora culture. By paying attention to the emotions, Trinidadian artworks and performances reveal more complex implications for the cultural. Even where ethnicity is so central to understanding national and transnational communities, as it is in Trinidad, I have shown why cultural practices deserve alternative analytic attention beyond models of representation, textuality and signification.

Conclusion: Ownership and the Emotions

I began by indicating that notions of Trinidadian national culture – with art making as its vanguard – were structured along multi-ethnic lines and derived indirectly from a desire for ever-sharpening distinctions between the 'overseas', or 'metropolitan', and 'local' components for cultural production. It was this condition of literal isolation which was thought to be enabling of national distinctiveness in Trinidad, since a major anti-colonial concern was to press cultural creativity into the service of domestic rather than outside interests. A leading proponent of this view was first prime minister of Trinidad and Tobago, Dr Eric Williams, who expressed the terms of this relationship to the outside in his many addresses, interviews and publications, such as in the following:

> Dependence on the outside world in the Caribbean in 1969 is not only economic. It is also cultural, institutional, intellectual and psychological. Political forms and social institutions, even in the politically independent countries, were imitated rather than created, borrowed rather than relevant, reflecting the forms existing in the particular metropolitan country from which they were derived. There is still no serious indigenous intellectual life. (Williams 1970: 501)

Williams's message encouraged the creation of forms and institutions capable of containing or generating indigenous cultural products. This leads me to suggest that it ought also to be read as part of a broader emotional discourse of ownership in the Caribbean. Williams insists on a move away from those products which are 'imitated rather than created, borrowed rather than relevant'. Such ideas have remained hegemonic in the aftermath of Empire and are central to anti-colonial politics, but what is unexplored about them is how they both couple ownership and production, and pay little attention to cultural consumption. The 'insiderism' of anti-colonial cultural debate focused on the rejection of outsider ideas and practices – preferring to replace them with home-grown ones. Far less emphasis was given to rejecting colonial patterns of consuming 'indigenous' products. In short, there was little confrontation of the categorization of the cultural (the divisions of art and craft; of fine art, popular arts and 'folk' art, as M.P. Alladin suggested) which Trinidad inherited at the moment of its independence. There was also little appreciation that the outcome of commodifying culture as a political resource would mean the reification of ethnic and racial differences.

Certainly much may be gained from avoiding such reification, given the sort of experiences among artists and performers that I have outlined here. I have suggested that this might begin by reflecting on the emotions as a register of what happens when the cultural is employed as a site of creating difference. The examples in this chapter suggest a need to unpick such categories of the cultural and to pursue the current turn away from models of cultural representation. In general, the emotional processes described here are part and parcel of political dynamics, such as the desire to create a creole, national identity, independent of the imperial legacy, and the yearning for an Indo-Trinidadian identity as a component of national community. Such emotions suggest how state-sanctioned forms of Trinidadian 'Indianness' are being felt as well as renegotiated in ways that throw light on patterns of the counter-hegemonic ownership of cultural practices within diasporic space.

At root, much rests on being able to see the limitations that result from identification with the Indian diaspora in Trinidad. Of course, these need to be evaluated alongside the benefits and opportunities that such an association has granted in the historic past. In either case, analysis of this context then becomes a matter of the need to pay more direct attention to cultural phenomena. This would avoid what cultural theorist Barbara Stafford has named the 'ruling metaphor of reading' (Stafford 1995: 6) – the apprehension of cultural objects for their representational, signifying and textual qualities. Dispensing with this model – of the legibility of cultural practices – in favour of a focus on the emotions has particular outcomes on the ground for Caribbean artists and performers. These individuals face demands among audiences for readable ethnic difference in a context where readability is germane to the cultural object becoming a commodity. However, once they are shown to be involved in a more complex emotional set of interactions (in which objects and images actively evoke particular emotions, rather than simply lend themselves to emotional demands, as vehicles or media in their service) then a fuller sense of the motivations for cultural production itself emerges.

The pressures as well as the opportunities to signify diasporic difference configure a discursive field which artists and performers are obliged to navigate. Why they should choose art making, song or performance in order to do so can be understood from the details of how cultural reception and the emotions intersect. This is where aesthetic experience can be relieved from the burden of discourses of difference in order to see more clearly the contrapuntal forms of emotional ownership that operate around cultural practices. To put this simply, artists and performers in spaces of diaspora live and work with the obstacles, as well as the opportunities, of ethnic identification. Their interest in cultural production stems in part from a desire to exceed those limits. Here I have tried to demonstrate the benefits of a greater awareness of the emotional dimension of the search for ownership of one's own cultural practices. Within overdeterminedly ethnicized spaces, cultural products are transformed by the emotions into less confined alternatives.

Notes

1. This chaper is a revised version of chapter 4 of Leon Wainwright, *Timed Out: Art and the Transnational Caribbean* (Manchester: Manchester University Press, pp. 122–46). Fieldwork was conducted with funding from the Leverhulme Trust (Early Career Fellowship) and the University of Sussex. The ideas were developed as part of the project 'Creativity and Innovation in a World of Movement', which was financially supported by the HERA Joint Research Programme and co-funded by AHRC, AKA, DASTI, ETF, FNR, FWF, HAZU, IRCHSS, MHEST, NWO, RANNIS, RCN, VR and The European Community FP7 2007–2013 under the Socio-economic Sciences and Humanities programme.
2. Compare the observation of Deborah Thomas in her account of 'folk Blackness' in Jamaica as a prevailing norm of identification (Thomas 2004).

3. 'Painting Contest on East Indian Life', *Trinidad Guardian*, 5 June, 1983.
4. '"Art in the Marketplace" at West Mall Today', *Trinidad Guardian*, 6 June 1983.
5. To see *Somewhere in Fyzabad* and further examples of Maharaj's work, go to his website: http://smfineart.com/.
6. See 'Boleh Murugwah', *Youtube*. Retrieved 7 June 2008 from: http://www.youtube.com/watch?v=G_qzWpbj7c4.
7. For examples of Ravi B's oeuvre, see the videos on *Youtube* for 'Karma Farewell Party: Rum is Meh Lova' (http://www.youtube.com/watch?v=sUCbWviISuQ&NR=1), 'Rum is Meh Lover' (http://www.youtube.com/watch?v=BGIYUWNHqsI&feature=r elated) and 'Hunter and Bunji Bring It' (http://www.youtube.com/watch?v=mVJnilB YiQc&feature=related). These videos were last retrieved on 7 June 2008.

References

Ahmed, S. *The Cultural Politics of Emotion*. London: Routledge.

Alladin, M.P. 1975. 'Artists and Craftsmen', in M. Anthony and A. Carr (eds), *David Frost Introduces Trinidad and Tobago*. London: Andre Deutsch Ltd, pp. 136–46.

Altieri, C. 2003. *The Particulars of Rapture: An Aesthetics of the Affects*. Ithaca, NY: Cornell University Press.

Araeen, R. 1991. 'From Primitivism to Ethnic Arts', in S. Hiller (ed.), *The Myth of Primitivism: Perspectives on Art*. London: Routledge, pp. 50–71.

Bhabha, H. 1994. *The Location of Culture*. London: Routledge.

Bourdieu, P. 1984. *Distinction: A Social Critique of the Judgement of Taste*, trans. R. Nice. London: Routledge.

Cozier, C. 1999 'Between Narratives and Other Spaces', *Small Axe* 6: 19–37.

de Certeau, M. 1984. *The Practice of Everyday Life*, trans. S. Rendall. Berkeley: University of California Press.

Fisher, P. 2002. *The Vehement Passions*. Princeton, NJ: Princeton University Press.

Freedberg, D. 1989. *The Power of Images: Studies in the History and Theory of Response*. Chicago: University of Chicago Press.

Gordon, W. 1983. 'On the Art of Real Life: In Pursuit of Real Subjects', *Trinidad Guardian*, 17 August.

Hallam, E., and T. Ingold (eds). 2007. *Creativity and Cultural Improvisation*. Oxford: Berg.

Harrison, C. 1983. *Art and Language*. Birmingham: Ikon Gallery.

Khan, A. 2004. *Callaloo Nation: Metaphors of Race and Religious Identity among South Asians in Trinidad*. Durham, NC: Duke University Press.

Lutz, C.A., and L. Abu-Lughod (eds). 1990. *Language and the Politics of Emotion*. Cambridge: Cambridge University Press.

Maharaj, S. 1992. 'Indo-Caribbean Visual Arts: Evolution and Change', *Trinidad Guardian*, 8 October.

Mohammed, P. 2002. 'The "Creolisation" of Indian Women in Trinidad', in V. Shepherd and G.L. Richards (eds), *Questioning Creole: Creolisation Discourses in Caribbean Culture*. London: James Currey, pp. 130–47.

Ngai, S. 2005. *Ugly Feelings*. Cambridge, MA: Harvard University Press.

Niranjana, T. 2006. *Mobilizing India: Women, Music, and Migration between India and Trinidad*. Durham, NC: Duke University Press.

Price, S. 1089. *Primitive Art in Civilised Places*. Chicago: University of Chicago Press.

Scher, P. 1999. 'Confounding Categories in the Caribbean Art Market: Reflections on Self-taught Artists in Trinidad and Tobago', *Small Axe* 6: 37–56.

Svašek, M. 2007 *Anthropology, Art and Cultural Production*. London: Pluto.

––––––– 2010. 'Improvising in a World of Movement: Transit, Transition, and Transformation', in H. Anheimer and Y.R. Isar (eds), *Cultural Expression, Creativity and Innovation*. London: Sage, pp. 62–77.

––––––– (ed.). 2006. *Postsocialism, Politics and Emotions in Central and Eastern Europe*. Oxford: Berghahn.

Stafford, B.M. 1995. *Good Looking: Essays on the Virtues of Images*. Cambridge, MA: MIT Press.

Thomas, D. 2004. *Modern Blackness: Nationalism, Globalization, and the Politics of Culture in Jamaica*. Durham, NC: Duke University Press.

Wainwright, L. 2007. '"Indian Art" in Trinidad? Ethnicity at Material Limits', *Creative Communications* 2(1/2): 163–88.

––––––– 2009a. 'Mutual Ground: Post-empire Canons of Art in Britain and the Caribbean', in B. Lalla and J. Rahim (eds), *Beyond Borders: Cross-culturalism and the Caribbean Canon*. Kingston: University of the West Indies Press, pp. 116–48.

––––––– 2009b. 'On Being Unique: World Art and its British Institutions', *Visual Culture in Britain* 10(1): 87–101.

Williams, E. 1970. *From Columbus to Castro: The History of the Caribbean, 1492–1969*. London: Andre Deutsch Ltd.

Williams, R. 1977. *Marxism and Literature*. Oxford: Oxford University Press.

Yelvington, K.A. 1993. *Trinidad Ethnicity*. London: Macmillan.

11

'WHAT YOU PERCEIVE IS WHAT YOU CONCEIVE': EVALUATING SUBJECTS AND OBJECTS THROUGH EMOTIONS

Maruška Svašek

Perception, Evaluation, Conception

In 2006, I asked my five-year-old son to tell me what he thought of some photographs of a performance by George Hughes, entitled 'What You Perceive Is What You Conceive'. I had invited the US-based Ghanaian artist to the conference 'Migrant Art, Artefacts and Emotional Agency', an AHRC-funded event organized at Queens University Belfast where anthropologists, art historians and artists, presented papers about material culture, emotions and human mobility. George's performance was one of the highlights and was held in the Performance Room of the then School of Anthropological Studies (now the School of History and Anthropology). As a temporary meeting place of people (subjects) and things (objects), the event stimulated interaction between human and non-human actors, all marked by histories of 'transit', or movement through time and space.

The performance began with the appearance of a barely dressed, well-built African man (George) wearing an enormous wig with his face hidden behind a mask. With him were two white 'student helpers' who were also wearing masks. The main performer and his assistants held up white robotic dogs for the audience to touch. Subsequently, the African performer took the robots that had pieces of cloth tied to their tails, and dipped the cloths in paint. Using a remote control device, he then made the 'dogs' walk over a prepared canvas on the floor, leaving trails of paint. After some minutes, the robots were put aside and two of the men lifted up the canvas, placing it upright against the wall. The performer then turned to the public and screamed loudly. In what seemed to be the second part of the performance, he finished the painting, interspersing this activity with dance movements and ending it with a second loud scream. During this latter half of the show, the two assistants stood motionless in the two corners of the room.

Figure 11.1: George Hughes performing 'What You Perceive Is What You Conceive', 2007. Photograph by Maruška Svašek.

Figure 11.2: George Hughes performing 'What You Perceive Is What You Conceive', 2007. Photograph by Maruška Svašek.

Looking at the photographs of the performance, my son displayed a mixture of fascination and disgust. He looked intensely at the pictures, turned up his nose, and said he did not like them one bit. In most of the pictures, George was wearing a large black wig and a golden mask, and his body was smeared with blue paint (Figure 11.1). According to my son, he looked 'dirty' (*vies*) and was 'being messy' (*aan het viezikken*). When he saw the image of George painting on what seemed to be the floor (Figure 11.2), he said he was doing 'something naughty' (*iets stouts*). Commenting on the resulting work of art, a large painting (Figure 11.3), he said it looked 'like a scary face, or is it something really dirty what he has done?' When I asked him whether he liked the end result he replied he did not, and added that he preferred a painting depicting 'many fish or rabbits or cats'. In response to the last photograph (Figure 11.4), the conversation ended as follows:

Figure 11.3: George Hughes and the painting made during 'What You Perceive Is What You Conceive', 2007. Photograph by Maruška Svašek.

Figure 11.4: George Hughes after the performance 'What You Perceive Is What you Conceive', 2007. Photograph by Maruška Svašek.

M: Is this a normal man?
T: No, he is still covered in blue.
M: Do you want blue on you?
T: No, I find it dirty.
M: Do you think he is a strong man?
T: No, because dirty things make you weaker and weaker.

The response illustrates a number of issues central to this chapter. First, confrontations with things (in this case photographs) can produce strong emotional reactions. As will be discussed later on, this phenomenon can be understood through Gell's concept of 'object agency' (Gell 1998). Secondly, factors such as age, educational background, gender, ethnicity and personal idiosyncrasies may influence how individuals understand and experience material culture (Bourdieu and Darbel 1969; Berger 1972; Gans 1974; Bourdieu 1984, 1993; Chadwick 1990; Coote and Shelton 1992; Halle 1993; Jordan and Weedon 1995). Audience perception is also influenced by the social framing and spatial contextualization of people and things (Clifford 1988; Hart 1995; Karp and Levine 1991). In the case above, I had taken the photographs home from work and looked at them, sitting on the couch in the living room. In this space we often read books or looked at pictures together, and discussed why we thought they were *leuk* (nice, attractive, captivating) or *stom* (stupid, silly, unattractive).

When exploring how individuals perceive objects and images, and why they are potentially stirred by them, it is important to note that 'perception can never be disinterested or purely contemplative' because '[t] he perceptually acute organism is one whose movements are closely tuned and ever responsive to environmental perturbations' (Ingold 2000: 206). Focusing on the relational process of vision, Ingold noted that two levels of seeing can be distinguished:

> [O]n the one hand, the ordinary sight of pre-existing things that comes from moving around in the environment and detecting patterns in the ambient light reflected off its outer surfaces; on the other hand, the revelatory sight experienced at those moments when the world opens up to the perceiver, as though he or she were caught up in the movement of its birth. (ibid.: 278)

Perceptual processes, in other words, draw situated subjects into life worlds, a process that can also be understood as emotional engagement. Kay Milton (2002, 2005) has argued that emotional dynamics are central to the ways in which people learn to perceive their changing environments, as 'knowledge unbiased by emotions cannot exist, for it is emotion that enables the development and use of knowledge' (Milton 2002: 66). In other words, people's experiences of changing human and non-human environments are shaped by specific interests and expectations that partially arise out of earlier experiences. A child born into a family that owns a friendly sheepdog, for example, will be inclined to like dogs, and expect affectionate interaction with new dogs it encounters. This emotional habitus can drastically change when the child is unexpectedly bitten, having learnt that some dogs are dangerous. This implies that embodied memories of earlier experiences influence how we perceive, evaluate and approach the world as it appears to us in different settings.

As mechanisms for engaging with and learning about those different settings, emotions are not be understood as psychological or physical states within the mind and bodies of individuals, but rather as interactive processes that shape people's perceptions. This view challenges rigid conceptual distinctions between mind and body, the individual and the social, and 'intrapsychic realms' and 'extrapsychic, external worlds' (Svašek 2007: 67). From this perspective, it is not surprising that a five year old, relatively unfamiliar with discourses and practices of contemporary art, would associate body paint with 'dirt' and 'naughtiness', especially when interviewed by his mum. Aware that he had been told off on previous occasions for being messy when smearing paint on the table, he (mis) understood George's action as a dirty act; the further association with 'weakness' was a telling result of my attempts to teach him the basic rules of hygiene. No doubt his physical dislike of stickiness and his general disinterest in drawing and painting also influenced his negative evaluation. When I e-mailed George about my son's reaction, he answered: 'It is very interesting to note that we react differently depending on our temperament. It is likely that I would have said the same thing at five, more so having grown up in a conservative Ghana. Many Ghanaians will be shocked at my performances'.

As illustrated by my son's view and George's statement, people's perception and evaluation of particular experiences change as they come to know the world in new ways. These 'transformations', defined here as dynamic processes in which people experience, shape and negotiate their subjectivity in dynamic ways as they appear in, co-create and react to social and material environments, may either be temporary and situationally specific, or may lead to a more permanent metamorphosis. Transformations can be dialectically related to what I call 'transitions', transit-related changes of objects or images in terms of their meaning, value and emotional efficacy (Svašek 2007, 2009; see also Introduction, this volume).

This chapter will focus in particular on the different ways in which George and various members of his audience conceptualized, perceived and reacted to 'What You Perceive Is What You Conceive' as they transformed into 'artist' and 'audience'. It will show that, while George took the major role in designing and acting out the performance, creating an environment in which he staged both people and things, the members of the audience drew on earlier experiences when making sense of what was happening.

But what exactly were George's motivations for using his body and the various props in these particular ways, and why did he create a painting? What was he trying to do to his audience, and how were his actions perceived by different individuals? How and in what different ways did the latter evaluate the show, and to what extent did their experiences lead to new conceptions? To answer these questions, I interviewed George before and after the show, observed audience behaviour during the performance, chatted with people immediately afterwards, examined opinions through a questionnaire, and approached some of the respondents for more information, either by e-mail or through semi-structured interviews.

George Hughes: A Brief History of Transit and Transformation

To understand artistic intentions and outcomes, it is necessary to look beyond the lives and outputs of individual artists and explore the wider social, economic and political contexts in which art is produced, sold, displayed and appreciated (Wolff 1981; Becker 1982; Bourdieu 1984). I first met George in 1989 while he was completing his final year in painting at the College of Art in Kumasi, Ghana. He appeared to be a promising young artist fully devoted to his chosen discipline. His creative potential was, however, limited by market demands, as most art buyers in Ghana (mainly tourists and expats, but also more affluent members of the Ghanaian middle classes) were interested in depictions of African village scenes, 'traditional' culture, and palm beaches. After a period during which he successfully improvised within these genres, he wanted to widen his horizon, aspiring to enter the world of international art.

He first moved to the UK and, after a brief spell back in Ghana, migrated to the US where he developed his career as an artist and professional art teacher (Svašek 2009). At the time of his performance in Belfast he was Assistant Professor in Painting in the Visual Studies Department of the University at Buffalo, Colorado. The university website described him as a versatile producer of paintings, installations and performances, and as an artist who set his experiences 'against his African heritage'.[6] In transit, George transformed himself from being a relatively unknown Ghanaian art graduate, mainly producing commissioned depictions of 'African scenes' for European expats, into a well-connected and relatively prestigious international artist with a broad portfolio, working on themes (violence, sexuality) that did not fulfil the expectations of most consumers in Ghana. His job at a prestigious American art department and his participation in exhibitions in Africa, the US and Europe indicated his growing status in an international network of 'contemporary art'.[7] Asked in 2009 about his professional transformation, he explained:

> The ability to be part of an international art scene has offered me a wider fluidity between locations: local and foreign. This fluidity of movement and accessibility has increasingly enabled exposure, and an expansive network, but also has brought a higher logistic expense since the playing field continuously gets bigger and more challenging. By being influenced by the local and adopted culture, I have also been able to interrelate ideas by using crossover experiments.[8]

One of the questions in this chapter is to what extent previous experiences can influence people's interests in new phenomena. George only had a vague knowledge of Western contemporary performance art before moving to the US. Learning more about it after he had arrived, he became fascinated by works by Chris Burden, Marina Abramovic and Joseph Beuys. His increasing enthusiasm motivated him to experiment with the art form, and his approach was partially based on his knowledge and understanding of ritual practices in Ghana. In his view, performance art offered a powerful route to personal empowerment and audience confrontation:

> I was astonished to realize how similar Western performance art was to some African traditional ritual practices such as during funerals, durbar, naming of a child, ancestral atonement, etc. The only difference was that the Western performance artist was in charge whereas in Ghana it is either an elder or traditional priest who officiates the process. I was so excited when I discovered that at long last I could explore activities and objects (performance art) in a manner reserved for priests and elders back home. Not to discount my other art genres, but performance art is the only dramatic way I can confront the audience evocatively and provocatively.

George made connections between performance art and ritual ceremonies even though he realized that the proceedings and effects were different. His approach was playful and in line with postmodern artistic modes of aesthetic appropriation and imagination: 'I "imagine" the audience to be one with me and that they would respond the same way Ghanaians would in a local ceremony. But that is not truly the case because it is my imagination at play. It is a parody with comic effect, a pastiche because it also has influences from other sources apart from Africa'.

George clearly did not intend to reproduce a particular ritual, and wished to undermine the notion of static 'traditional' identity. He emphasized that moving between different countries had taught him that people's perceptions were always shaped by outside factors. This insight informed the performance in Belfast, which was meant to challenge spectator expectations. In George's words:

> The performance presented to the viewer an encounter outside the expected everyday narrative. By borrowing from specific seemingly unrelated objects and practices of varied cultures, the performance challenged our familiar perceptual interpretation and also critiqued the validity of the generalization of meaning and how it affects us based on our acquired conception and autonomy.

His acts of destabilization through what he thought to be a series of unpredictable actions were intended to evoke shock and surprise in the audience. As such, he aimed to strategically employ emotional dynamics as artistic tools.

Subjects and Objects in Performative Contexts

'What You Perceive Is What You Conceive' was an 'intercultural' event, a concept that has been used to describe activities in multi-ethnic and diasporic settings in which cultural producers appropriate elements from different sources and traditions (Um 2005). The performance was also 'interpersonal', in the sense that individuals of different age groups, with outlooks and emotional habituses shaped by idiosyncratic life histories, interacted in a singular space–time frame. The gathering included the US-based Ghanaian migrant artist, two anthropology students who took active part in the performance (an Italian on a MA scholarship and a Spanish migrant who had moved to Northern Ireland as a child), and about forty members of the public, including people from Northern Ireland, the Republic of Ireland, England, the Netherlands, Ghana, Brazil and the United States.

The performance included numerous objects, more specifically masks and robotic dogs. George appropriated these mass-produced commodities, altering them to suit his artistic ends. In this process of transition they were given new meanings and efficacy. As noted earlier, George's main aim was to empower himself in order to challenge the viewers, and he used and created material things as part of his own transformation. Gell's

Figure 11.5: Members of the audience during the performance 'What You Perceive Is What you Conceive', 2007. Photograph by Maruška Svašek.

theory of object agency (Gell 1998) is useful here, as it draws attention to the fact that people can influence others through objects and images that stir and potentially mobilize viewers. In Gell's terminology, primary agents (individuals) can distribute their agency through things (secondary agents), and in causal milieux, subject and objects exist in temporary 'agent–patient' relations. As agents, people shape material realities, and as patients they are affected by them (ibid.: 21). Object agency has an emotional dimension, as images and artefacts can be active triggers and mediators of feelings.

In an analysis of the emotional impact of Yoruba artefacts, Robert Armstrong argued that an object's potential impact, defined by him as 'affecting presence', 'enacts its being only in interchange between itself and a perceptor, appropriately when that perceptor is co-cultural to it, probably wrongly when the opposite case is true' (Armstrong 1971: 31). In this chapter, the question is not whether George and his public reacted accurately to the artefacts and images used in the performance, as George had not stipulated a 'correct reaction', apart from expecting them to be destabilized. Instead, this analysis aims to find out whether individual spectators were indeed challenged, and how their transformative reactions were informed by previous knowledge and experience. Evidently, the discursive and spatial contextualization of the event as an 'art performance' also served to create an already atmospheric setting. As Armstrong pointed out, artefacts intended to have emotional impact on viewers are often presented in 'special' spaces, such as shrines, art galleries or museums (ibid.: 8–9; cf. Napier 1992: xvi).

Artists' Judgements: Insider Knowledge and Critical Reflection

Apart from myself and a Ghanaian friend of George who had come over from London for the occasion, the only other person in the audience who knew the artist prior to his visit to Belfast was Anna, a 61-year-old Dutch artist. In the past, Anna had organized exhibitions of Ghanaian art in the Netherlands that had included George's works, so participation in crossing networks of art defined their relationship. She had never attended any of his performances, which made her 'very curious' and 'excited'. She said she had expected to see a powerful performance, knowing that George was 'looking for drama, "crazy things" as he would call it, to shake up the audience'. These expectations and her professional art background shaped her perception of the event.

Anna had enjoyed the eclectic mix, describing 'the strong scream before George started painting' as 'a good act of *ur*-creativity'. Her reaction to the sudden scream stood in sharp contrast to that of a terrified little girl, who burst out in tears and had to be taken out of the room by her mother. This illustrates how familiarity with the artist's work and age were important factors in its perception and impact. Asked for her own emotional responses during the event, Anna admitted to feelings of fear, although they had not been caused by George's shouting, and had been far less overwhelming than those experienced by the six-year-old: 'I was excited in the beginning by George's appearance with a wig and painted body, it also scared me a little (the unknown...) and I was very curious what would happen next. The outbursts [or] screams gave me a good strong feeling of an act of creativity, and the robots amused me a lot'.

Expecting more 'crazy things', she was less excited by the second half of the performance in which George turned his back to the audience, finishing the now upturned painting. Anna expressed her disappointment through critical reflection on George's artistic choices, as may be expected from a fellow artist. In her view, the two parts of the performance had not been well integrated: 'The beginning was very strong and had great drama, especially the robots were significant, a metaphor for the mechanical world, a loss of control? However I missed a connection in the second part, no robots there, no relevance of the painted body to the canvas'.

The above illustrates that emotions often function as evaluative judgements. As Michelle Rosaldo (1984: 143) noted, emotional processes are informed by the pragmatics of social life and can be highly normative. These judgements may be positive (as in curiosity and joy) or negative (as in fright or discontent). Anna's emotional judgements were also influenced by her more general knowledge of art history. She compared George's performance to work by well-established artists, a common interpretative convention in art criticism. 'His blue body reminded me of Yves Klein', she said, 'but nothing happened here, just painting'. She added that George could have made more of the body paint: 'it could have become another act or interaction of creativity in relation to the robots or to the canvas'. Anna's comments show very clearly that audiences are not passive sponges, simply taking in information. By contrast, perception is productive and judgemental, triggering new trains of thought.

It is interesting to compare Anna's experience with the views of Andrew, a 44-year-old Irish artist and art lecturer. Andrew's latest conceptual art works dealt with the theme of refugees and marginalization, and his interest in discrimination and knowledge of postcolonial theory clearly coloured his perception of George's performance. In his description of the event, he commented on its 'non-specific ritualistic reference to "tribal" African tradition', which he understood as playful critical commentary on racial stereotyping: 'I perceived it as a tongue-in-cheek Western perception of African tribal ritual. I think George is aware of this and is referring to colonial perceptions of the African male as 'other'.

Andrew was, however, not really challenged, but simply recognized George's intentions. In his response to the questionnaire, he discussed George's interaction with the audience in detail. This was not surprising as in his own artistic work community involvement was a central aim.

George involves the audience by ritualistically touching the sacred objects (robot animals) therefore implicating the audience in the making of his artwork – a large-scale painting on canvas ... The performance included an eclectic mix of recorded music styles from a CD player, which informed the pace, timing and duration of his performance. George alternated between addressing the audience with high-energy vocal sounds, impromptu dance movements and turning his back on the audience to apply swathes of paint to a previously prepared canvas.

The above indicates that the audience did not just rely on vision during the performance, but also experienced touch and sound. This alludes to the fact that perceptual activities are commonly multi-sensorial (Ingold 2000).

Without going into detail, Andrew remarked that he had observed 'a strong physical and emotional response to George's physique, especially from female members of the audience'. When I asked George in 2009 whether he had consciously played out his gender or sexuality in his choice of near nakedness, he replied:

The near nakedness is my poor attempt to imitate a return to the simplicity of tribal life which I deeply respect. In my performances I try to put on make-up which makes no particular reference to any specific tribe but rather reminiscent of an imaginary tribe. The attempt to use make-up and also to reveal my body has little to do with eroticism; rather, I try to present a bizarre outlook to intensify the ritualistic potency of the performance.[18]

He claimed that he had only become aware of the impact of his physicality on the audience when members of the public had commented on his muscularity. He regarded associations with gender, sexuality, masculinity or eroticism as accidental or coincidental effects.

As with Anna, Andrew's understanding of the performance was partly based on his familiarity with particular discourses of artistic creativity. Referring to expressionism, he noted that 'George was attempting to return to the fundamental raw energy of applying paint to a surface (canvas) which presupposes that by returning to a meditative state of being [he] will create a pure form of expression'. Whilst he had enjoyed the event, he was 'not particularly drawn to further performances' because he had 'not [learned] anything new from his performance – perhaps the ultimate weakness of Georges' performance for me'. His negative perception was clearly embodied and emotional, as it was experienced through feelings of disappointment.

It is striking that out of the ten people I spoke to in more detail about their reactions to the performance it was artists who seemed to be least impressed. The fact that they were judging a 'colleague', and that they based their critique on aesthetic preferences in their own work, might have been a factor. Despite their critical notes, both artists had, however, enjoyed the show. Anna liked the first half of the performance, and Andrew had appreciated the 'upbeat energetic performance aided by the eclectic mix of popular and classical music and humour'. Some musical pieces, he added, had 'evoked personal memories which encouraged me to project emotive episodes of my past within the performance'. As we will see in the next section, Andrew was not the only person who was struck by the mix of musical fragments.

'Cool': A Teenage Perspective

A third member of the audience, Bruce, was a 45-year-old former newspaper editor. At the time, Bruce was an anthropology student, and he had brought his two sons, Robert (13) and John (12) to George's performance. Bruce explained that 'Robert had recognized some of the music he and John love in the soundtrack (not the Beethoven!) and wondered aloud why there was such a mix. The punk and metal was not out of place to him and he enjoyed the association with something "weird" and "cool" and, I think, "grown-up". The wonder came with the inclusion of different genres'. He further reported:

> The event clearly had a great impact on each of them, though getting detailed answers was like pulling hen's teeth ... Both enthusiastically summed up the performance in one word: 'cool', child-speak reserved for something which impressed, and not used lightly. The first thing that caught Robert's attention when George walked into the room was his wig, which he said was 'weird'. John loved the dogbots.

The lack of knowledge of a more 'sophisticated' art-criticism discourse (as employed by Anna and Andrew) did not stop the boys responding to the props and expressing their views. Like my son, they had a clear opinion and judged the event through emotional engagement, using terms like 'cool' and 'weird' to express their feelings. Bruce recalled that '[t]hey each immediately said they would love to see George in performance again, no hesitation, their expression showing they felt no explanation was necessary'. He reflected on their positive experience, emphasizing the unusualness of the event and its liberating potential.

> My interpretation is they were totally engrossed in the whole event - something way outside of what they are familiar with, lively, at times loud. Neither spoke at any stage of any puzzle as to what George was doing. That didn't seem to matter. I think a huge part of the enjoyment for them was that the performance was unscheduled, unpredictable and fascinating because of that. Their lives have so much within boundaries, time limits and expected behaviours; this [event] stood out.

The children's transformation as they experienced the unexpected was fully in line with George's intentions, as he had meant to create a 'bridge to the unknown', and provide 'an experience familiar only by the bits and pieces of the visual puzzle, one that is capable of stretching our imagination beyond its chartered boundaries'. Their enthusiasm, rising from the unpredictable environment of the performance, produced cognition of 'art' as something that could potentially capture their attention and excite them. This perception was radically different to experiences of boredom when seeing dusty paintings in an 'uncool' museum.

While observing an artist paint a canvas was an exceptional and uplifting occasion for the boys, the previous section demonstrated that the artists in the audience had found it less stimulating as they had 'seen it all before'. This demonstrates that memories of prior experiences feed into interconnected processes of transition and transformation.

Anthropology Students: Learning about 'Art' and 'Other Cultures'

Bruce, who described himself as someone 'without any particular interest in art', had decided to come to the performance because he had been attracted by the 'dramatic posters with [an] enticing title' that advertised the event. In Gell's perspective, he was a patient impacted upon by the agency of the visual and textual announcement. Bruce was also attracted because he intended to gain a new perspective that could feed into his university coursework, so he expected an event with transformative potential. In his view, the performance had been 'a powerful mixture of drama, physical presence, live art and suggestions of an "other" culture with which I am unfamiliar'. His reference to '"other" culture' was a telling sign of his training in anthropology and the inverted commas around 'other' revealed his knowledge of critical theories of identity formation and cultural difference.

Bruce had attended George's conference presentation, which had also clearly influenced his anticipation. He noted that prior to the performance, he had 'high expectations of [George's] ability as an artist, both in painting and physical performance, after having heard his talk and seen samples of his work. Previous works shown on slides were neatly finished, so I was keen to see how a "raw" first product would look'. His expectations had been shaped further by George's African background and his 'tribal' presentation on the poster. He speculated that George had 'perhaps deliberately draw[n] attention to this difference from almost every member of the audience, staging his 'difference' through the startling screams, the body paint and the use of masks. Interestingly, Bruce argued that while George's playful reference to a racial stereotype had been potentially challenging, seeing him paint on canvas had been even more powerful, as this kind of art is 'not usually associated with [an African] background'. His comment made me realize that the performance structure split into two parts could also be read as an attempt to first reinforce and then break the stereotypical Western notion of 'African art'.

Bruce mentioned four reasons for having appreciated the performance. He had experienced it as an 'unusual' event; he had liked the 'audience closeness' and the 'feeling of having been a part of the event'; and he had enjoyed his children's visible pleasure. His words illustrate that artistic events are social occasions, where bodies sharing space interact and are affected by each other's physicality and body language. Members of the public communicated, for example, by smiling, cringing and raising their eyebrows. No doubt these visible emotional practices influenced their judgements.

Referring to the large painting, Bruce said he had enjoyed 'feeling part of a particular event during which an object holding memories of the evening was fashioned'. The latter remark demonstrates the potential power of objects in the making, when people's histories become intertwined through concrete experiences and shared memories of co-presence and cultural production. He noted that the fact that George had painted the word 'Belfast' on the painting at the very end could be understood as an 'exercise in encouraging a memory of his performance for the audience'. Interestingly, the word 'Belfast' added additional emotional potency to the art work as I discovered a few days after the performance, when three employees from the Estates Department came over to attach the painting to the wall. Seeing the explosion of colours and textures in combination with the word 'Belfast', one of the men said half-jokingly that the artist had succeeded very well in expressing the essence of Northern Ireland's troubled political history.

Performing with George: Eduardo

Two students had agreed to be George's assistants and were briefed by the artist an hour before the performance. As George explained, he had to improvise as he could only give them instructions after he had seen the space in which they would perform together. He asked them to wear black clothes and golden masks, and made them walk around with the robotic dogs for the public to touch. The two students were thus transformed into ritual players, partially through their staged engagement with objects that functioned as transformative agents.

One of the assistants, Eduardo, was an anthropology student from Italy in his thirties with a background in web-based journalism. Eduardo had not only been enthusiastic about the prospect of working with an artist, but he also thoroughly enjoyed George's company. Describing his own role in the performance, he explained how he had gone around with the robotic dogs 'to make the audience bless them'. He added that when the robotic dogs 'stroll[ed] around the canvas' and George danced and yelled 'crazily', he and the other assistant had to stand motionless 'like two sort of priests'. When I asked George whether he had used religious imagery in his brief to his helpers, he replied:

'blessing' and 'priest' were probably implied by my choice of description before the performance. I do not remember the exact words I used when I was telling them what to do. But I can be hyperbolic sometimes. In studying Eduardo's phrase 'like two sort of priests' one can deduce that it is a 'simile' and therefore role playing. Whatever the interpretation, [the two assistants] were not actual priests but they were like priests. My intention was to make them to be my 'guardians' during the performance for the purpose of 'security by numbers'. I never had a religious connotation even though it could be interpreted as such. [I probably hoped] to involve the audience by empowering them with the collective role of what a tribal 'priest' or 'elder' would do at a ceremony.[24]

Eduardo found George's use of body paint, masks, the wig, the dog toys, different musical genres and his screams 'funny, as they were cleverly connected together', and it seemed to him that 'the none-sense of connecting all this stuff was meaningful as an act of rebellion and denunciation of our stereotypical views about rites, Africa, art and, in particular, mass-produced objects like the toys'. He noted that Richard Schechner's writings about the role of performers and their relation with the audience had been very relevant to his understanding of the performance. Schechner (1985) has argued that the neat separation between theatre and ritual should be questioned, and that in experimental theatre the distance between performers and spectators is often overcome through audience participation. George had utilized the robotic dogs for that purpose, turning the public into 'patients' as they were confronted by the agency of dogs. As such, he stimulated emotional interaction.

When I asked Eduardo whether he had learned anything new from his involvement in the performance, he pointed out that it had made him reflect on the nature of artistic intentions and audience perception. Describing George as a 'source of thoughts and creativeness', and judging the performance to be 'brilliant [and] well-conceived', he wondered, however, whether more explanation in advance of the performance might have been useful 'for making the audience understand the jumble of music, dances, robots, yells, colours [and] shapes on the canvas'. The lack of explicit meaning, he suggested, might have put people off. He would have liked George to 'exaggerate more and more in all the aspects of it all: more music, more colours, more meaningful jumble and none-sense (if there was any), more yells, more dance, etc.'. His comments again demonstrate that art audiences are not passive viewers, and may be inspired to think creatively.

Sophie: Anthropology and Thick Description

Sophie, a British anthropologist in her fifties, pointed out that she had come to the performance because she was interested in art and had wanted to support activities put on by the department. Her description of the performance revealed her skills in ethnographic observation, and is worth quoting in full.

The artist came in wearing a mask, a tall wig and a sort of loincloth. He was extremely muscular and gave the impression of solid strength which was in no way threatening. He was accompanied by two attendants who carried three small metal robots. His unexpected initial scream and generally impressive appearance covered up the awkwardness of the fumbling attempts to dip in paint the rags attached to the robots. Operating on remote control, the robots trailed paint on the large painting lying on the floor (it already had a background of browns and greens). Then the painting was raised onto the wall, and the artist removed his mask and wig and proceeded (mostly using a broad brush) to develop the picture. It was clear to me that the picture 'took shape' without clear premeditation, as the artist worked on what was already there and the accidental dripping of paint. There was a bit of a tug of war between artistic openness (haziness?) and the artist's concern with obvious regimentality (for instance, he muddied up the word 'Belfast' when it wrote itself too clearly, as in a poster). This labour was interspersed with dancing and screaming. Though both these activities were fun to watch and hear, the connection with the painting was not clear. (I could go on and on – but this will become an essay!)

Several factors mentioned earlier in this chapter were brought up in the quote. Sophie noted that the artist's body was muscular but 'in no way threatening'. Her emotional judgement was of course influenced by the fact that he had presented himself as 'art performer' in an art environment; she obviously would have reacted differently had she encountered a half-naked man in a dark street. This was also picked up by Bruce, who pointed out that '[t]here was a comfort, too, in the setting. If someone, especially of George's size, had stood in front of them in a street and screamed as he did they would have been frightened, but this was a controlled environment with others there who were intrigued by such outbursts'.

I wondered whether gender had influenced Sophie's response to George's physicality, especially when reading her statement that 'the muscular body of the artist in its near-nakedness was open to more interpretations than I care to go into'. When I asked her this question in 2009 she replied:

Gender influenced my response, but his gender rather than mine (discounting for the moment the view that gender is a relation). Muscular men (at least in Western culture) tend to be portrayed as macho. There was no machismo here, only solid strength and an earthy rootedness, exemplified in the grounded stance. The noises he made might have come from the bowels of the earth, the voice of thunder, or exotic birds. They didn't invite interpretation; they simply created a mood. At the same time there was a humorous lightness, a quirky whimsicality accentuated by the artist's disarming smile and the stuff with the robots. The disparate elements created uncertainty and expectation, but were not threatening or erotic.

Knowing that George was an artist, Sophie had tried to read his artistic intentions. Describing the event as a mixture of entertainment and artistic experiment in which the development of artistic ideas was more important that the final product, the entertainment factor, she noted, lowered her expectations of the final output. Her association of art with seriousness informed her emotional response to the unfolding event. Judging the performance as a whole, she wondered how an 'entertaining performance' could be part of 'serious painting'. Perhaps typical of an anthropologist trained in reflexivity, acknowledging the impact of her own views on her interpretation of the event, she questioned her own thoughts: 'Is it a weakness or a strength that it pushed me to formulate ideas about what the artist meant with all this? So that rather than respond to it as a performance, I kept thinking that the artist had a motive and wanted to get something across by presenting himself in this way'.

Sophie also reflected on the questions George took from the audience after the performance. He had planned no to do so but had changed his mind during the show. Sophie stated enthusiastically:

> I was particularly pleased that he took questions at the end of the performance. The mode of his response, especially to questions by children, was engaging, as he treated all as equal. Some aspects of his explanation – especially concerning how he himself felt while performing, and generally his attitude to his art and his own development – was an addendum to the performance rather than part of it. His assertion that he could become free as an artist only when he gained mastery of his technique was an excellent and sobering point, but also didactic – this is why I say it is not part of the performance.

Turning to the audience to answer questions transformed George from a 'spectacle' into a discussion partner. His thoughtful and well-articulated answers no doubt further influenced audience perception, undermining the idea that his performance had been a product of irrational primitive artistic passion. In the words of Sophie, hearing George's explanations had also made a vast difference to her appreciation of his work as it 'revealed him more intimately as a person'. I suspect that during the question-and-answer session, most if not all of the members of the public (except perhaps the young terrified girl) came to perceive him as a fellow human being, with whom they could more or less easily communicate across cultural, professional, ethnic and age-related boundaries. In my own view, this was the most valuable, exciting and potentially transformative outcome of the event.

Conclusion

This chapter has explored the social and emotional dynamics of an intercultural performance that brought subjects and objects together and resulted in creative improvisation and the making of a large painting. The analysis examined processes of perception, evaluation and conception and argued that perception is tightly linked to conception. Humans are reflective and judgemental beings who create ideas as they evaluate experience. This does not imply that the analytic distinction between perception and conception should be dissolved. After all, there may be time lapses between the two processes, especially when people have new or undefined perceptual experiences (hearing an unfamiliar sound, seeing a blurred image), thereby perhaps needing time to place and build on them.

Trying to understand how individual members of the audience came to experience and evaluate the performance in distinct ways, it proved useful to include a perspective on emotions as learning processes. This approach highlights the ways in which individuals come to understand and react to changing environments, and how their bodily engagement and judgemental practices are partially shaped by embodied memories of earlier experiences.

The performance allowed for multi-sensorial engagement, not only with moving subjects and objects but also with the unfolding soundscape. The handling and creation of objects and images was central. In this process, both people and things, regarded as forces in causal relationships, influenced the ways in which the environment was shaped and experienced. Appropriated by the performer and his assistants, the masks, the wig and other mass-produced items gained new meanings and emotional efficacy, triggering fascination, puzzlement, fear and joy.

Various discourses with a global (albeit selective) reach made the performance meaningful to at least some of the participants. Knowledge about the existence of 'international performance art', for example, coloured some people's interpretations. Anthropological knowledge of rituals and mask traditions also influenced how some individuals understood the event, opening up the possibility of a more or less familiar debate. Various members of the audience recognized George's use of parody as a form of cultural critique. In addition, familiarity with globally recognized musical genres and songs also seemed to draw in some members of the audience.

The framing of the event as 'art performance' also influenced audience perception as it meant that George and the public had specific expectations about their relationship. These were reinforced when the spectators entered the room that had been divided into a seating area and a space for the performance. The conventional set-up influenced the emotional dynamics of the event, opening up a space for intense but 'safe' experiences. Structural factors were essential, as the event was staged thanks to the fact that the performing artist (George) and the organizer (myself) were both embedded in institutional settings that willingly provided the necessary resources. As transnationally operating actors and players in global networks of art and academia, they had used their positions to promote the occasion, also producing a poster as an extension of their agencies.

New conceptions that arose before, during and after the performance were based on previous understandings and active imagination, as exemplified by the various suggestions for improving the performance. Taking inspiration from his own life, George had decided to zoom in on larger questions of perception and conception in a world of hybridity and movement. His conceptualization of the performance was influenced by experiences that had ignited a fascination with rituals, a desire for personal empowerment and direct contact with audiences, as well as an interest in challenging people's world-views. While George was no doubt the main force of improvisation and artistic creation, individual members of the public were also involved in creative imagination, not only through inner reflections but also by brainstorming with others about the strengths and weaknesses of the performance. Reflecting on past and present experiences, and combining different discourses – of, for example, African art, art, ritual and entertainment – they built new ideas, using their creativity to form judgements and to think up alternatives.

Notes

1. As we will see, in transnational settings both subjects and objects are marked by specific histories of production. In the case of people, this includes both physiological processes (conception and birth) and social processes (family dynamics, class and other conditions influencing personal development). In the case of things, 'production' may involve chemical reactions, mechanical construction and industrial manufacture. In addition, things make unique trajectories through time and space, living 'social lives', to use Appadurai's terminology (Appadurai 1986; see also Introduction, this volume).

2. George's performance can be classified as 'image-oriented spectacle' (Carlson 1996: 105) along the lines of the 'theatre of mixed means' (Kostelanetz 1968). The artist himself described his performance as follows: 'In "What You Perceive Is What You Conceive", the canvas is not the only surface that takes the paint but also my brown skin which was painted blue mimicking the sky. Also, I am not the only painter but the small robots representing technology. At one point I also paused and painted the space around me as if the air was canvas, extending the image on the canvas beyond its boundaries, emphasizing the idea of the existence of the unseen image. By playing different genres of music, rock 'n' roll, reggae, rap, classical etc. to accompany the performance, I sought to dissolve the comforts of my own musical taste and that of the audience if any. My wig, mask, body paint, loin cloth and boots served as ritual objects meant to induce specific cultural meaning, often associated with fashion, tribal adornment, military gear, body art and the like' (personal communication, 2009).

3. George Hughes (personal communication, 2009).

4. The initial idea for this chapter came out of the conference 'Migrant Art, Artefacts, and Emotional Agency', which took place at Queens University, Belfast, in 2007. The conference was one in a series of three in the 'Diasporas, Migration and Identities' programme and funded by the AHRC. I would like to thanks George Hughes and other interviewees for their help. This chapter was partially developed as part of the project 'Creativity and Innovation in a World of Movement', which is financially supported by the HERA Joint Research Programme which is co-funded by AHRC, AKA, DASTI, ETF, FNR, FWF, HAZU, IRCHSS, MHEST, NWO, RANNIS, RCN, VR and The European Community FP7 2007-2013, under the Socio-economic Sciences and Humanities programme. An earlier version of this chapter was presented at the Anthropology and Ethnomusicology Research Seminars at Queens University Belfast in 2009. I am grateful for the financial and intellectual support of both the AHRC and HERA and for the feedback given by members of the audience at the seminar presentation. I would also like to thank Justin I'Anson-Sparks and the two anonymous reviewers for their insightful comments on an earlier version of this chapter.

5. The questionnaire I employed asked for gender, age, professional background and national/ethnic background, and included the questions:
   a. Why did you come to the performance?
   b. Could you describe the performance?
   c. How did you experience the performance?
   d. What were in your opinion the strengths and weaknesses of the performance?
   e. Did you have any particular emotional responses to (parts of) the performance (anger, fear, joy, disgust, boredom, admiration, any others; please describe and explain)
   f. Did any of the following influence your perception of the performance and the performer (if so please explain in what sense):
      – the performer's status as an artist
      – his African background
      – his use of body paint, masks, the wig, the dog toys, different musical genres, his screams, etc. (please refer to each)
      – other information you had about George or memories of earlier interaction with him
   g. would you be interested in seeing another performance by George (why, why not)
   h. Other comments.
6. Retrieved 9 September 2009 from: http://visualstudies.buffalo.edu/.
7. George's work has been shown extensively at the following places: Mabee Gerer Museum, Shawnee, OK; Toledo Museum of Art, Toledo, OH; The Butler Institute of American Art, Youngstown; Park Art Gallery, New York; Gallery 128, New York; Artooteek Zuidoost, Amsterdam; Livingston Gallery, The Hague; Gemeente Museum, The Hague; Galerie Xenios, Frankfurt am Main; Humboldt University, Berlin; Museum voor Zuid, Goes, Germany; Artists Alliance Gallery, Ghana; and several other locations. He is represented in Germany, Luxemburg, Austria and Switzerland by Artco, based in Herzogenrath, Germany. In Ghana his work is represented by Artists Alliance Gallery.
8. George Hughes (personal conversation, 2009).
9. By 2005, performance art was a well-established art form that had emerged in the 1970s and 1980s in the United States, Western Europe and Japan (Carlson 1996: 100; Marranca and Dasgupta 1999; Shepherd 2006; cf. Napier 1992), but performance art (meaning the 'contemporary art' type) was uncommon in West Africa and non-existent in Ghana. George's involvement with performance art began with his 'Dead Man' actions in 2005, when he posed as a corpse on Park Avenue in New York, exploring 'the boundaries of pedestrian reaction to a well-dressed man dead on the pavement'. His interest in performance art arose from the fact that his experiences in painting began to cross over into other activities (personal communication, 2007). When I asked him in 2009 whether he was also exploring issues of 'race', he replied: 'No, race was not on my mind at the time. In Dead Man Series I was just dealing with the concept of death and inner-city cultural perceptions of a dead body. My skin colour of course always affects the way I am perceived but in this case it was not part of my premise even though I was aware of the implications of my ethnicity' (personal communication, 2009). The reactions of the passers-by, ignoring or making fun of him, taught him that 'meaning is imputed by the individual based on one's knowledge of an experience' (personal communication 2005, quoted in Svašek 2007: 119).
10. George Hughes (personal communication, 2009). George also noted: 'I decided to use performance art as a medium to express myself because I realized it was convenient to combine all other art forms (familiar and unfamiliar) including life-like situations and collaborations with other artists'.
11. Travel between different continents is common practice amongst those involved in intercultural performances. Richard Schechner noted that 'the roads East–West/

South–North are crowded with traffic going both ways', with African, Asian and South American studying western theatrical styles, and North American and European performers travelling to Africa, Asia and South America to learn a variety of performance techniques (Schechner 1985: 23). The result is often an intercultural mix of stylistic features. It must be emphasized that the notion of the 'intercultural' must be handled with caution. Various scholars, including anthropologists such as Victor Turner and performance theorists like Richard Schechner, have used the term 'intercultural performance' to project idealized images of performers from different 'cultures' freely exchanging knowledge about performance styles. In their optimistic analyses of transnational artistic flows, they have overlooked the complex histories of specific performance traditions and have ignored the political dynamics of cultural appropriation and representation (Bharucha 1990: 2; Um 2005: 8; Svašek 2007: 191). As I have argued elsewhere (Svašek 2009), a more critical approach should focus on the ways in which globalization and inherent forces of inequality stimulate or hamper specific forms of improvisation and cultural production. In the case of 'What You Perceive Is What You Conceive', the relationship between George (as invited artist) and myself (as organizer of the event) was relatively equal. We were both embedded in local academic structures, were financially supported by our institutions and research councils, and had agreed in advance on the aims and conditions of George's visit. Indirectly, the event did, however, unveil North–South economic inequality, as George would most likely not have been able to get financial support for the project if he had stayed in Ghana.

12. George described the performance as: 'an aesthetic discourse probing the significance of the irrational in relation to myths that govern our belief systems. These cultural belief systems often determine how meaning is imputed in our everyday interaction with the environment and also with fellow human beings' (personal communication, 2009).

13. George Hughes (personal communication, 2009).

14. The spectators came to the performance for various reasons. Some were speakers at the conference, and for them it was a social event they were expected to attend. Not wanting to frame George as 'add on', however, I had given him a slot in the conference as a paper presenter, when he had the opportunity to impress them and raise interest in his work. At least some of the people who had heard him had felt curious. Obviously, their perception of him as a passionate speaker and a producer of what some regarded as aesthetically pleasing works of art shaped their expectation. Other members of the audience were anthropology students taking a course in the anthropology of art, some of whom had attended the paper presentation, and others who had listened to paper presentations by two other presenters, which I had made a compulsory part of the course. The performance was optional, so those who showed up were clearly driven by interest and curiosity, and possibly by the desired effect of the poster. The remaining crowd were, as far as I know, mostly people interested in art and colleagues from my department and school who wanted to show their support.

15. Influenced by phenomenology, Armstrong defined the term as the 'actualization of … form via the flux of sensations, a form whose only significant apperception is in terms of feeling' (Armstrong 1971: 31). Armstrong emphasized that 'affecting presence' must not be confused with conceptualization, as it does not refer to anything at all and is therefore non-representational. He further explained: 'The affecting presence is a thing-in-itself – a *presence* as I have called it here – and not a symbol because the creator does not build into his work cues to some real or imagined affective estate external to the work itself, but rather strives to achieve in that work the embodiment of those physical conditions which generate or are causative or constitutive of that emotion, feeling, or value with which he is concerned' (ibid.: 31).

16. Anna used '*ur*-creativity' assuming that some elements of George's creative act stemmed from the realm of the deeply unconscious. The reference to *ur* comes from Freud's psychoanalytic theory: 'In the German term *Urverdrängung*, "primal repression," the prefix *ur-* denotes this primordial aspect, for it means "original," "of the origins." It does not, however, provide any key to the meaning of primal repression. In parallel with *Urvater*, primal father of the horde, and *Urszene*, primal scene, *Urverdrägung* designates the matrix, as it were, of the prohibition on knowledge of that which was formerly known' ('Primal Repression', *International Dictionary of Psychoanalysis*. Retrieved 13 November 2009 from: http://www.enotes.com/psycho-analysis-encyclopedia/primal-repression).

17. Andrew pointed out that 'the wig, body paint and mask extend[ed] the performer's spatio-temporal location and reinforce[d] the notion of "exotic otherness" which could be interpreted as a negative colonial stereotype'. He added that 'a further interpretation may suggest an empowered subject reinforced by the acquiescence of George's masked assistants'. Artists of African descent like George, who have purposefully appropriated the label 'black', have done this from a diversity of subject positions, as works by Bet Saar and others show (Cooks 1997). Their appropriation of 'blackness' as a medium of resistance indicates that 'black' is a culturally constructed category, not a fixed natural entity (Hall 1988). In Paul Gilroy's view, to battle overt and covert racism it is necessary to examine 'the place which [European intellectual traditions] provide for the images of their racialized others as objects of knowledge, power, and cultural criticism' (Gilroy 1993: 5–6).

18. George Hughes (personal communication, 2009).

19. George Hughes (personal communication, 2009).

20. Bruce also mentioned that he saw an opportunity to do something interesting with his two sons. Bruce's experience of the performance was partly influenced by his children's presence: 'My enjoyment of the entire performance was in part due to the unusual, partly the audience closeness and feeling of having been a part of the event, and partly due to the obvious enjoyment of my children and their active participation by taking photos and a video'.

21. Bruce noted that 'body paint emphasized his exotic appeal and fitted with European conceptions of African males (on the photograph); the blue body paint used for the performance was possibly his way of saying he was "playing around" with the stereotypes of African male and Western artistic expression'.

22. George Hughes (personal communication, 2009).

23. The Italian student was quite overwhelmed by George's powerful presence. He mentioned that he 'had admiration for the energetic and creatively powerful skills of George', and added that 'happiness and energy were a relevant part of the whole of George's performance'. He also mentioned: 'I was happy with the idea of the performance also before seeing his brochure with the picture of his works. Then he gave me one of these brochures and I really enjoyed his paintings. And definitely in the days I knew him here in Belfast I had always the feeling of talking with a creative and brilliant mind. This should have influenced my enjoyment of the performance before it'.

24. George Hughes (personal communication, 2009).

25. Eduardo commented: '[T]he performance and the previous and after discussions with George about it left me with a lot of thoughts about it: the sense of it, the role of the performers, the planning of it ... how the planning differs from the perceived reality by the audience, the theorization of it ("it was not a ritual") ... But he also said to me that he felt "like a shaman"'.

26. With regard to his physicality, George had told me in 2007 that, three months ahead of the performance, he had started training sessions in his local gym, so the transformation of his body shape had been part and parcel of it. His main aim had not been to embody 'ideal' masculinity, but rather, to prevent injuries. He explained: 'Since

some of the aspects of my performance art always has to do with spontaneous kicks and physical endurance, I am more interested not to injure myself rather than show up without any precautions. I have had in the past serious injuries due to a lack of physical preparation or warm-up when as a teenager I practised martial arts'.

27. Sophie put it like this: 'The fact that he was an artist prepared me to expect an artistic end product, beyond the performance. That is to say, I didn't think he would simply throw a lot of paint on a canvas; I expected him to produce something of artistic value at the end. So I continually looked for form and meaning to emerge as the painting took shape'.

28. Sophie noted: 'although I enjoyed the performance, I wondered about the articulation between the screaming, the dancing, the music and the painting. Perhaps the performance itself weakened the painting. How can an entertaining performance be part of serious painting?'

References

Appadurai, A. (ed.). 1986. *The Social Life of Things: Commodities in Cultural Perspective.* Cambridge: Cambridge University Press.

Armstrong, R.P. 1971. *The Affecting Presence: An Essay in Humanistic Anthropology.* Urbana: University of Illinois Press.

Becker, H. 1982. *Art Worlds.* Berkeley: University of California Press.

Berger, J. 1972. *Ways of Seeing.* London: BBC Books.

Bharucha, R. 1990. *Theatre and the World: Essays on Performance and Politics of Culture.* New Delhi: Manohar Publications.

Bourdieu, P. 1984. *Distinction: A Social Critique of the Judgement of Taste,* trans. R. Nice. London: Routledge and Kegan Paul.

———— 1993. *The Field of Cultural Production: Essays on Art and Literature.* New York: Columbia University Press.

Bourdieu, P., and A. Darbel. 1969. *L'Amour de l'Art: Le Musée et Son Public.* Paris: Editions de Minuit.

Carlson, M. 1996. *Performance: A Critical Introduction.* London: Routledge.

Chadwick, W. 1990. *Women, Art and Society.* London: Thames and Hudson.

Clifford, J. 1988. *The Predicament of Culture: Twentieth-century Ethnography, Literature, and Art.* Cambridge, MA: Harvard University Press.

Cooks, B.R. 1997. 'Complicated Shadows: Challenging Histories of Cultural Representation in Contemporary Art', *Focaal* 29: 25–36.

Coote, J., and A. Shelton (eds). 1992. *Anthropology, Art and Aesthetics.* Oxford: Oxford University Press.

Gans, H. 1974. *Popular Culture and High Culture: An Analysis and an Evaluation of Taste.* New York: Basic Books.

Gell, A. 1998. *Art and Agency. An Anthropological Theory.* Oxford: Clarendon Press.

Gilroy, P. 1993. *The Black Atlantic.* Cambridge, MA: Harvard University Press.

Hall, S. 1988. 'New Ethnicities', in K. Mercer (ed.), *Black Film: British Cinema*. London: Institute for Contemporary Arts.

Halle, D. 1993. *Inside Culture: Art and Class in the American Home*. Chicago: University of Chicago Press.

Hart, L.M. 1995. 'Three Walls: Regional Aesthetics and the International Art World', in G.E. Marcus and F.R. Myers (eds.), *The Traffic in Culture: Refiguring Art and Anthropology*. Berkeley: University of California Press, pp. 127–50.

Ingold, T. 2000. *The Perception of the Environment. Essays on Livelihood, Dwelling and Skill*. London: Routledge.

Jordan, G., and C. Weedon. 1995. *Cultural Politics: Class, Gender, Race and the Postmodern World*. Oxford: Blackwell.

Karp, I., and S.D. Levine (eds). 1991. *Exhibiting Cultures: The Poetics and Politics of Museum Display*. Washington, DC: Smithsonian Institution.

Kostelanetz, R. 1968. *The Theatre of Mixed Means*. New York: Dial.

Marranca, B., and G. Dasgupta (eds). 1999. *Conversations on Art and Performance*. Baltimore, MD: Johns Hopkins University Press.

Milton, K. 2002. *Loving Nature: Towards an Ecology of Emotion*. London: Routledge.

———— 2005 'Meanings, Feelings and Human Ecology', in K. Milton and M. Svašek (eds), *Mixed Emotions: Anthropological Studies of Feeling*. Oxford: Berg, pp. 25–42.

Napier, D.A. 1992. *Foreign Bodies: Performance, Art and Symbolic Anthropology*. Berkeley: University of California Press.

Rosaldo, M.Z. 1984. 'Toward an Anthropology of Self and Feeling', in R.A. Shweder and R.A. LeVine (eds), *Culture Theory: Essays on Mind, Self, and Emotion*, Cambridge: Cambridge University Press, pp. 137–57.

Schechner, R. 1985. *Between Theater and Anthropology*. Philadelphia: University of Pennsylvania Press.

Shepherd, S. 2006. *Theatre, Body and Pleasure*. London: Routledge.

Svašek, M. 2007. *Anthropology, Art and Cultural Production*. London: Pluto.

———— 2009. 'Improvising in a World of Movement: Transit, Transition and Transformation', in H.K. Anheier and Y.R. Isar (eds), *Cultural Expression, Creativity and Innovation*. London: Sage, pp. 62–77.

Um, H. 2005. *Diasporas and Interculturalism in Asian Performing Arts: Translating Traditions*. New York: Routledge Curzon.

Wolff, J. 1981. *The Social Production of Art*. London: MacMillan.

NOTES ON CONTRIBUTORS

Kathy Burrell is Reader in Migration and Material Culture at the School of Humanities, De Montfort University, Leicester. She is currently writing up her research on different waves of Polish migration to the Midlands region of Britain, having interviewed people who migrated during the socialist era, the periods of 'transition' and post-EU accession. Her research interests include changing experiences of travel and migration, and the material dimensions of migrants' lives and relationships. Her publications include the edited volume *Polish Migration to the UK in the 'New' European Union: After 2004* (2009) and several articles on different aspects of life in socialist and transition-era Poland and Polish migration to the UK.

Anne Sigfrid Grønseth is Associate Professor of Social Anthropology in the Department of Health and Social Science at University College Lillehammer, Norway, where she directs the Research Unit on Health, Culture and Identity. Her research is focused on Tamil refugees in Norway and the world-wide diaspora with special interests in identity, illness, well-being, embodiment, religion, existentialism and humanism. Her recent publications include *Lost Selves and Lonely Persons: Experiences of Illness and Well-being among Tamil Refugees in Norway* (2007). She also recently co-edited the volume *Mutuality and Empathy: Self and Other in the Ethnographic Encounter* (2010) and published articles in the *Journal of Ethnic and Migration Studies* and *Anthropology in Action*.

Timm Lau studied Ethnology in Hamburg (Germany), took his M.Sc. in Social Anthropology at the London School of Economics and Political Science, and his Ph.D. in Social Anthropology at the University of Cambridge. His publications include *How Do We Know? Evidence, Ethnography and the Making of Anthropological Knowledge* (co-edited with L. Chua and C. High, 2008, Cambridge Scholars Publishing), 'Tibetan Fears and Indian Foes: Fears of Cultural Extinction and Antagonism as Discursive Strategy' (2009, in *vis-à-vis: Explorations in Anthropology*), and 'The Hindi Film's Romance and Tibetan Notions of Harmony: Emotional Attachments and Personal Identity in the Tibetan Diaspora in India' (2010, in *Journal of Ethnic and Migration Studies*). From 2010 to 2011, Dr. Lau held a Postdoctoral Research Fellow funded by the AXA Research Fund at the University of Calgary, undertaking research on Tibetan economic adaptation in Canada.

Sameera Maiti is Assistant Professor in the Department of Anthropology, University of Lucknow, India, and also a National Associate at the Indian Institute of Advanced Studies, Shimla. Her research interests broadly lie in the study of anthropology and art (including material culture and performing arts), marginalized and indigenous cultures in changing situations, gender issues (especially in tribal and rural areas), medical anthropology among indigenous peoples, and demographic issues. She is also the author of a number of books and research papers.

Enrico Maria Milič holds an MA in social anthropology from Queen's University, Belfast, and currently works as a journalist in the Italian media. He is the author of a number of articles on the themes of storytelling, embodiment, the internet and online communities.

Maggie O'Neill is Professor in Criminology at Durham University and has a longstanding interest and engagement in collaborating with artists through ethnographic research (specifically biographical narrative research), participatory action research and participatory arts. She has published extensively on sex work, forced migration, arts, migration and diaspora, cultural criminology, critical theory and participatory methodologies. Her latest book is *Asylum, Migration and Community* (2010).

Fiona Parrott is Research Fellow in Anthropology at the University of Amsterdam and the London School of Hygiene and Tropical Medicine. Her research focuses on the material and sensory dynamics of memory in relation to household and relationship change in London, and she has also conducted research with patients in secure psychiatric care. She has recently published articles in the *Journal of the Royal Anthropological Institute*, and *Culture, Medicine and Psychiatry*.

Eddy Plasquy is currently completing a Ph.D. in social anthropology at the University of Leuven, Belgium. His current research focuses on pilgrimage in El Rocío, southern Spain, over the last fifty years, and he has also conducted fieldwork among Spanish migrants in Vilvoorde, Belgium. His research interests include ritual dynamics and transformation, pilgrimage, transnational migration and religion.

Deborah Schultz is Assistant Professor of Art History at Richmond University and Regent's College, London. Her primary areas of study focus on word–image relations, photography and memory in twentieth-century and contemporary art. She is the author of *Marcel Broodthaers: Strategy and Dialogue* (2007), co-author of *Pictorial Narrative in the Nazi Period: Felix Nussbaum, Charlotte Salomon and Arnold Daghani* (2009) and co-editor of *Arnold Daghani's Memories of Mikhailowka: The Illustrated Diary of a Slave Labour Camp Survivor* (2009).

Maruška Svašek is Reader in the School of History and Anthropology, Queens University, Belfast. Svašek is currently project leader of a large two-year HERA/AHRC-funded project entitled 'Creativity and Innovation in a World of Movement', and in 2007 she co-founded the Cultural Dynamics and Emotions Network. Her main research interests include emotional dynamics, migration, art and artefacts. Her recent publications include *Anthropology, Art and Cultural Production* (2007), the edited volumes *Emotions and Human Mobility. Ethnographies of Movement* (2012), *Postsocialism: Politics and Emotions in Central and Eastern Europe* (2006) and the co-edited volume *Mixed Emotions: Anthropological Studies of Feeling* (2005).

Leon Wainwright is Lecturer in Art History at The Open University and a member of the editorial board of the journal *Third Text*. He is the OU Principal Investigator for 'Creativity and Innovation in a World of Movement' (CIM), a two-year collaborative research project funded by the European Science Foundation (HERA JRP). His monograph *Timed Out: Art and the Transnational Caribbean* was published by Manchester University Press in 2011, and he is co-editor, with Charles Harrison and Paul Wood, of a forthcoming volume in the series 'Art in Theory: An Anthology of Changing Ideas' (Wiley Blackwell).

INDEX